Hana-Kimi

For You in Full Blossom

16

story and art by
HISAYA NAKAJO

HANA-KIMI

For You in Full Blossom
VOLUME 16

STORY & ART BY HISAYA NAKAJO

Translation & English Adaptation/David Ury
Touch-up Art & Lettering/Primary Graphix
Design/Izumi Evers
Editor/Jason Thompson

Managing Editor/Megan Bates
Editorial Director/Elizabeth Kawasaki
Editor in Chief/Alvin Lu
Sr. Director of Acquisitions/Rika Inouye
Sr. VP of Marketing/Liza Coppola
Exec. VP of Sales & Marketing/John Easum
Publisher/Hyoe Narita

Printed in the U.S.A.

Published by VIZ Media, LLC, P.O. Box 77010, San Francisco, CA 94107

Shôjo Edition
10 9 8 7 6 5 4 3 2 1

First printing, February 2007

www.viz.com
store.viz.com

PARENTAL ADVISORY
HANA-KIMI is rated T+ for Older Teen and is recommended for ages 16 and up. Contains strong language, sexual themes and alcohol and tobacco usage.

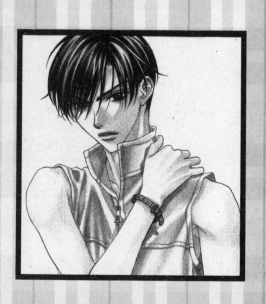

CONTENTS

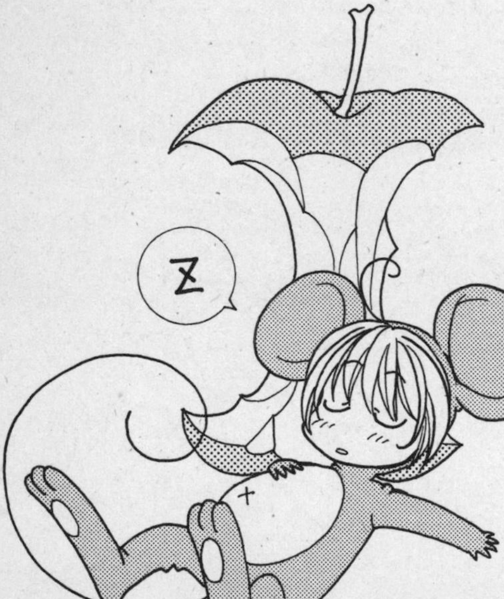
Z

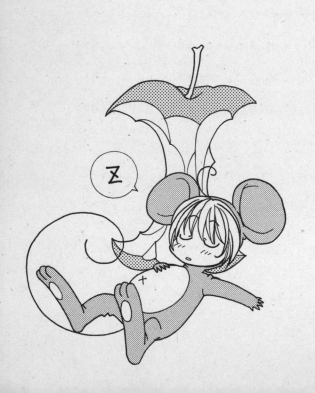

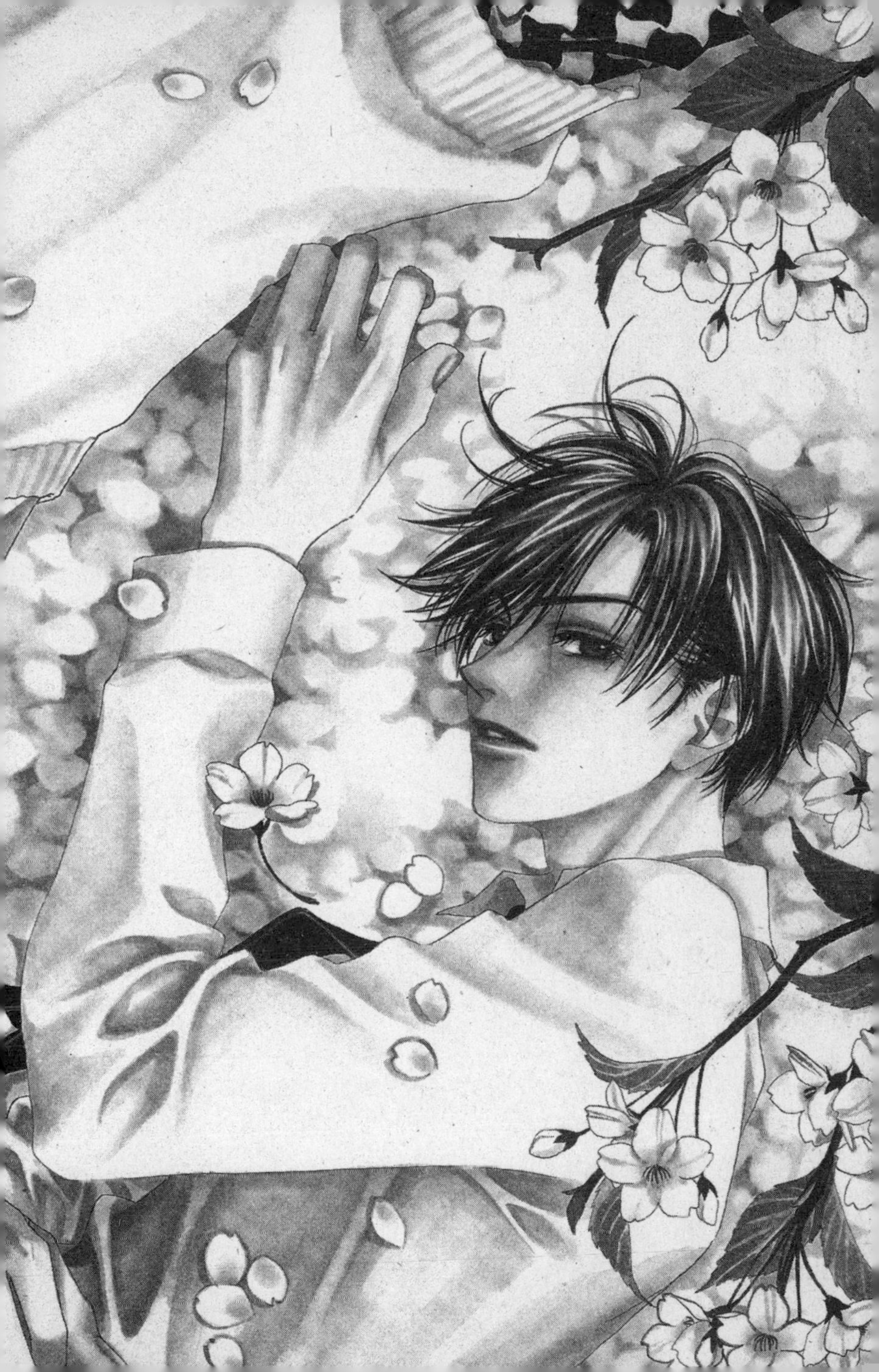

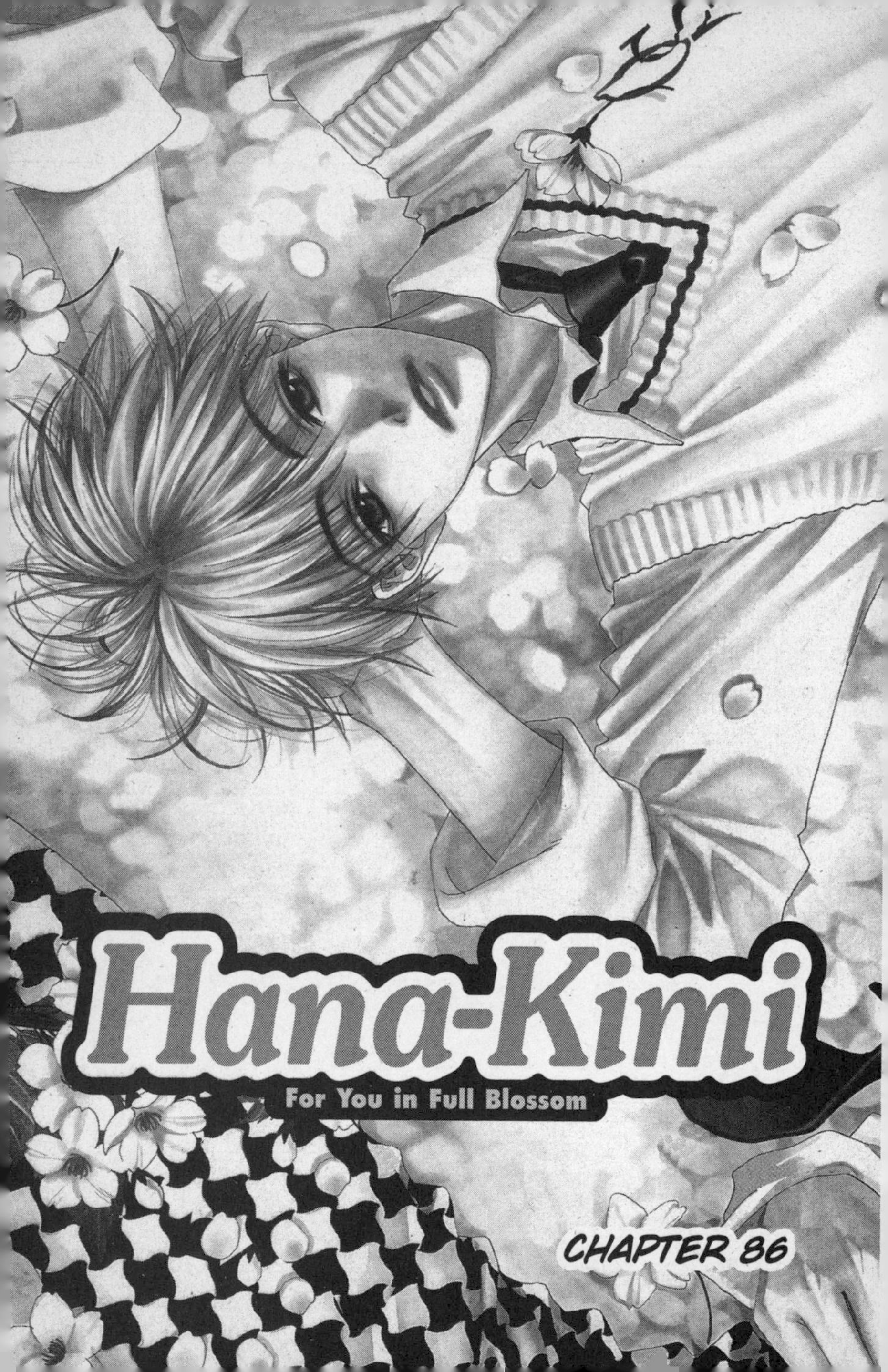

Hana-Kimi
For You in Full Blossom
CHAPTER 86

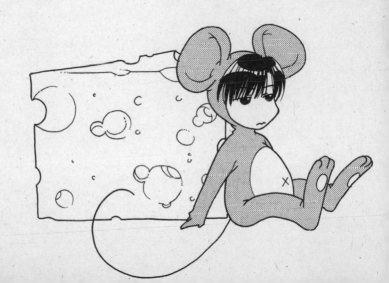

ERASE ERASE
HEY ERASE
ERASE

TEACHER--!

ART ROOM

DRIED ANCHOVIES

It may be silly to share this with you guys, but whenever I buy a bag of dried anchovies, I love looking for other kinds of fish that accidentally got mixed in. Yep. You can usually buy anchovies by the pound, you know? I often find shrimp, octopus, squid and sea bream mixed in. It's so much fun to find them. It's not like I buy anchovies all the time, but the most exciting thing I've ever found was a one-centimeter-long sea horse!

It ← looked like this.

Attention! You have a much better chance of finding different kinds of fish when you buy the cheap anchovies, not the expensive ones. (I always buy the cheap ones ♥)

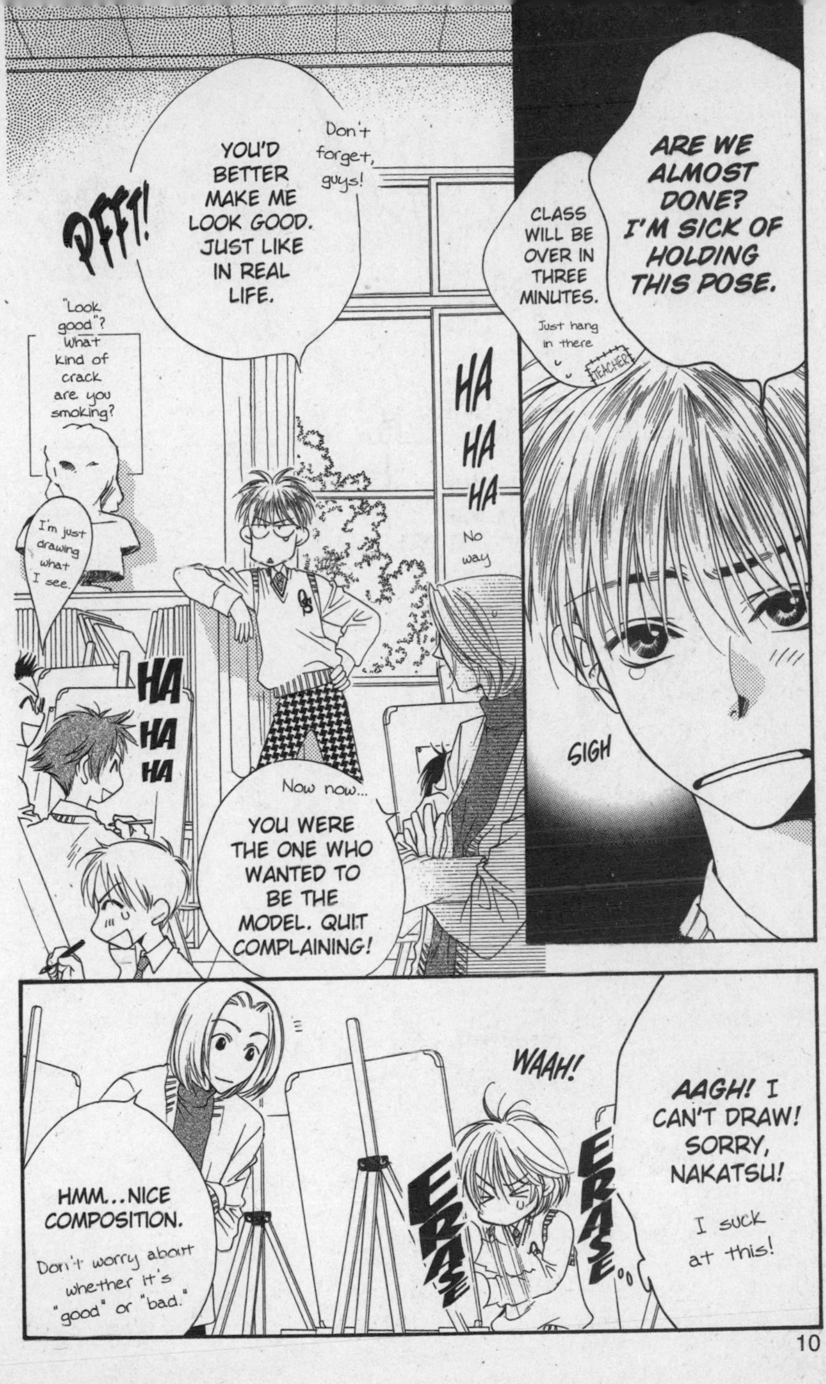
ARE WE ALMOST DONE? I'M SICK OF HOLDING THIS POSE.
CLASS WILL BE OVER IN THREE MINUTES.
Just hang in there
TEACHER
SIGH
HA HA HA
No way
Don't forget, guys!
YOU'D BETTER MAKE ME LOOK GOOD. JUST LIKE IN REAL LIFE.
PFFT!
"Look good"? What kind of crack are you smoking?
I'm just drawing what I see.
HA HA HA
Now now...
YOU WERE THE ONE WHO WANTED TO BE THE MODEL. QUIT COMPLAINING!
AAGH! I CAN'T DRAW! SORRY, NAKATSU!
I suck at this!
ERASE
WAAH!
ERASE
HMM...NICE COMPOSITION.
Don't worry about whether it's "good" or "bad."

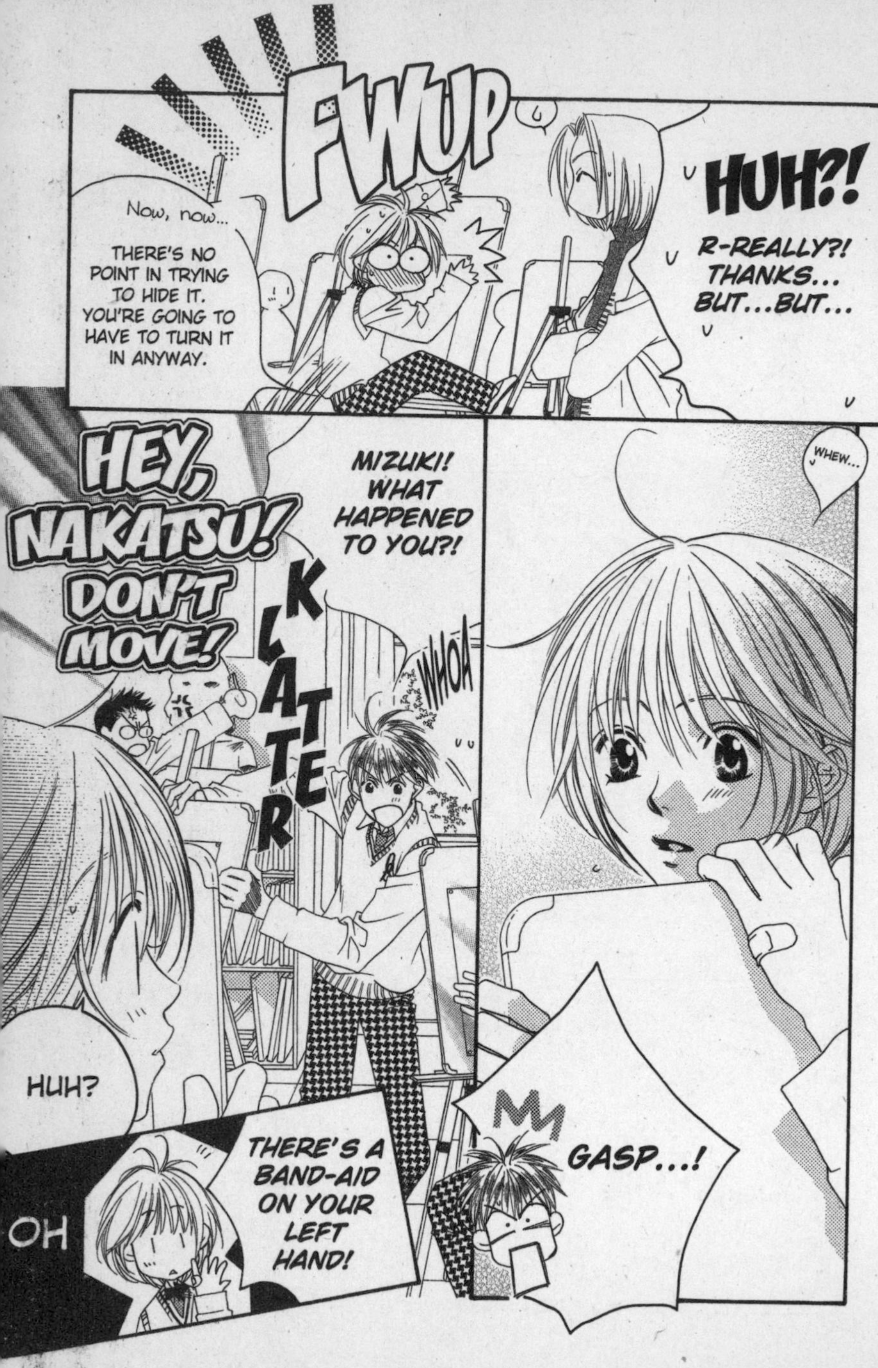
HUH?!
R-REALLY?! THANKS... BUT...BUT...
FWUP
Now, now...
THERE'S NO POINT IN TRYING TO HIDE IT. YOU'RE GOING TO HAVE TO TURN IT IN ANYWAY.
WHEW...
GASP...!
MIZUKI! WHAT HAPPENED TO YOU?!
HEY, NAKATSU! DON'T MOVE!
KLATTER
WHOA
HUH?
THERE'S A BAND-AID ON YOUR LEFT HAND!
OH

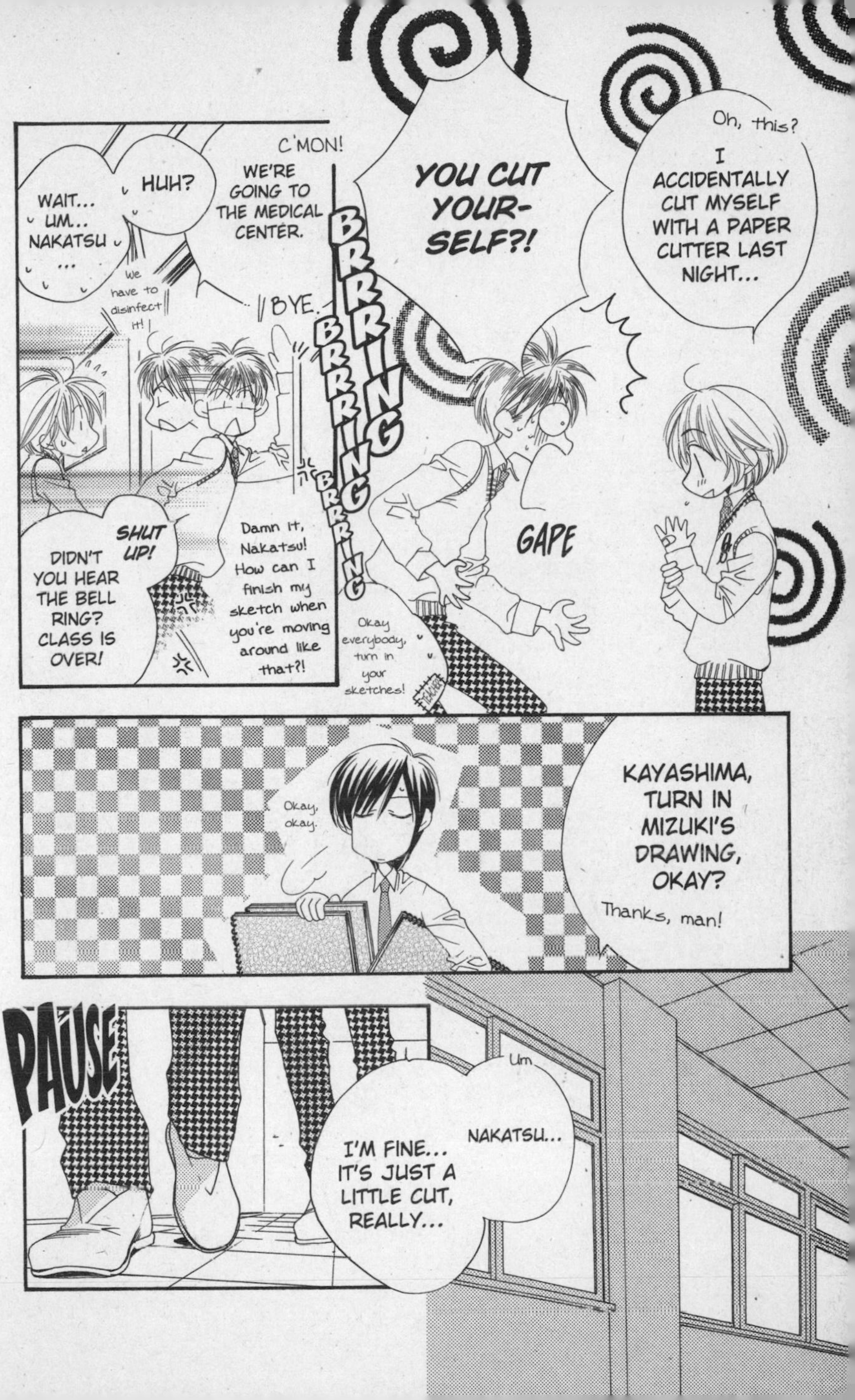
Oh, this? I ACCIDENTALLY CUT MYSELF WITH A PAPER CUTTER LAST NIGHT...
YOU CUT YOUR-SELF?!
BRRRING
BRRRING
BRRRING
GAPE
Okay everybody, turn in your sketches!
TEACHER
C'MON! WE'RE GOING TO THE MEDICAL CENTER.
HUH?
WAIT... UM... NAKATSU...
We have to disinfect it!
BYE.
Damn it, Nakatsu! How can I finish my sketch when you're moving around like that?!
SHUT UP! DIDN'T YOU HEAR THE BELL RING? CLASS IS OVER!
KAYASHIMA, TURN IN MIZUKI'S DRAWING, OKAY? Thanks, man!
Okay, okay.
Um NAKATSU...
I'M FINE... IT'S JUST A LITTLE CUT, REALLY...
PAUSE

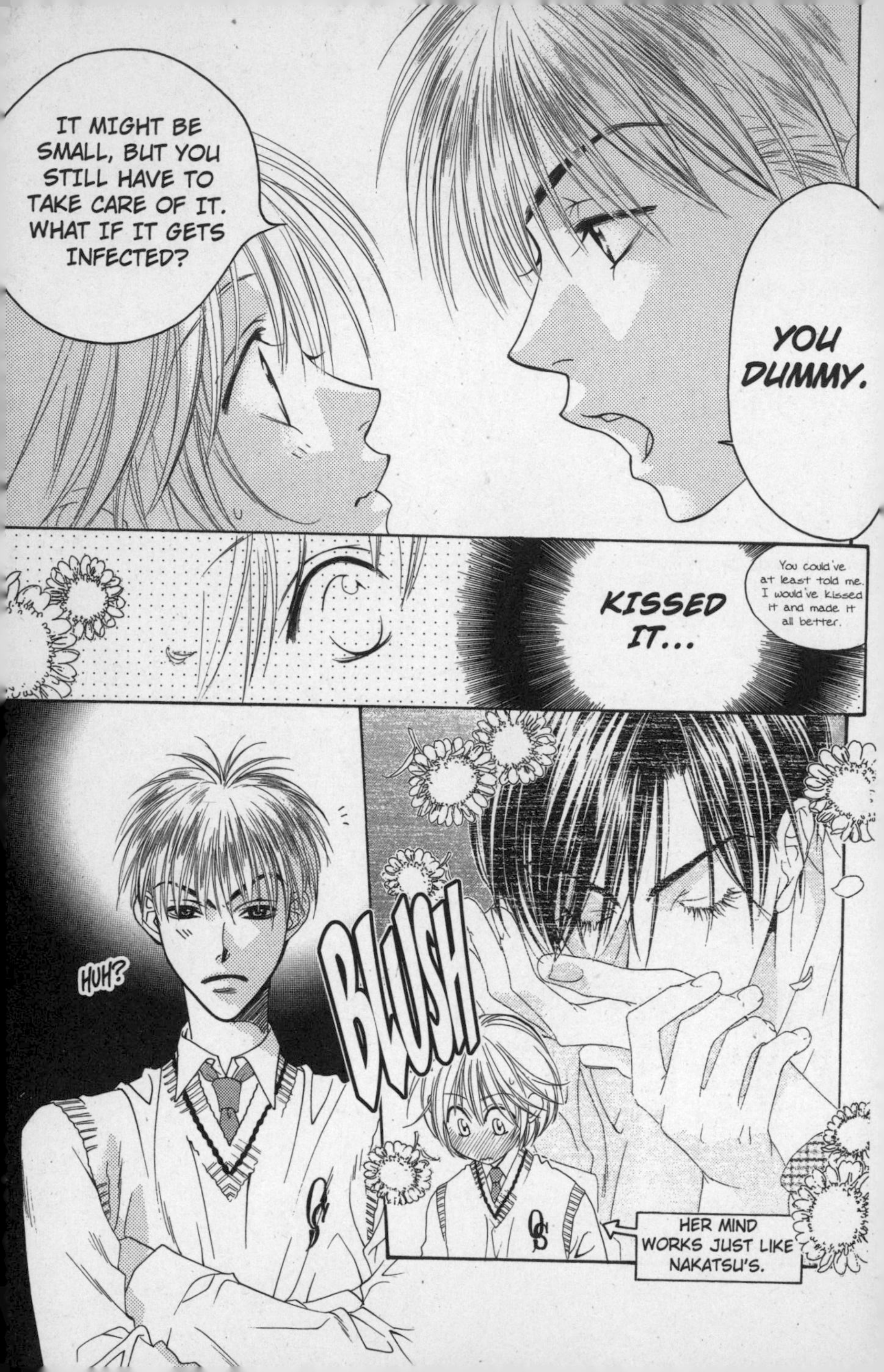
YOU DUMMY.
IT MIGHT BE SMALL, BUT YOU STILL HAVE TO TAKE CARE OF IT. WHAT IF IT GETS INFECTED?
You could've at least told me. I would've kissed it and made it all better.
KISSED IT...
BLUSH
HER MIND WORKS JUST LIKE NAKATSU'S.
HUH?

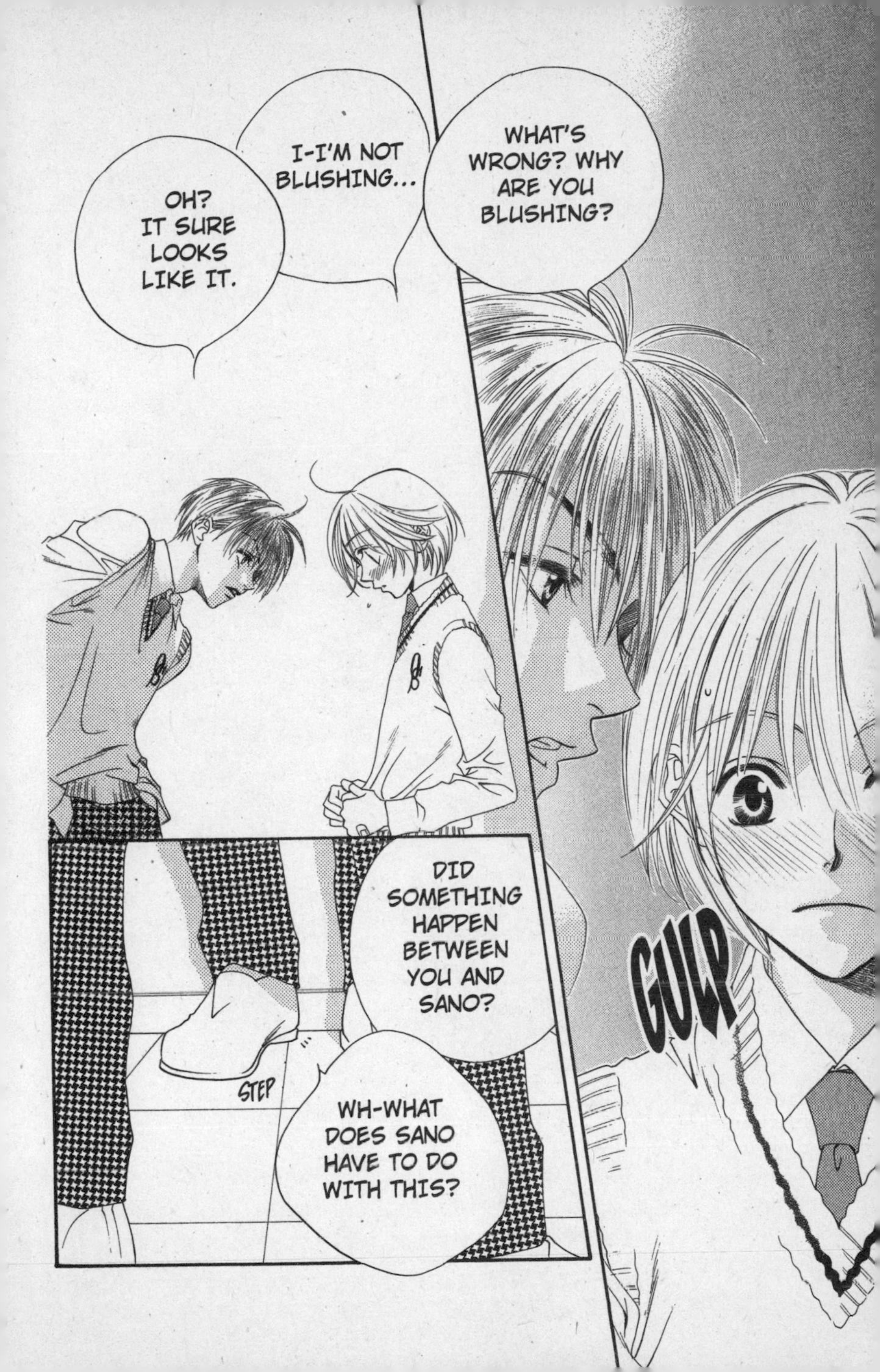
WHAT'S WRONG? WHY ARE YOU BLUSHING?
GULP
I-I'M NOT BLUSHING...
OH? IT SURE LOOKS LIKE IT.
DID SOMETHING HAPPEN BETWEEN YOU AND SANO?
STEP
WH-WHAT DOES SANO HAVE TO DO WITH THIS?

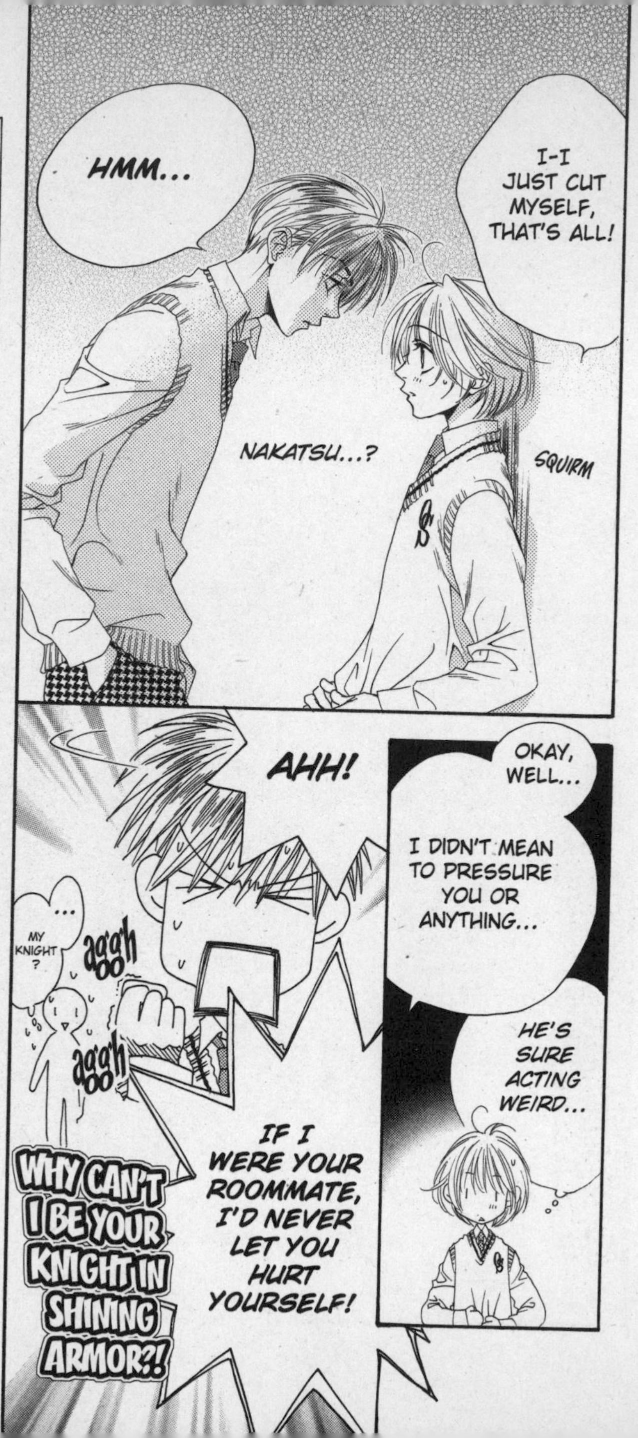
I-I JUST CUT MYSELF, THAT'S ALL!
HMM...
SQUIRM
NAKATSU...?
OKAY, WELL...
I DIDN'T MEAN TO PRESSURE YOU OR ANYTHING...
HE'S SURE ACTING WEIRD...
AHH!
...
MY KNIGHT ?
IF I WERE YOUR ROOMMATE, I'D NEVER LET YOU HURT YOURSELF!
WHY CAN'T I BE YOUR KNIGHT IN SHINING ARMOR?!

16

Hello! Welcome to **Hana-Kimi** book 16. Shin is on the cover this time! Did you guess that it'd be him? I bet a lot of you guessed that it would be Shin. (I gave you so many hints in the last volume...) The flowers in the background are called babianas. They look a little bit like freesias. (The petals are different, though.) I drew the flowers and the character separately, so it was hard to balance out the composition... I learned my lesson for next time.

16

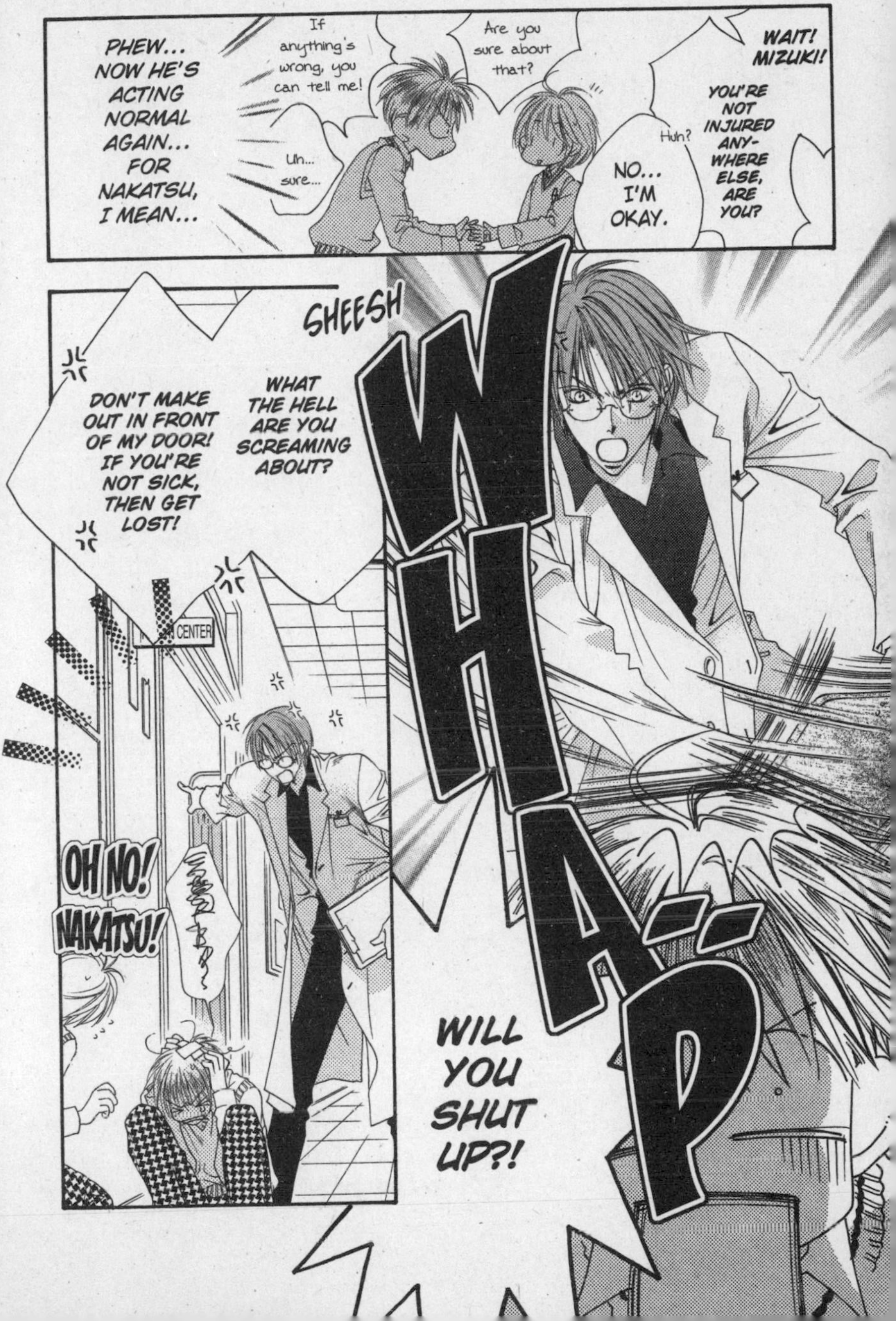

WAIT! MIZUKI!
YOU'RE NOT INJURED ANYWHERE ELSE, ARE YOU?
Huh?
NO... I'M OKAY.
Are you sure about that?
If anything's wrong, you can tell me!
Uh... sure...
PHEW... NOW HE'S ACTING NORMAL AGAIN... FOR NAKATSU, I MEAN...
WHAP
WILL YOU SHUT UP?!
SHEESH
WHAT THE HELL ARE YOU SCREAMING ABOUT?
DON'T MAKE OUT IN FRONT OF MY DOOR! IF YOU'RE NOT SICK, THEN GET LOST!
CENTER
OH NO! NAKATSU!

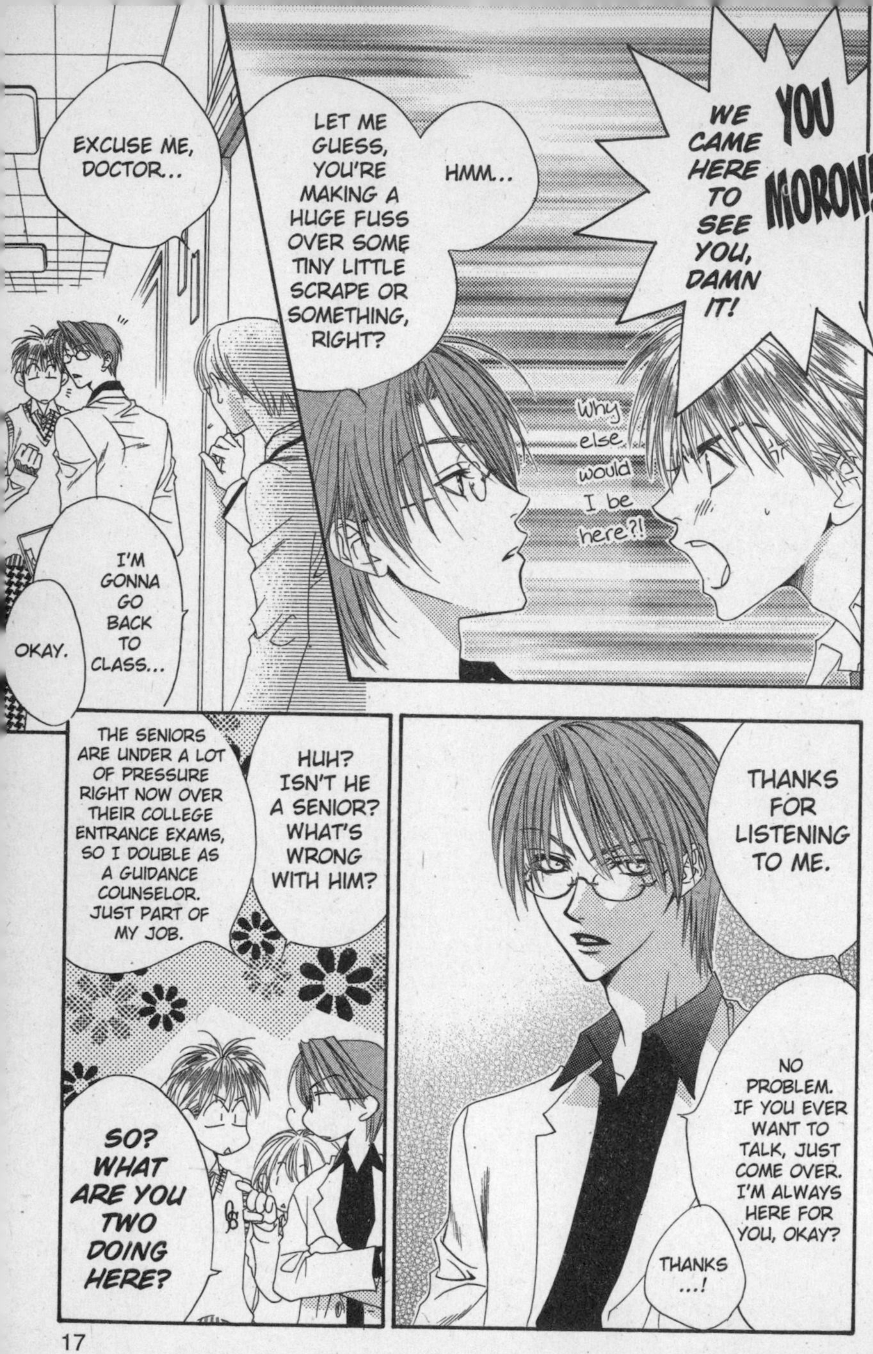
HMM...
LET ME GUESS, YOU'RE MAKING A HUGE FUSS OVER SOME TINY LITTLE SCRAPE OR SOMETHING, RIGHT?
WE CAME HERE TO SEE YOU, DAMN IT!
YOU MORON!
Why else would I be here?!
EXCUSE ME, DOCTOR...
I'M GONNA GO BACK TO CLASS...
OKAY.
THANKS FOR LISTENING TO ME.
NO PROBLEM. IF YOU EVER WANT TO TALK, JUST COME OVER. I'M ALWAYS HERE FOR YOU, OKAY?
THANKS ...!
HUH? ISN'T HE A SENIOR? WHAT'S WRONG WITH HIM?
THE SENIORS ARE UNDER A LOT OF PRESSURE RIGHT NOW OVER THEIR COLLEGE ENTRANCE EXAMS, SO I DOUBLE AS A GUIDANCE COUNSELOR. JUST PART OF MY JOB.
SO? WHAT ARE YOU TWO DOING HERE?

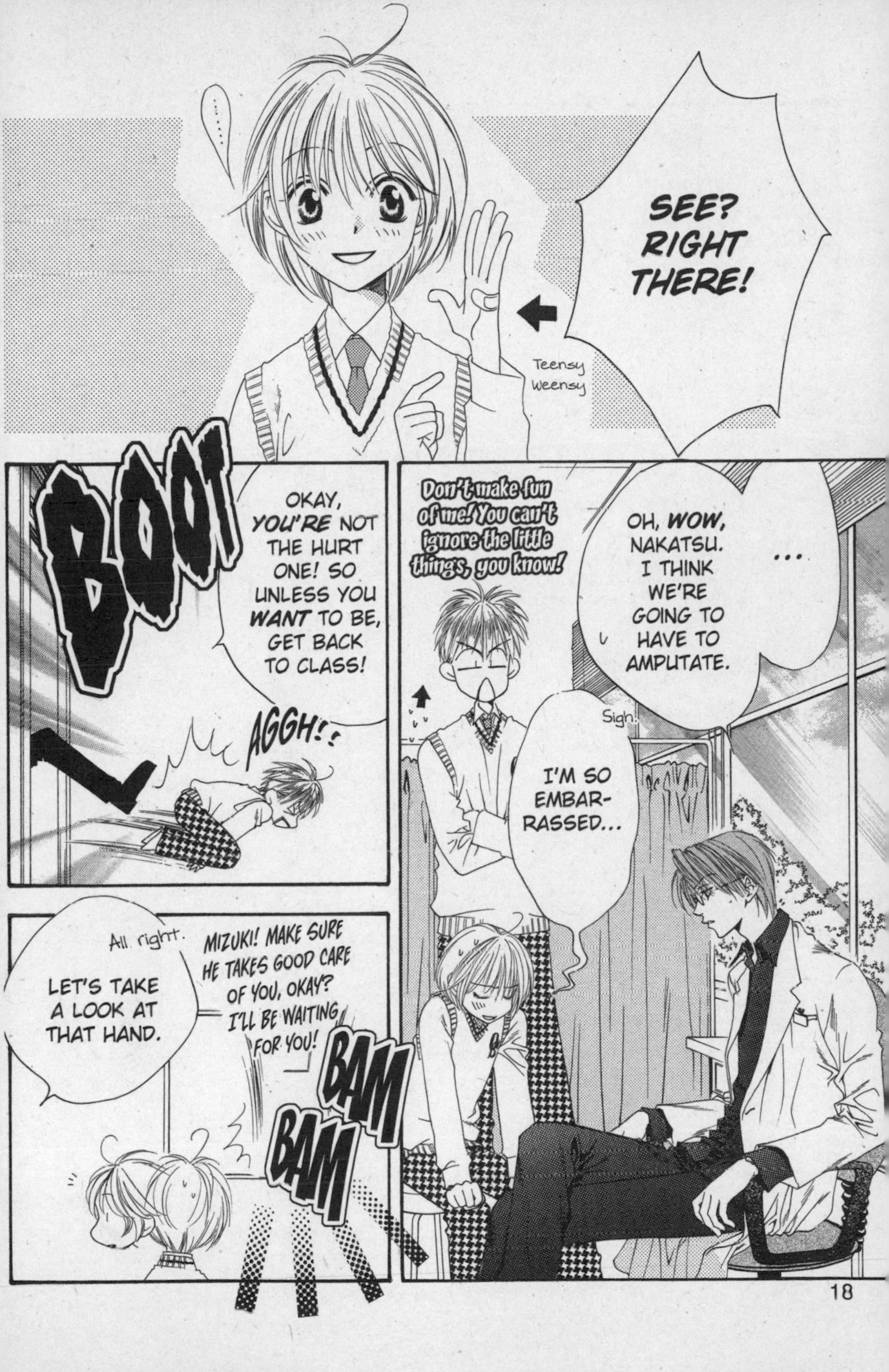
SEE? RIGHT THERE!
Teensy Weensy
...
OH, WOW, NAKATSU. I THINK WE'RE GOING TO HAVE TO AMPUTATE.
Don't make fun of me! You can't ignore the little things, you know!
Sigh
I'M SO EMBARRASSED...
OKAY, YOU'RE NOT THE HURT ONE! SO UNLESS YOU WANT TO BE, GET BACK TO CLASS!
BOOT
AGGH!!
MIZUKI! MAKE SURE HE TAKES GOOD CARE OF YOU, OKAY? I'LL BE WAITING FOR YOU!
All right.
LET'S TAKE A LOOK AT THAT HAND.
BAM
BAM
BAM

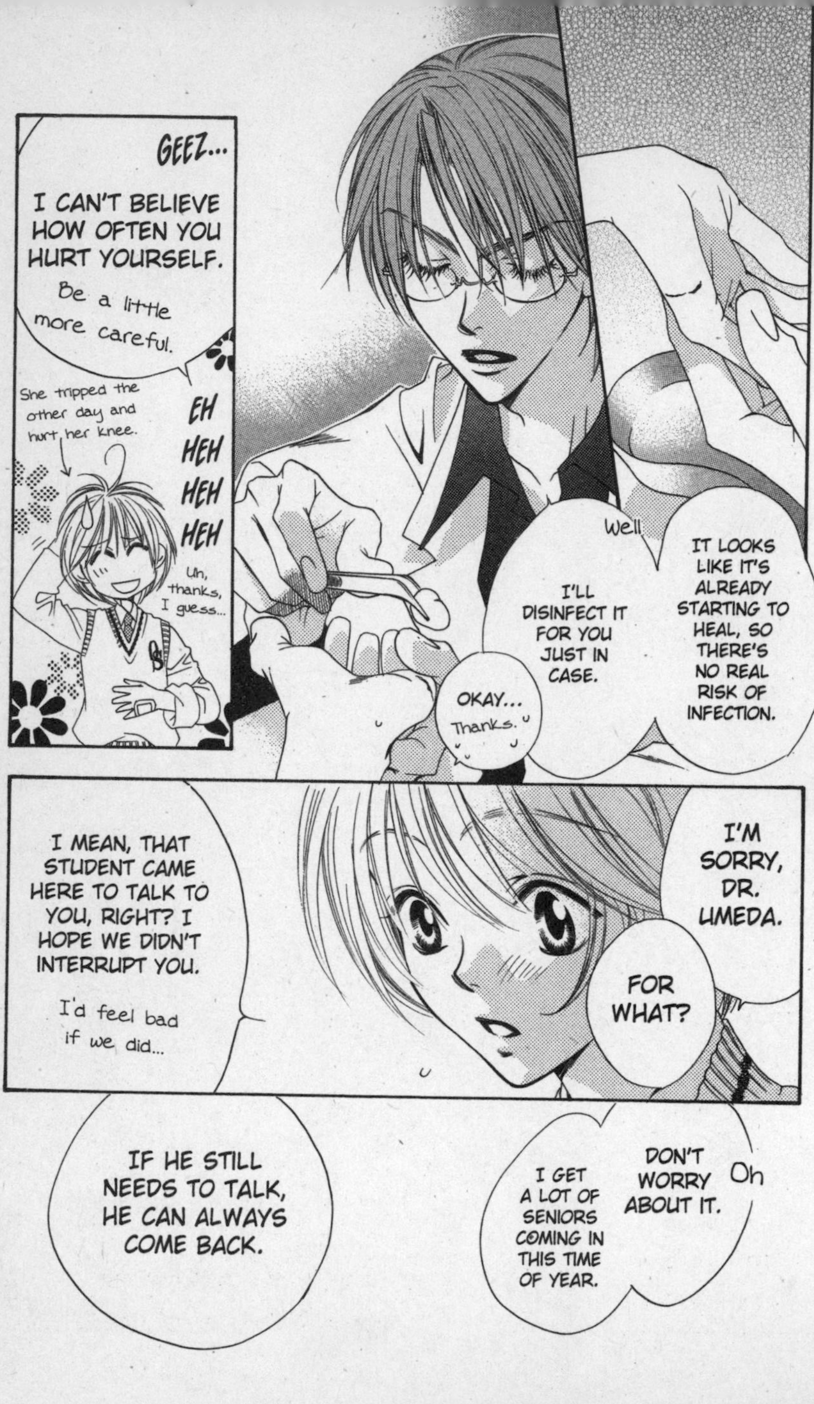
Well
IT LOOKS LIKE IT'S ALREADY STARTING TO HEAL, SO THERE'S NO REAL RISK OF INFECTION.
I'LL DISINFECT IT FOR YOU JUST IN CASE.
OKAY... Thanks.
GEEZ...
I CAN'T BELIEVE HOW OFTEN YOU HURT YOURSELF.
Be a little more careful.
EH HEH HEH HEH
Uh, thanks, I guess...
She tripped the other day and hurt her knee.
I'M SORRY, DR. UMEDA.
FOR WHAT?
I MEAN, THAT STUDENT CAME HERE TO TALK TO YOU, RIGHT? I HOPE WE DIDN'T INTERRUPT YOU.
I'd feel bad if we did...
Oh
DON'T WORRY ABOUT IT.
I GET A LOT OF SENIORS COMING IN THIS TIME OF YEAR.
IF HE STILL NEEDS TO TALK, HE CAN ALWAYS COME BACK.

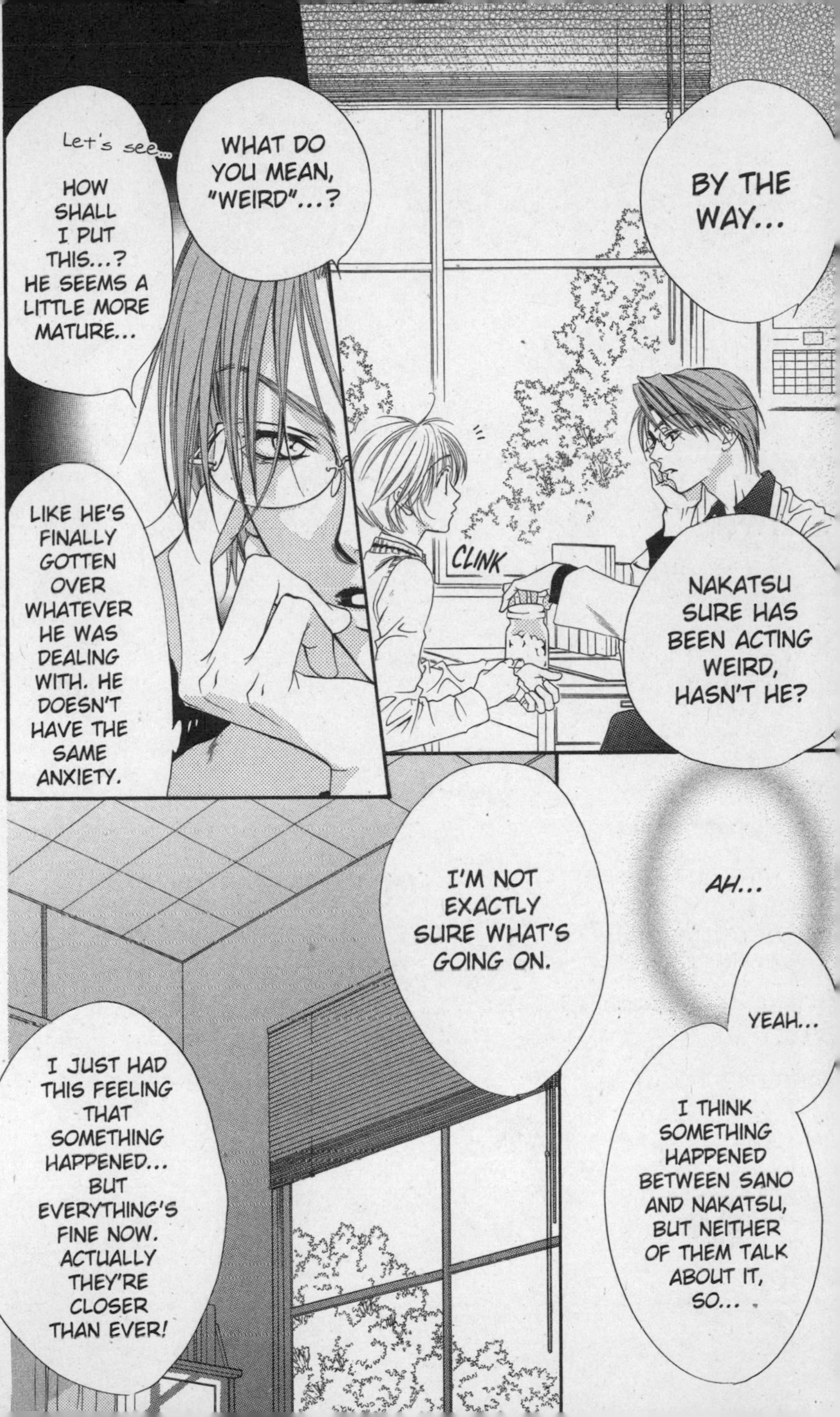
BY THE WAY...
NAKATSU SURE HAS BEEN ACTING WEIRD, HASN'T HE?
CLINK
WHAT DO YOU MEAN, "WEIRD"...?
Let's see... HOW SHALL I PUT THIS...? HE SEEMS A LITTLE MORE MATURE...
LIKE HE'S FINALLY GOTTEN OVER WHATEVER HE WAS DEALING WITH. HE DOESN'T HAVE THE SAME ANXIETY.
AH...
YEAH...
I THINK SOMETHING HAPPENED BETWEEN SANO AND NAKATSU, BUT NEITHER OF THEM TALK ABOUT IT, SO...
I'M NOT EXACTLY SURE WHAT'S GOING ON.
I JUST HAD THIS FEELING THAT SOMETHING HAPPENED... BUT EVERYTHING'S FINE NOW. ACTUALLY THEY'RE CLOSER THAN EVER!

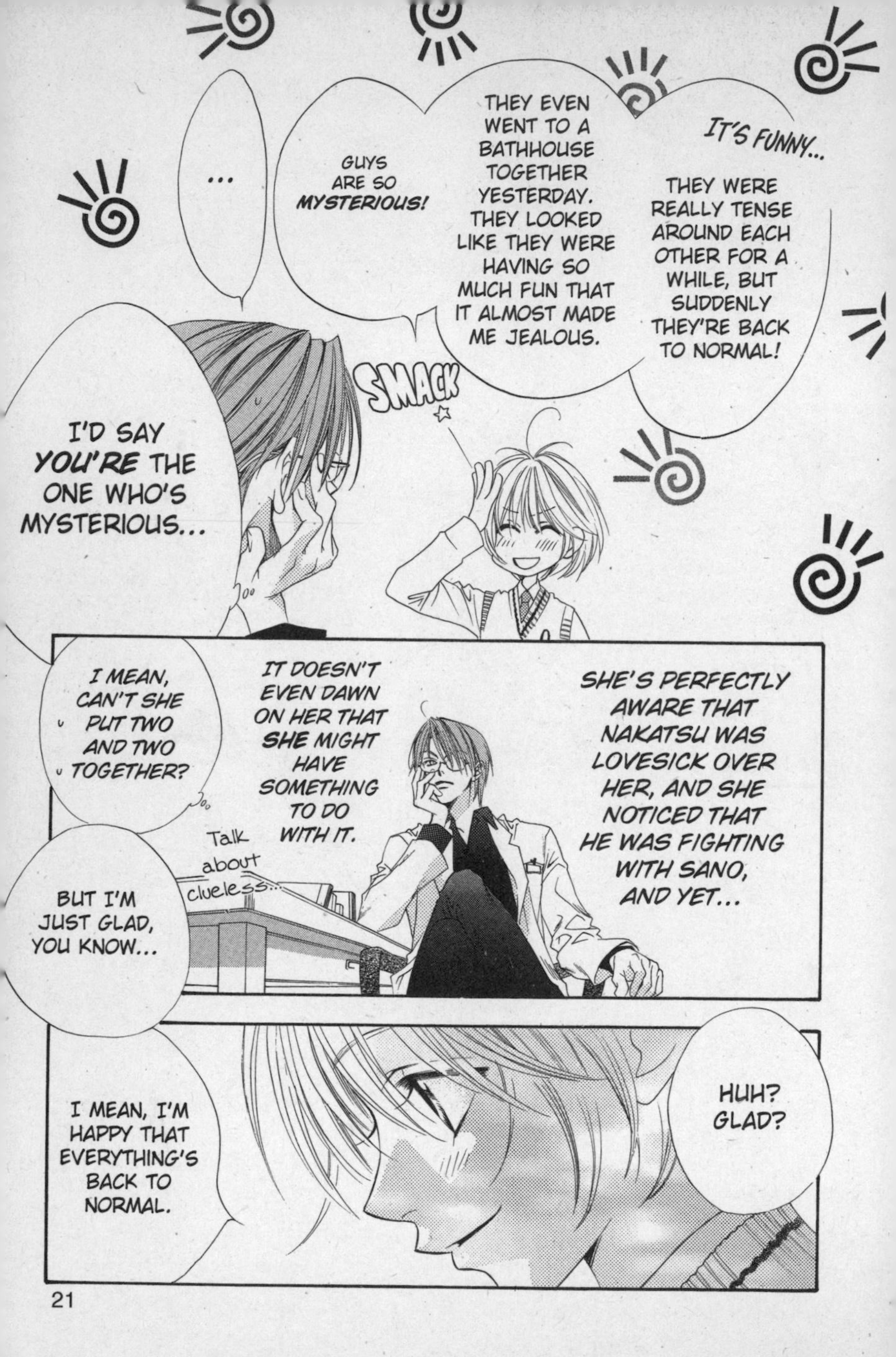
IT'S FUNNY... THEY WERE REALLY TENSE AROUND EACH OTHER FOR A WHILE, BUT SUDDENLY THEY'RE BACK TO NORMAL!
THEY EVEN WENT TO A BATHHOUSE TOGETHER YESTERDAY. THEY LOOKED LIKE THEY WERE HAVING SO MUCH FUN THAT IT ALMOST MADE ME JEALOUS.
GUYS ARE SO MYSTERIOUS!
SMACK
...
I'D SAY YOU'RE THE ONE WHO'S MYSTERIOUS...
SHE'S PERFECTLY AWARE THAT NAKATSU WAS LOVESICK OVER HER, AND SHE NOTICED THAT HE WAS FIGHTING WITH SANO, AND YET...
IT DOESN'T EVEN DAWN ON HER THAT SHE MIGHT HAVE SOMETHING TO DO WITH IT.
I MEAN, CAN'T SHE PUT TWO AND TWO TOGETHER?
Talk about clueless...
BUT I'M JUST GLAD, YOU KNOW...
HUH? GLAD?
I MEAN, I'M HAPPY THAT EVERYTHING'S BACK TO NORMAL.

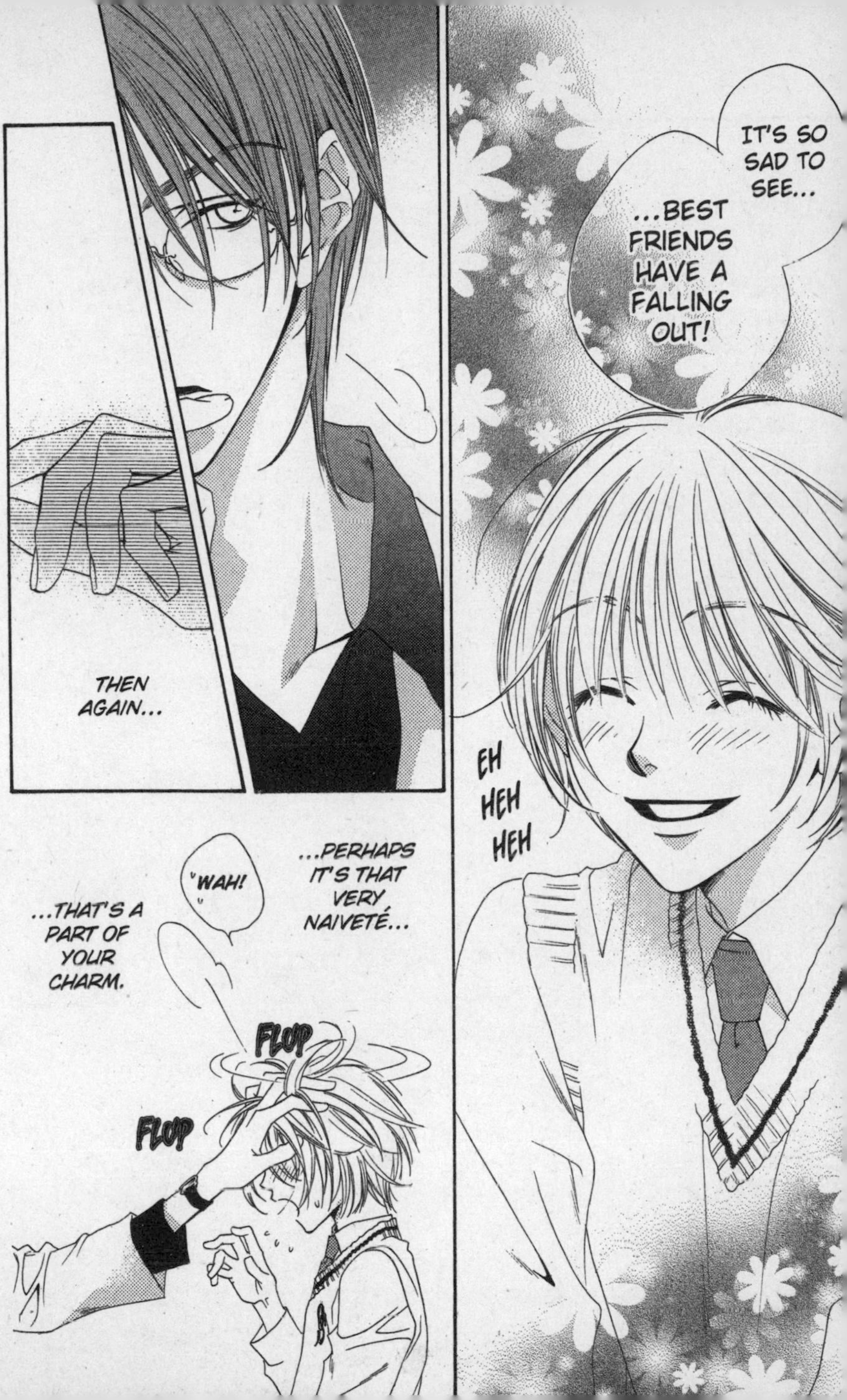
IT'S SO SAD TO SEE...
...BEST FRIENDS HAVE A FALLING OUT!
EH HEH HEH
THEN AGAIN...
...PERHAPS IT'S THAT VERY NAIVETÉ...
WAH!
...THAT'S A PART OF YOUR CHARM.
FLOP
FLOP

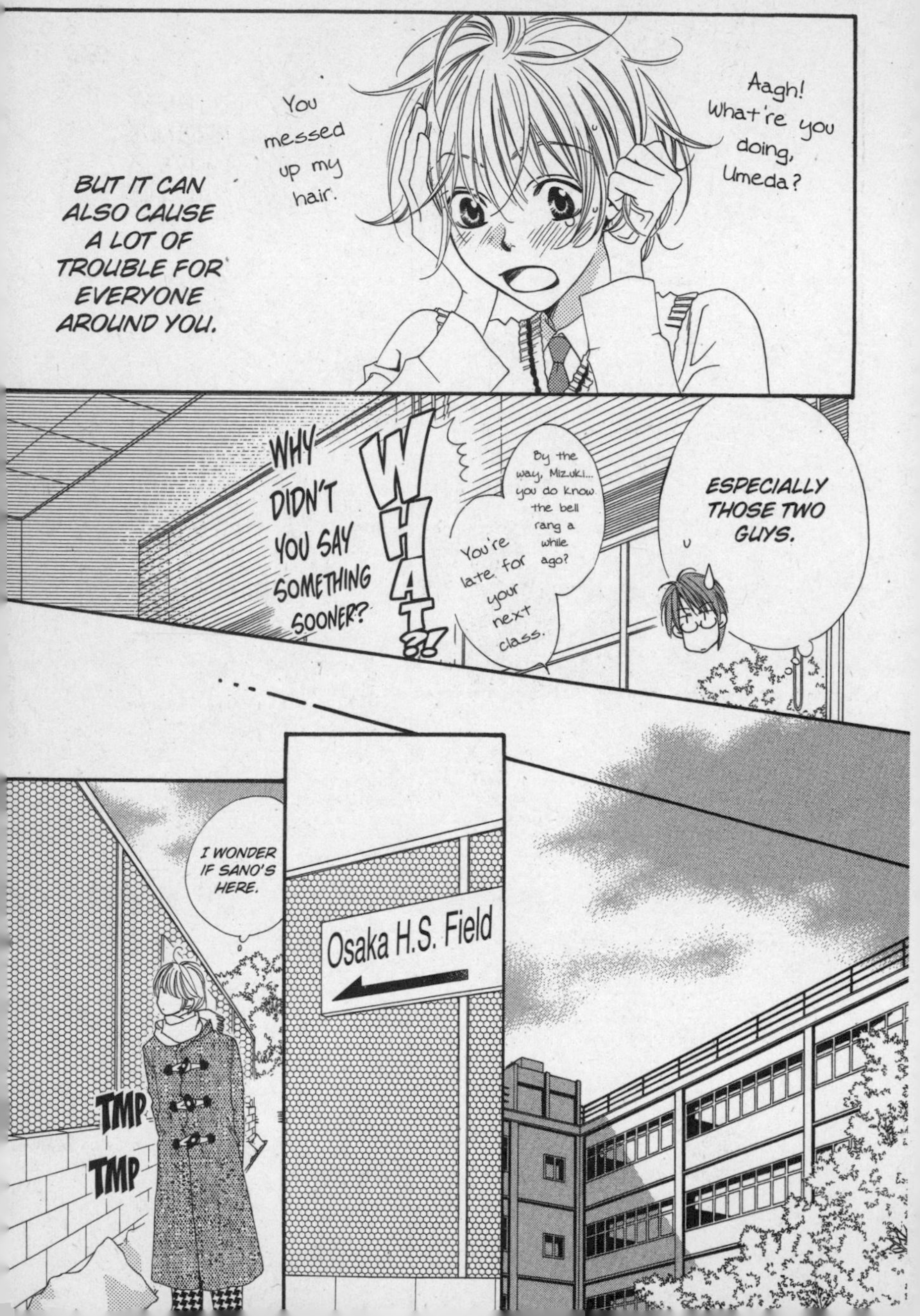
Aagh! What're you doing, Umeda?
You messed up my hair.
BUT IT CAN ALSO CAUSE A LOT OF TROUBLE FOR EVERYONE AROUND YOU.
ESPECIALLY THOSE TWO GUYS.
By the way, Mizuki... you do know the bell rang a while ago?
You're late for your next class.
WHAT?!
WHY DIDN'T YOU SAY SOMETHING SOONER?
Osaka H.S. Field
I WONDER IF SANO'S HERE.
TMP
TMP

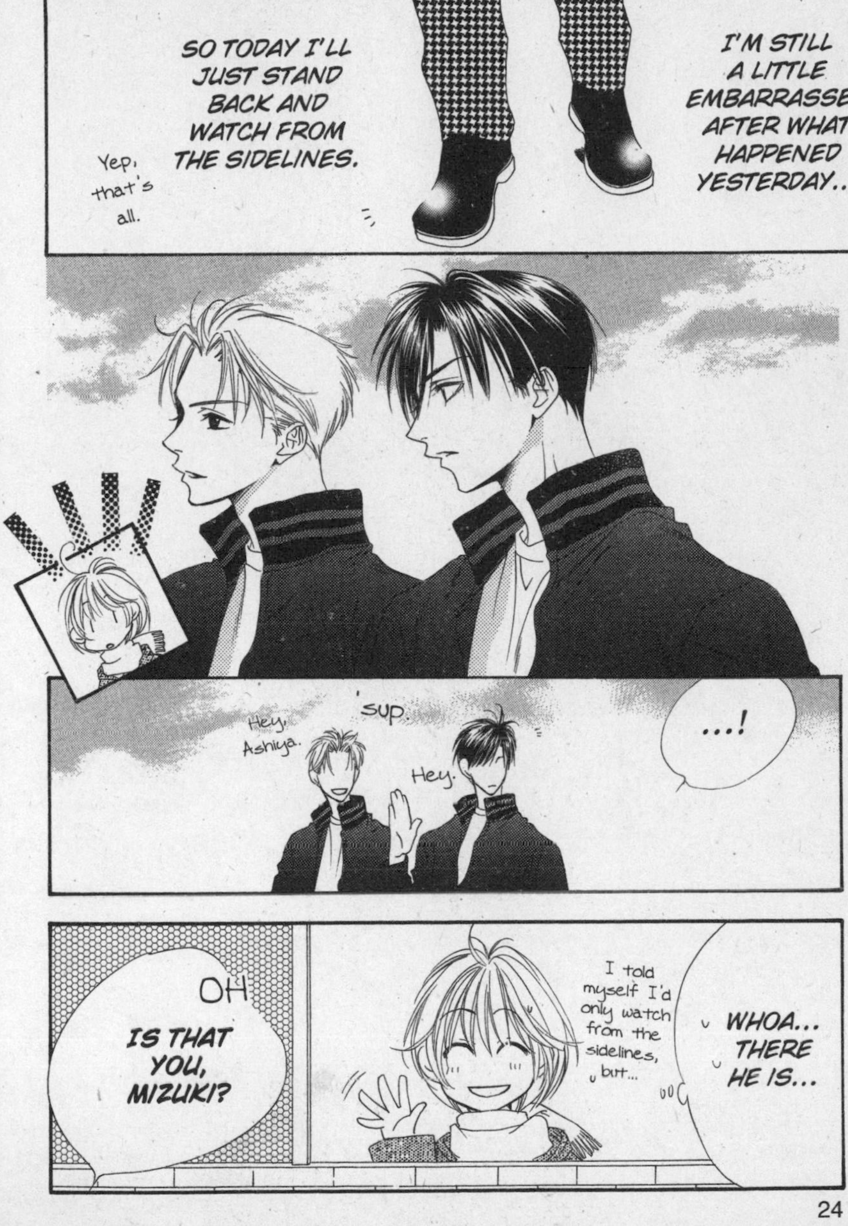
I'M STILL A LITTLE EMBARRASSED AFTER WHAT HAPPENED YESTERDAY...
SO TODAY I'LL JUST STAND BACK AND WATCH FROM THE SIDELINES.
Yep, that's all.
...!
'sup.
Hey.
Hey, Ashiya.
WHOA... THERE HE IS...
I told myself I'd only watch from the sidelines, but...
OH
IS THAT YOU, MIZUKI?

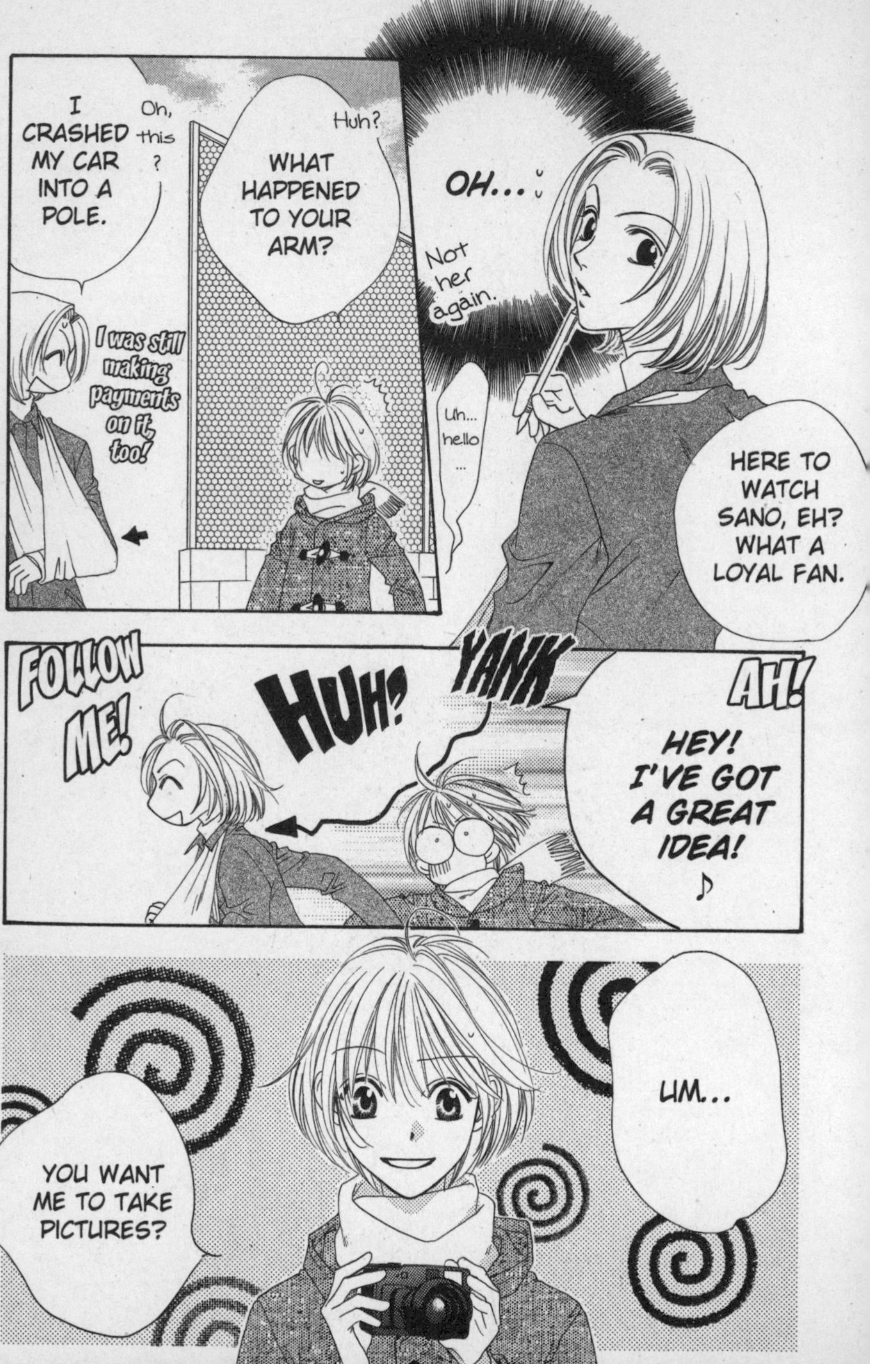
OH...
Not her again.
HERE TO WATCH SANO, EH? WHAT A LOYAL FAN.
Uh... hello...
Huh?
WHAT HAPPENED TO YOUR ARM?
Oh, this?
I CRASHED MY CAR INTO A POLE.
I was still making payments on it, too!
AH!
HEY! I'VE GOT A GREAT IDEA! ♪
YANK
HUH?
FOLLOW ME!
UM...
YOU WANT ME TO TAKE PICTURES?

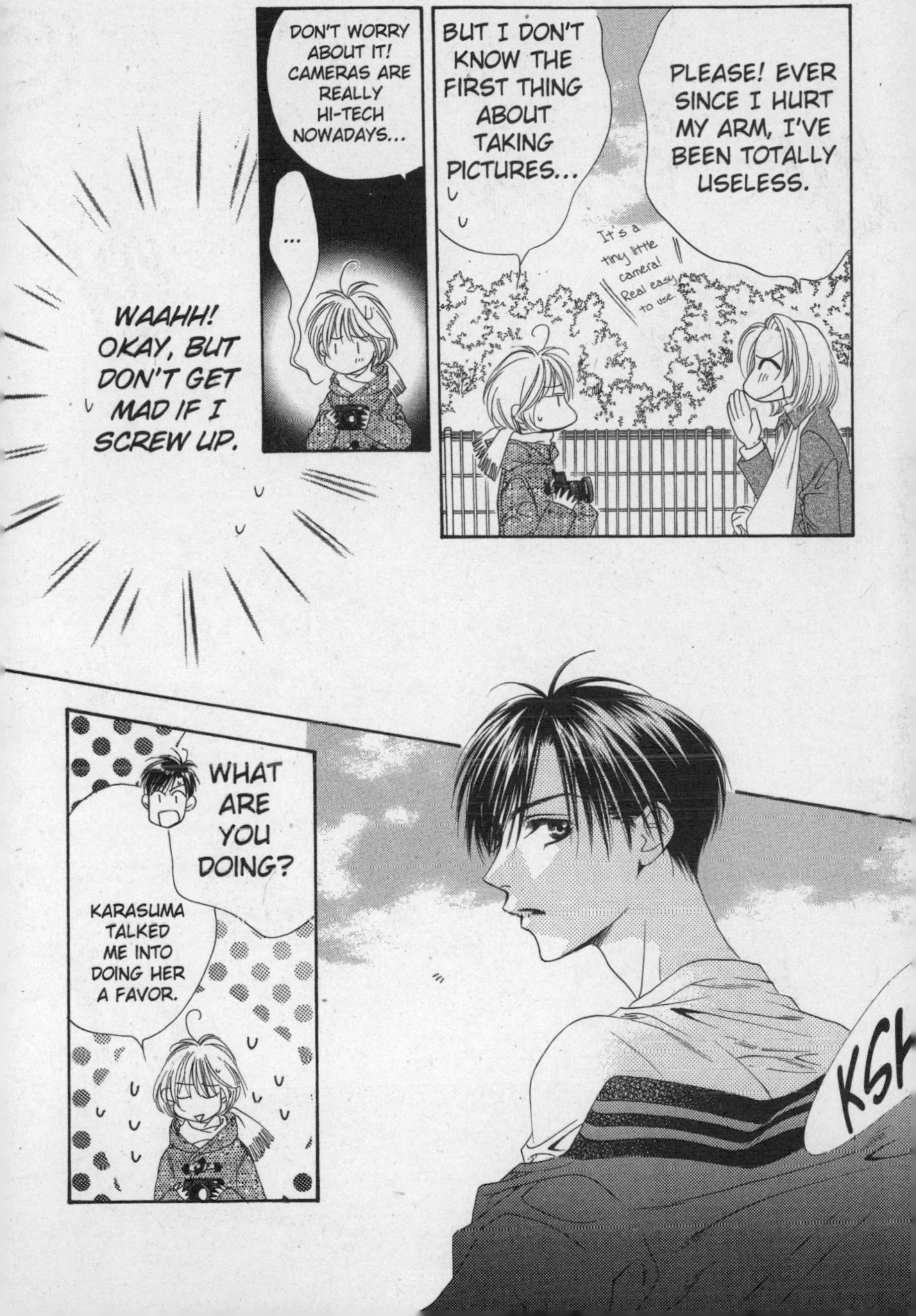
PLEASE! EVER SINCE I HURT MY ARM, I'VE BEEN TOTALLY USELESS.
BUT I DON'T KNOW THE FIRST THING ABOUT TAKING PICTURES...
It's a tiny little camera! Real easy to use.
DON'T WORRY ABOUT IT! CAMERAS ARE REALLY HI-TECH NOWADAYS...
...
WAAHH! OKAY, BUT DON'T GET MAD IF I SCREW UP.
KSH
WHAT ARE YOU DOING?
KARASUMA TALKED ME INTO DOING HER A FAVOR.

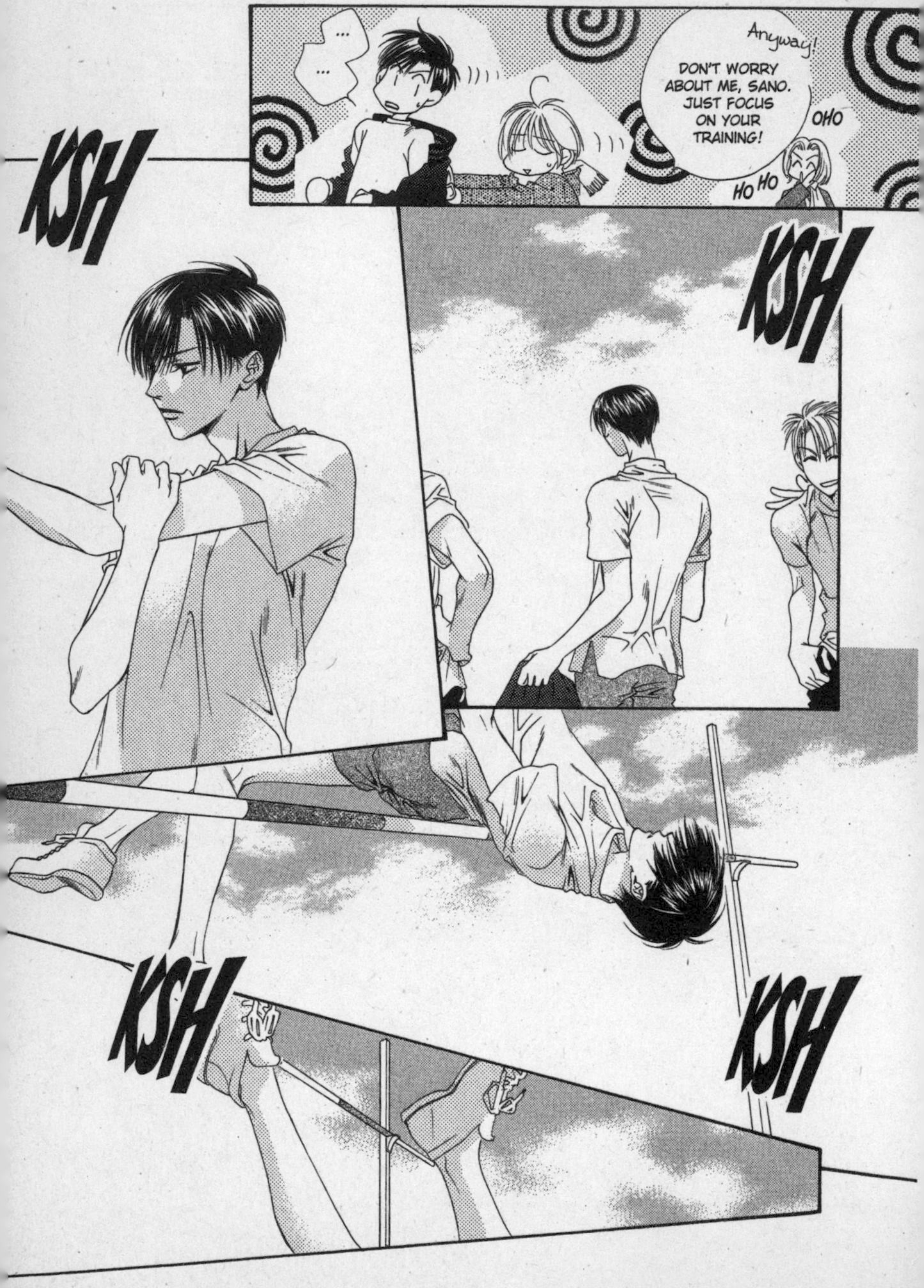

Anyway!
DON'T WORRY ABOUT ME, SANO. JUST FOCUS ON YOUR TRAINING!
OHO HO HO
...
...
KSH
KSH
KSH
KSH

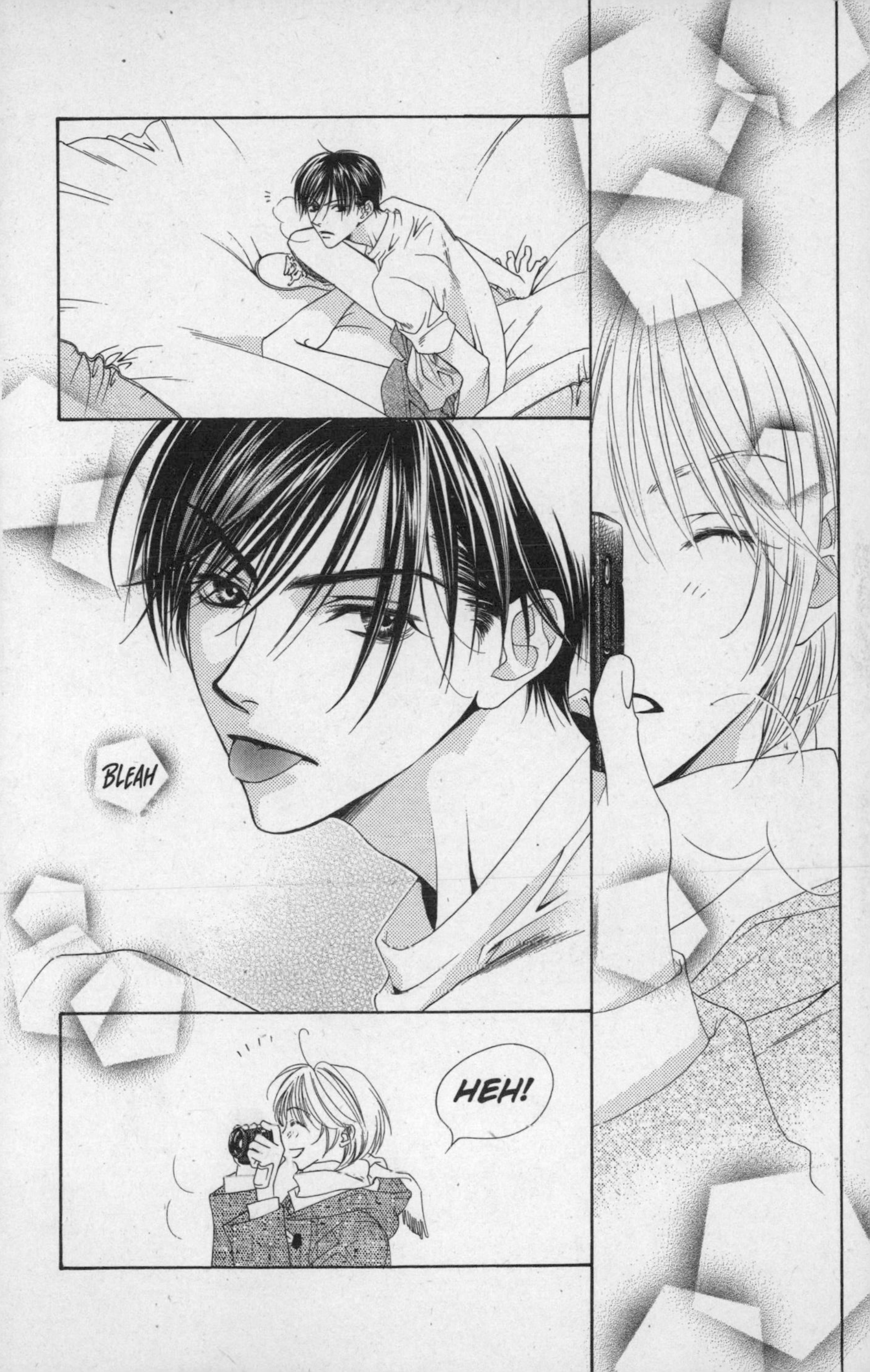
BLEAH
HEH!

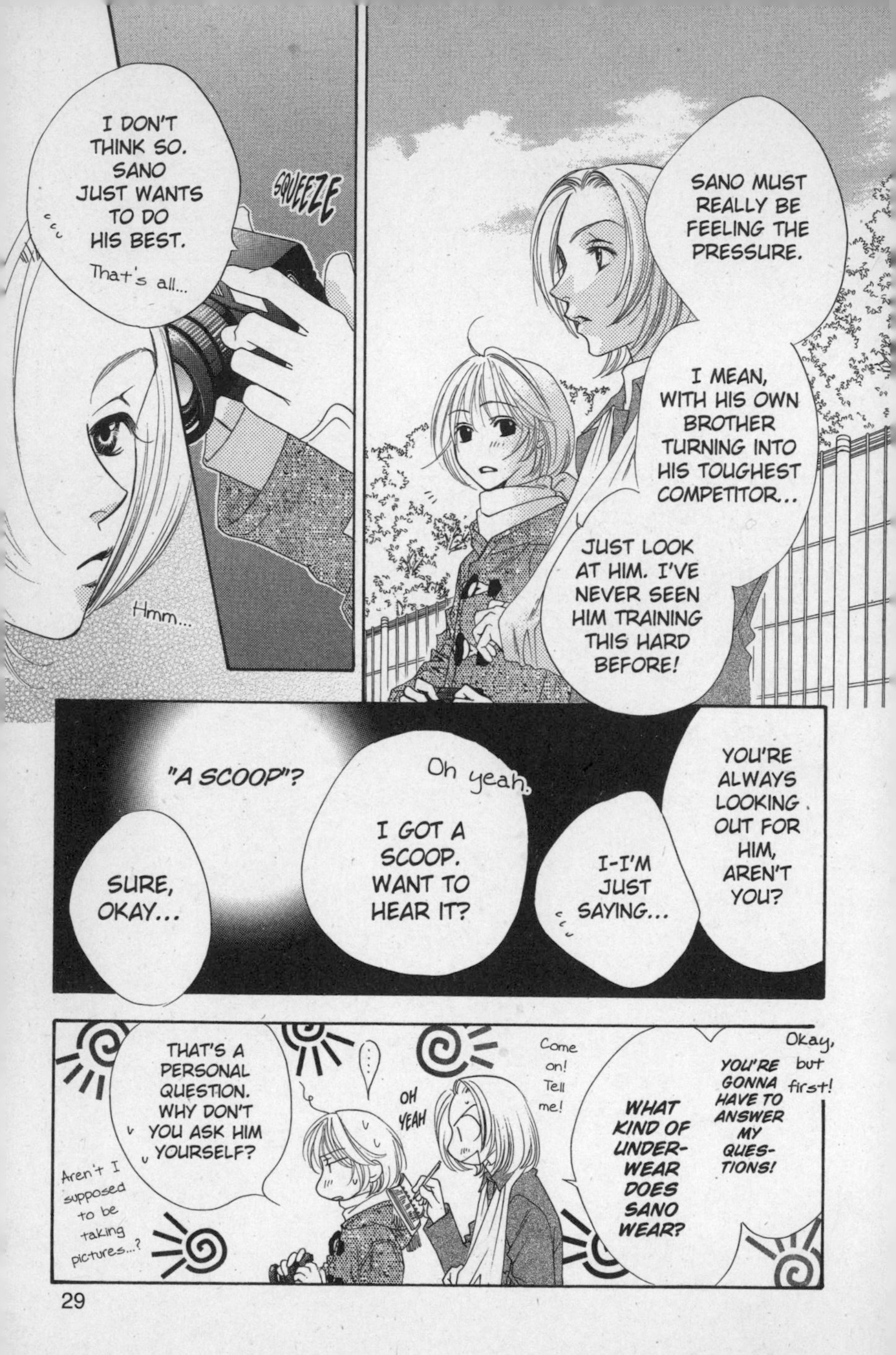
SANO MUST REALLY BE FEELING THE PRESSURE.
I MEAN, WITH HIS OWN BROTHER TURNING INTO HIS TOUGHEST COMPETITOR...
JUST LOOK AT HIM. I'VE NEVER SEEN HIM TRAINING THIS HARD BEFORE!
SQUEEZE
I DON'T THINK SO. SANO JUST WANTS TO DO HIS BEST.
That's all...
Hmm...
YOU'RE ALWAYS LOOKING OUT FOR HIM, AREN'T YOU?
I-I'M JUST SAYING...
Oh yeah.
I GOT A SCOOP. WANT TO HEAR IT?
"A SCOOP"?
SURE, OKAY...
Okay, but first!
YOU'RE GONNA HAVE TO ANSWER MY QUES-TIONS!
WHAT KIND OF UNDER-WEAR DOES SANO WEAR?
Come on! Tell me!
OH YEAH
...
THAT'S A PERSONAL QUESTION. WHY DON'T YOU ASK HIM YOURSELF?
Aren't I supposed to be taking pictures...?

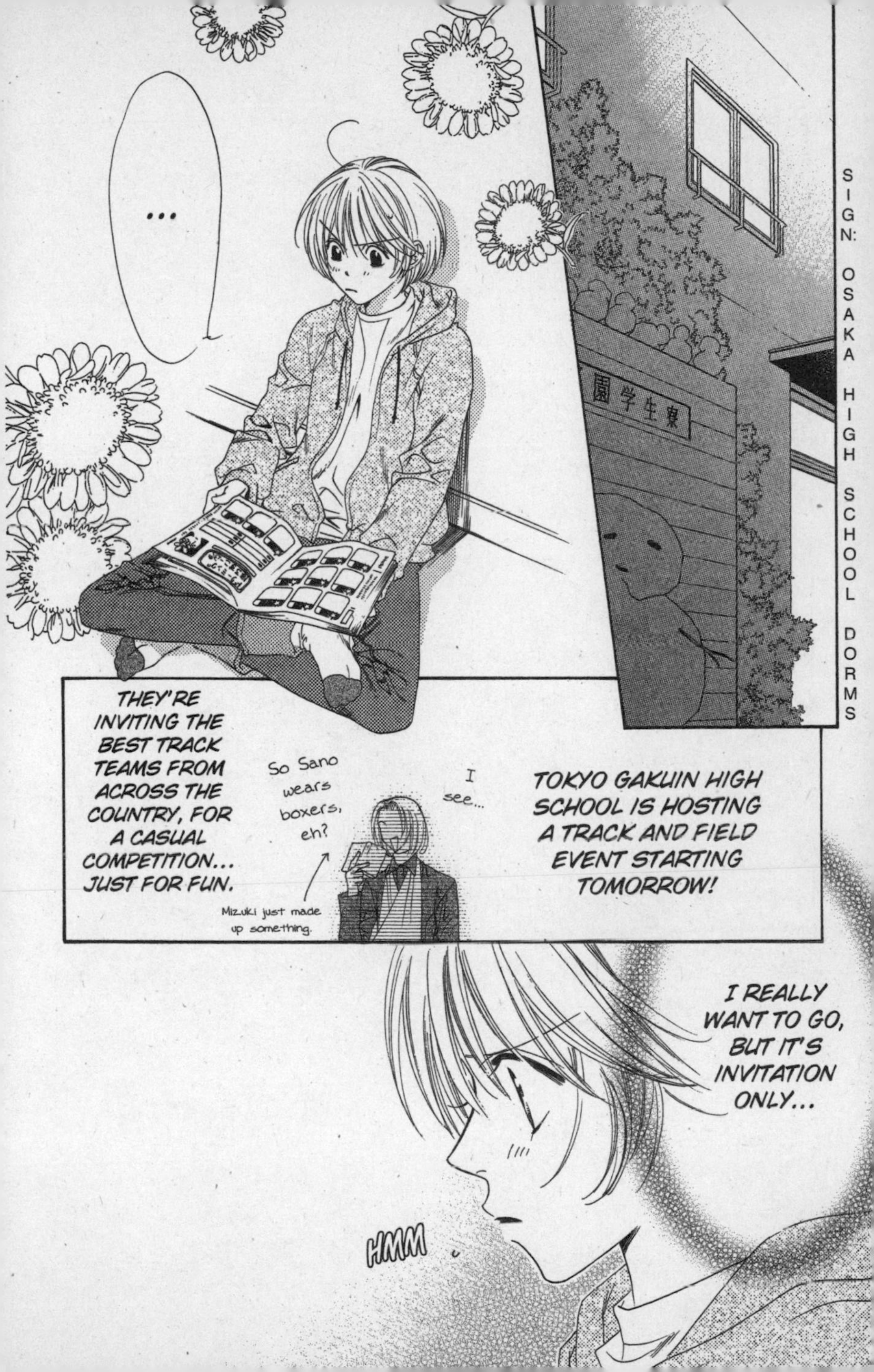

SIGN: OSAKA HIGH SCHOOL DORMS
東生学園
...
TOKYO GAKUIN HIGH SCHOOL IS HOSTING A TRACK AND FIELD EVENT STARTING TOMORROW!
I see...
So Sano wears boxers, eh?
Mizuki just made up something.
THEY'RE INVITING THE BEST TRACK TEAMS FROM ACROSS THE COUNTRY, FOR A CASUAL COMPETITION... JUST FOR FUN.
I REALLY WANT TO GO, BUT IT'S INVITATION ONLY...
HMM

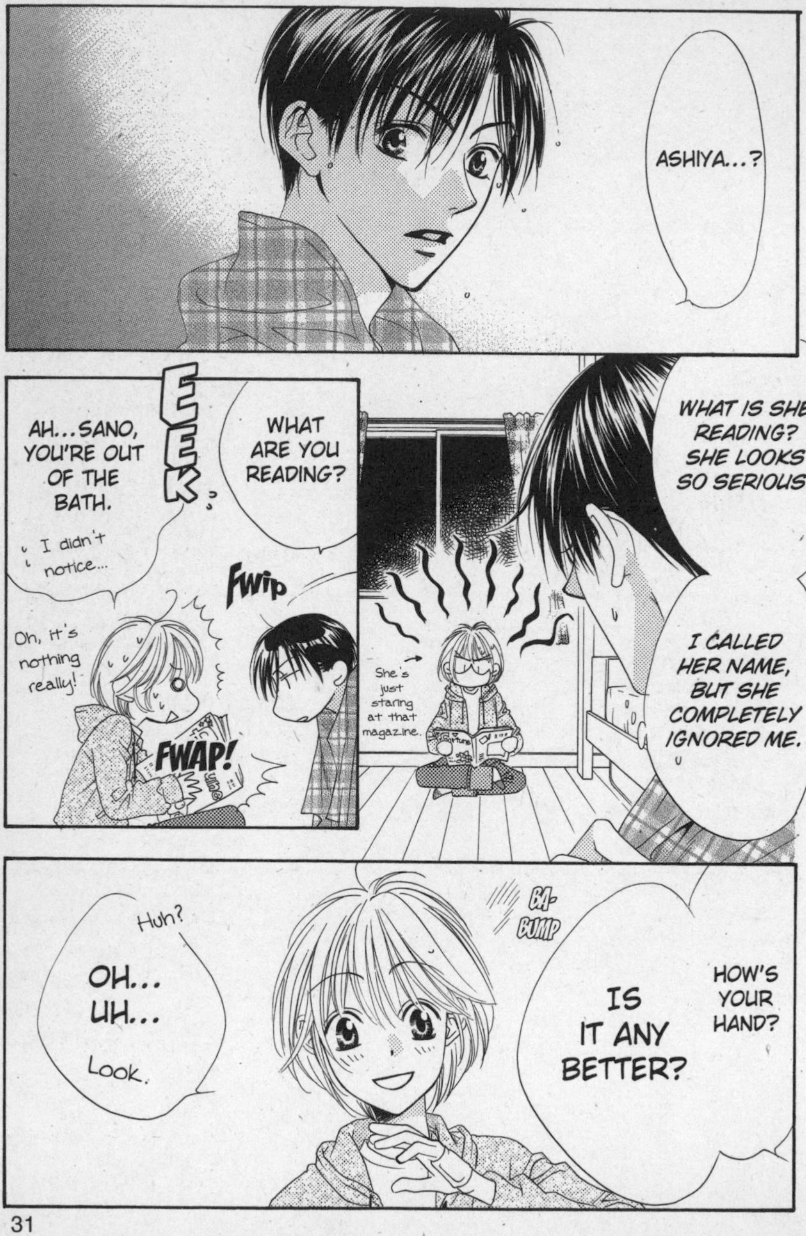
ASHIYA...?
WHAT IS SHE READING? SHE LOOKS SO SERIOUS.
I CALLED HER NAME, BUT SHE COMPLETELY IGNORED ME.
She's just staring at that magazine.
WHAT ARE YOU READING?
EEK
AH...SANO, YOU'RE OUT OF THE BATH.
I didn't notice...
FWIP
Oh, it's nothing really!
FWAP!
HOW'S YOUR HAND?
IS IT ANY BETTER?
BA-BUMP
Huh?
OH... UH...
Look.

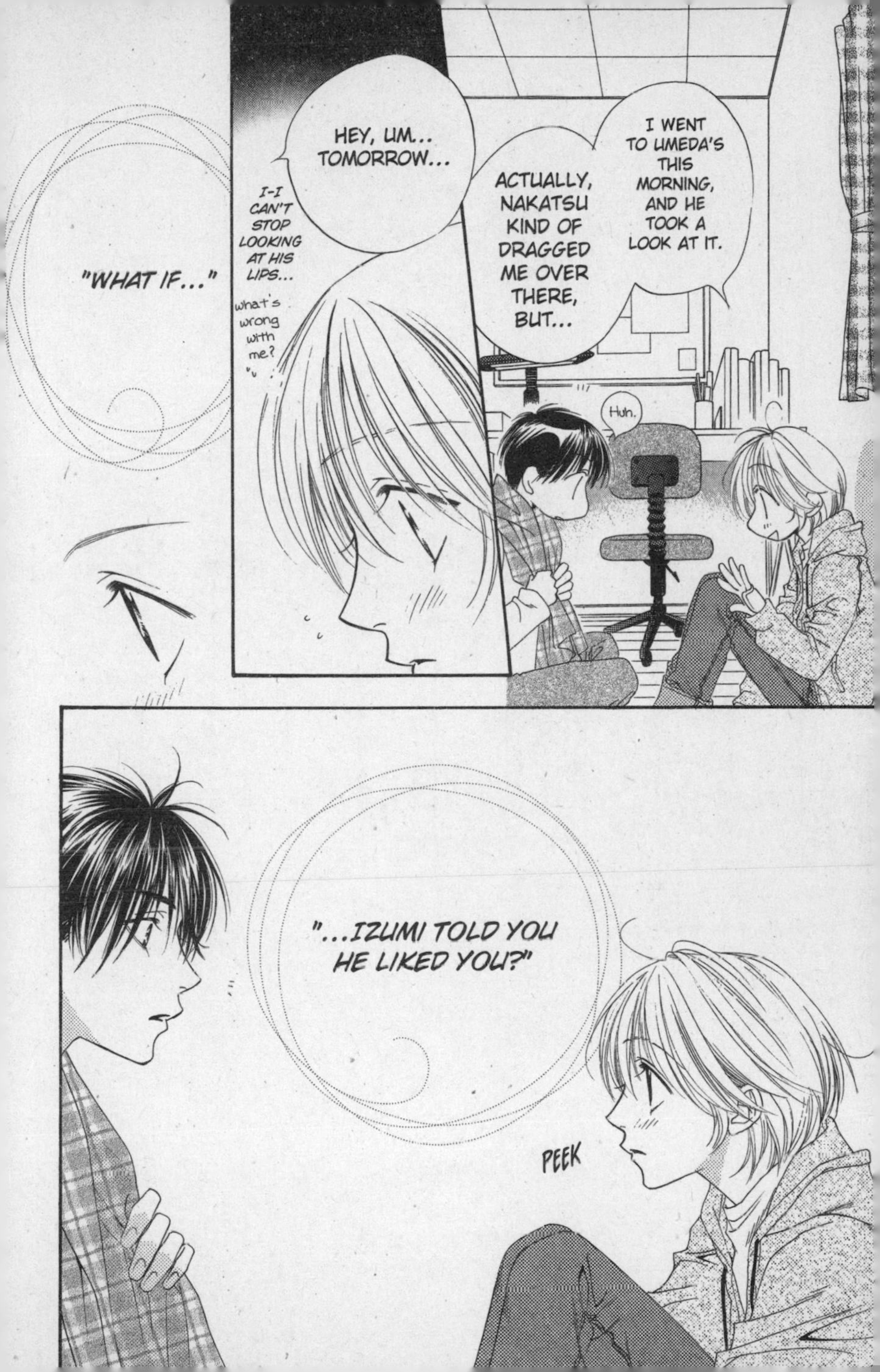
I WENT TO UMEDA'S THIS MORNING, AND HE TOOK A LOOK AT IT.
ACTUALLY, NAKATSU KIND OF DRAGGED ME OVER THERE, BUT...
Huh.
HEY, UM... TOMORROW...
I-I CAN'T STOP LOOKING AT HIS LIPS...
what's wrong with me?
"WHAT IF..."
"...IZUMI TOLD YOU HE LIKED YOU?"
PEEK

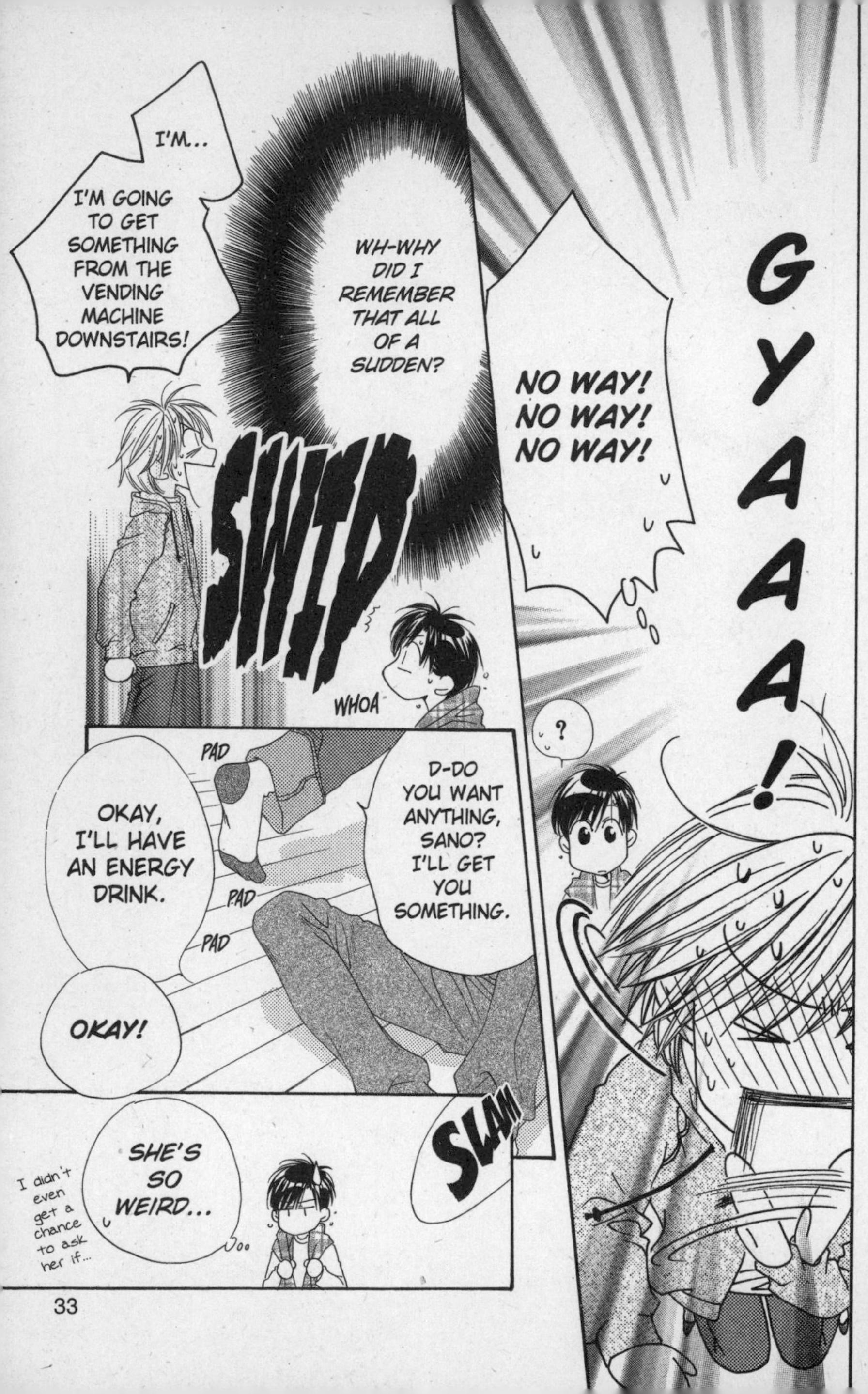
NO WAY!
NO WAY!
NO WAY!
GYAAAA!
?
I'M...
I'M GOING TO GET SOMETHING FROM THE VENDING MACHINE DOWNSTAIRS!
WH-WHY DID I REMEMBER THAT ALL OF A SUDDEN?
SWIP
WHOA
D-DO YOU WANT ANYTHING, SANO? I'LL GET YOU SOMETHING.
PAD
OKAY, I'LL HAVE AN ENERGY DRINK.
PAD
PAD
OKAY!
SLAM
SHE'S SO WEIRD...
I didn't even get a chance to ask her if...

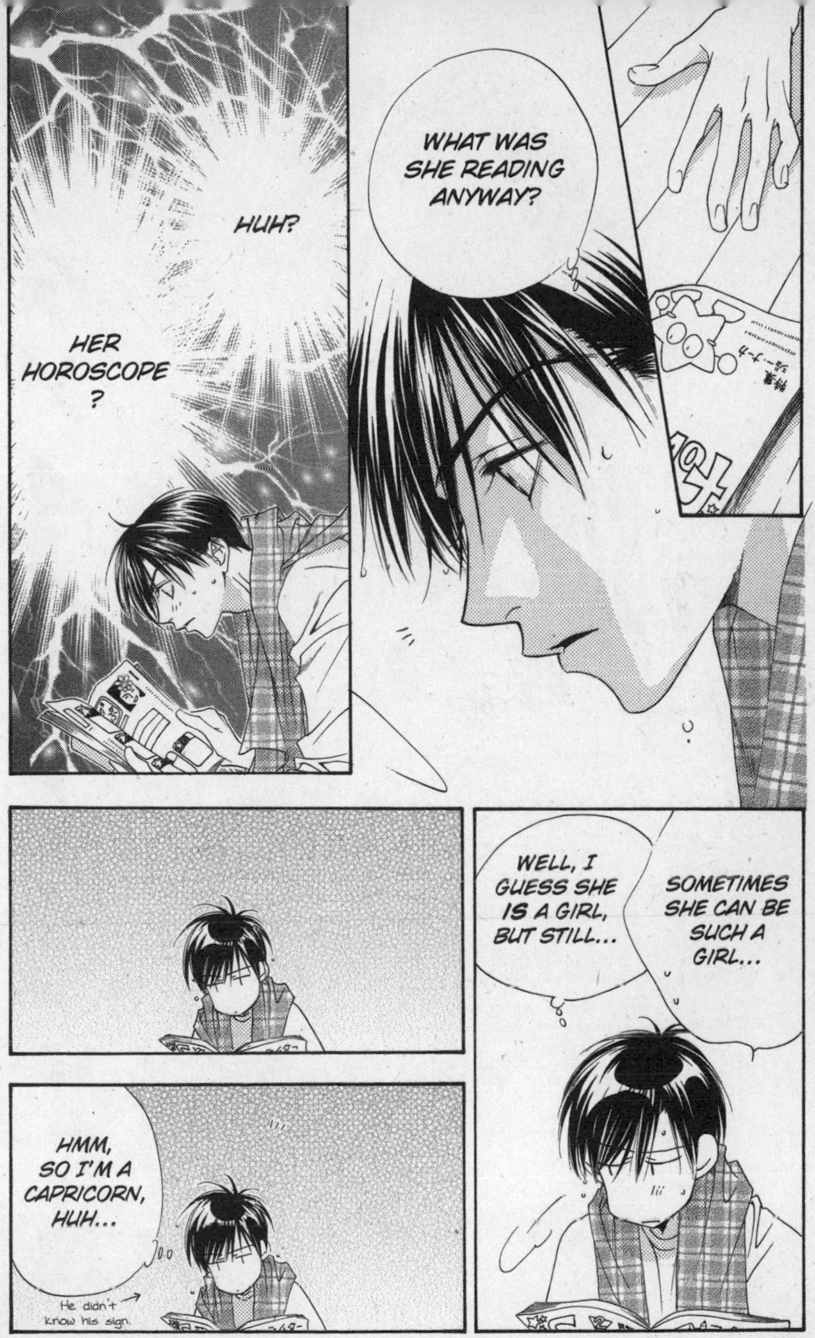
WHAT WAS SHE READING ANYWAY?
HUH?
HER HOROSCOPE?
SOMETIMES SHE CAN BE SUCH A GIRL...
WELL, I GUESS SHE IS A GIRL, BUT STILL...
HMM, SO I'M A CAPRICORN, HUH...
He didn't know his sign.

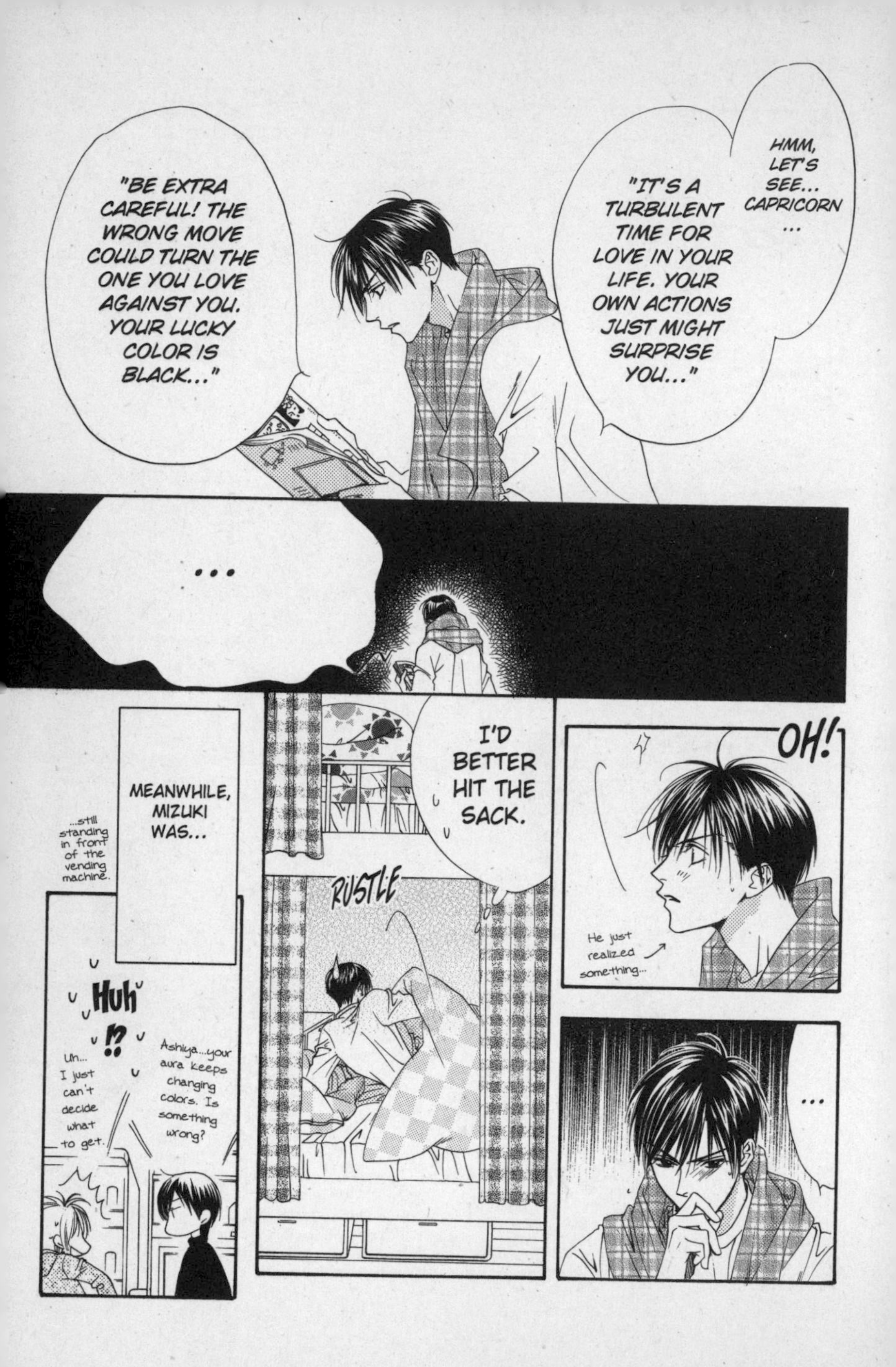
HMM, LET'S SEE... CAPRICORN ...
"IT'S A TURBULENT TIME FOR LOVE IN YOUR LIFE. YOUR OWN ACTIONS JUST MIGHT SURPRISE YOU..."
"BE EXTRA CAREFUL! THE WRONG MOVE COULD TURN THE ONE YOU LOVE AGAINST YOU. YOUR LUCKY COLOR IS BLACK..."
...
OH!
He just realized something...
I'D BETTER HIT THE SACK.
RUSTLE
...
MEANWHILE, MIZUKI WAS...
...still standing in front of the vending machine.
Huh !?
Ashiya...your aura keeps changing colors. Is something wrong?
Uh... I just can't decide what to get.

SIGN=Tokyo Gakuin High School

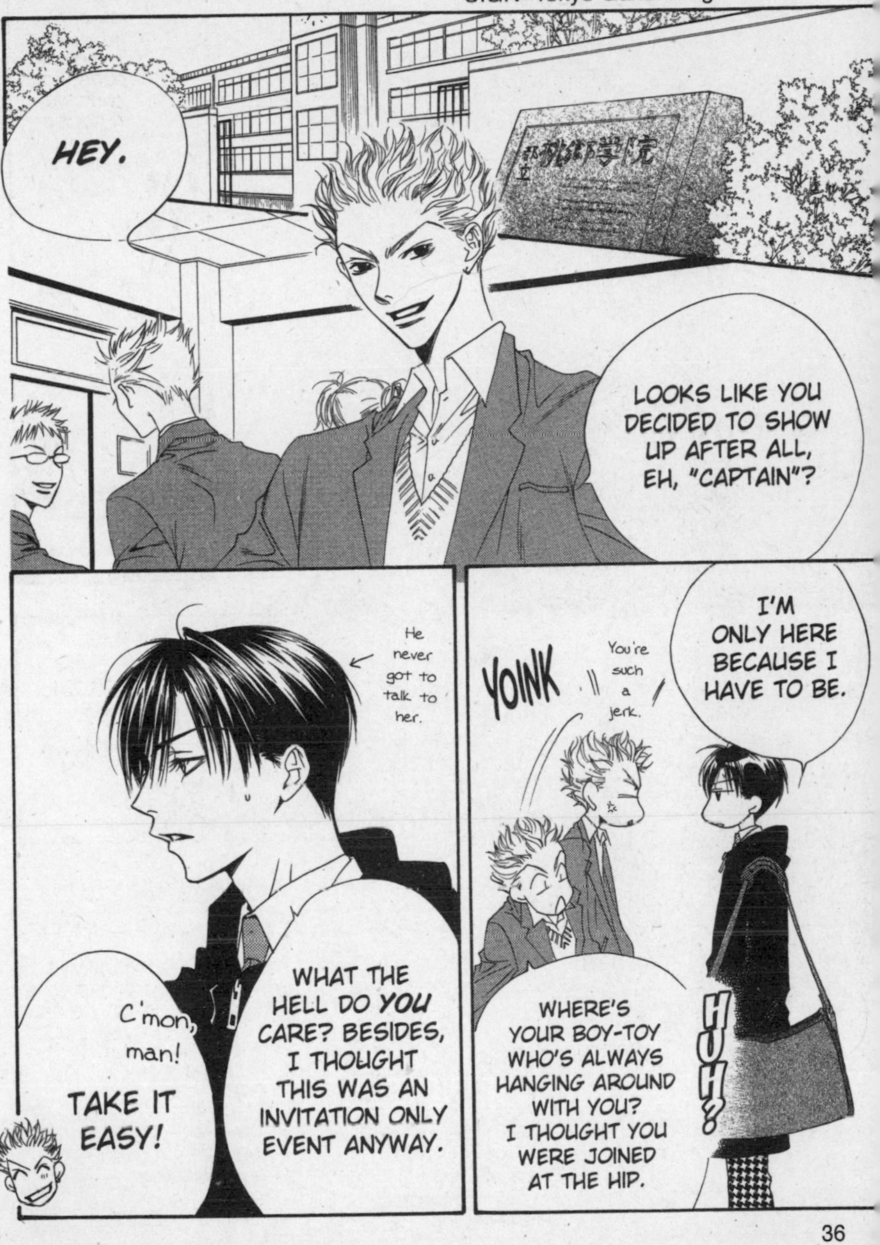
HEY.
LOOKS LIKE YOU DECIDED TO SHOW UP AFTER ALL, EH, "CAPTAIN"?
I'M ONLY HERE BECAUSE I HAVE TO BE.
YOINK
You're such a jerk.
HUH?
WHERE'S YOUR BOY-TOY WHO'S ALWAYS HANGING AROUND WITH YOU? I THOUGHT YOU WERE JOINED AT THE HIP.
He never got to talk to her.
WHAT THE HELL DO *YOU* CARE? BESIDES, I THOUGHT THIS WAS AN INVITATION ONLY EVENT ANYWAY.
C'mon, man!
TAKE IT EASY!

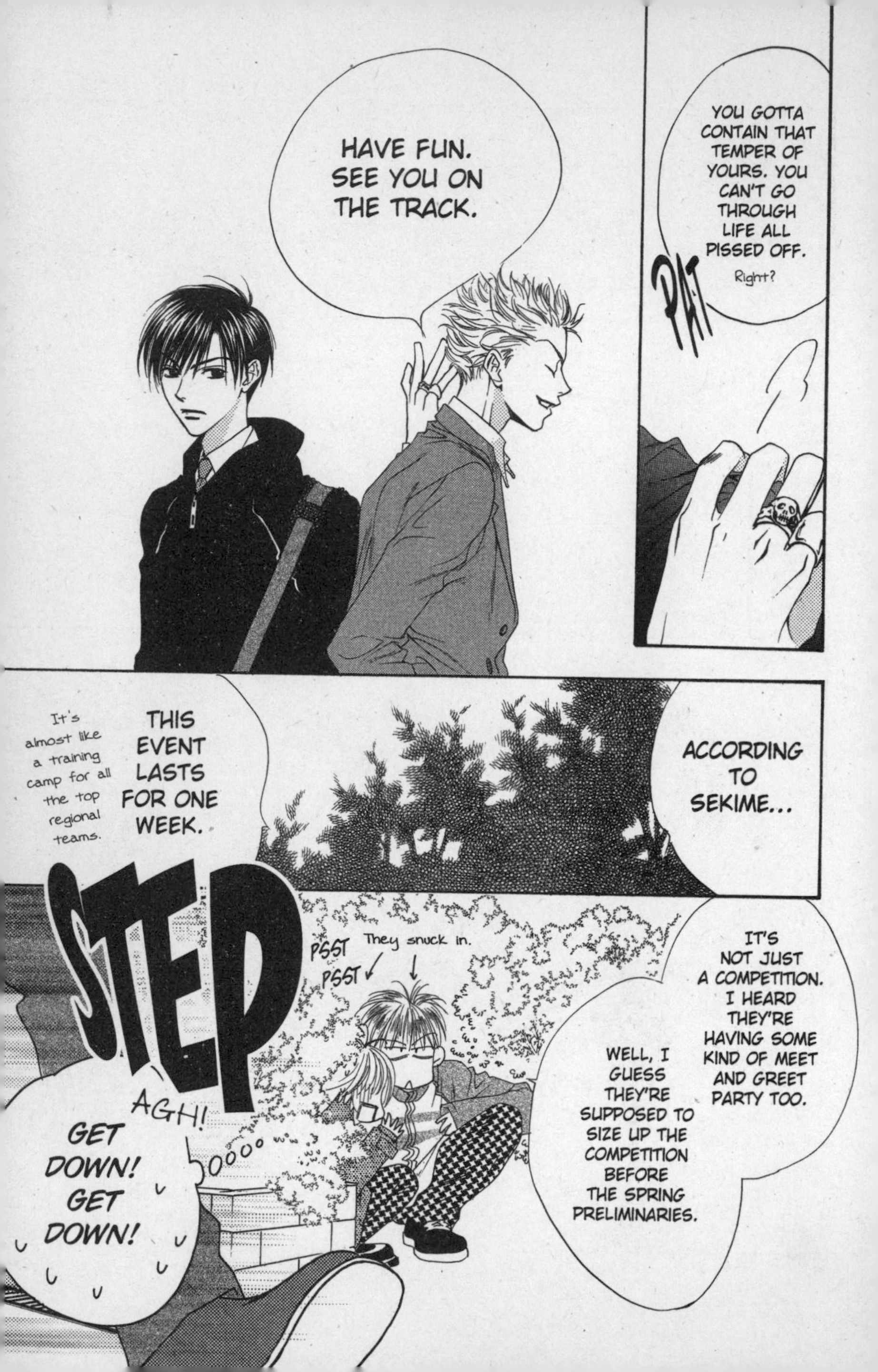
YOU GOTTA CONTAIN THAT TEMPER OF YOURS. YOU CAN'T GO THROUGH LIFE ALL PISSED OFF.
Right?
PAT
HAVE FUN. SEE YOU ON THE TRACK.
ACCORDING TO SEKIME...
THIS EVENT LASTS FOR ONE WEEK.
It's almost like a training camp for all the top regional teams.
IT'S NOT JUST A COMPETITION. I HEARD THEY'RE HAVING SOME KIND OF MEET AND GREET PARTY TOO.
WELL, I GUESS THEY'RE SUPPOSED TO SIZE UP THE COMPETITION BEFORE THE SPRING PRELIMINARIES.
They snuck in.
PSST PSST
STEP
AGH!
GET DOWN! GET DOWN!

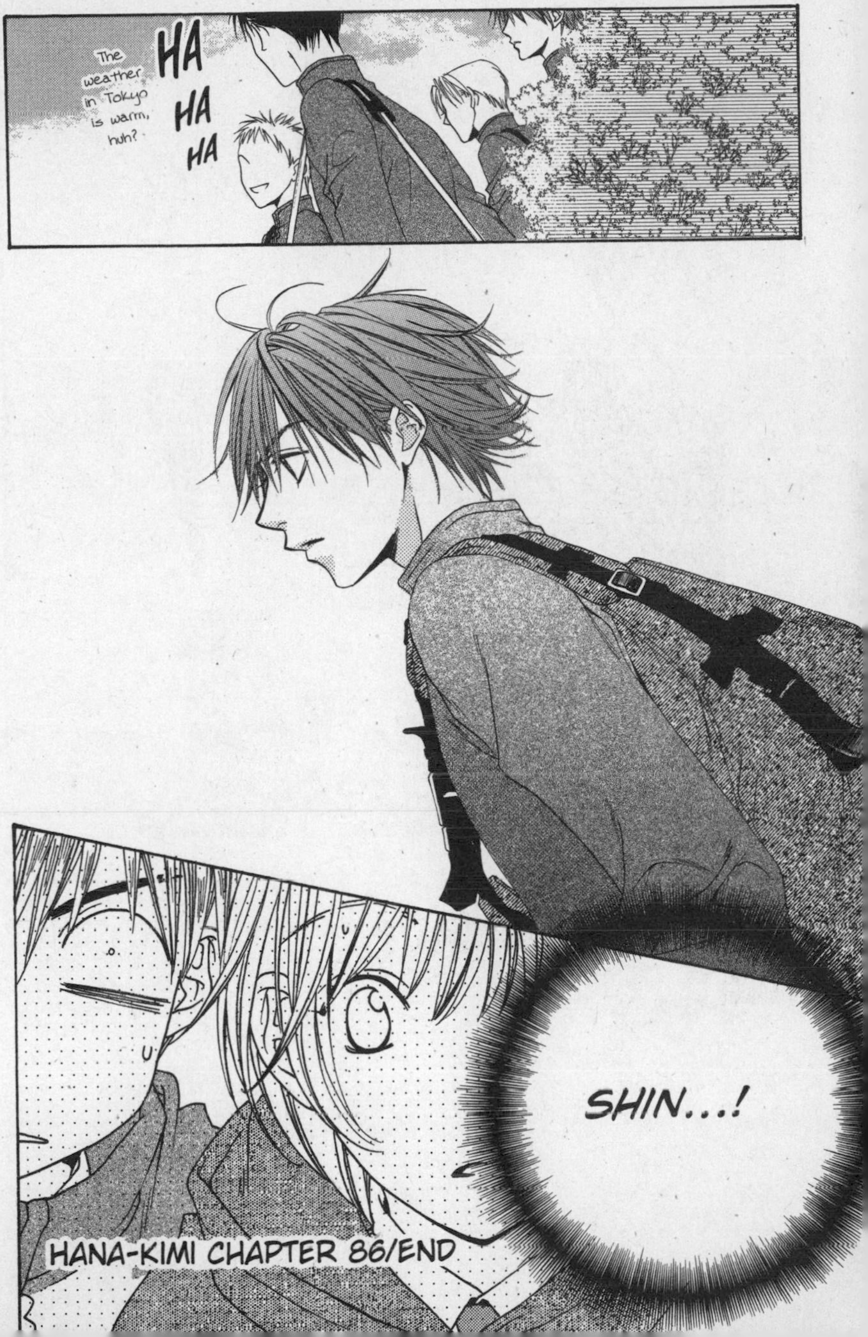
HA HA HA
The weather in Tokyo is warm, huh?
SHIN...!
HANA-KIMI CHAPTER 86/END

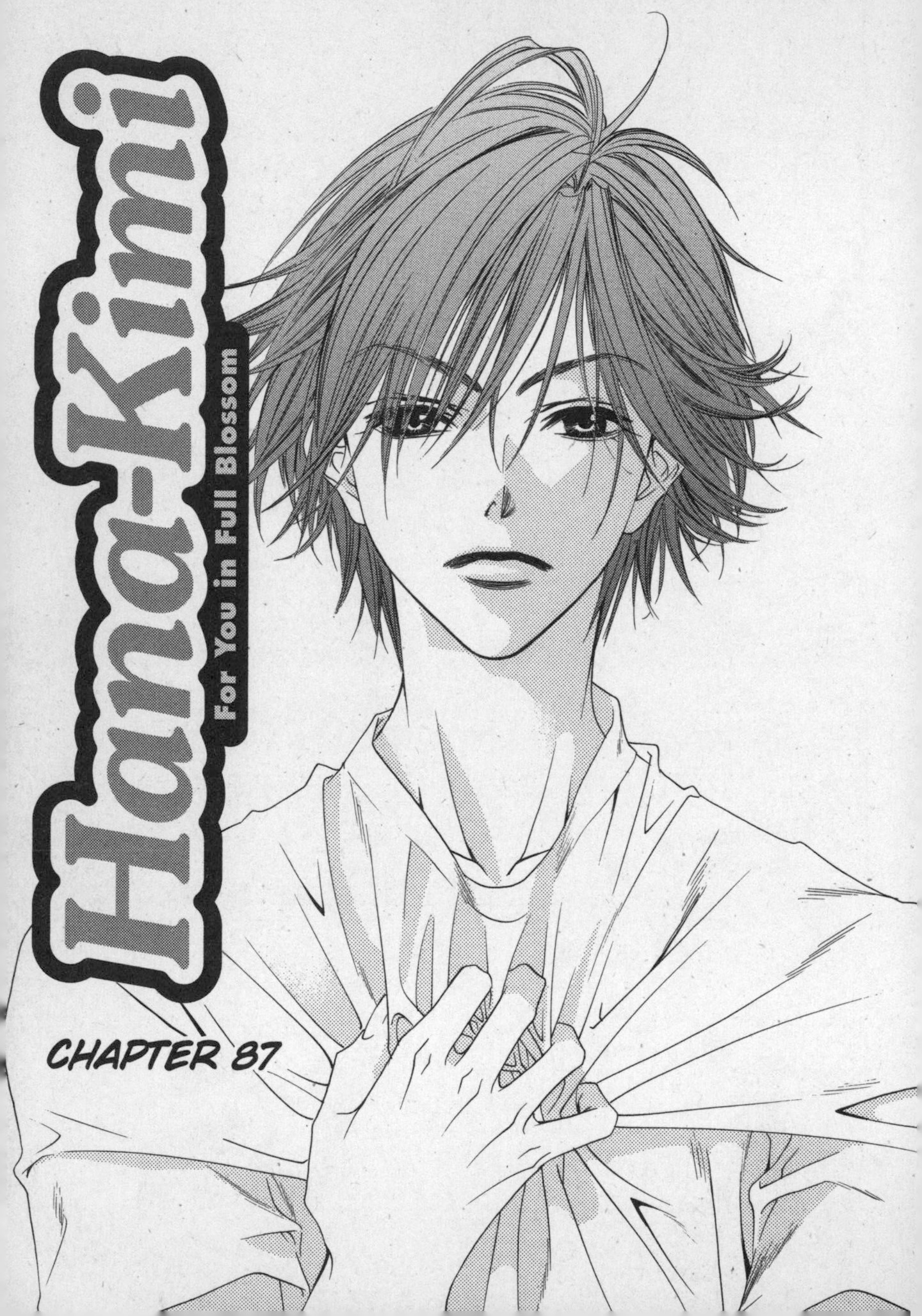
Hana-Kimi
For You in Full Blossom
CHAPTER 87

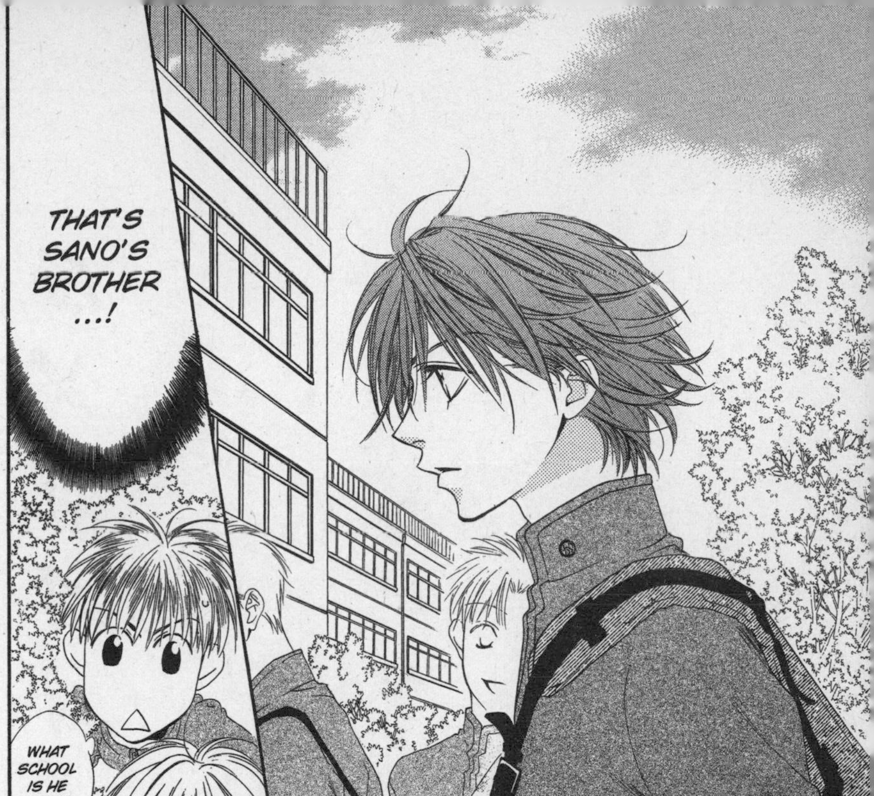
THAT'S SANO'S BROTHER ...!
WHAT SCHOOL IS HE FROM?

SHOTARO MORIKUBO

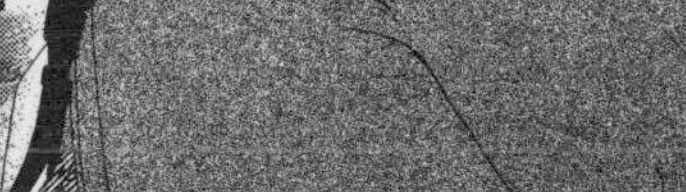

This doesn't really look like him...sorry.

I went to see Shotaro Morikubo's "Okubyomono no G-Koi" (Coward's Action G) tour. I went twice. One show was at Shibuya Deseo and the other was at the Takadanobaba Arena. I really enjoyed both shows! It was the best concert I've ever seen!

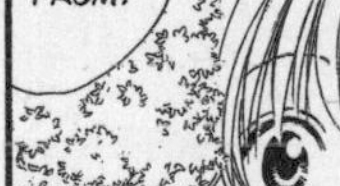
SM

I love seeing bands play at tiny little venues. (I hadn't been to a tiny venue like that in 7 or 8 years). It really gives the performer a chance to connect with the audience.

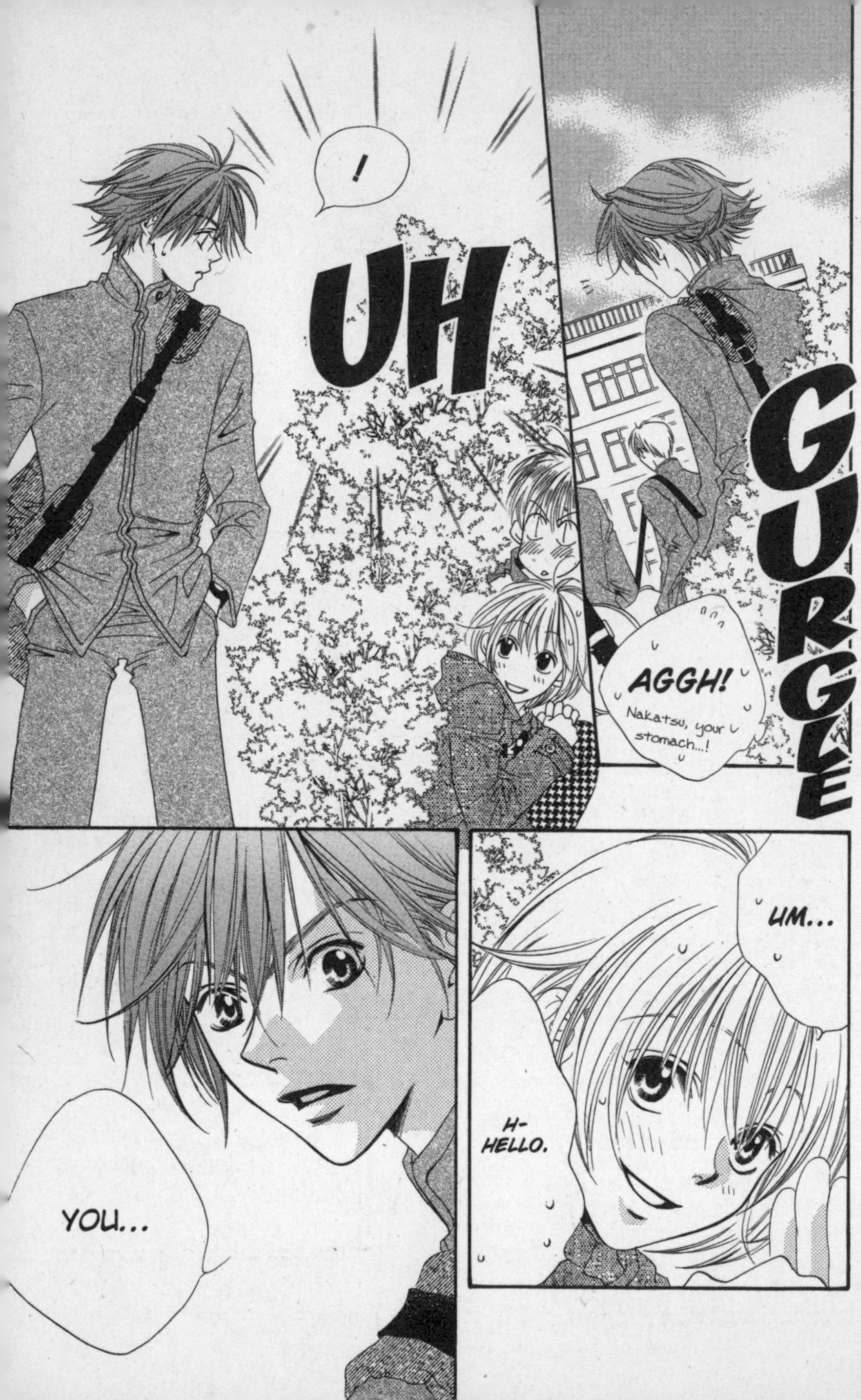
GURGLE
AGGH!
Nakatsu, your stomach...!
UH
!
UM...
H-HELLO.
YOU...

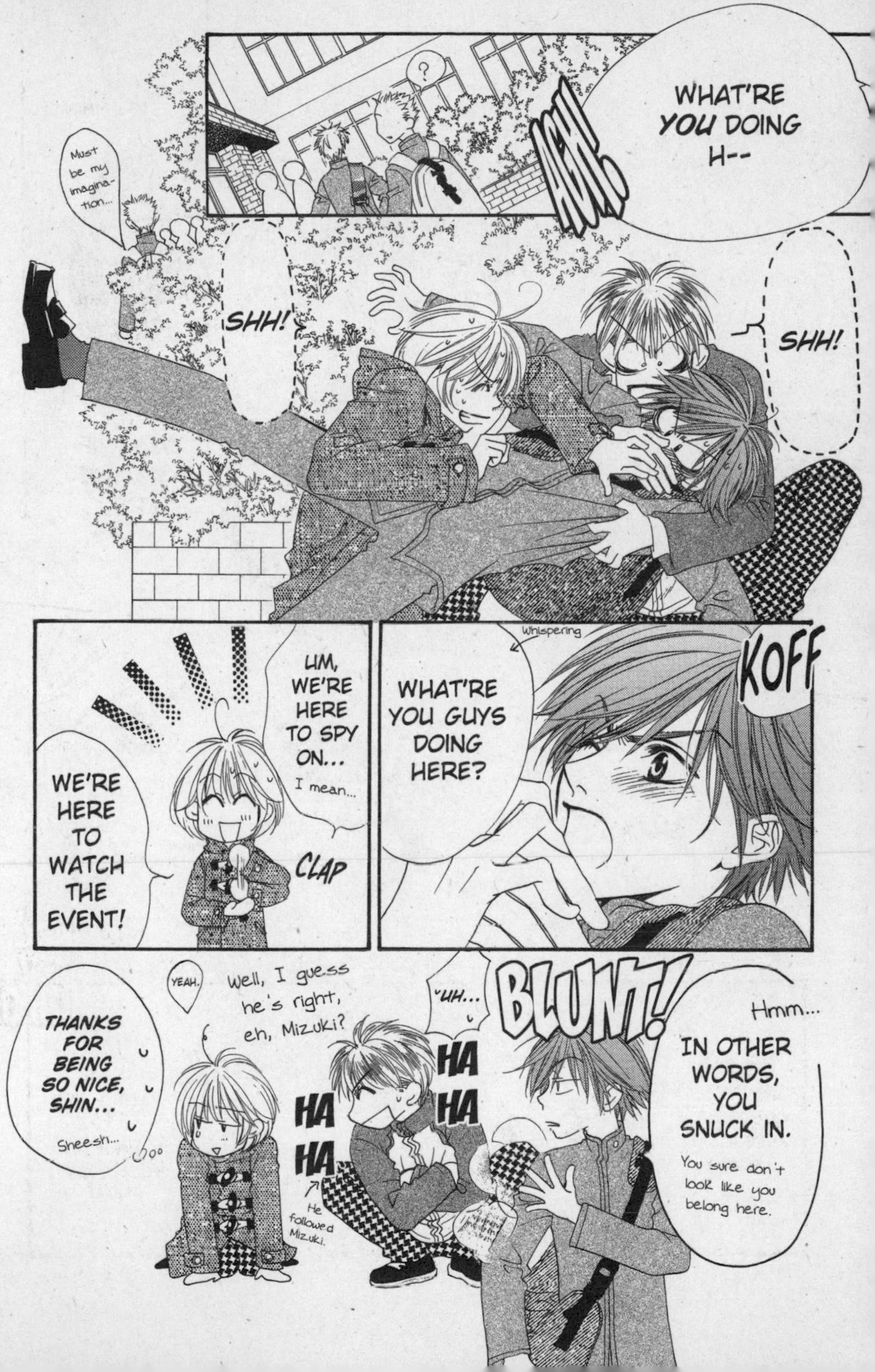
WHAT'RE YOU DOING H--
AGH!
?
Must be my imagination...
SHH!
SHH!
Whispering
WHAT'RE YOU GUYS DOING HERE?
KOFF
UM, WE'RE HERE TO SPY ON... I mean...
WE'RE HERE TO WATCH THE EVENT!
CLAP
Hmm...
IN OTHER WORDS, YOU SNUCK IN.
You sure don't look like you belong here.
BLUNT!
UH...
HA HA HA HA
He followed Mizuki.
Well, I guess he's right, eh, Mizuki?
YEAH.
THANKS FOR BEING SO NICE, SHIN...
Sheesh...

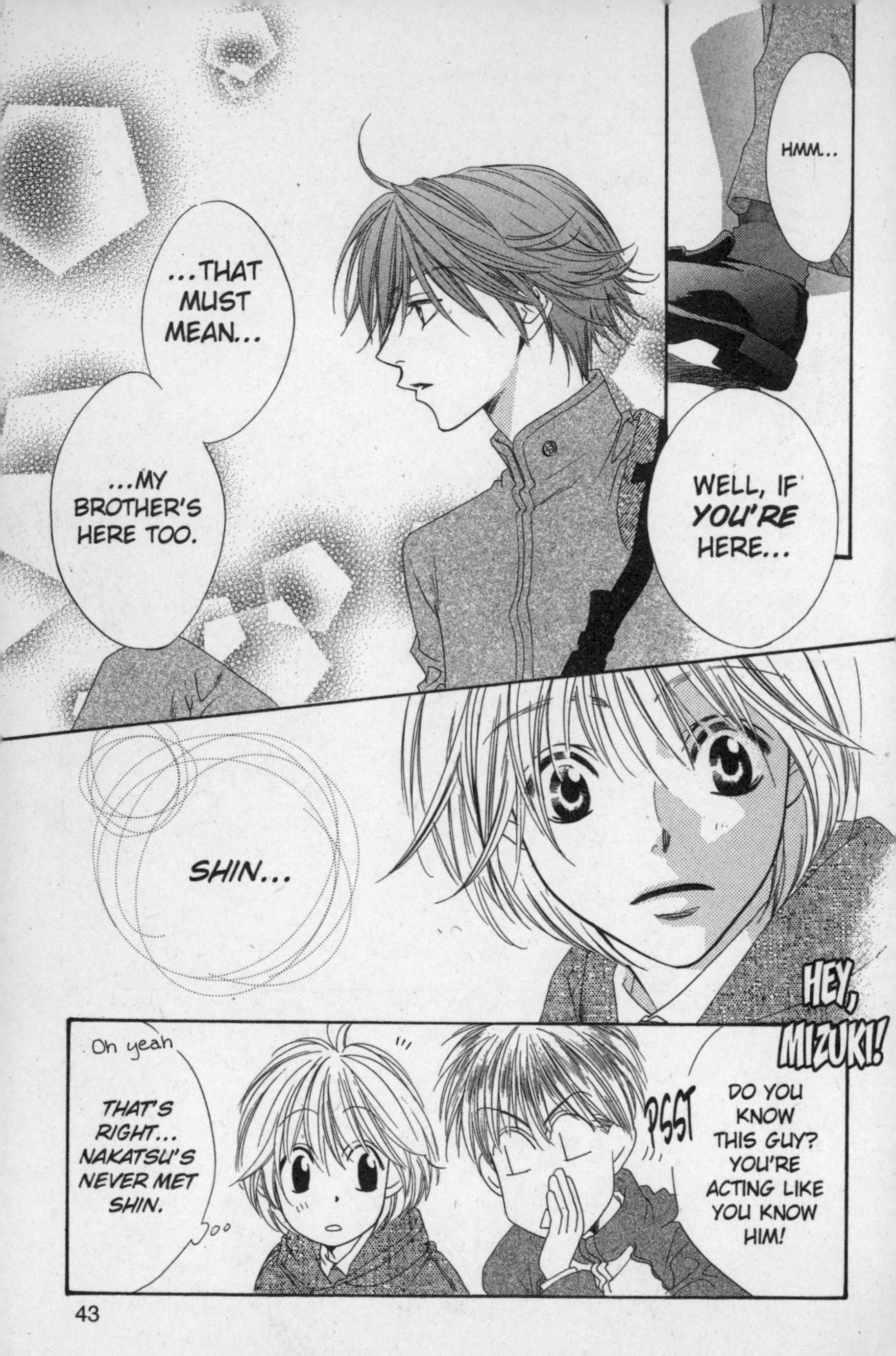
HMM...
WELL, IF *YOU'RE* HERE...
...THAT MUST MEAN...
...MY BROTHER'S HERE TOO.
SHIN...
HEY, MIZUKI!
PSST
DO YOU KNOW THIS GUY? YOU'RE ACTING LIKE YOU KNOW HIM!
Oh yeah
THAT'S RIGHT... NAKATSU'S NEVER MET SHIN.

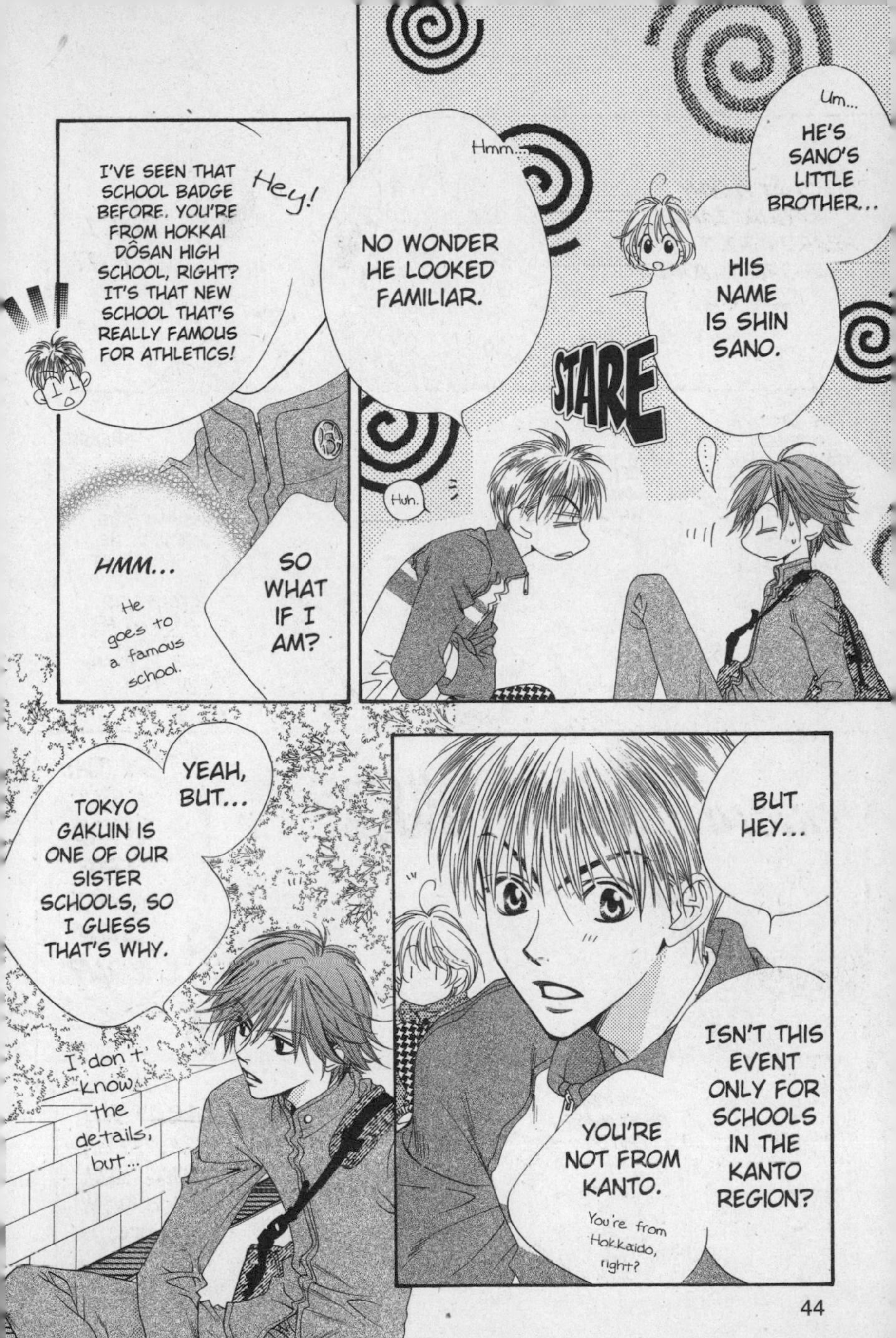
Um... HE'S SANO'S LITTLE BROTHER...
HIS NAME IS SHIN SANO.
Hmm...
NO WONDER HE LOOKED FAMILIAR.
STARE
...
Huh.
Hey!
I'VE SEEN THAT SCHOOL BADGE BEFORE. YOU'RE FROM HOKKAI DÔSAN HIGH SCHOOL, RIGHT? IT'S THAT NEW SCHOOL THAT'S REALLY FAMOUS FOR ATHLETICS!
SO WHAT IF I AM?
HMM...
He goes to a famous school.
BUT HEY...
ISN'T THIS EVENT ONLY FOR SCHOOLS IN THE KANTO REGION?
YOU'RE NOT FROM KANTO.
You're from Hokkaido, right?
YEAH, BUT...
TOKYO GAKUIN IS ONE OF OUR SISTER SCHOOLS, SO I GUESS THAT'S WHY.
I don't know the details, but...

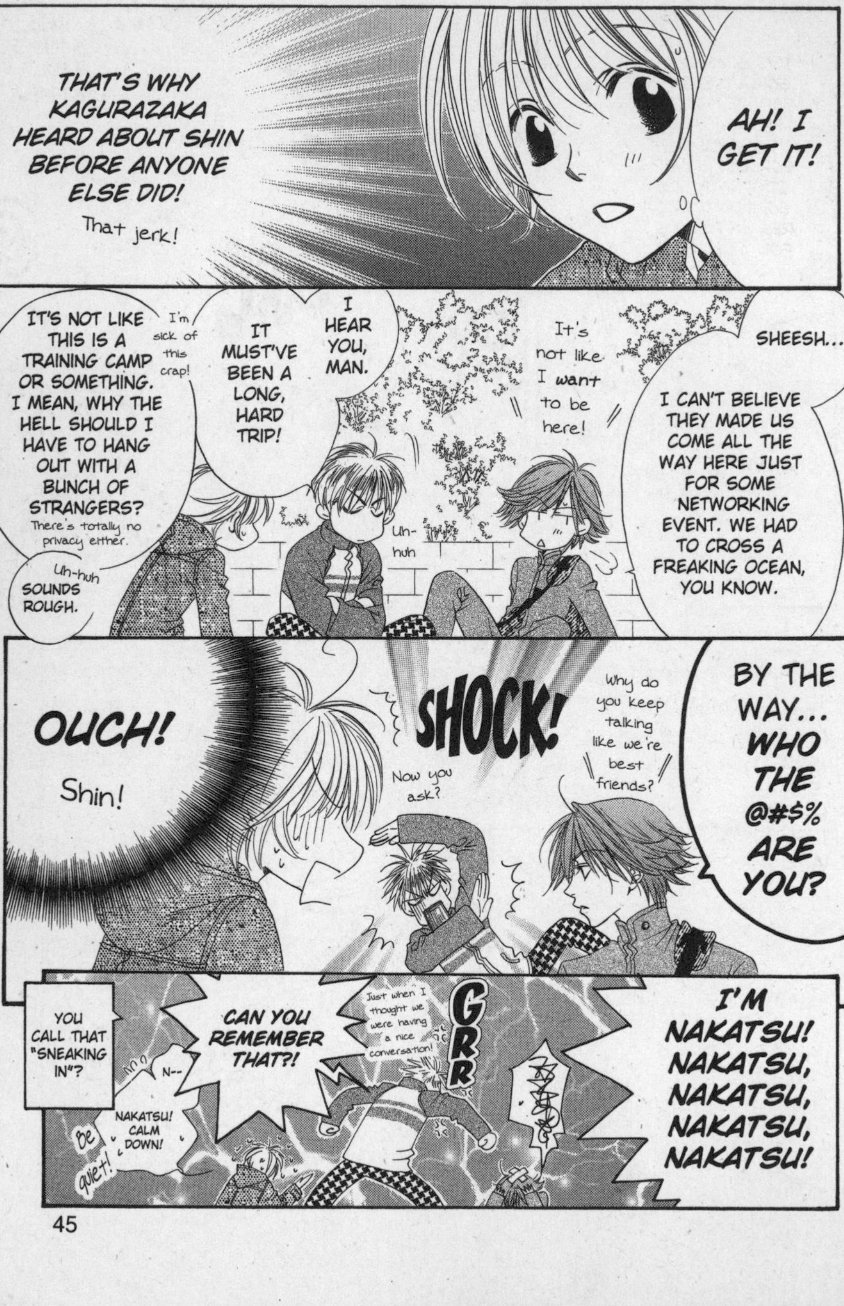
AH! I GET IT!
THAT'S WHY KAGURAZAKA HEARD ABOUT SHIN BEFORE ANYONE ELSE DID!
That jerk!
SHEESH...
I CAN'T BELIEVE THEY MADE US COME ALL THE WAY HERE JUST FOR SOME NETWORKING EVENT. WE HAD TO CROSS A FREAKING OCEAN, YOU KNOW.
It's not like I want to be here!
Uh-huh
I HEAR YOU, MAN.
IT MUST'VE BEEN A LONG, HARD TRIP!
I'm sick of this crap!
IT'S NOT LIKE THIS IS A TRAINING CAMP OR SOMETHING. I MEAN, WHY THE HELL SHOULD I HAVE TO HANG OUT WITH A BUNCH OF STRANGERS?
There's totally no privacy either.
Uh-huh SOUNDS ROUGH.
BY THE WAY... WHO THE @#$% ARE YOU?
Why do you keep talking like we're best friends?
SHOCK!
Now you ask?
OUCH!
Shin!
I'M NAKATSU! NAKATSU, NAKATSU, NAKATSU, NAKATSU!
GRR
Just when I thought we were having a nice conversation!
CAN YOU REMEMBER THAT?!
N--
NAKATSU! CALM DOWN!
Be quiet!
YOU CALL THAT "SNEAKING IN"?

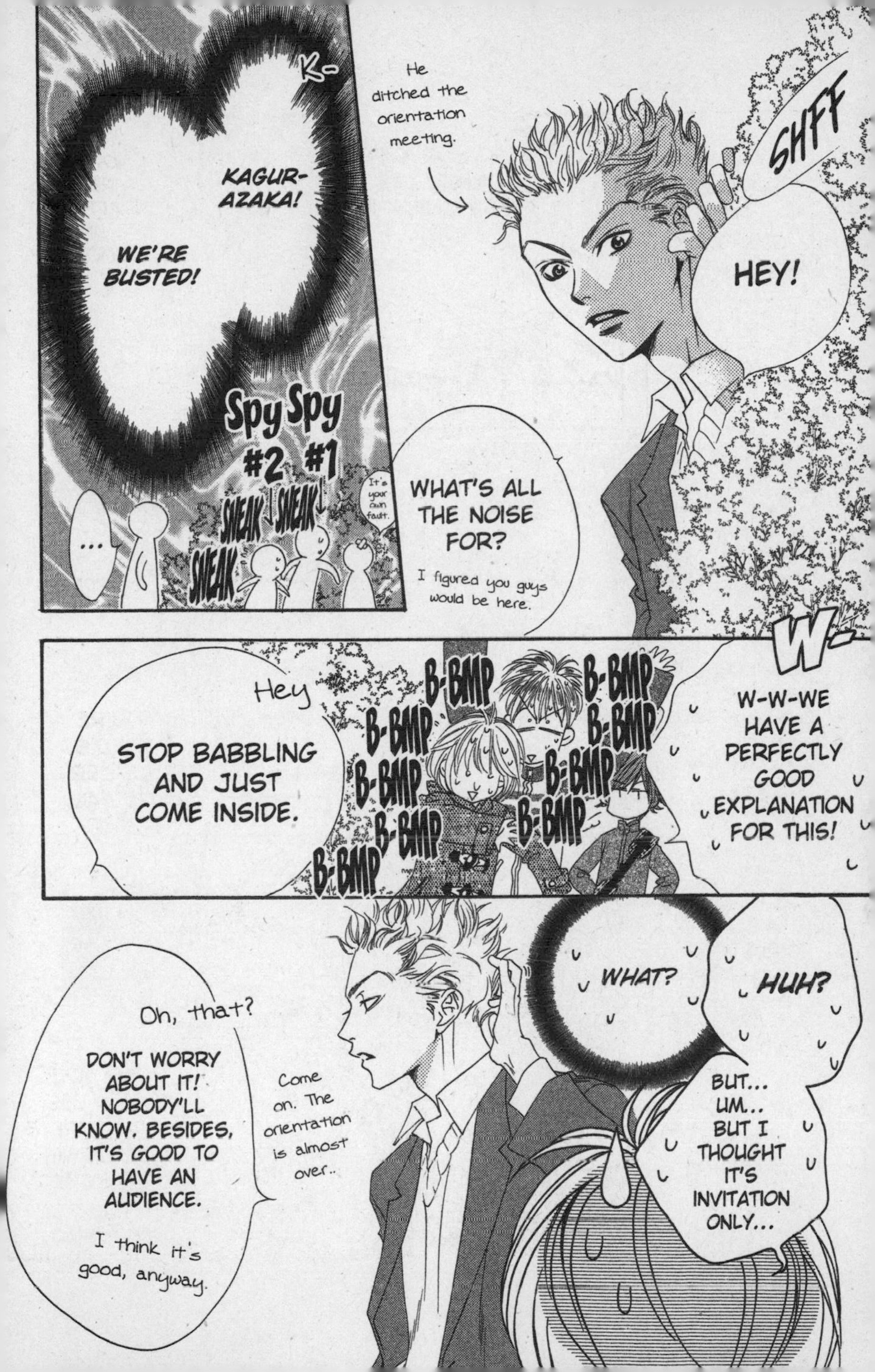
SHFF
HEY!
He ditched the orientation meeting.
WHAT'S ALL THE NOISE FOR?
I figured you guys would be here.
K-
KAGUR-AZAKA!
WE'RE BUSTED!
Spy #1
Spy #2
SNEAK
SNEAK
SNEAK
It's your own fault.
...
W-
W-W-WE HAVE A PERFECTLY GOOD EXPLANATION FOR THIS!
B-BMP B-BMP B-BMP B-BMP B-BMP
B-BMP B-BMP B-BMP B-BMP B-BMP
Hey
STOP BABBLING AND JUST COME INSIDE.
HUH?
WHAT?
BUT... UM... BUT I THOUGHT IT'S INVITATION ONLY...
Come on. The orientation is almost over..
Oh, that?
DON'T WORRY ABOUT IT! NOBODY'LL KNOW. BESIDES, IT'S GOOD TO HAVE AN AUDIENCE.
I think it's good, anyway.

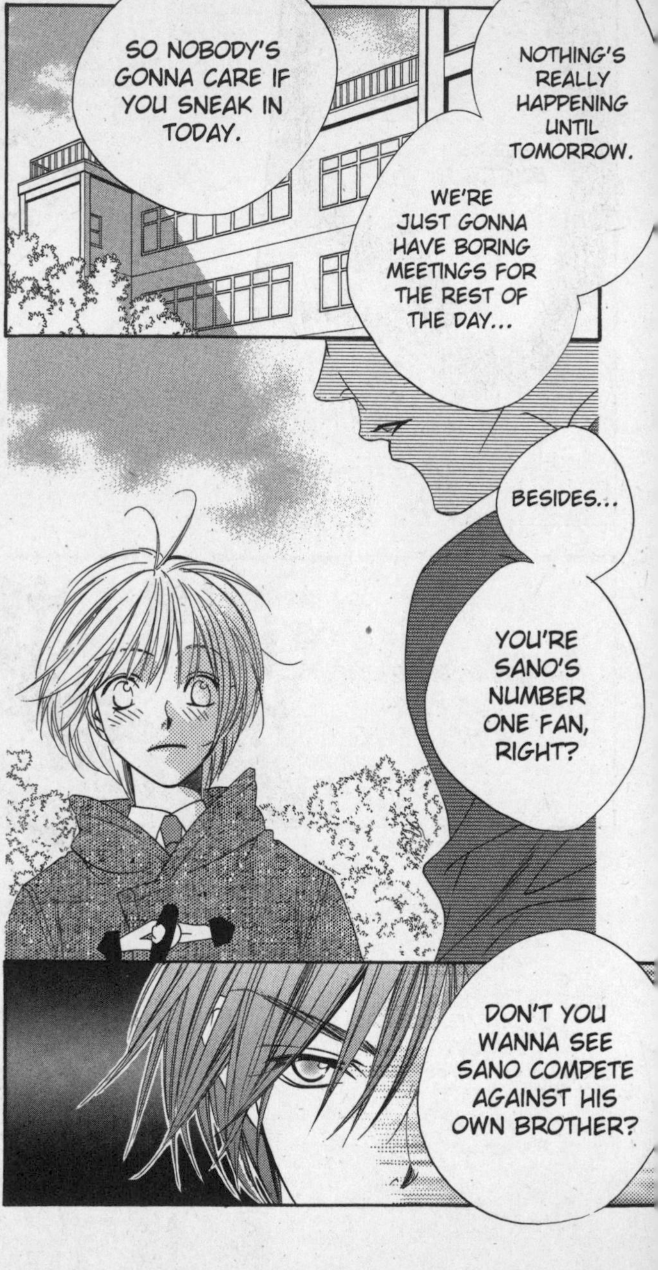
NOTHING'S REALLY HAPPENING UNTIL TOMORROW.
WE'RE JUST GONNA HAVE BORING MEETINGS FOR THE REST OF THE DAY...
SO NOBODY'S GONNA CARE IF YOU SNEAK IN TODAY.
BESIDES...
YOU'RE SANO'S NUMBER ONE FAN, RIGHT?
DON'T YOU WANNA SEE SANO COMPETE AGAINST HIS OWN BROTHER?

SHIN SANO

Birthday: February 4th
Grade: First Year Japanese H.S. (equivalent of 10th grade in America)
Blood Type: A
Sign: Aquarius
Height: 174cm
Favorite Foods: Beef Bowl, Milk, Stew
Favorite Colors: Khaki, Gray
Favorite Celebrities: Maki Gotou, Takako Uehara
Favorite Season: Summer
Favorite Subject: Chemistry (especially experiments)
Least Favorite Subject: Math
Least Favorite Foods: Onions, Bell peppers, Beans, Shiitake Mushrooms, Sprouts
Flower: Babiana

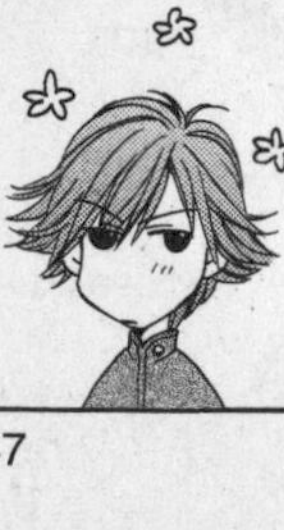

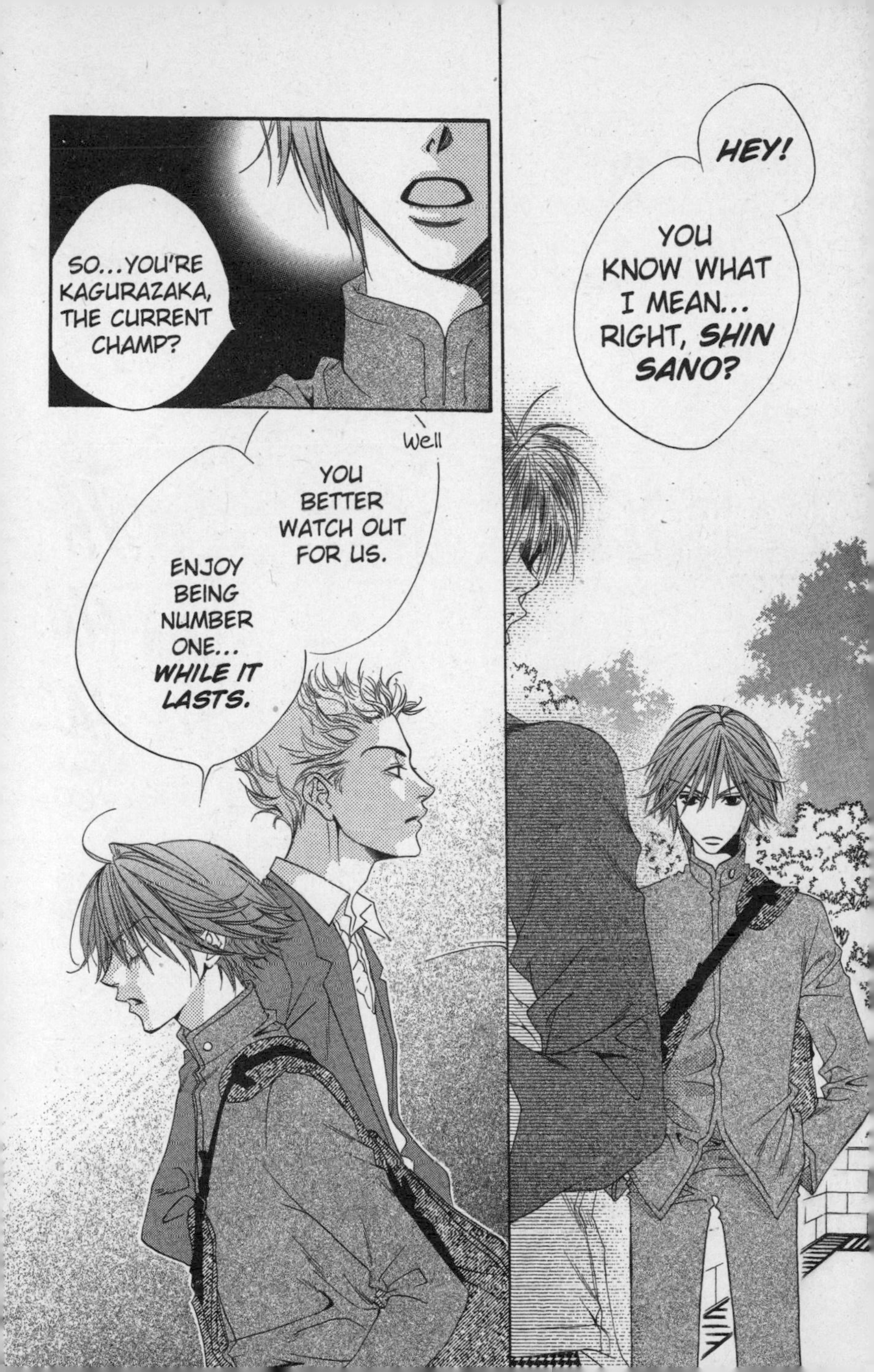
HEY!
YOU KNOW WHAT I MEAN... RIGHT, SHIN SANO?
SO...YOU'RE KAGURAZAKA, THE CURRENT CHAMP?
Well
YOU BETTER WATCH OUT FOR US.
ENJOY BEING NUMBER ONE... WHILE IT LASTS.

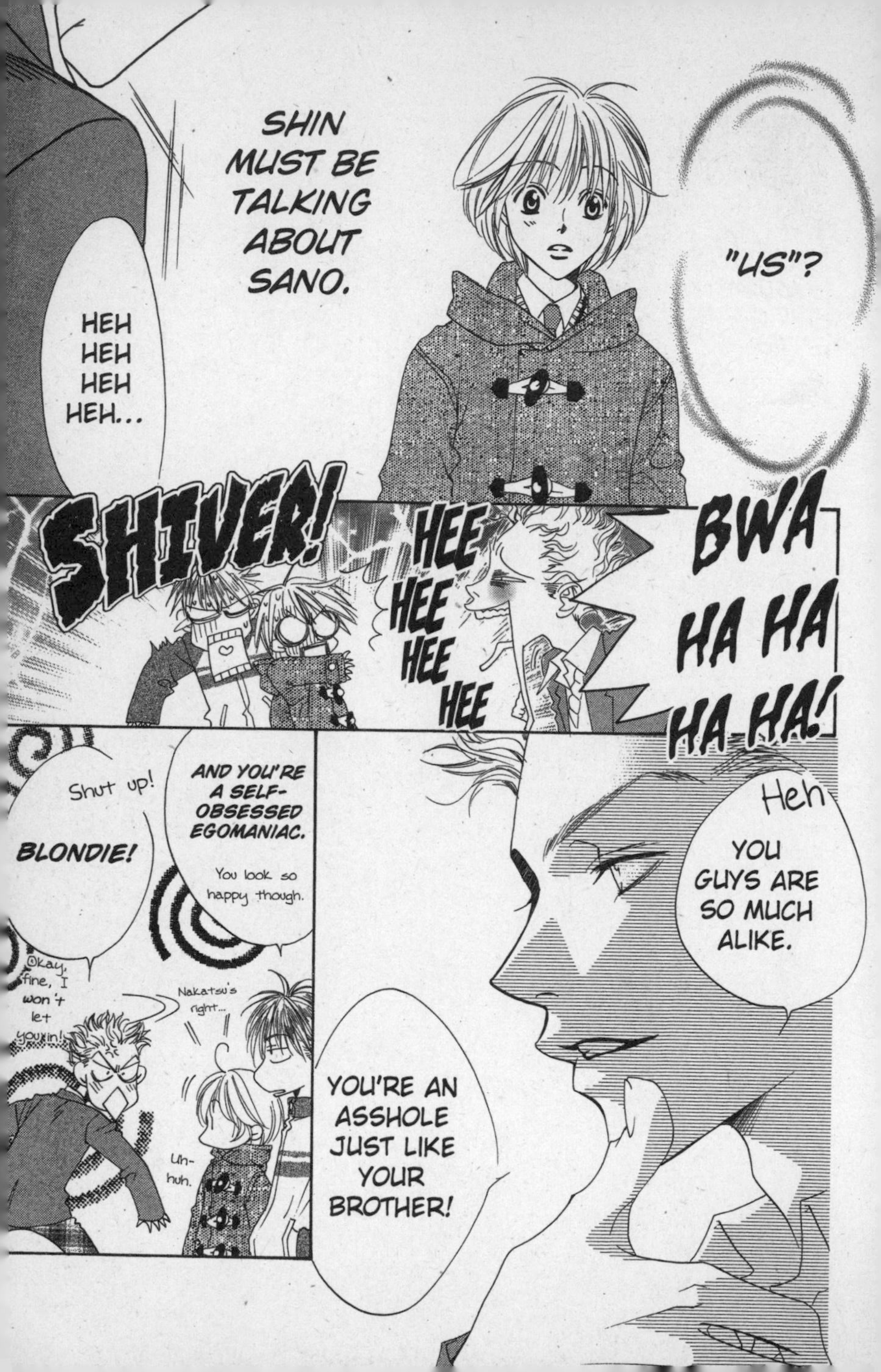
"US"?
SHIN MUST BE TALKING ABOUT SANO.
HEH HEH HEH HEH...
BWA HA HA HA HA!
HEE HEE HEE HEE
SHIVER!
Heh
YOU GUYS ARE SO MUCH ALIKE.
YOU'RE AN ASSHOLE JUST LIKE YOUR BROTHER!
AND YOU'RE A SELF-OBSESSED EGOMANIAC.
You look so happy though.
Shut up!
BLONDIE!
Nakatsu's right...
Okay, fine, I won't let you in!
Uh-huh.

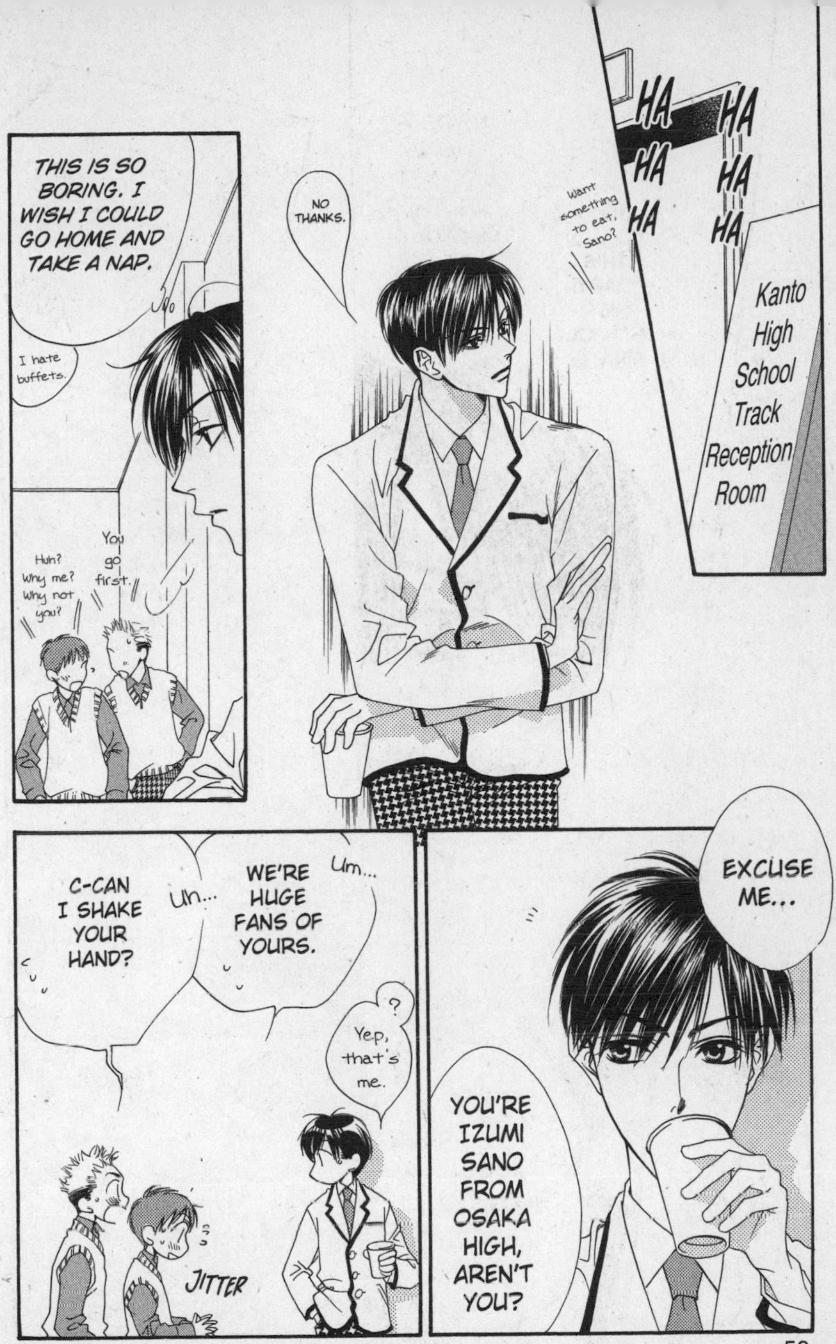
HA HA HA
HA HA HA
Kanto High School Track Reception Room
Want something to eat, Sano?
NO THANKS.
THIS IS SO BORING. I WISH I COULD GO HOME AND TAKE A NAP.
I hate buffets.
You go first.
Huh? Why me? Why not you?
EXCUSE ME...
YOU'RE IZUMI SANO FROM OSAKA HIGH, AREN'T YOU?
Um...
WE'RE HUGE FANS OF YOURS.
Uh...
C-CAN I SHAKE YOUR HAND?
?
Yep, that's me.
JITTER

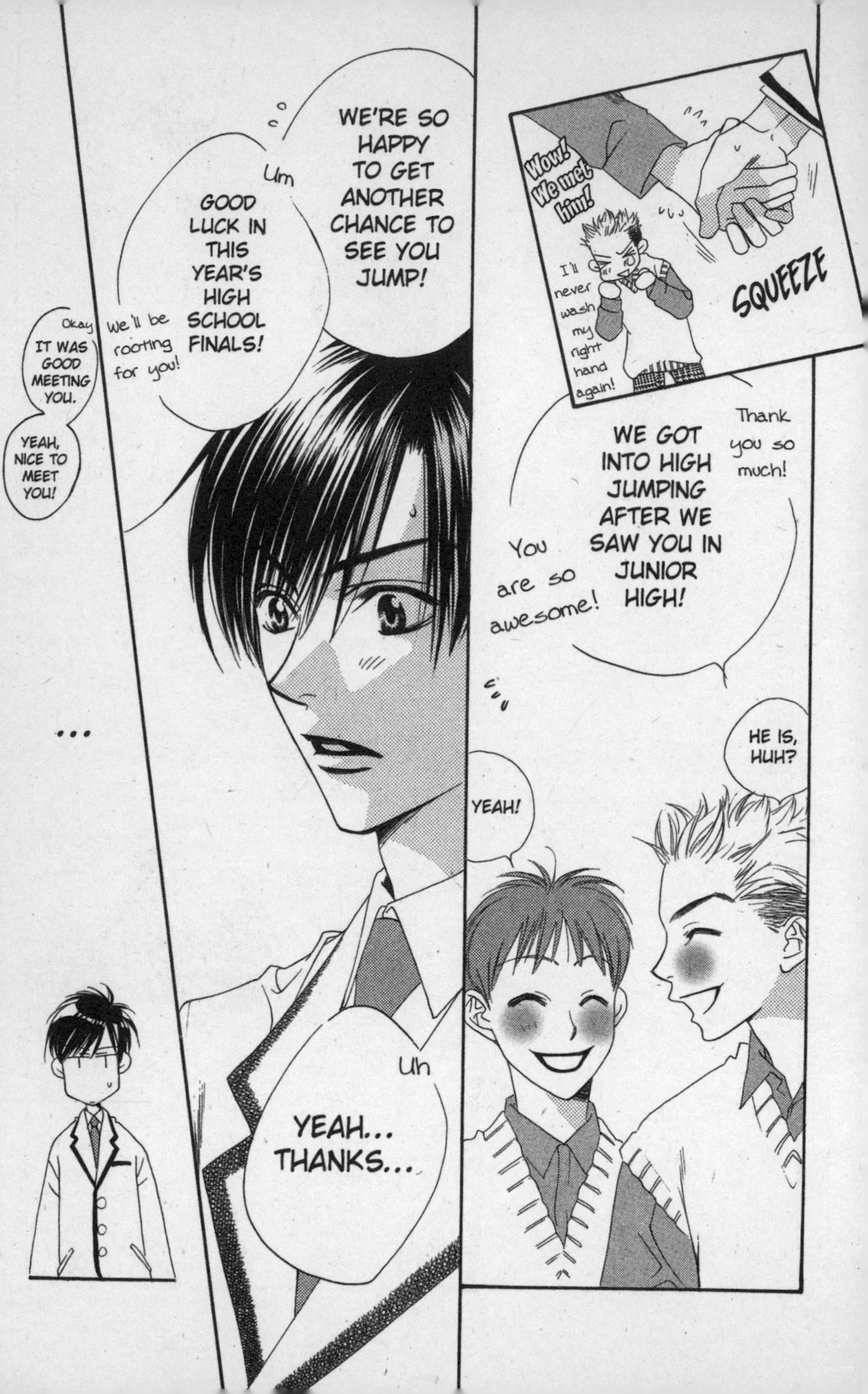

Wow! We met him!
I'll never wash my right hand again!
SQUEEZE
Thank you so much!
WE GOT INTO HIGH JUMPING AFTER WE SAW YOU IN JUNIOR HIGH!
You are so awesome!
HE IS, HUH?
YEAH!
WE'RE SO HAPPY TO GET ANOTHER CHANCE TO SEE YOU JUMP!
Um
GOOD LUCK IN THIS YEAR'S HIGH SCHOOL FINALS!
We'll be rooting for you!
Uh
YEAH... THANKS...
Okay
IT WAS GOOD MEETING YOU.
YEAH, NICE TO MEET YOU!
...

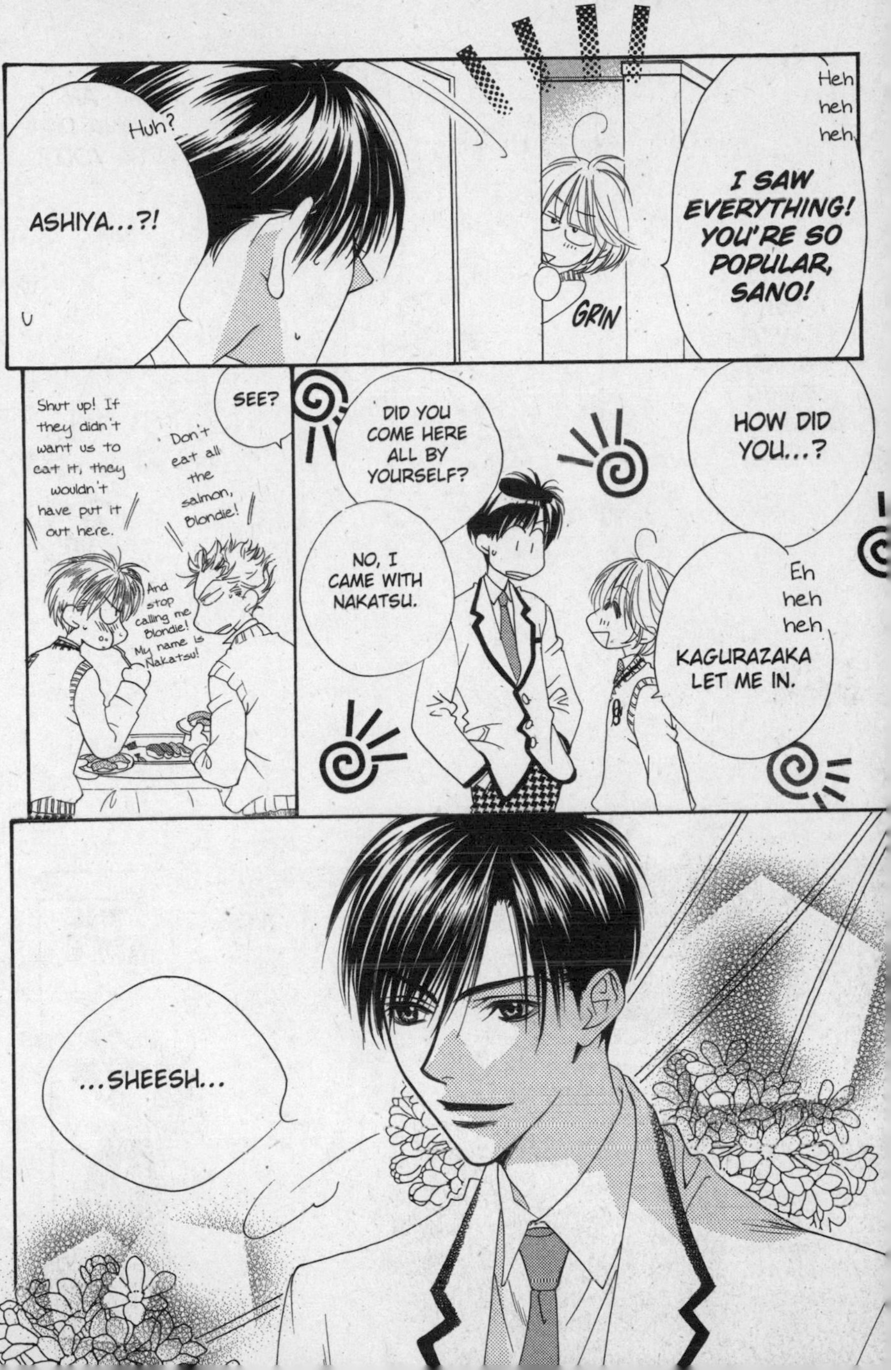
Heh heh heh
I SAW EVERYTHING! YOU'RE SO POPULAR, SANO!
GRIN
Huh?
ASHIYA...?!
HOW DID YOU...?
Eh heh heh
KAGURAZAKA LET ME IN.
DID YOU COME HERE ALL BY YOURSELF?
NO, I CAME WITH NAKATSU.
SEE?
Don't eat all the salmon, Blondie!
Shut up! If they didn't want us to eat it, they wouldn't have put it out here.
And stop calling me Blondie! My name is Nakatsu!
...SHEESH...

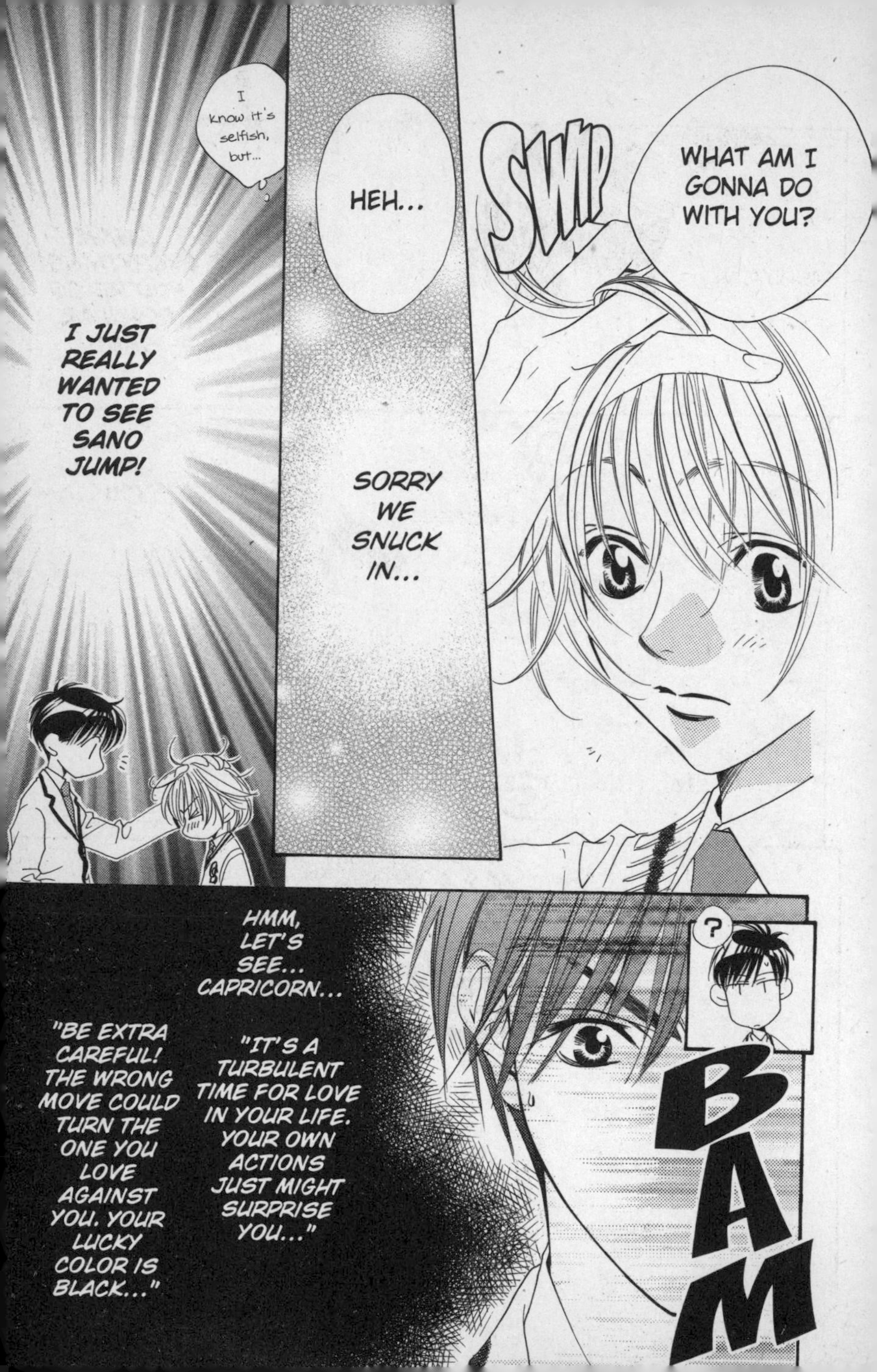
WHAT AM I GONNA DO WITH YOU?
SWIP
HEH...
SORRY WE SNUCK IN...
I know it's selfish, but...
I JUST REALLY WANTED TO SEE SANO JUMP!
?
BAM
HMM, LET'S SEE... CAPRICORN...
"IT'S A TURBULENT TIME FOR LOVE IN YOUR LIFE. YOUR OWN ACTIONS JUST MIGHT SURPRISE YOU..."
"BE EXTRA CAREFUL! THE WRONG MOVE COULD TURN THE ONE YOU LOVE AGAINST YOU. YOUR LUCKY COLOR IS BLACK..."

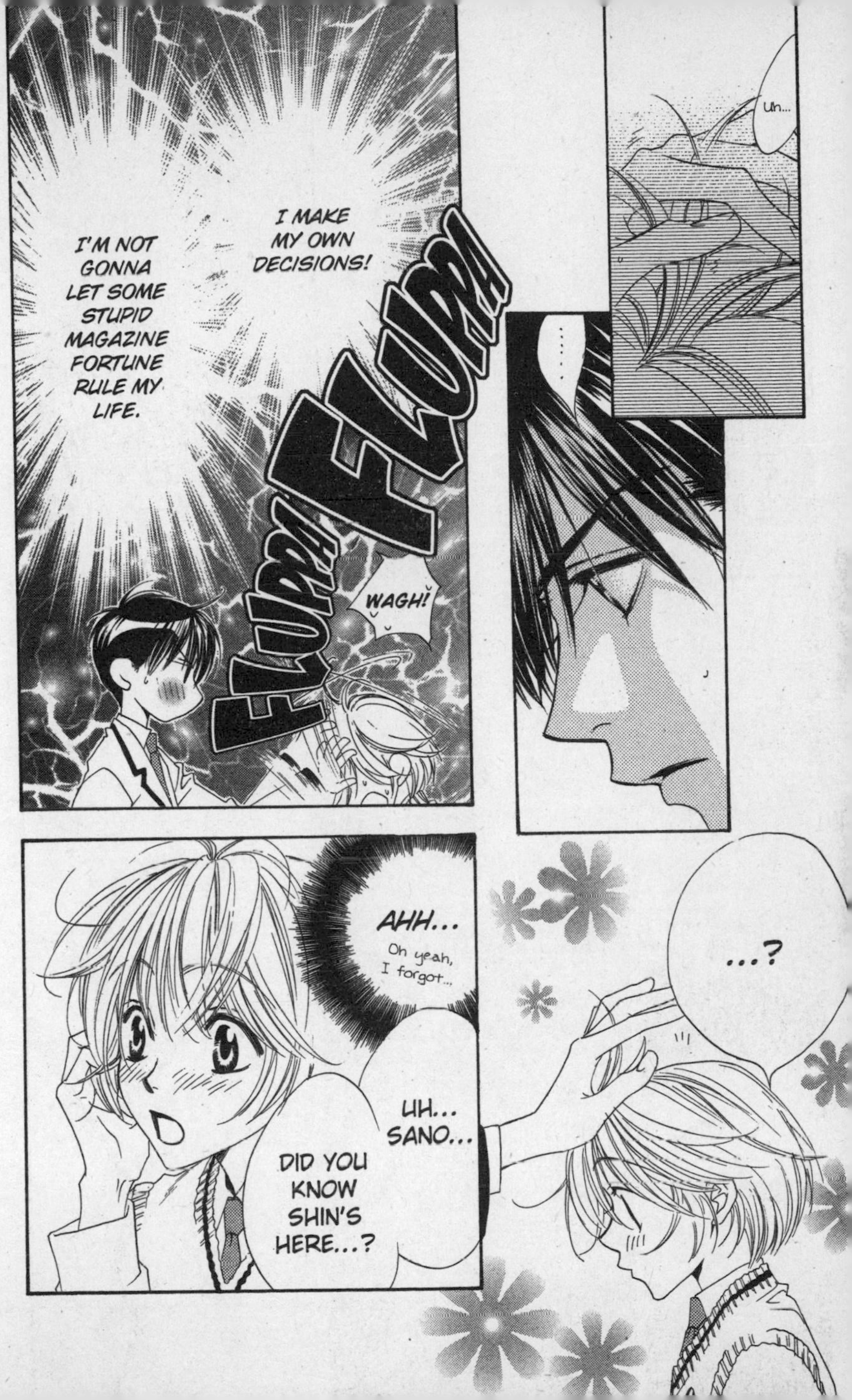
Un...
...
I MAKE MY OWN DECISIONS!
I'M NOT GONNA LET SOME STUPID MAGAZINE FORTUNE RULE MY LIFE.
FLUPPA FLUPPA
WAGH!
...?
AHH...
Oh yeah, I forgot...
UH... SANO...
DID YOU KNOW SHIN'S HERE...?

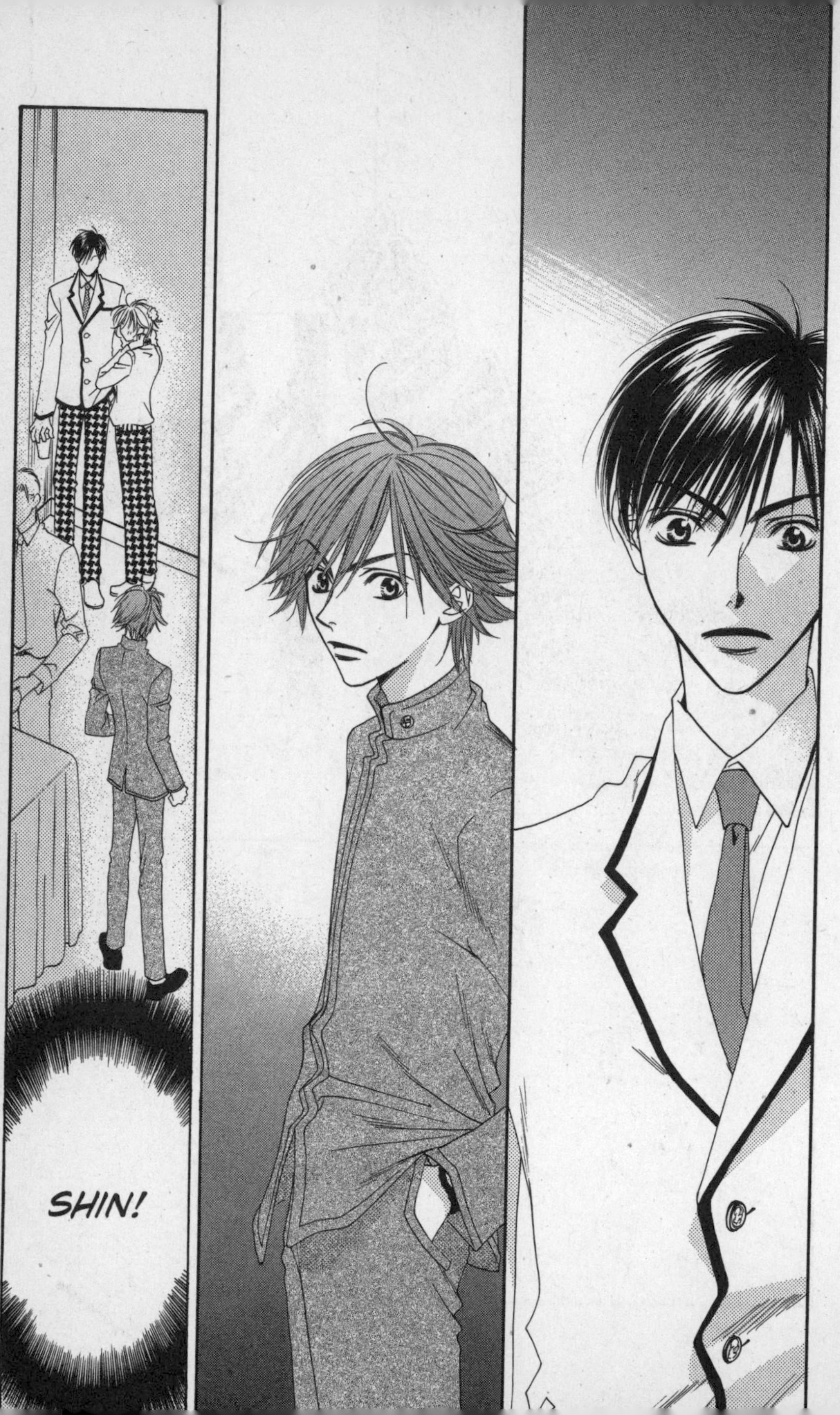
SHIN!

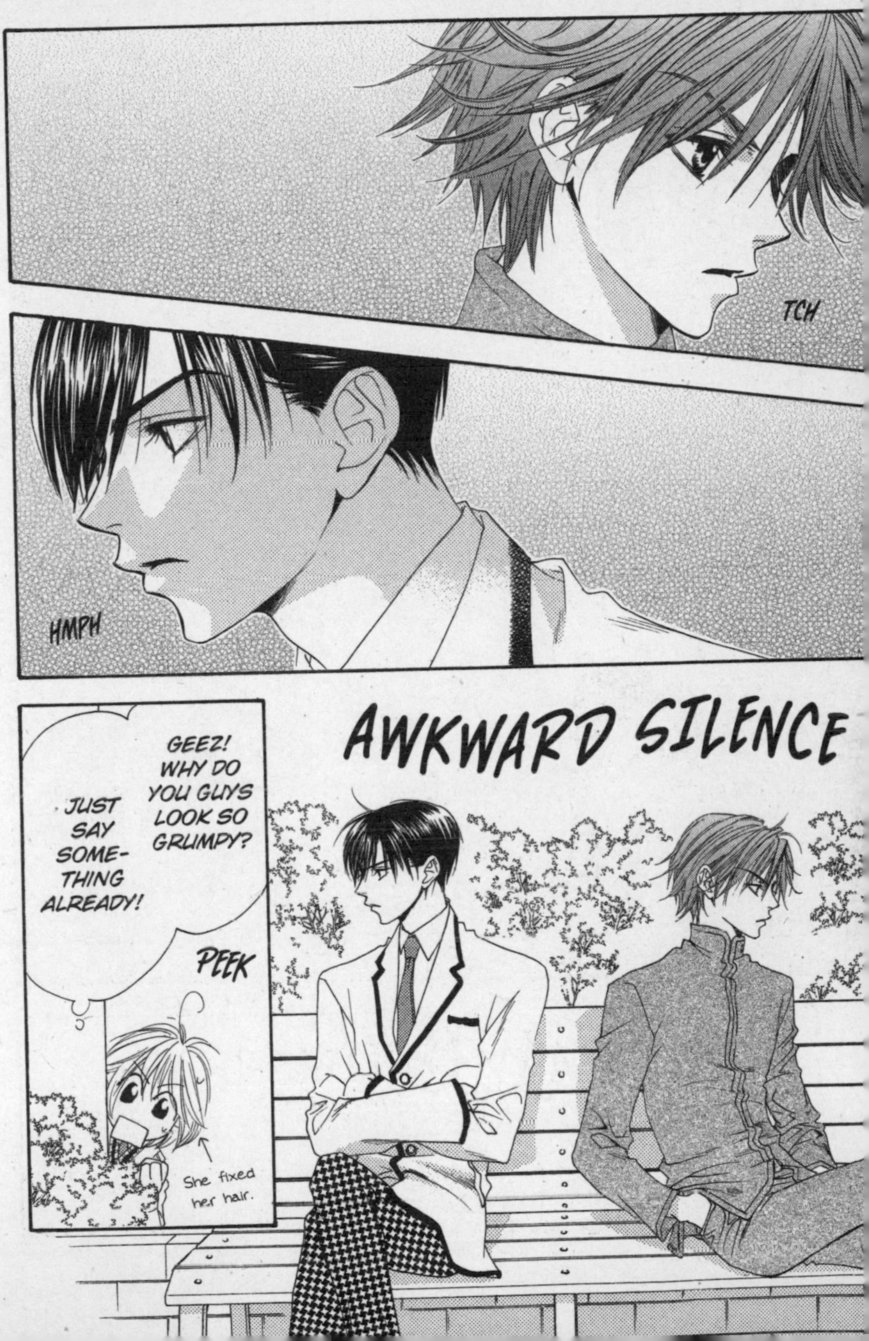
TCH
HMPH
AWKWARD SILENCE
GEEZ! WHY DO YOU GUYS LOOK SO GRUMPY?
JUST SAY SOME-THING ALREADY!
PEEK
She fixed her hair.

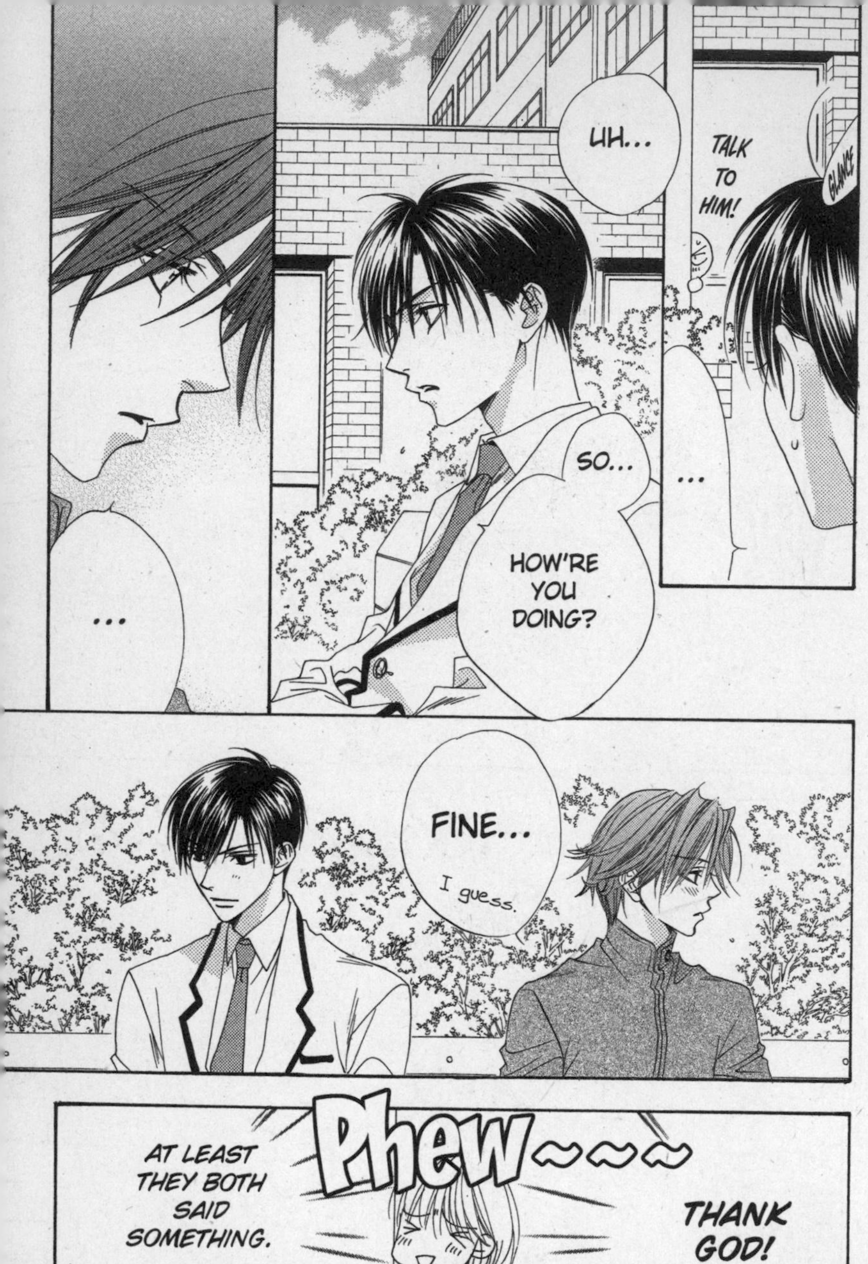

GLANCE
TALK TO HIM!
...
UH...
SO...
HOW'RE YOU DOING?
...
FINE...
I guess.
Phew~~~
THANK GOD!
AT LEAST THEY BOTH SAID SOMETHING.
That's it, guys. Keep going!

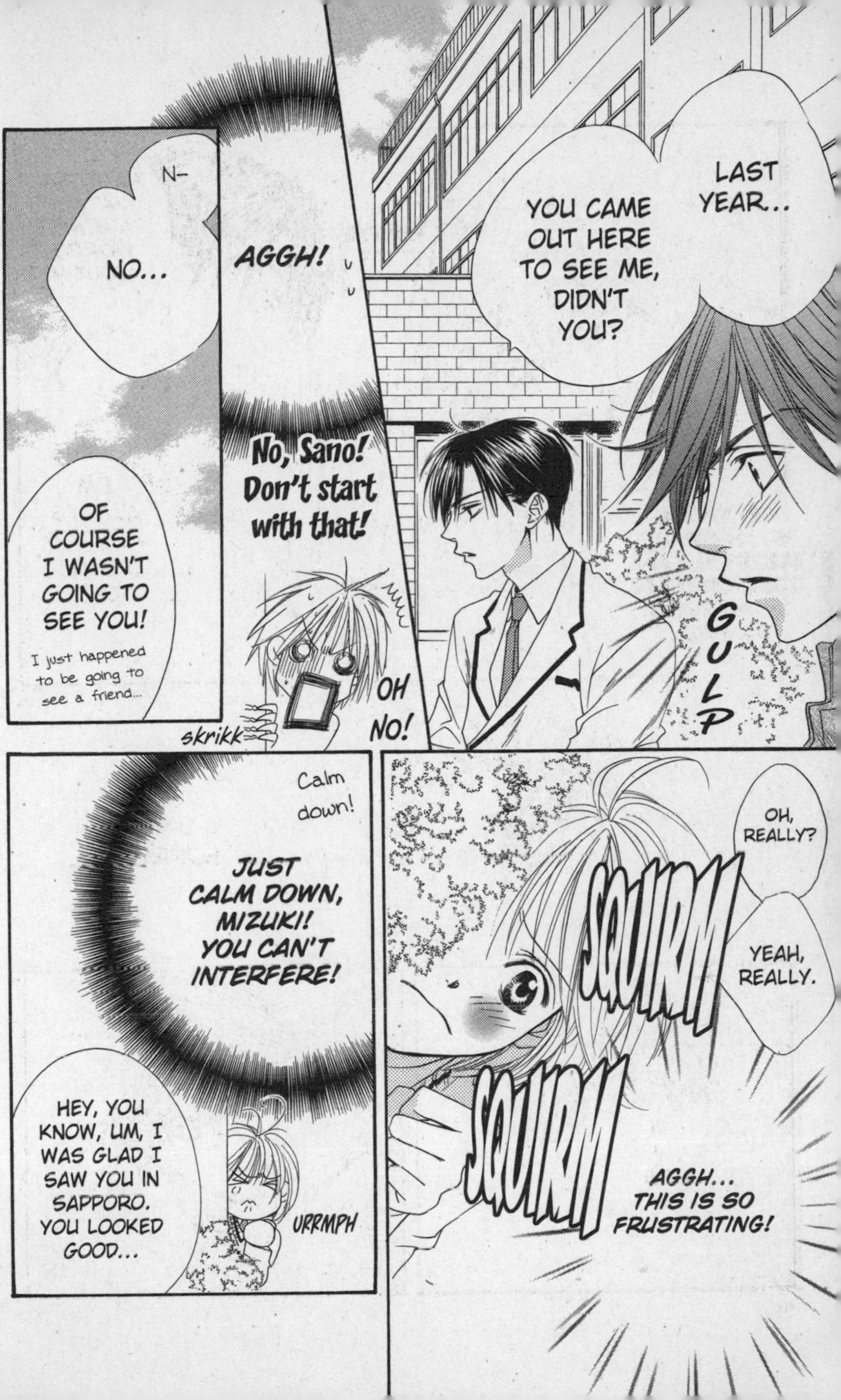
LAST YEAR...
YOU CAME OUT HERE TO SEE ME, DIDN'T YOU?
GULP
AGGH!
No, Sano! Don't start with that!
OH NO!
skrikk
N-
NO...
OF COURSE I WASN'T GOING TO SEE YOU!
I just happened to be going to see a friend...
OH, REALLY?
YEAH, REALLY.
SQUIRM
SQUIRM
AGGH... THIS IS SO FRUSTRATING!
Calm down!
JUST CALM DOWN, MIZUKI! YOU CAN'T INTERFERE!
HEY, YOU KNOW, UM, I WAS GLAD I SAW YOU IN SAPPORO. YOU LOOKED GOOD...
URRMPH

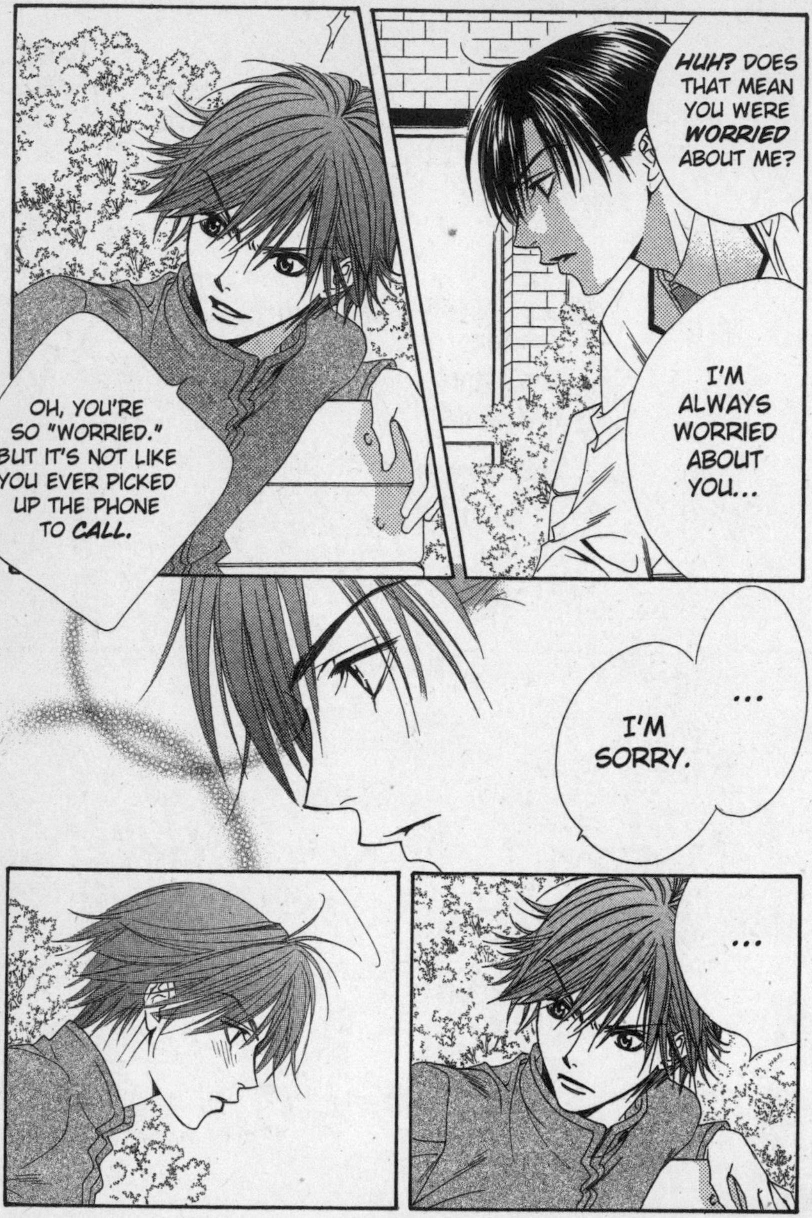
HUH? DOES THAT MEAN YOU WERE *WORRIED* ABOUT ME?
I'M ALWAYS WORRIED ABOUT YOU...
OH, YOU'RE SO "WORRIED." BUT IT'S NOT LIKE YOU EVER PICKED UP THE PHONE TO *CALL.*
...
I'M SORRY.
...

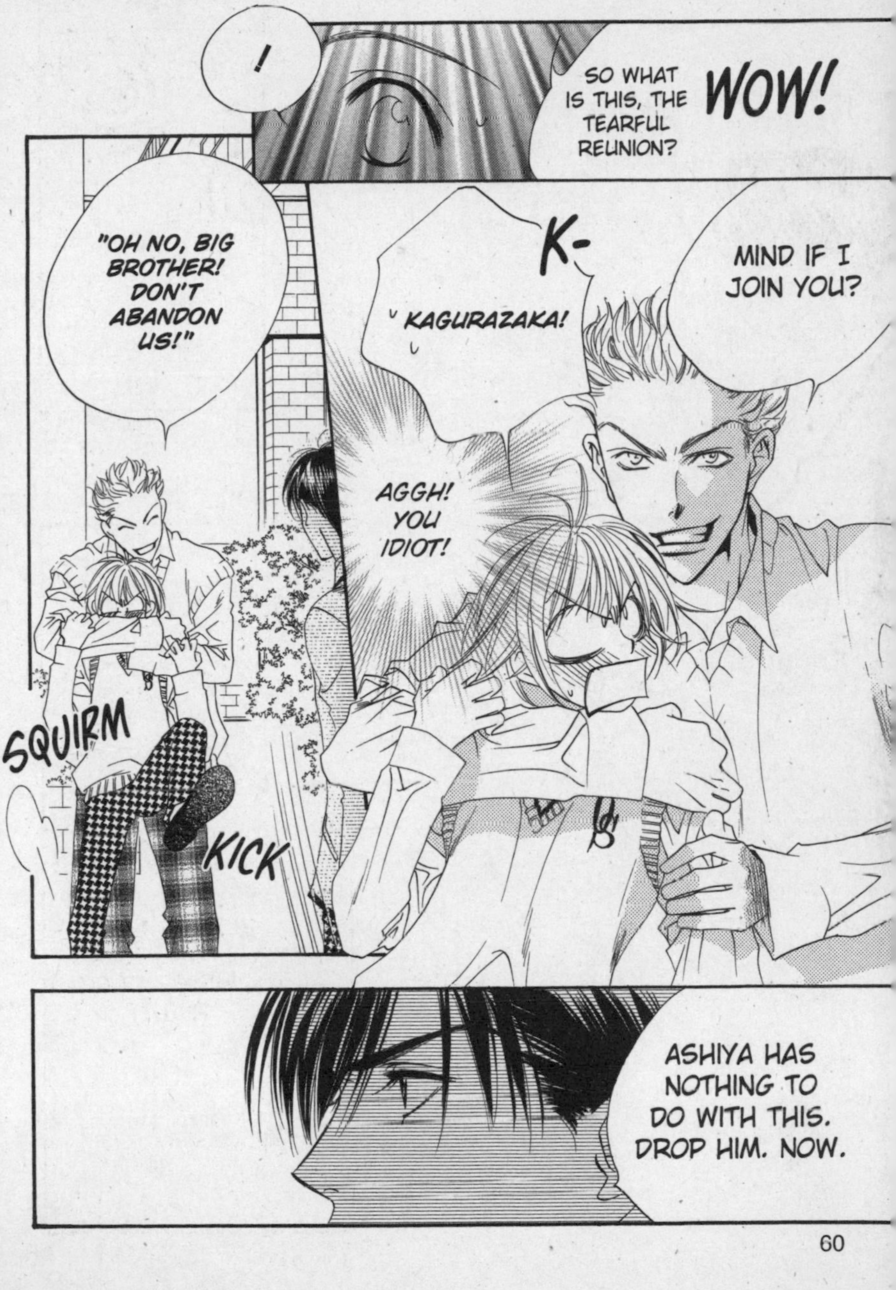

WOW!
SO WHAT IS THIS, THE TEARFUL REUNION?
!
MIND IF I JOIN YOU?
K-
KAGURAZAKA!
AGGH! YOU IDIOT!
"OH NO, BIG BROTHER! DON'T ABANDON US!"
SQUIRM
KICK
ASHIYA HAS NOTHING TO DO WITH THIS. DROP HIM. NOW.

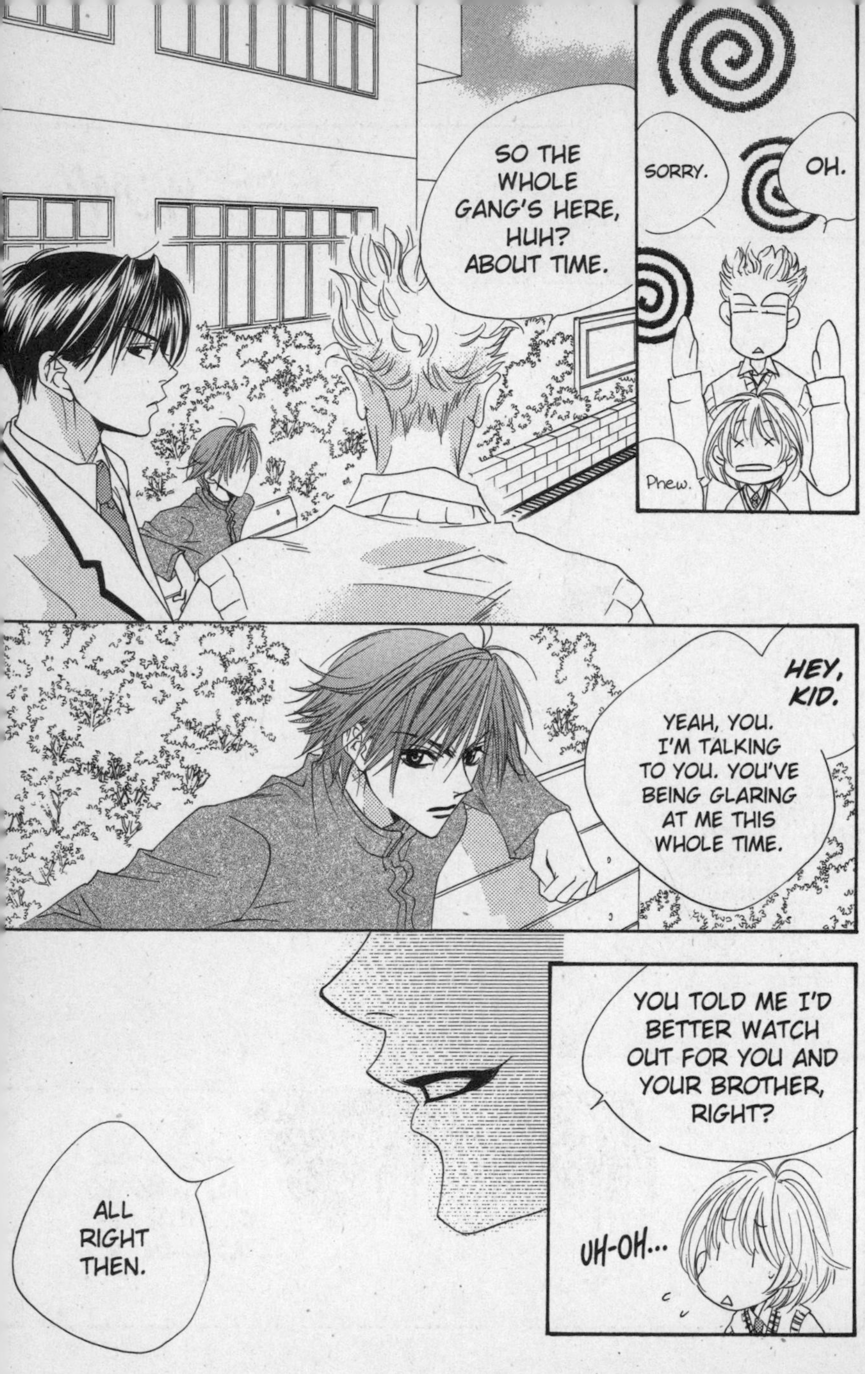
OH.
SORRY.
Phew.
SO THE WHOLE GANG'S HERE, HUH? ABOUT TIME.
HEY, KID.
YEAH, YOU. I'M TALKING TO YOU. YOU'VE BEING GLARING AT ME THIS WHOLE TIME.
YOU TOLD ME I'D BETTER WATCH OUT FOR YOU AND YOUR BROTHER, RIGHT?
UH-OH...
ALL RIGHT THEN.

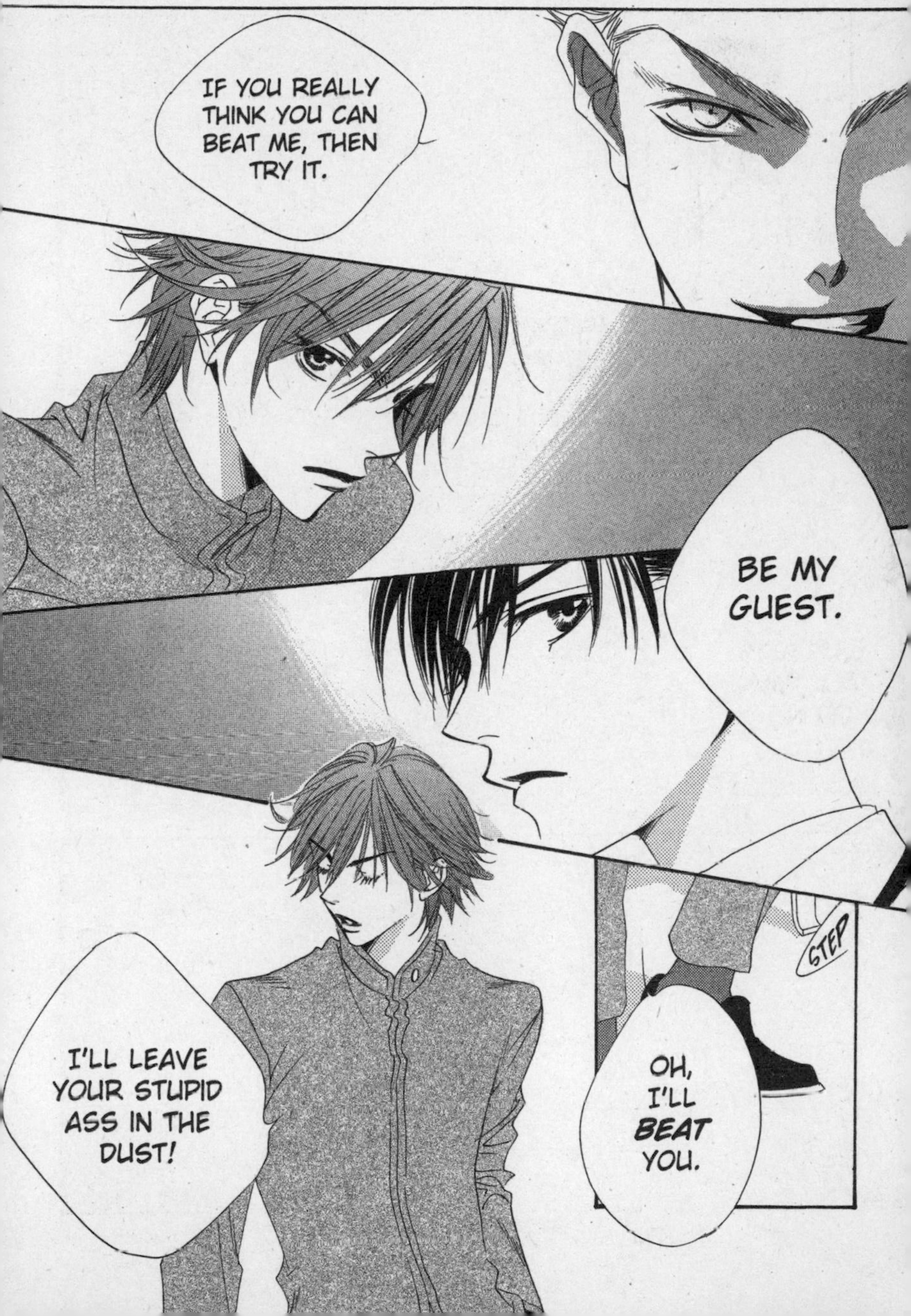
IF YOU REALLY THINK YOU CAN BEAT ME, THEN TRY IT.
BE MY GUEST.
STEP
OH, I'LL *BEAT* YOU.
I'LL LEAVE YOUR STUPID ASS IN THE DUST!

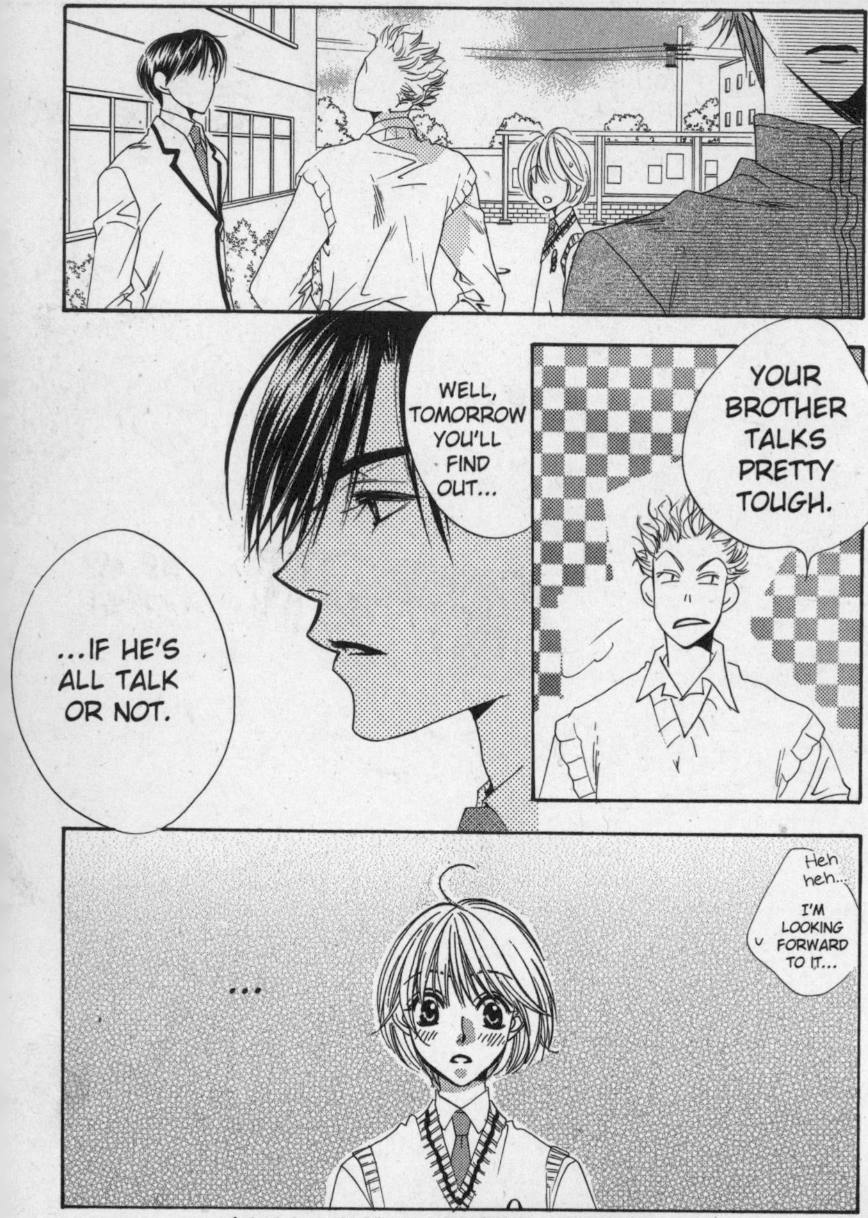
YOUR BROTHER TALKS PRETTY TOUGH.
WELL, TOMORROW YOU'LL FIND OUT...
...IF HE'S ALL TALK OR NOT.
Heh heh...
I'M LOOKING FORWARD TO IT...
...

HANA-KIMI CHAPTER 87/END

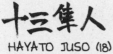

十三隼人
HAYATO JUSO (18)

Many of you sent in letters asking, "Who's that guy with the tan?" Well, here he is. He's an upperclassman who's on Nakatsu's soccer team. He used to be the captain. He still coaches the team but he doesn't play anymore. Lot of students look up to him, so he's got a bunch of friends. (Everybody still calls him Captain)

I was trying to make him look like my assistant Mo-chan's ideal type of guy (wild guys with dark tans). What do you think?

I like him. ♥ --Mo

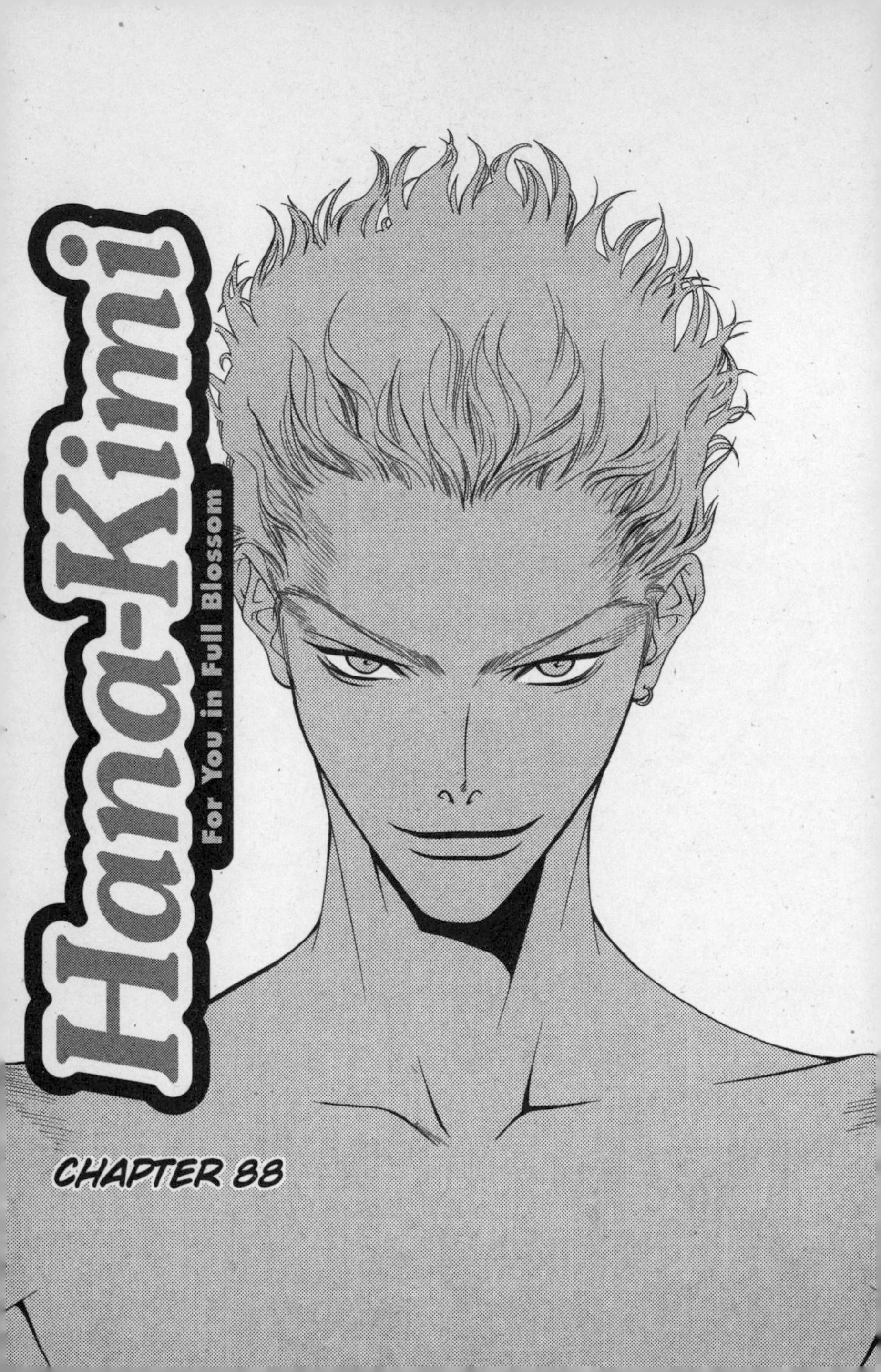
Hana-Kimi
For You in Full Blossom
CHAPTER 88

"IF YOU REALLY THINK YOU CAN BEAT ME, THEN TRY IT!"

JOE ODAGIRI

I didn't even realize it, but it looks like I've become a real fan of his. I kept telling my friends, "I'm not that big a fan," but I bought his photo book and all his CDs. Well, I used to watch "Kamen Rider Kuuga" every week, even though I'm not really into tokusatsu (special effects) shows, so I guess it makes sense! (Sigh!)

This is how he looked when he was doing "Kuuga."
What am I doing here?

Ah, Kuuga...I bought the DVD box set of the series. I guess that makes me a fan.

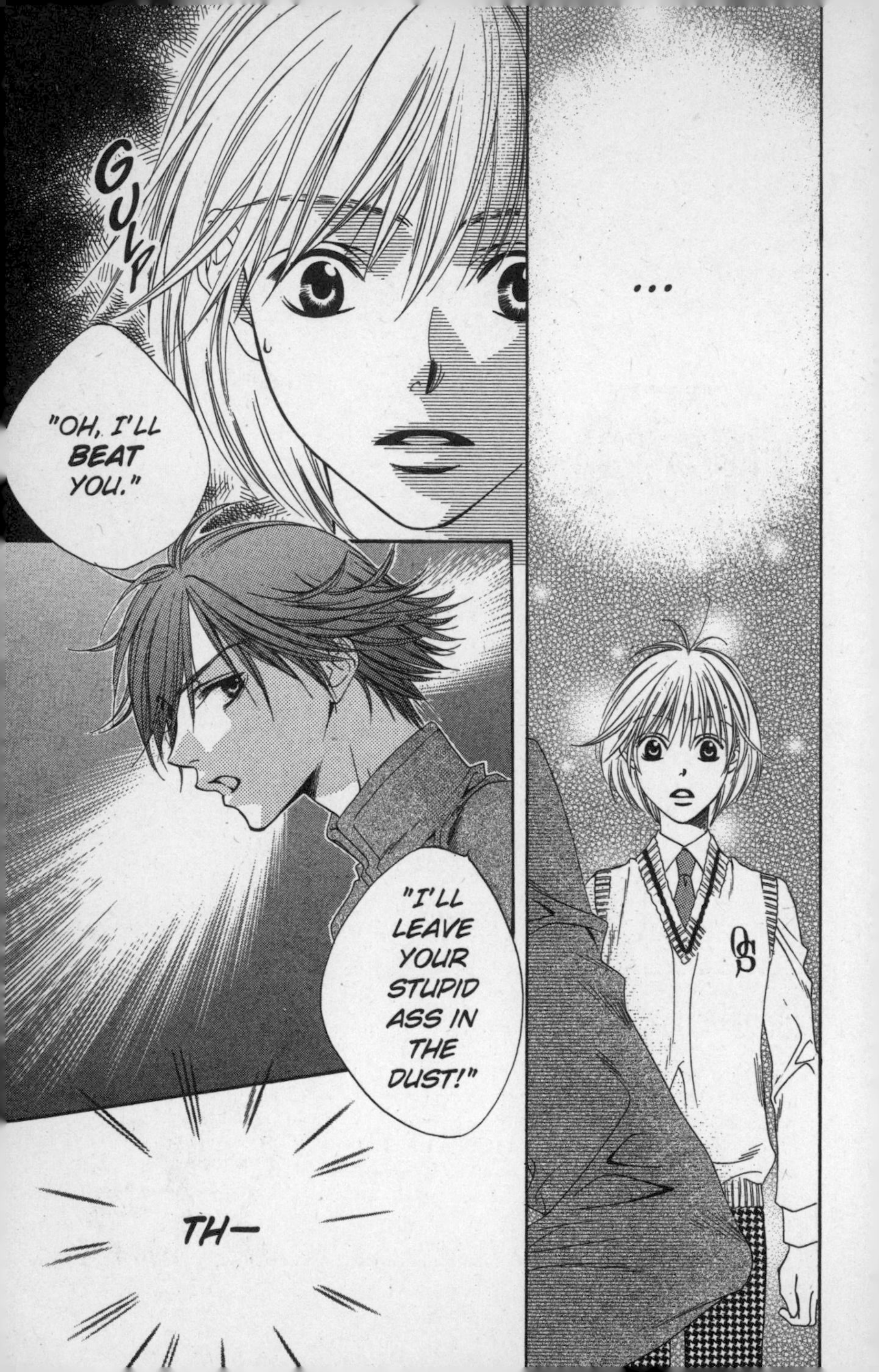
...
GULP
"OH, I'LL BEAT YOU."
"I'LL LEAVE YOUR STUPID ASS IN THE DUST!"
TH—

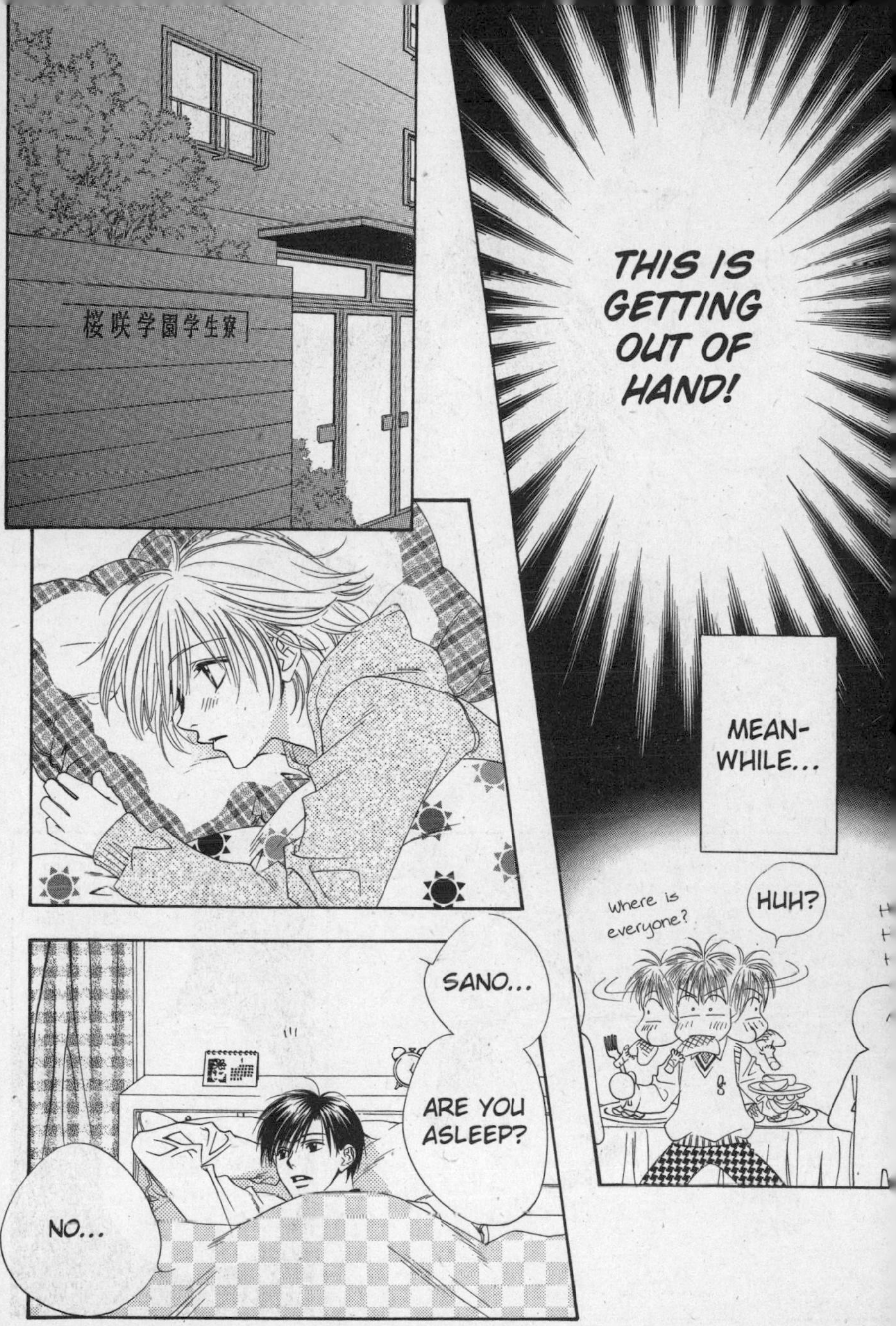
THIS IS GETTING OUT OF HAND!
MEAN-WHILE...
HUH?
Where is everyone?
桜咲学園学生寮
SANO...
ARE YOU ASLEEP?
NO...

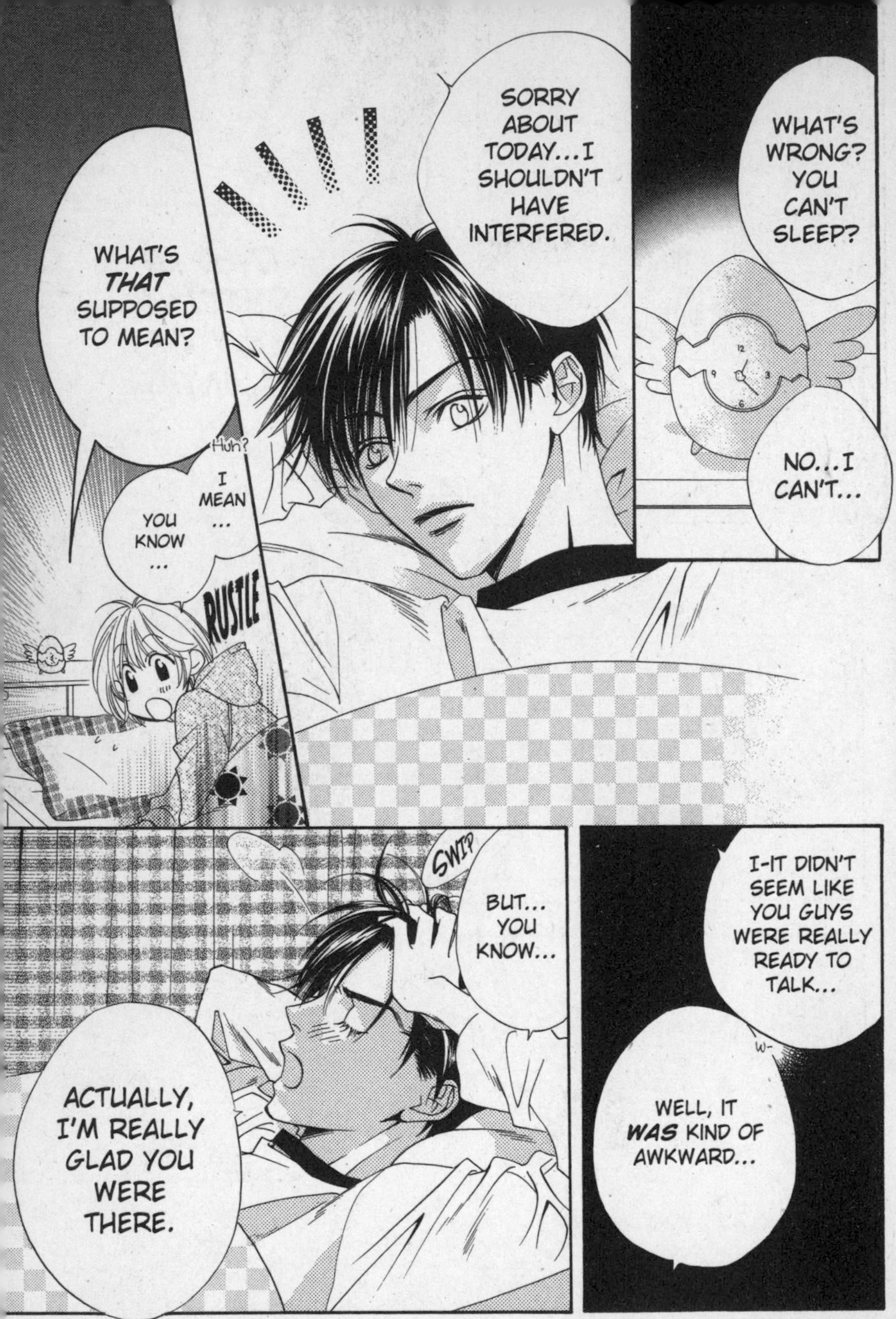
WHAT'S WRONG? YOU CAN'T SLEEP?
NO... I CAN'T...
SORRY ABOUT TODAY... I SHOULDN'T HAVE INTERFERED.
WHAT'S *THAT* SUPPOSED TO MEAN?
Huh?
I MEAN ...
YOU KNOW ...
RUSTLE
I-IT DIDN'T SEEM LIKE YOU GUYS WERE REALLY READY TO TALK...
W-
WELL, IT *WAS* KIND OF AWKWARD...
SWIP
BUT... YOU KNOW...
ACTUALLY, I'M REALLY GLAD YOU WERE THERE.

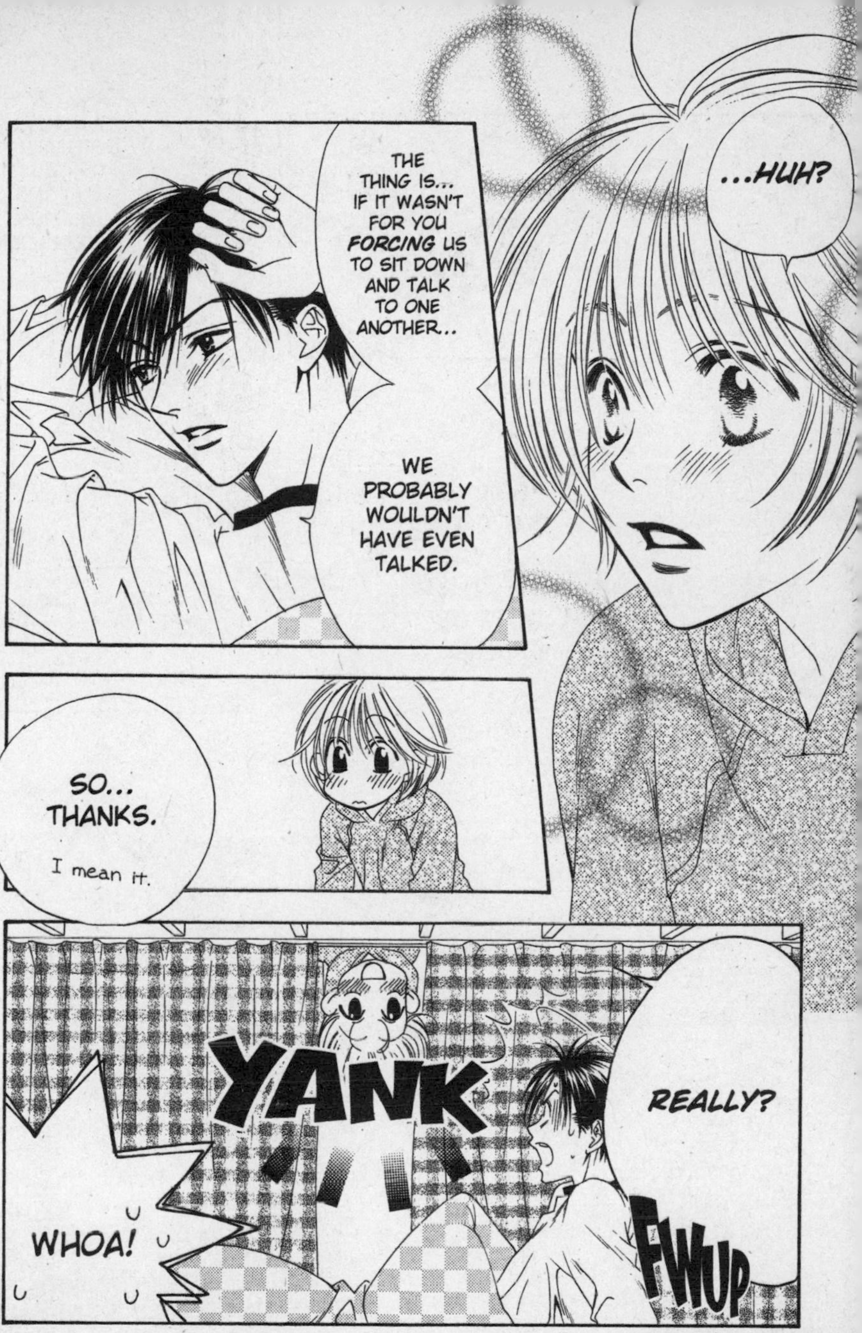
...HUH?
THE THING IS... IF IT WASN'T FOR YOU *FORCING* US TO SIT DOWN AND TALK TO ONE ANOTHER...
WE PROBABLY WOULDN'T HAVE EVEN TALKED.
SO... THANKS.
I mean it.
REALLY?
YANK
FWUP
WHOA!

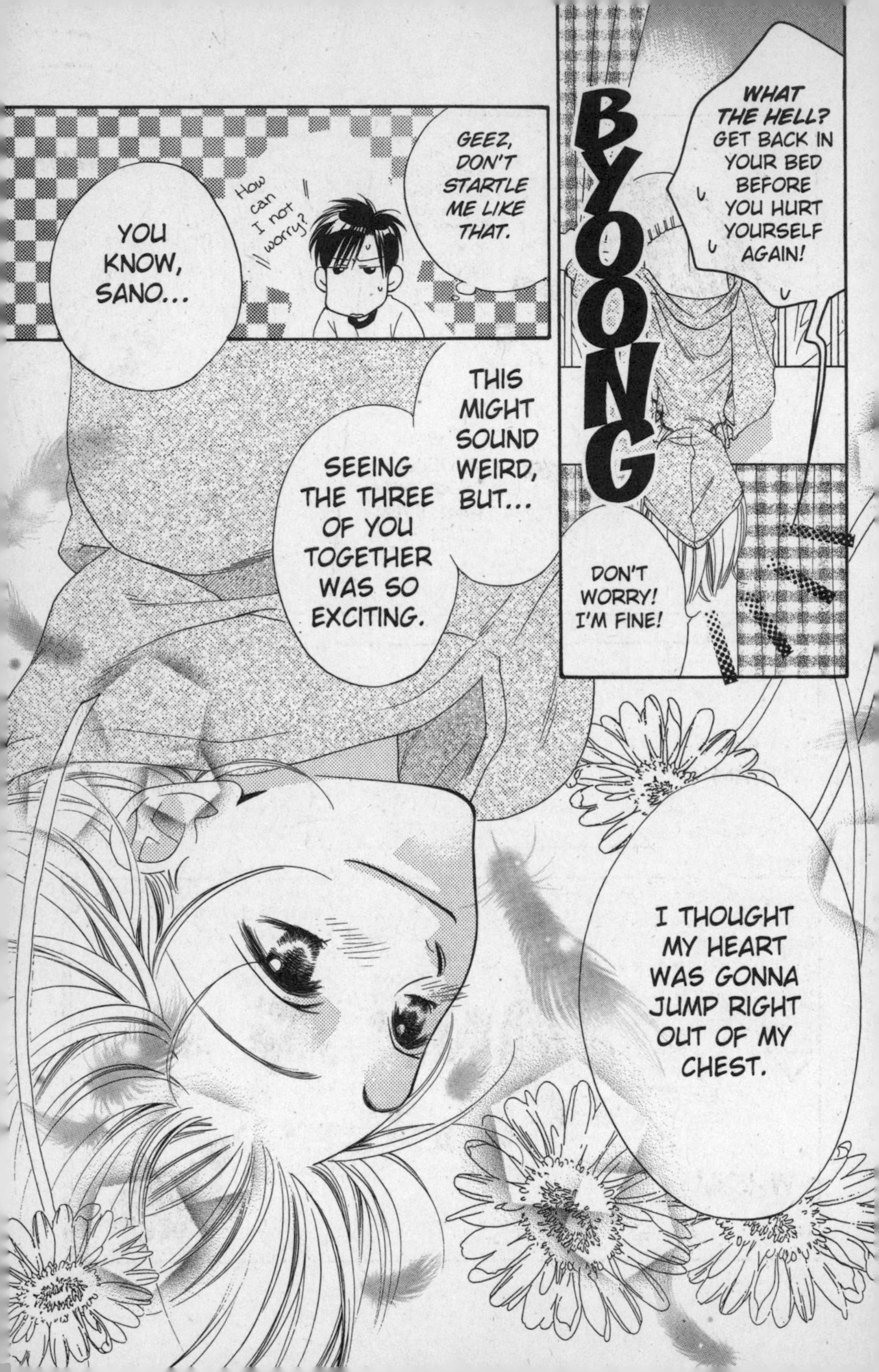
WHAT THE HELL? GET BACK IN YOUR BED BEFORE YOU HURT YOURSELF AGAIN!
BYOONG
DON'T WORRY! I'M FINE!
GEEZ, DON'T STARTLE ME LIKE THAT.
How can I not worry?
YOU KNOW, SANO...
THIS MIGHT SOUND WEIRD, BUT...
SEEING THE THREE OF YOU TOGETHER WAS SO EXCITING.
I THOUGHT MY HEART WAS GONNA JUMP RIGHT OUT OF MY CHEST.

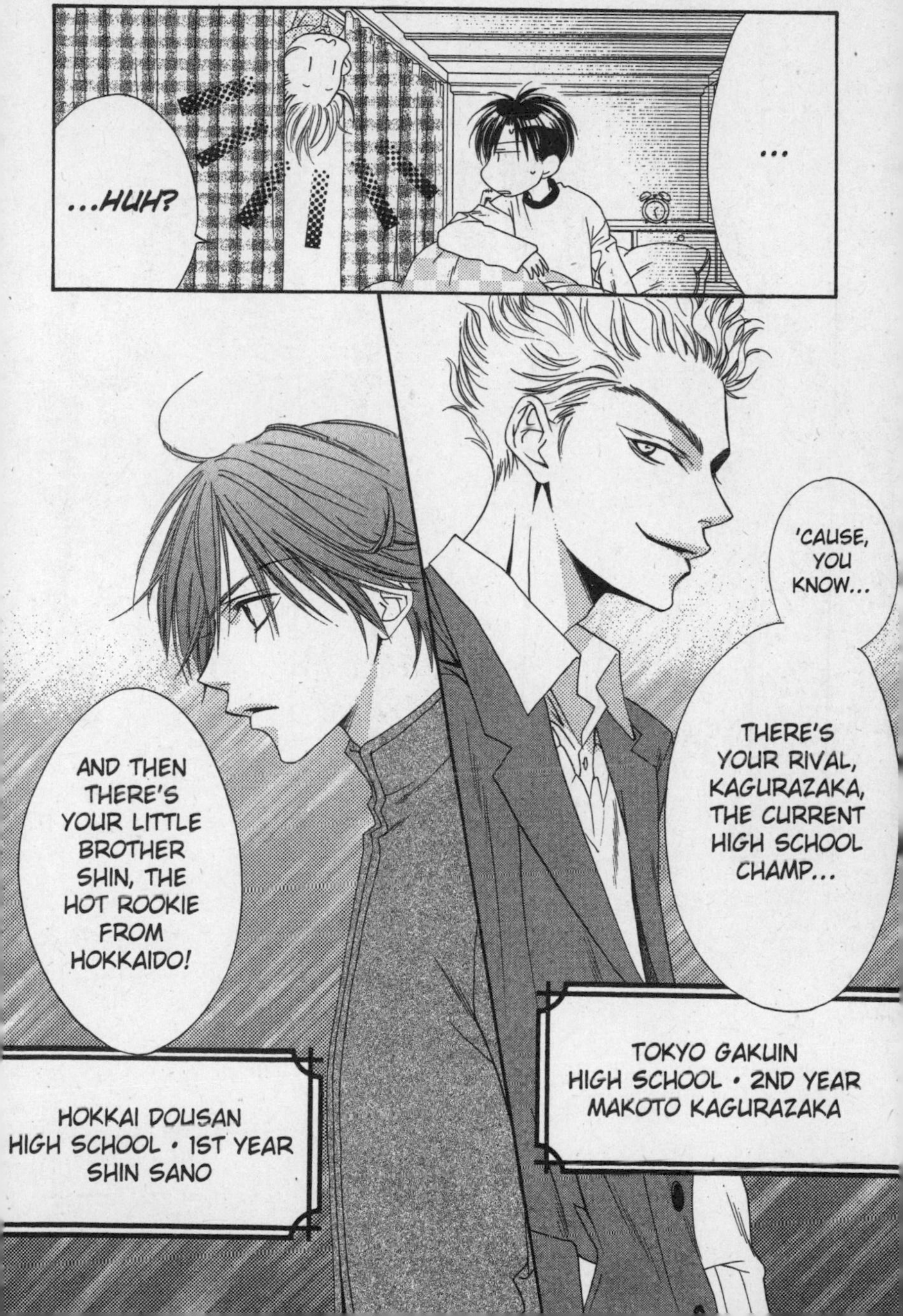
...
...HUH?
'CAUSE, YOU KNOW...
THERE'S YOUR RIVAL, KAGURAZAKA, THE CURRENT HIGH SCHOOL CHAMP...
TOKYO GAKUIN HIGH SCHOOL • 2ND YEAR MAKOTO KAGURAZAKA
AND THEN THERE'S YOUR LITTLE BROTHER SHIN, THE HOT ROOKIE FROM HOKKAIDO!
HOKKAI DOUSAN HIGH SCHOOL • 1ST YEAR SHIN SANO

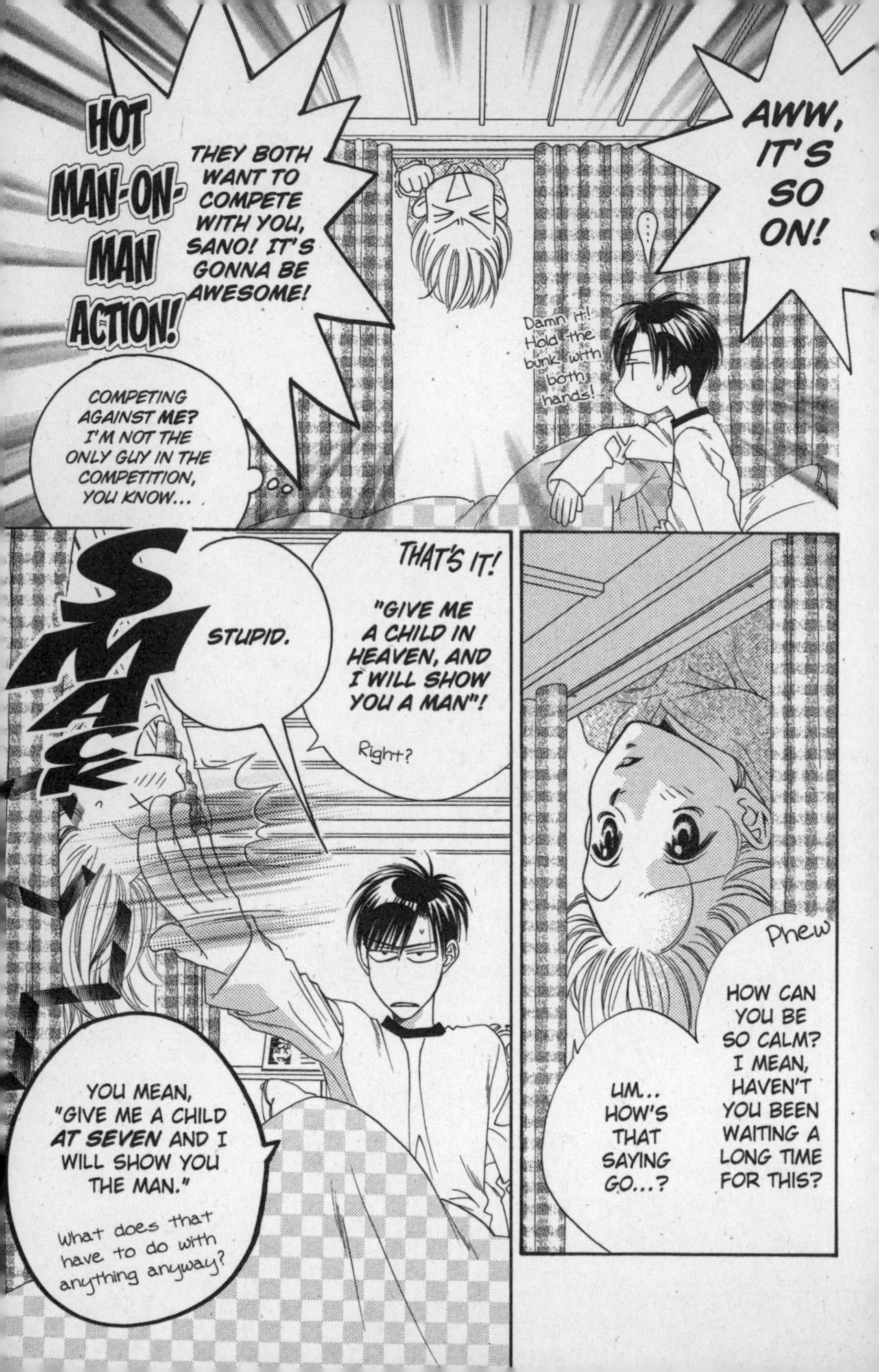
AWW, IT'S SO ON!
Damn it! Hold the bunk with both hands!
THEY BOTH WANT TO COMPETE WITH YOU, SANO! IT'S GONNA BE AWESOME!
HOT MAN-ON-MAN ACTION!
COMPETING AGAINST ME? I'M NOT THE ONLY GUY IN THE COMPETITION, YOU KNOW...
Phew
HOW CAN YOU BE SO CALM? I MEAN, HAVEN'T YOU BEEN WAITING A LONG TIME FOR THIS?
UM... HOW'S THAT SAYING GO...?
THAT'S IT!
"GIVE ME A CHILD IN HEAVEN, AND I WILL SHOW YOU A MAN"!
Right?
STUPID.
SMACK
YOU MEAN, "GIVE ME A CHILD AT SEVEN AND I WILL SHOW YOU THE MAN."
What does that have to do with anything anyway?

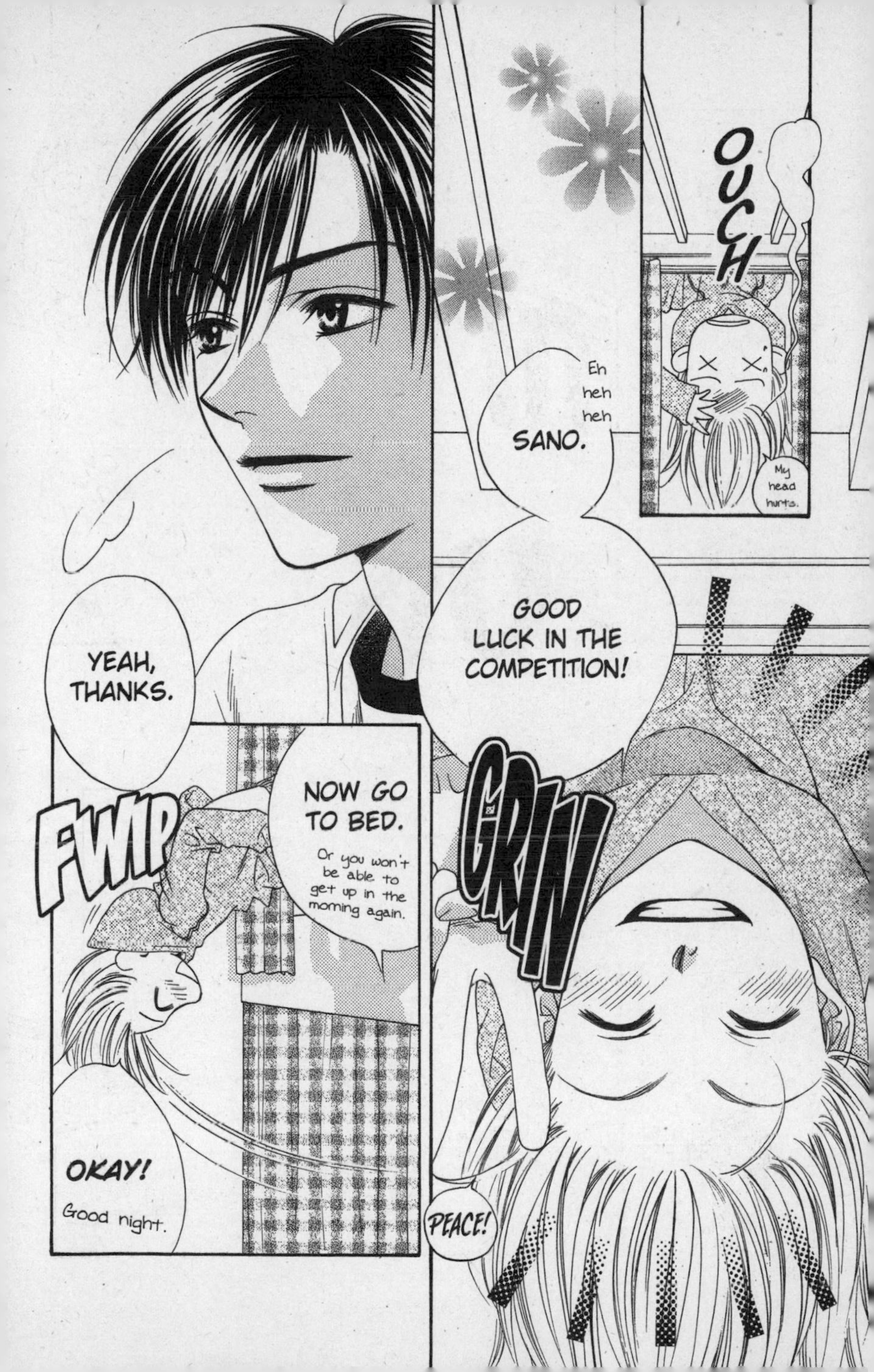
OUCH
My head hurts.
Eh heh heh
SANO.
GOOD LUCK IN THE COMPETITION!
GRIN
PEACE!
YEAH, THANKS.
NOW GO TO BED.
Or you won't be able to get up in the morning again.
FWIP
OKAY!
Good night.

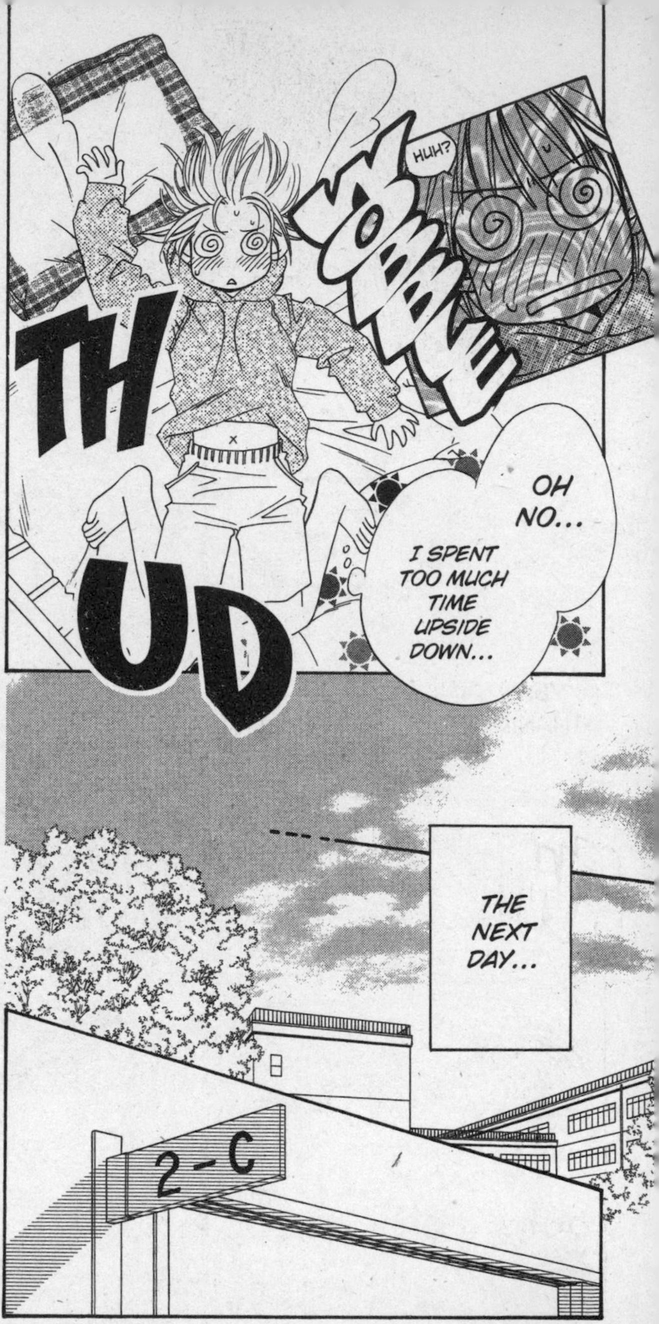
HUH?
WOBBLE
OH NO...
I SPENT TOO MUCH TIME UPSIDE DOWN...
THUD
THE NEXT DAY...
2-C

SHOTARO KADOMA

Birthday: May 18th
Grade: First Year Japanese H.S. (equivalent of 10th grade in America)
Blood Type: O
Sign: Taurus
Height: 158cm
Favorite Foods: Cherries, Stir-fried Udon
Favorite Colors: Navy Blue, White
Favorite Celebrities: Kein Kosugi, Andy Fugu
Favorite Season: Summer
Favorite Subject: Japanese
Least Favorite Subject: Biology
Favorite Foods: Pickled Ginger, Liver, Conch
Flower: Tulip

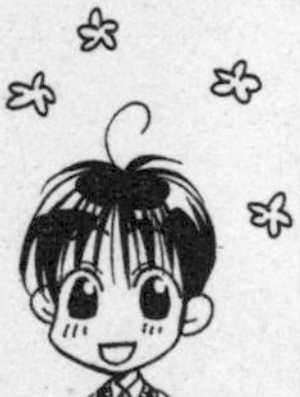

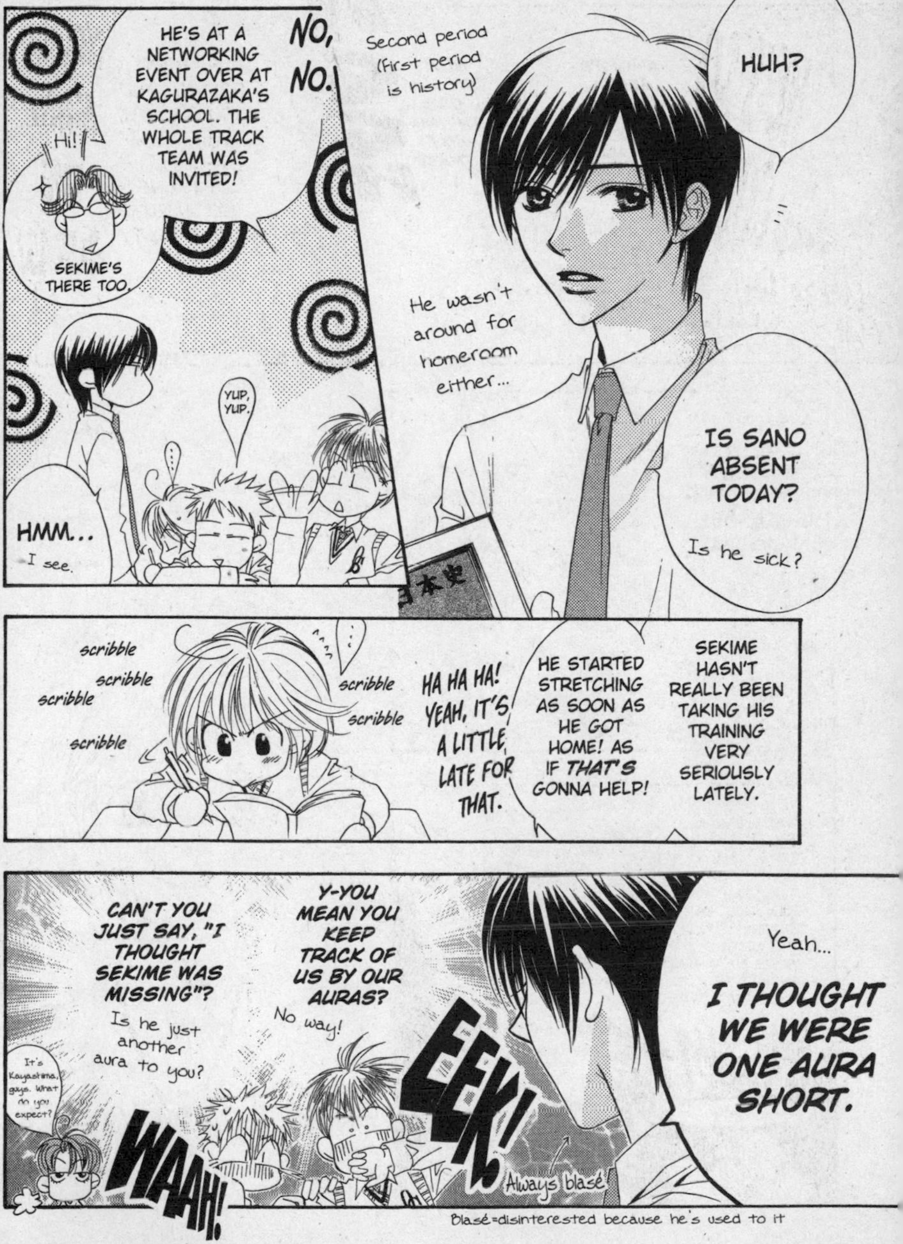
HUH?
Second period (first period is history)
IS SANO ABSENT TODAY?
Is he sick?
He wasn't around for homeroom either...
NO, NO.
HE'S AT A NETWORKING EVENT OVER AT KAGURAZAKA'S SCHOOL. THE WHOLE TRACK TEAM WAS INVITED!
Hi!
SEKIME'S THERE TOO.
YUP, YUP.
HMM...
I see.
SEKIME HASN'T REALLY BEEN TAKING HIS TRAINING VERY SERIOUSLY LATELY.
HE STARTED STRETCHING AS SOON AS HE GOT HOME! AS IF *THAT'S* GONNA HELP!
HA HA HA! YEAH, IT'S A LITTLE LATE FOR THAT.
scribble
scribble
scribble
scribble
scribble
scribble
Yeah...
I THOUGHT WE WERE ONE AURA SHORT.
Always blasé
EEK!
Y-YOU MEAN YOU KEEP TRACK OF US BY OUR AURAS?
No way!
CAN'T YOU JUST SAY, "I THOUGHT SEKIME WAS MISSING"?
Is he just another aura to you?
WAAH!
It's Kayashima, guys. What do you expect?

Blasé=disinterested because he's used to it

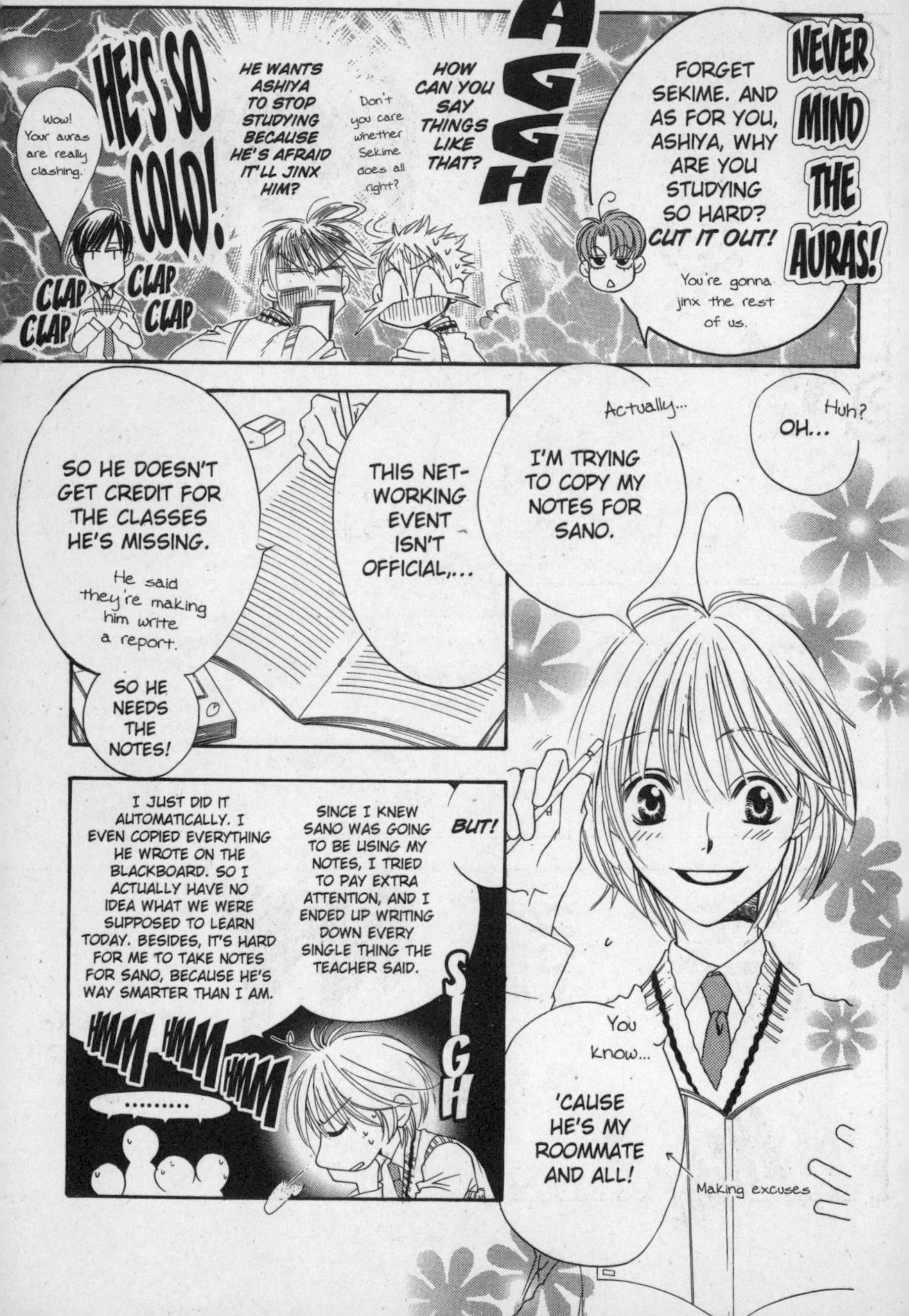
NEVER MIND THE AURAS!
FORGET SEKIME. AND AS FOR YOU, ASHIYA, WHY ARE YOU STUDYING SO HARD? CUT IT OUT!
You're gonna jinx the rest of us.
AGGH
HOW CAN YOU SAY THINGS LIKE THAT?
Don't you care whether Sekime does all right?
HE WANTS ASHIYA TO STOP STUDYING BECAUSE HE'S AFRAID IT'LL JINX HIM?
HE'S SO COLD!
Wow! Your auras are really clashing.
CLAP CLAP CLAP CLAP
Huh?
OH...
Actually...
I'M TRYING TO COPY MY NOTES FOR SANO.
You know...
'CAUSE HE'S MY ROOMMATE AND ALL!
Making excuses
THIS NET-WORKING EVENT ISN'T OFFICIAL,...
SO HE DOESN'T GET CREDIT FOR THE CLASSES HE'S MISSING.
He said they're making him write a report.
SO HE NEEDS THE NOTES!
BUT!
SINCE I KNEW SANO WAS GOING TO BE USING MY NOTES, I TRIED TO PAY EXTRA ATTENTION, AND I ENDED UP WRITING DOWN EVERY SINGLE THING THE TEACHER SAID.
I JUST DID IT AUTOMATICALLY. I EVEN COPIED EVERYTHING HE WROTE ON THE BLACKBOARD. SO I ACTUALLY HAVE NO IDEA WHAT WE WERE SUPPOSED TO LEARN TODAY. BESIDES, IT'S HARD FOR ME TO TAKE NOTES FOR SANO, BECAUSE HE'S WAY SMARTER THAN I AM.
SIGH
HMM HMM HMM
....

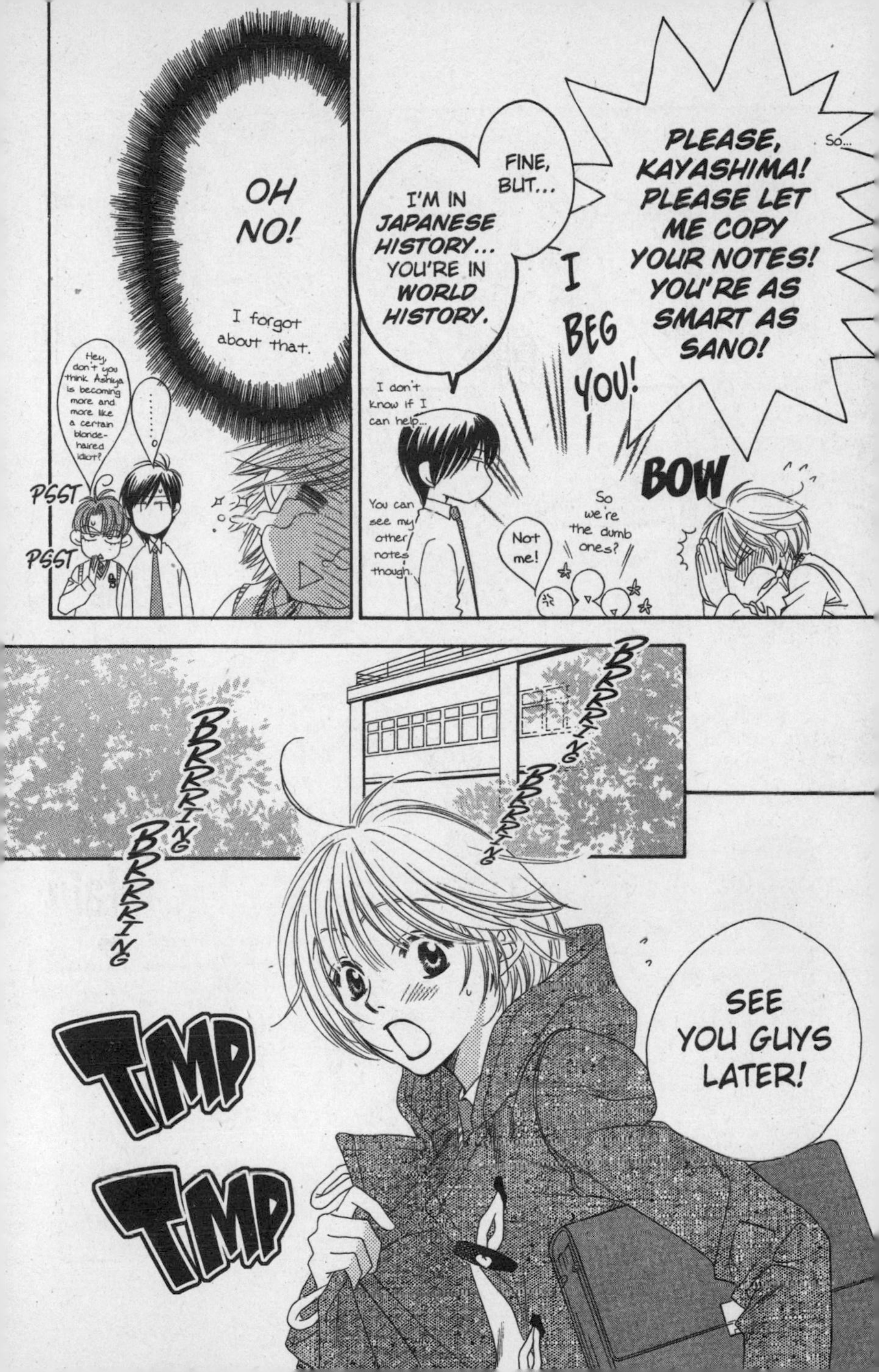
PLEASE, KAYASHIMA! PLEASE LET ME COPY YOUR NOTES! YOU'RE AS SMART AS SANO!
So...
I BEG YOU!
BOW
FINE, BUT...
I'M IN JAPANESE HISTORY... YOU'RE IN WORLD HISTORY.
I don't know if I can help...
You can see my other notes though.
So we're the dumb ones?
Not me!
OH NO!
I forgot about that.
......
Hey, don't you think Ashiya is becoming more and more like a certain blonde-haired idiot?
PSST
PSST
BRRRRING
BRRRRING
BRRRRING
BRRRRING
SEE YOU GUYS LATER!
TMP
TMP

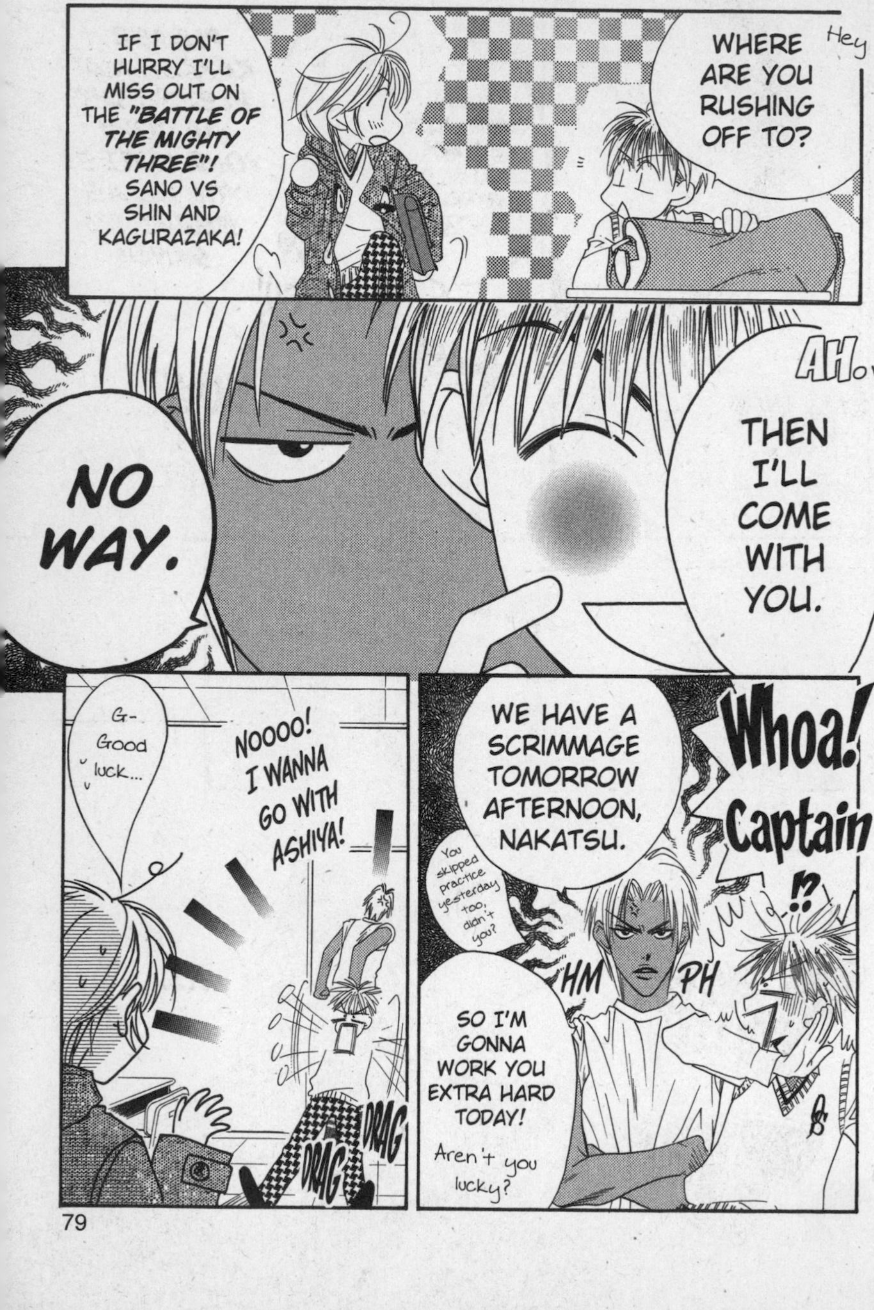

Hey
WHERE ARE YOU RUSHING OFF TO?
IF I DON'T HURRY I'LL MISS OUT ON THE *"BATTLE OF THE MIGHTY THREE"!* SANO VS SHIN AND KAGURAZAKA!
AH.
THEN I'LL COME WITH YOU.
NO WAY.
Whoa! Captain
!?
WE HAVE A SCRIMMAGE TOMORROW AFTERNOON, NAKATSU.
You skipped practice yesterday too, didn't you?
HM PH
SO I'M GONNA WORK YOU EXTRA HARD TODAY!
Aren't you lucky?
NOOOO! I WANNA GO WITH ASHIYA!
G-Good luck...
DRAG DRAG

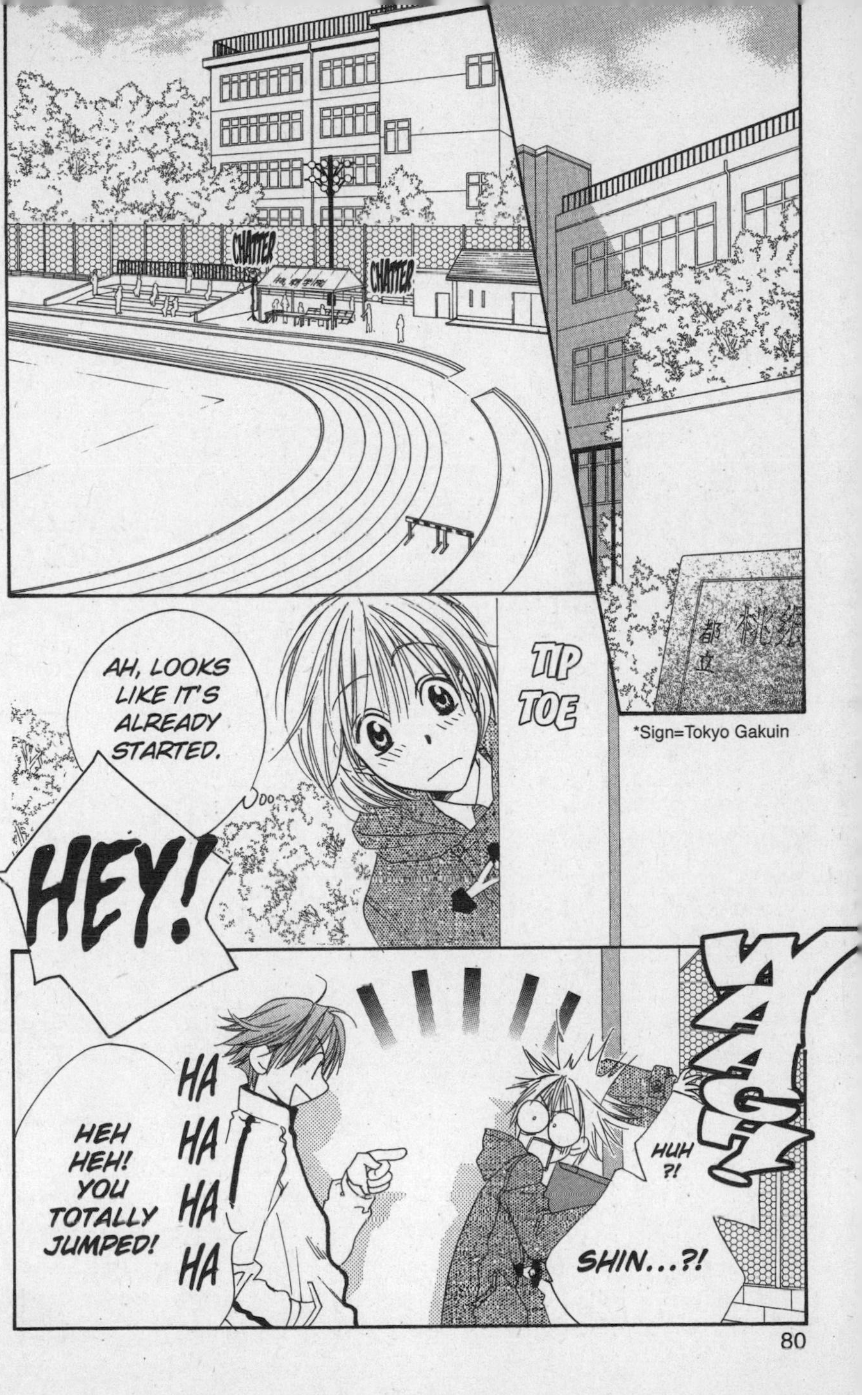
*Sign=Tokyo Gakuin
CHATTER
CHATTER
TIP TOE
AH, LOOKS LIKE IT'S ALREADY STARTED.
DO
HEY!
HUH ?!
SHIN...?!
HA HA HA HA
HEH HEH! YOU TOTALLY JUMPED!

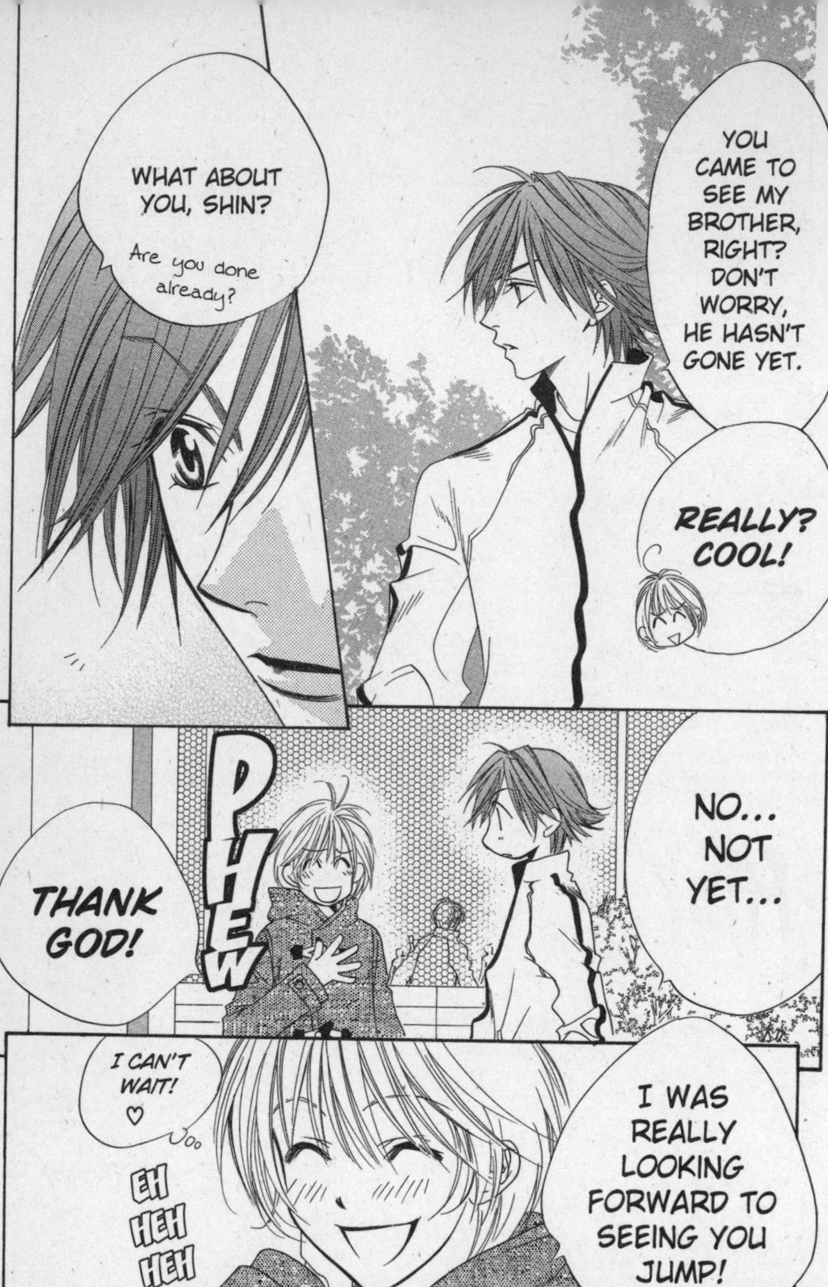
YOU CAME TO SEE MY BROTHER, RIGHT? DON'T WORRY, HE HASN'T GONE YET.
REALLY? COOL!
WHAT ABOUT YOU, SHIN?
Are you done already?
NO... NOT YET...
PHEW
THANK GOD!
I WAS REALLY LOOKING FORWARD TO SEEING YOU JUMP!
I CAN'T WAIT! ♡
EH HEH HEH

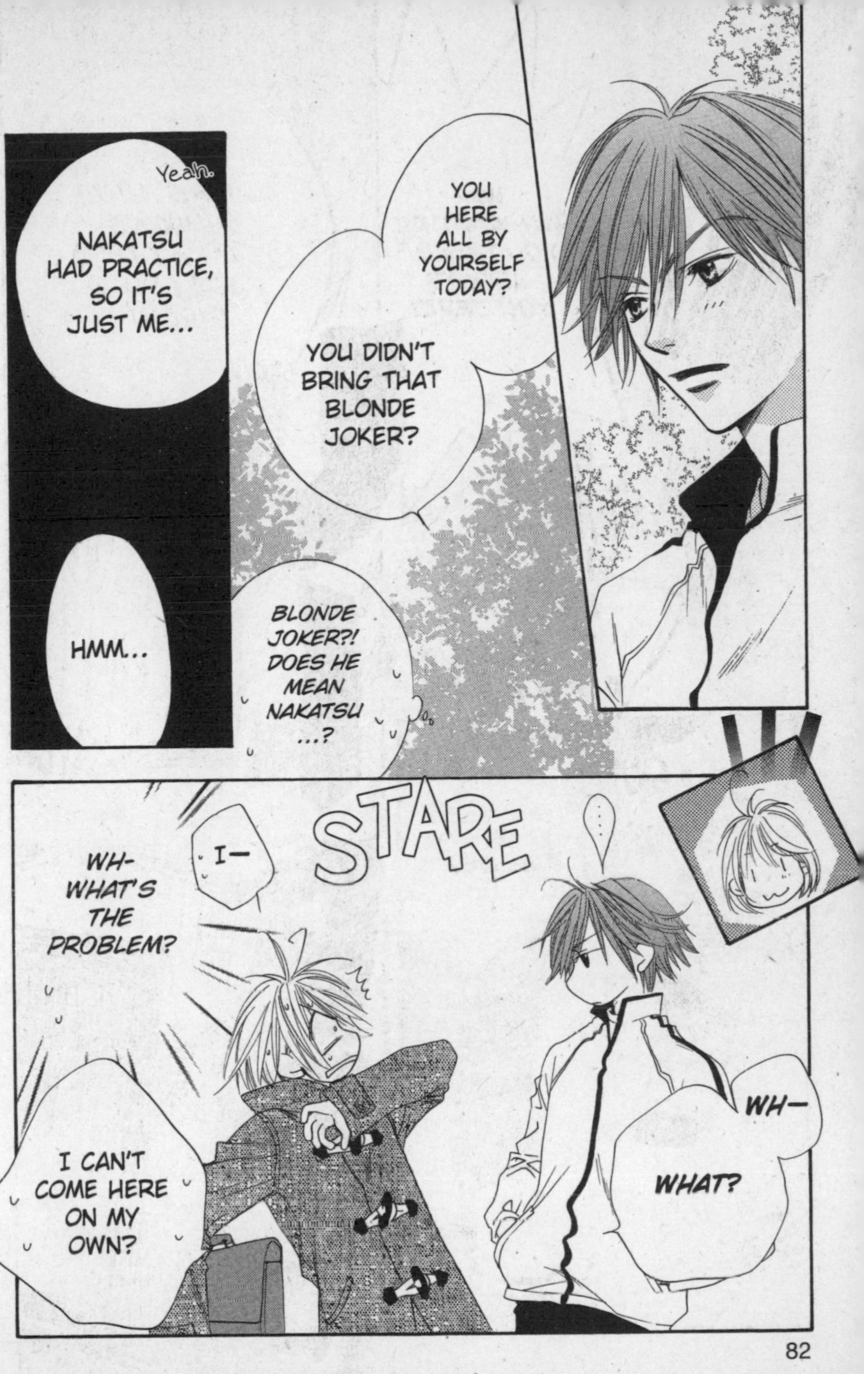
YOU HERE ALL BY YOURSELF TODAY?
YOU DIDN'T BRING THAT BLONDE JOKER?
Yeah.
NAKATSU HAD PRACTICE, SO IT'S JUST ME...
BLONDE JOKER?! DOES HE MEAN NAKATSU ...?
HMM...
STARE
WH- WHAT?
I—
WH- WHAT'S THE PROBLEM?
I CAN'T COME HERE ON MY OWN?

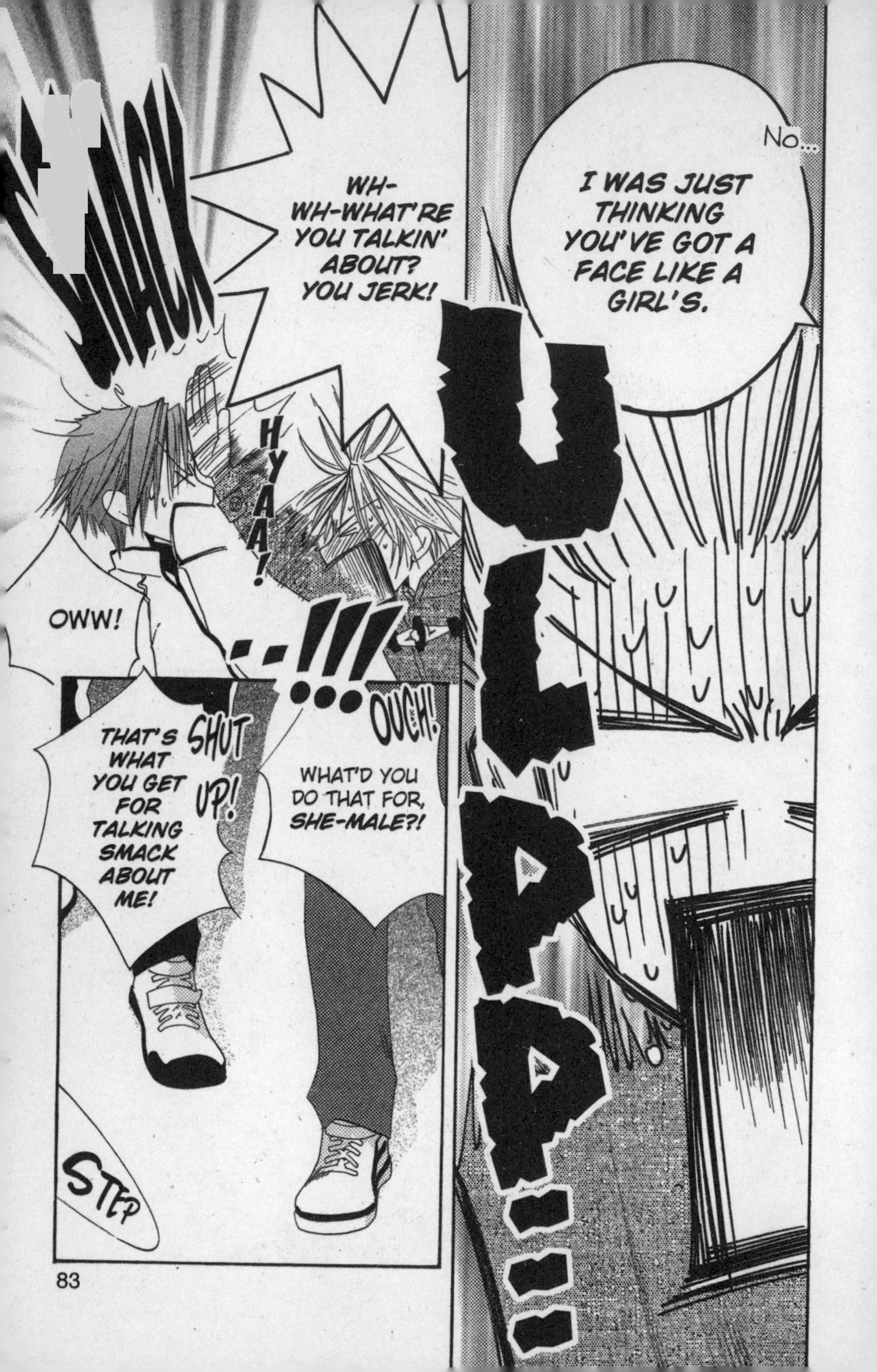

No...
I WAS JUST THINKING YOU'VE GOT A FACE LIKE A GIRL'S.
ULPP!!!
SMACK
WH- WH-WHAT'RE YOU TALKIN' ABOUT? YOU JERK!
HYAA!
OWW!
..!!!
...
OUCH!
SHUT UP!
THAT'S WHAT YOU GET FOR TALKING SMACK ABOUT ME!
WHAT'D YOU DO THAT FOR, SHE-MALE?!
STEP

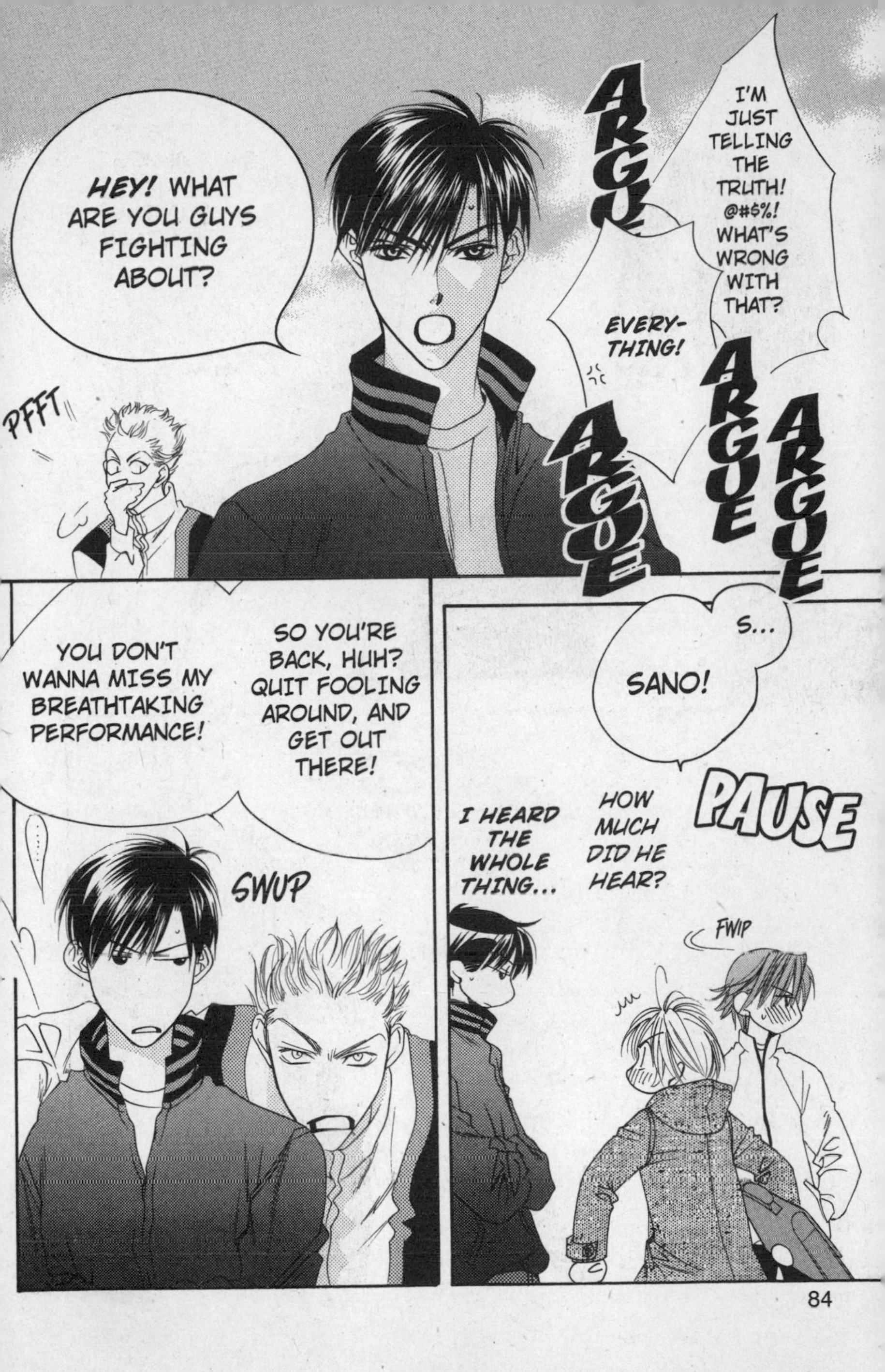
ARGUE
I'M JUST TELLING THE TRUTH! @#$%! WHAT'S WRONG WITH THAT?
EVERY-THING!
ARGUE
ARGUE
ARGUE
HEY! WHAT ARE YOU GUYS FIGHTING ABOUT?
PFFT
S...
SANO!
PAUSE
HOW MUCH DID HE HEAR?
I HEARD THE WHOLE THING...
FWIP
SO YOU'RE BACK, HUH? QUIT FOOLING AROUND, AND GET OUT THERE!
YOU DON'T WANNA MISS MY BREATHTAKING PERFORMANCE!
SWUP

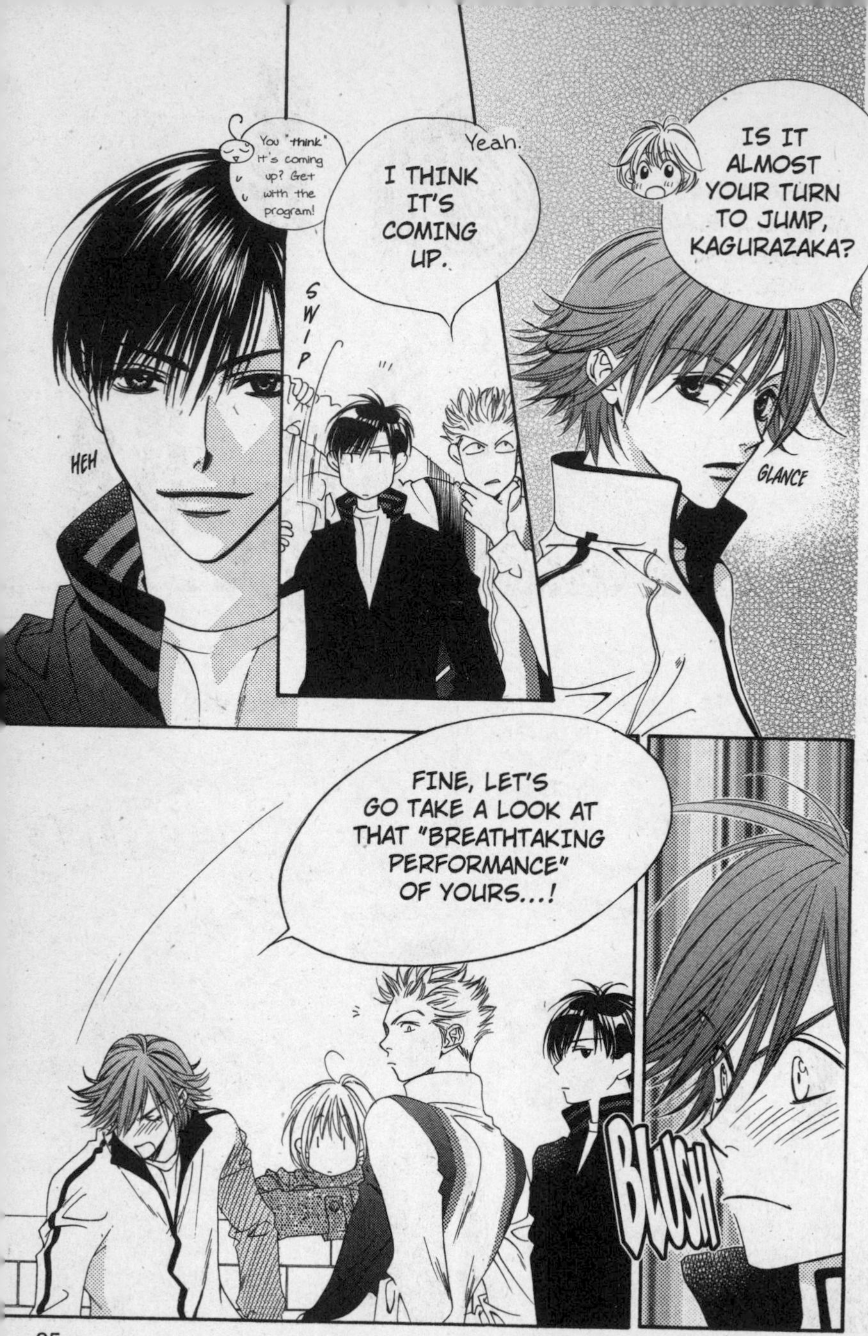
IS IT ALMOST YOUR TURN TO JUMP, KAGURAZAKA?
GLANCE
Yeah.
I THINK IT'S COMING UP.
SWIP
You "think" it's coming up? Get with the program!
HEH
BLUSH
FINE, LET'S GO TAKE A LOOK AT THAT "BREATHTAKING PERFORMANCE" OF YOURS...!

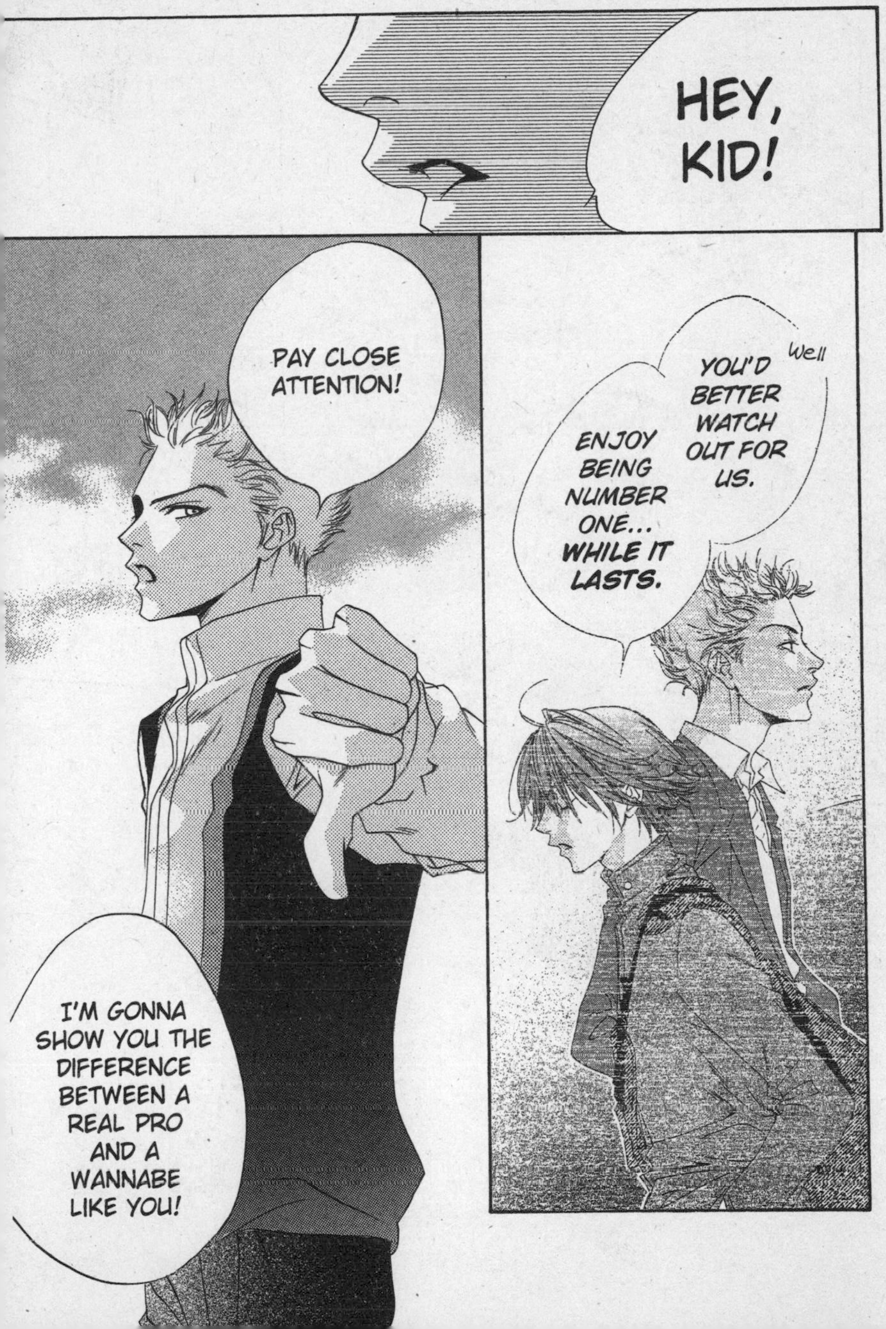
HEY, KID!
Well
YOU'D BETTER WATCH OUT FOR US.
ENJOY BEING NUMBER ONE... WHILE IT LASTS.
PAY CLOSE ATTENTION!
I'M GONNA SHOW YOU THE DIFFERENCE BETWEEN A REAL PRO AND A WANNABE LIKE YOU!

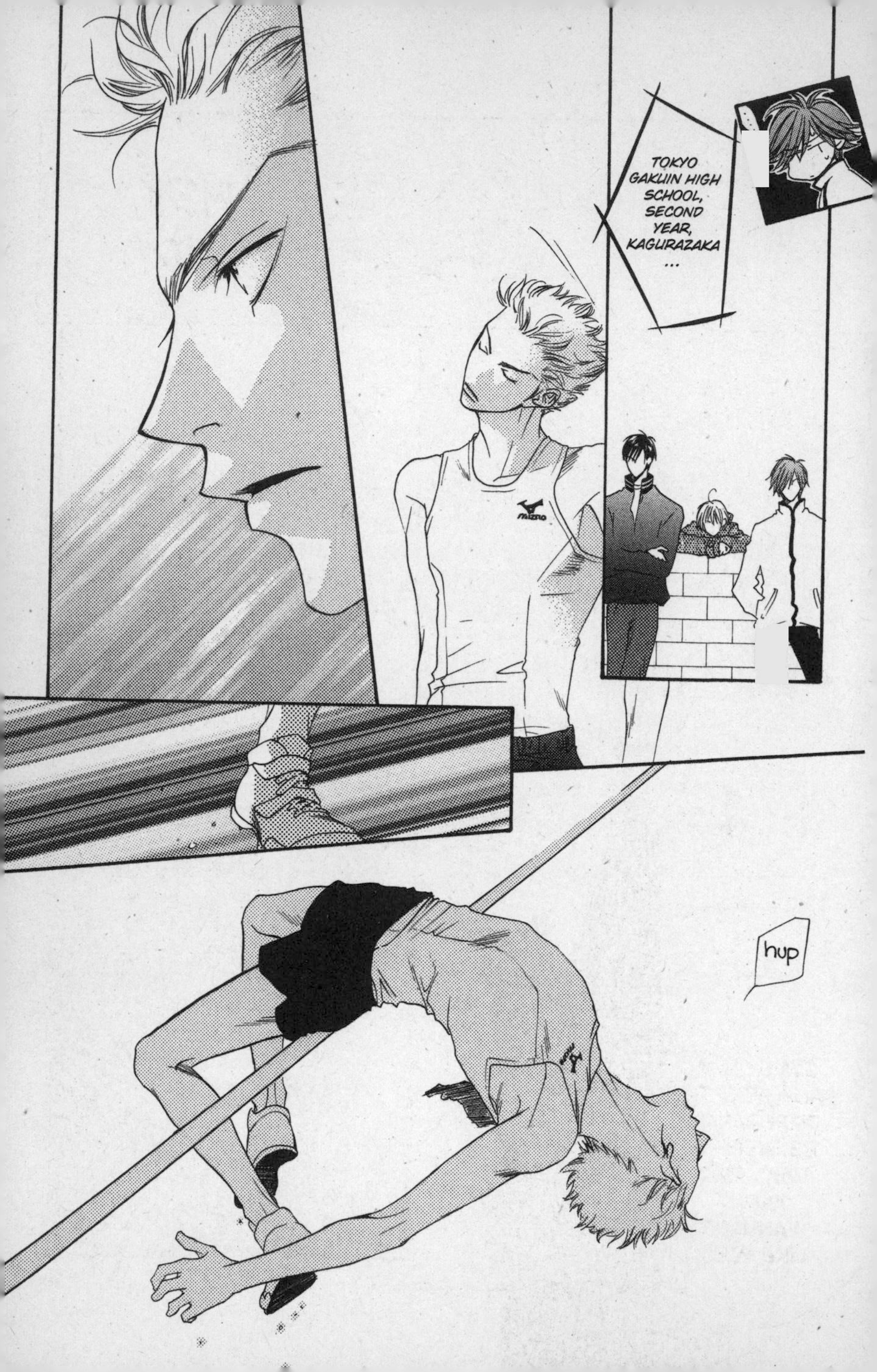
TOKYO GAKUIN HIGH SCHOOL, SECOND YEAR, KAGURAZAKA ...
hup

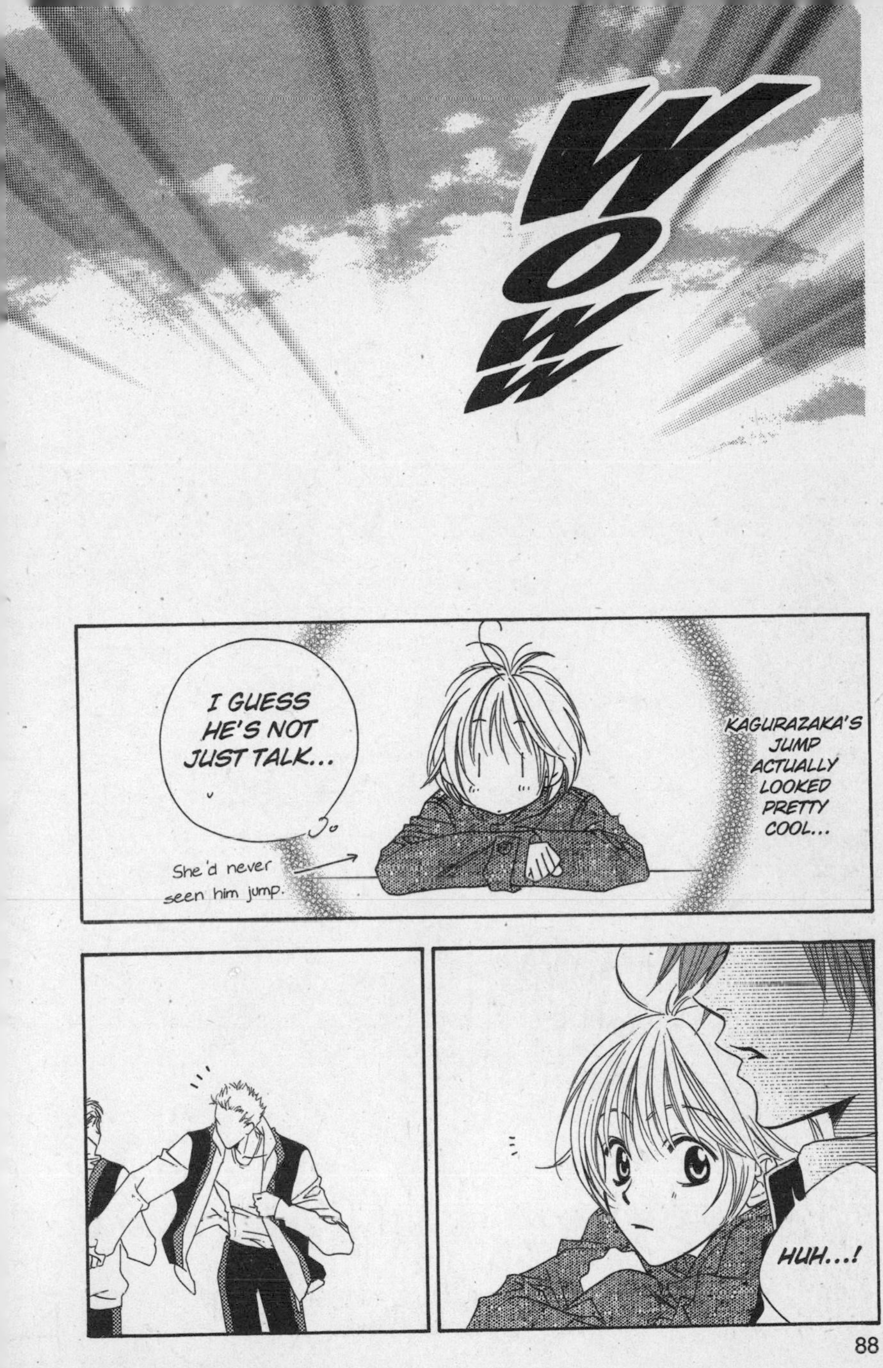
WOW
KAGURAZAKA'S JUMP ACTUALLY LOOKED PRETTY COOL...
I GUESS HE'S NOT JUST TALK...
She'd never seen him jump.
HUH...!

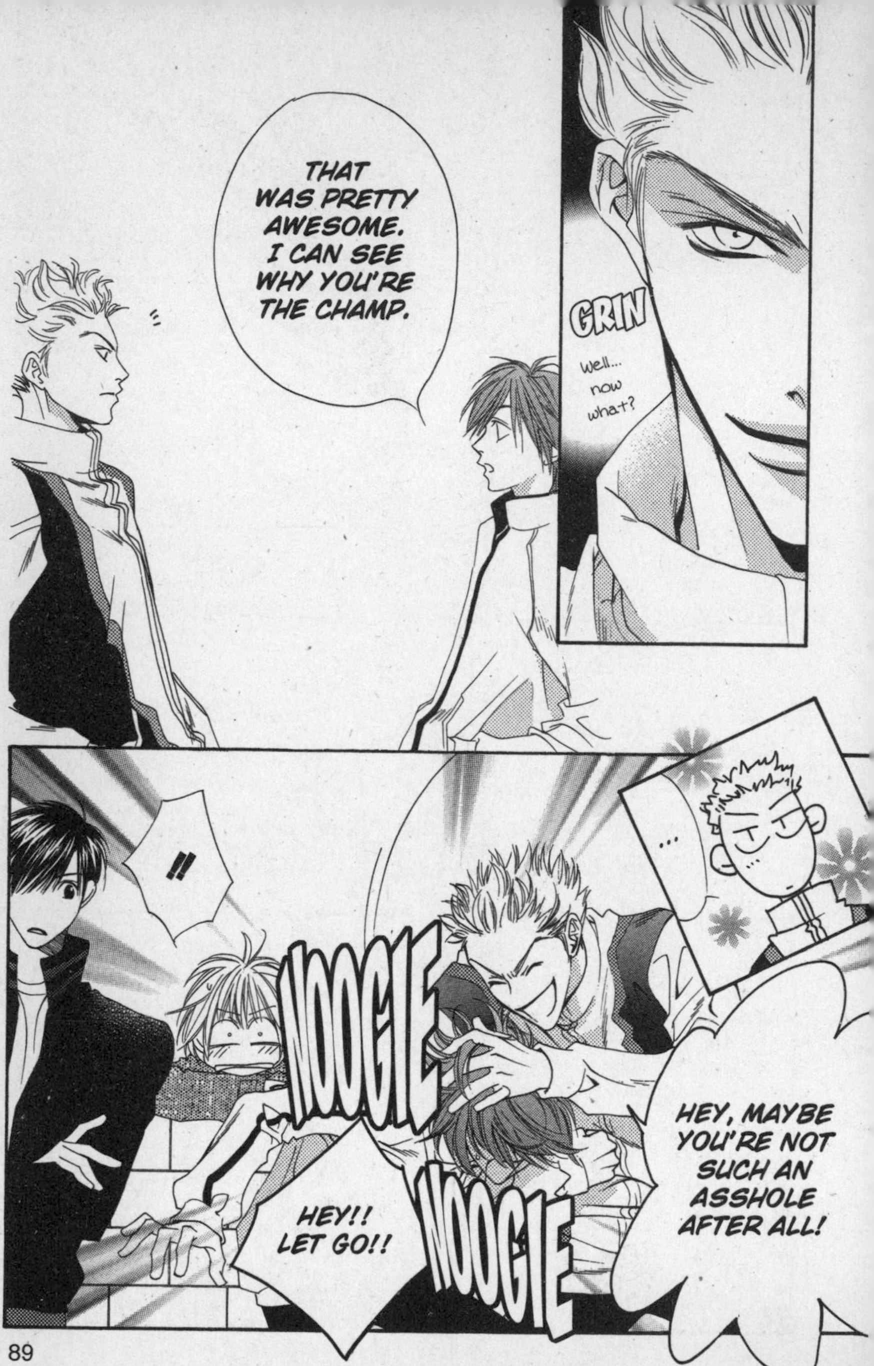
GRIN
Well... now what?
THAT WAS PRETTY AWESOME. I CAN SEE WHY YOU'RE THE CHAMP.
...
!!
NOOGIE
HEY, MAYBE YOU'RE NOT SUCH AN ASSHOLE AFTER ALL!
NOOGIE
HEY!! LET GO!!

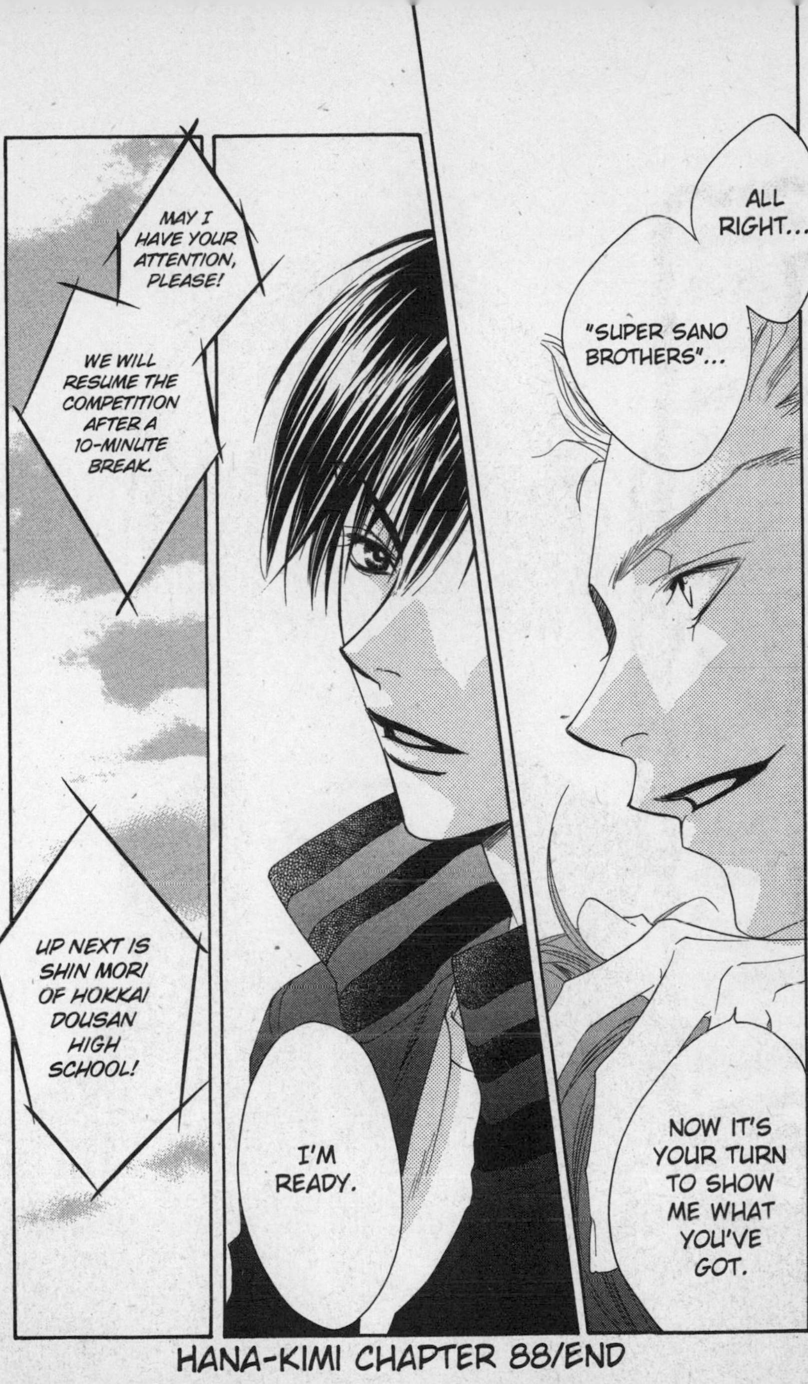
ALL RIGHT...
"SUPER SANO BROTHERS"...
NOW IT'S YOUR TURN TO SHOW ME WHAT YOU'VE GOT.
I'M READY.
MAY I HAVE YOUR ATTENTION, PLEASE!
WE WILL RESUME THE COMPETITION AFTER A 10-MINUTE BREAK.
UP NEXT IS SHIN MORI OF HOKKAI DOUSAN HIGH SCHOOL!

HANA-KIMI CHAPTER 88/END

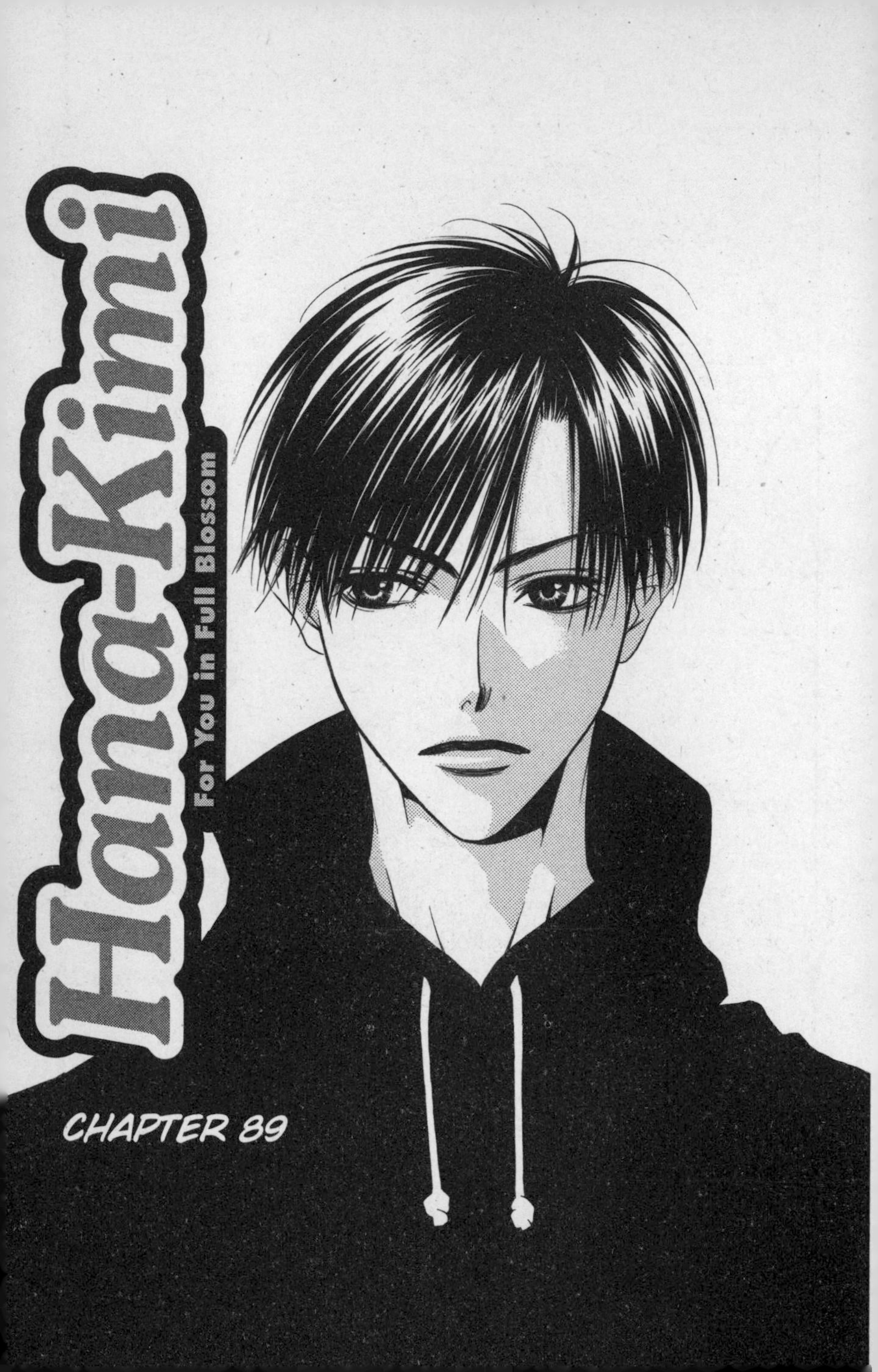
Hana-Kimi
For You in Full Blossom
CHAPTER 89

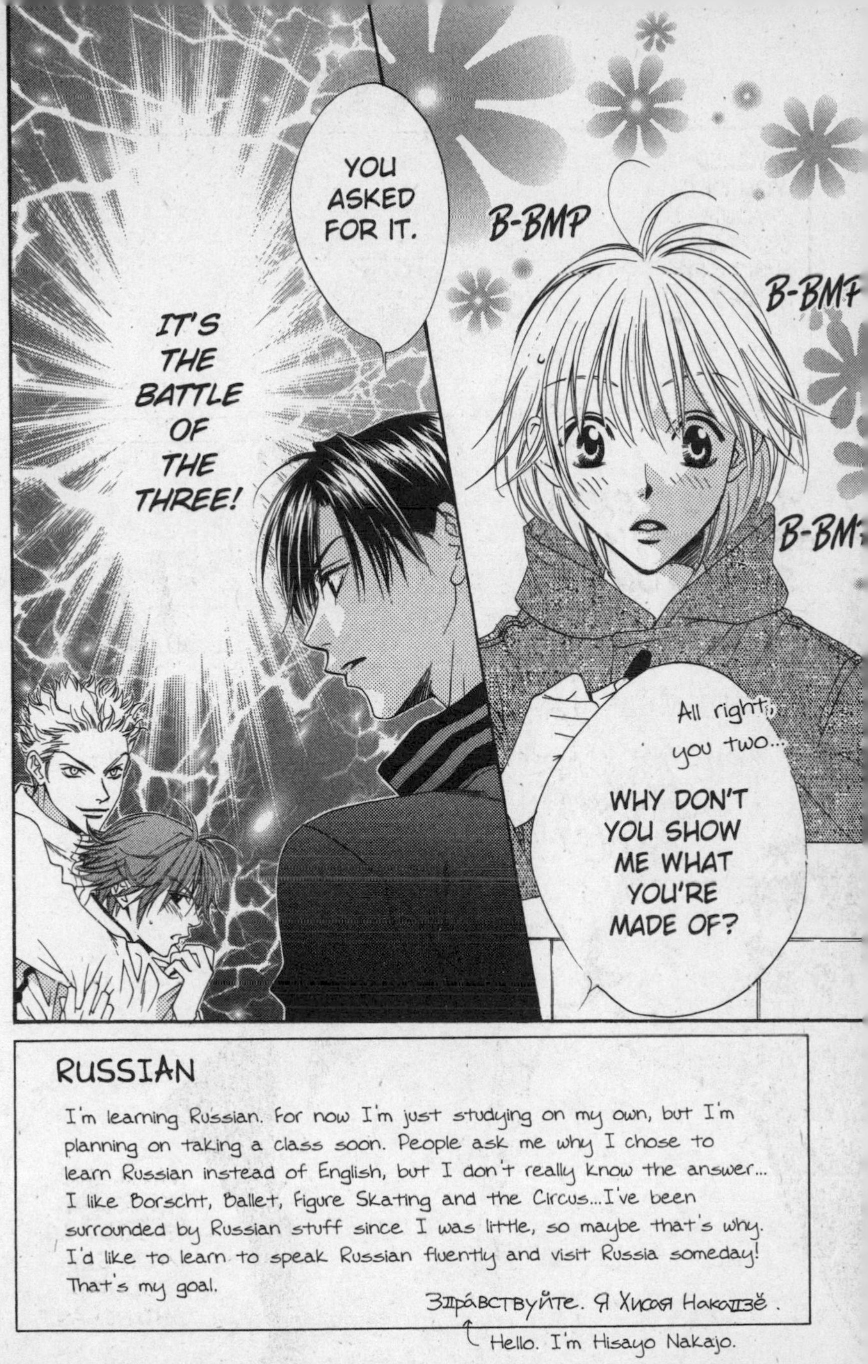
B-BMP
B-BMP
B-BM
All right, you two...
WHY DON'T YOU SHOW ME WHAT YOU'RE MADE OF?
YOU ASKED FOR IT.
IT'S THE BATTLE OF THE THREE!

RUSSIAN

I'm learning Russian. For now I'm just studying on my own, but I'm planning on taking a class soon. People ask me why I chose to learn Russian instead of English, but I don't really know the answer... I like Borscht, Ballet, Figure Skating and the Circus...I've been surrounded by Russian stuff since I was little, so maybe that's why. I'd like to learn to speak Russian fluently and visit Russia someday! That's my goal.

Здра́вствуйте. Я Хисая Накадзё.

Hello. I'm Hisayo Nakajo.

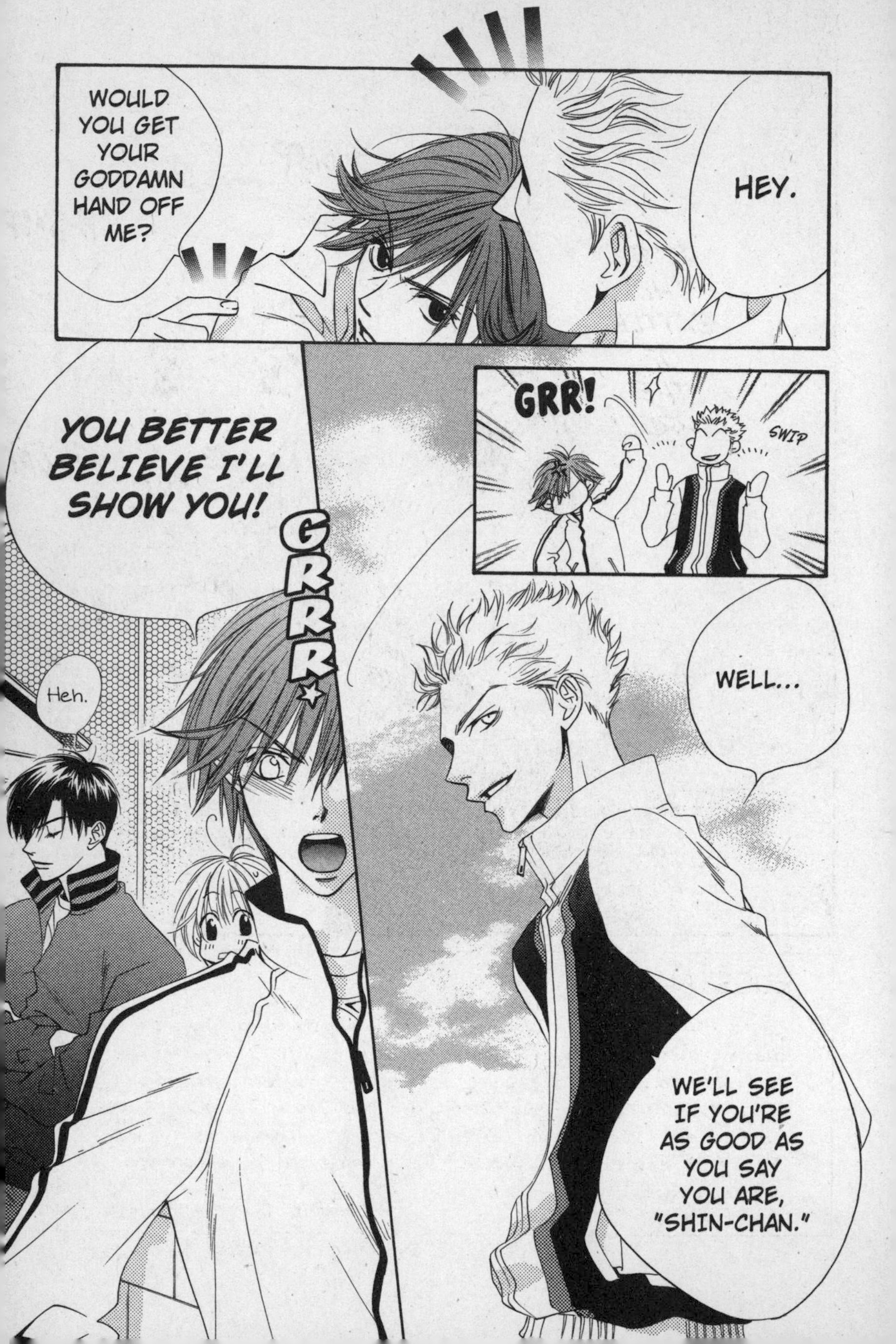
HEY.
WOULD YOU GET YOUR GODDAMN HAND OFF ME?
GRR!
SWIP
WELL...
WE'LL SEE IF YOU'RE AS GOOD AS YOU SAY YOU ARE, "SHIN-CHAN."
YOU BETTER BELIEVE I'LL SHOW YOU!
GRRR
Heh.

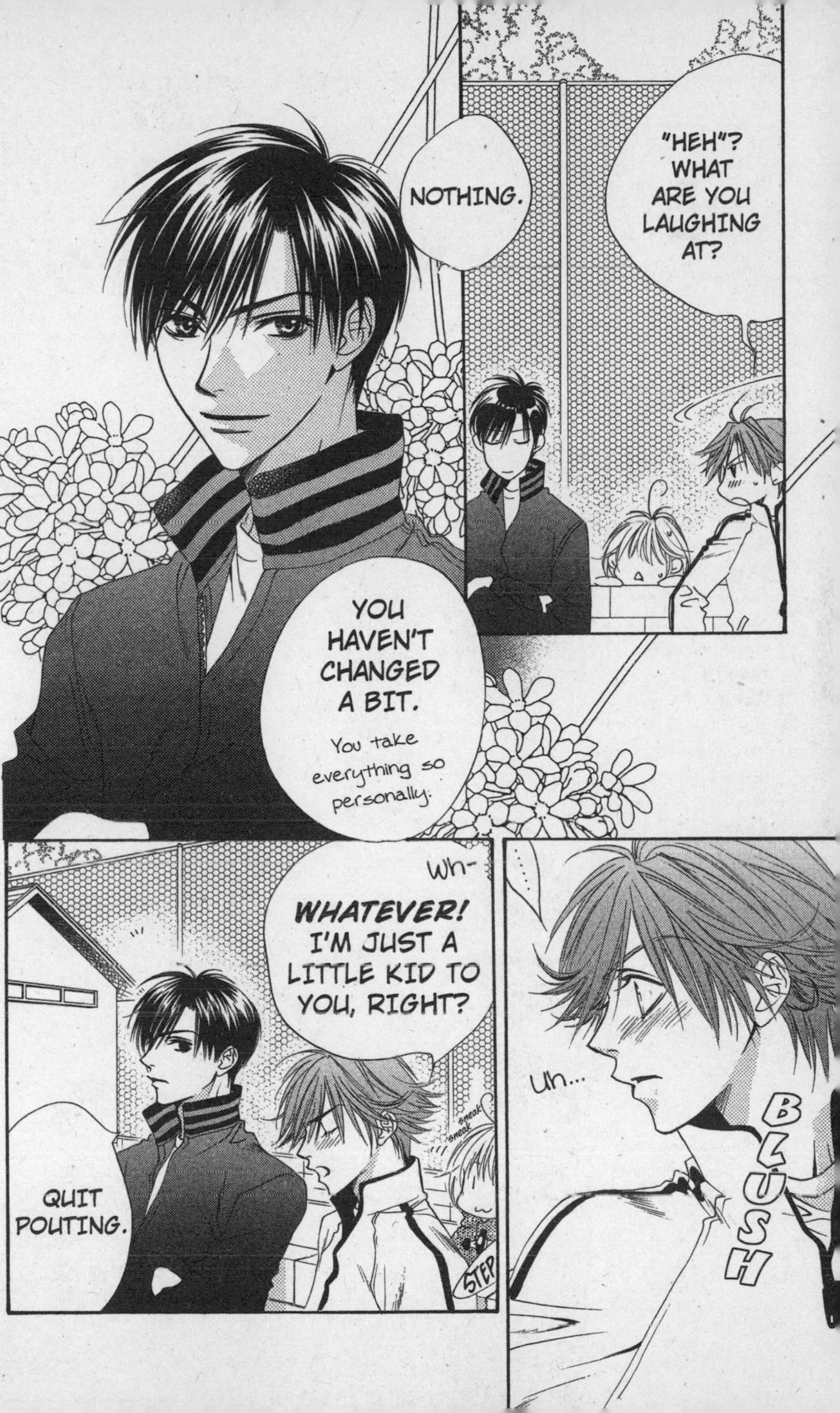
"HEH"? WHAT ARE YOU LAUGHING AT?
NOTHING.
YOU HAVEN'T CHANGED A BIT.
You take everything so personally.
Uh...
BLUSH
Wh-
WHATEVER! I'M JUST A LITTLE KID TO YOU, RIGHT?
sneak sneak
STEP
QUIT POUTING.

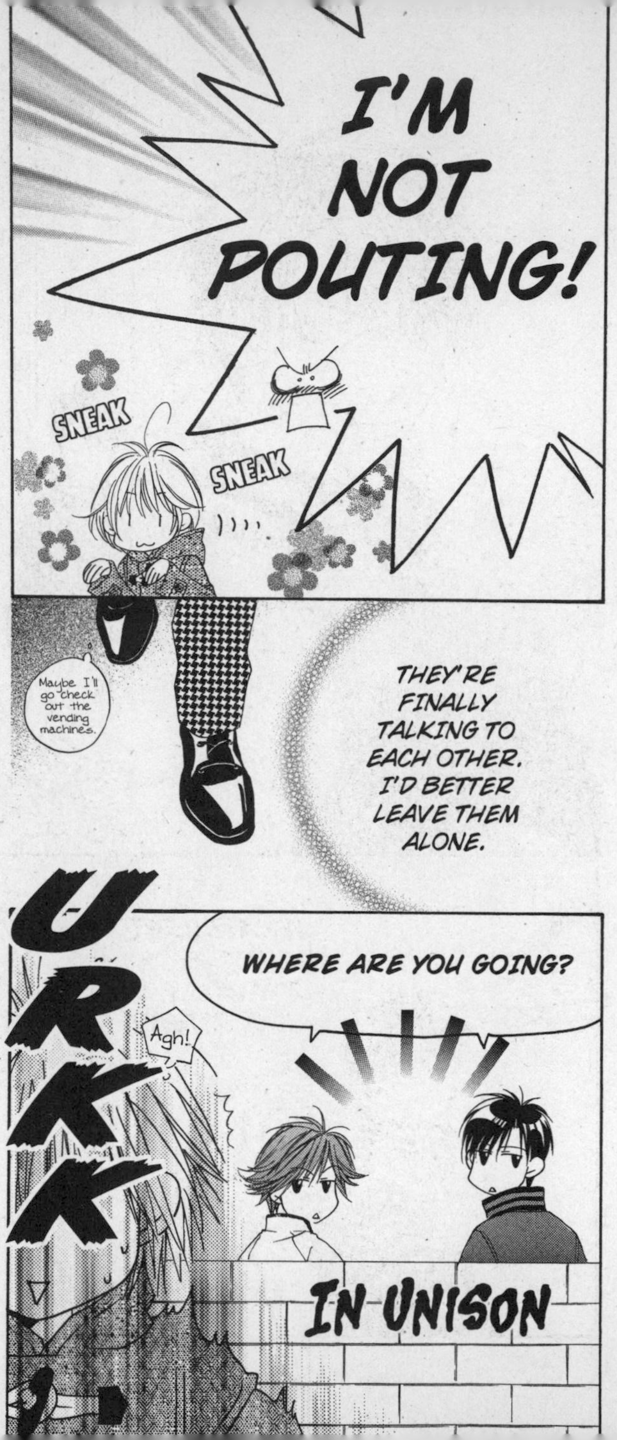
I'M NOT POUTING!
SNEAK
SNEAK
THEY'RE FINALLY TALKING TO EACH OTHER. I'D BETTER LEAVE THEM ALONE.
Maybe I'll go check out the vending machines.
WHERE ARE YOU GOING?
IN UNISON
Agh!
URKK

Itsuki Kujo

Birthday: January 31st
Grade: Third Year Japanese H.S. (equivalent of 12th grade in America)
Blood Type: AB
Sign: Aquarius
Height: 180cm
Favorite Foods: Vinegary salads, anything spicy
Favorite Celebrities: None
Favorite Season: Winter
Favorite Subject: Classical Literature
Least Favorite Subject: None
Least Favorite Foods: None
Flower: Iris

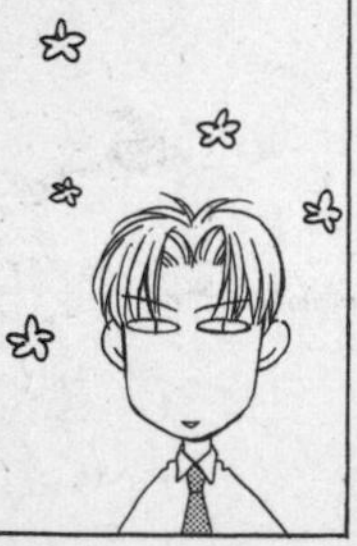

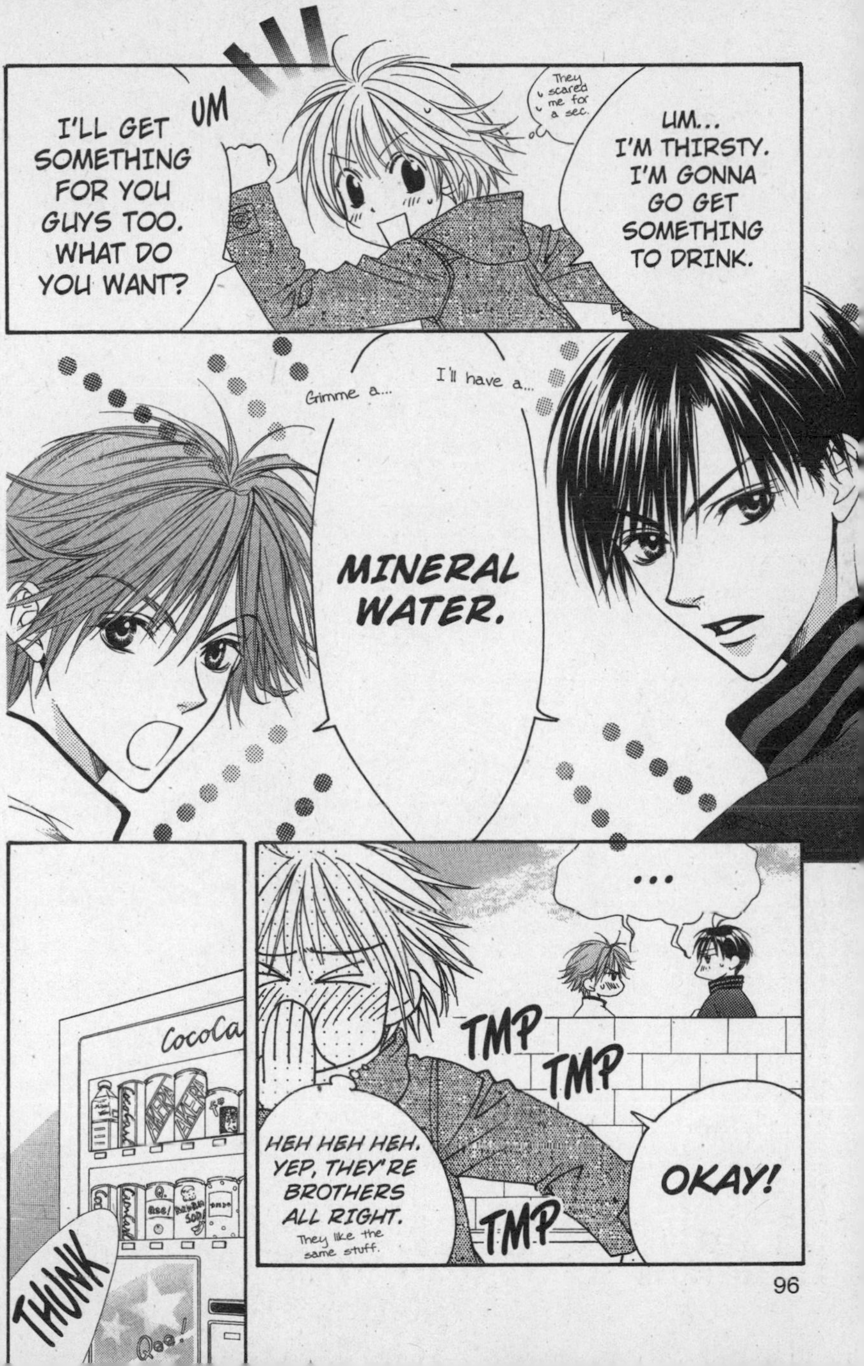
UM... I'M THIRSTY. I'M GONNA GO GET SOMETHING TO DRINK.
They scared me for a sec.
UM
I'LL GET SOMETHING FOR YOU GUYS TOO. WHAT DO YOU WANT?
I'll have a...
Gimme a...
MINERAL WATER.
...
OKAY!
TMP
TMP
TMP
HEH HEH HEH. YEP, THEY'RE BROTHERS ALL RIGHT.
They like the same stuff.
THINK

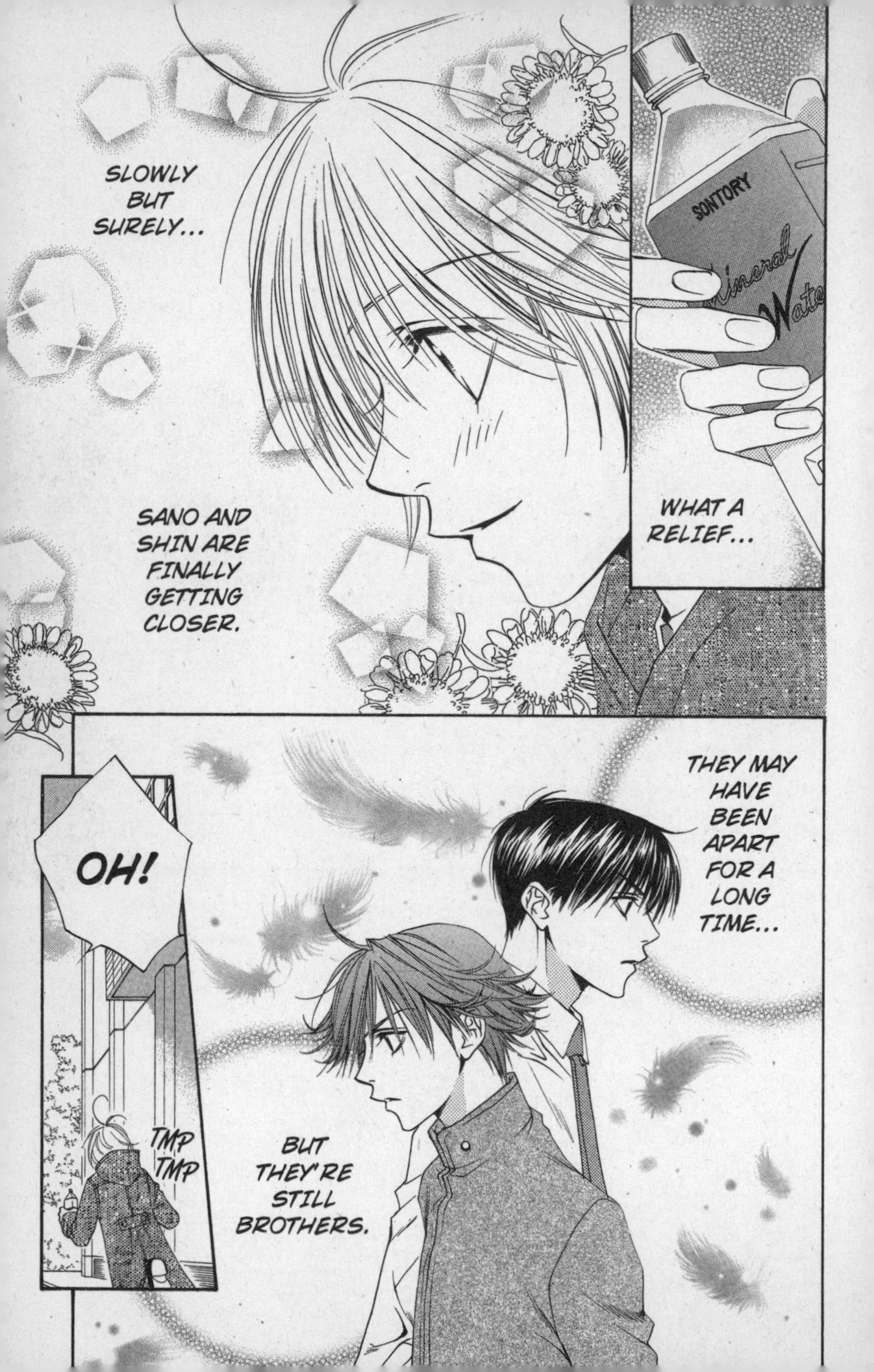
SONTORY
Mineral Water
WHAT A RELIEF...
SLOWLY BUT SURELY...
SANO AND SHIN ARE FINALLY GETTING CLOSER.
THEY MAY HAVE BEEN APART FOR A LONG TIME...
BUT THEY'RE STILL BROTHERS.
OH!
TMP TMP

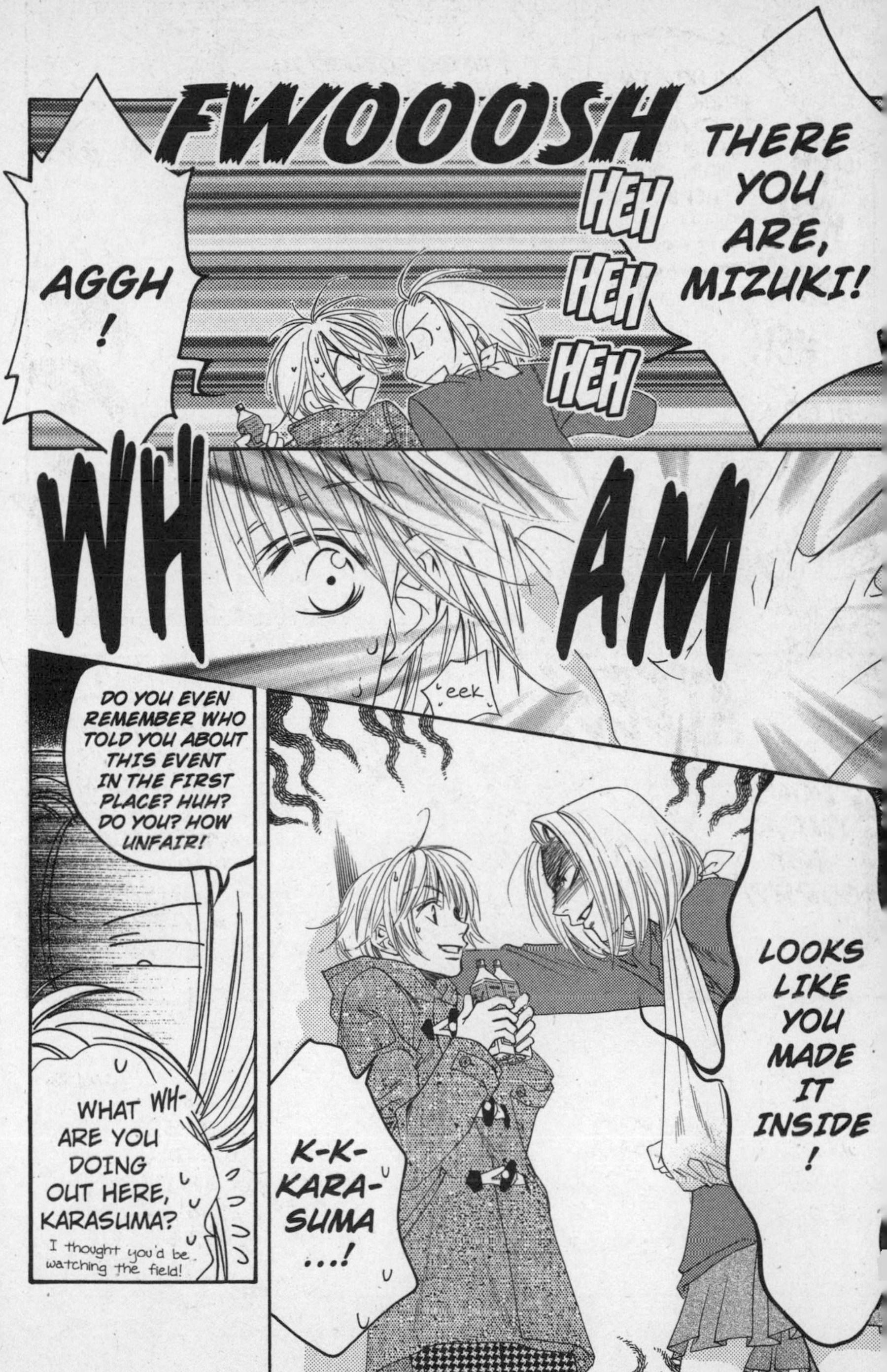
THERE YOU ARE, MIZUKI!
HEH HEH HEH
FWOOOSH
AGGH!
WHAM
eek
LOOKS LIKE YOU MADE IT INSIDE!
K-K-KARA-SUMA...!
DO YOU EVEN REMEMBER WHO TOLD YOU ABOUT THIS EVENT IN THE FIRST PLACE? HUH? DO YOU? HOW UNFAIR!
WH-
WHAT ARE YOU DOING OUT HERE, KARASUMA?
I thought you'd be watching the field!

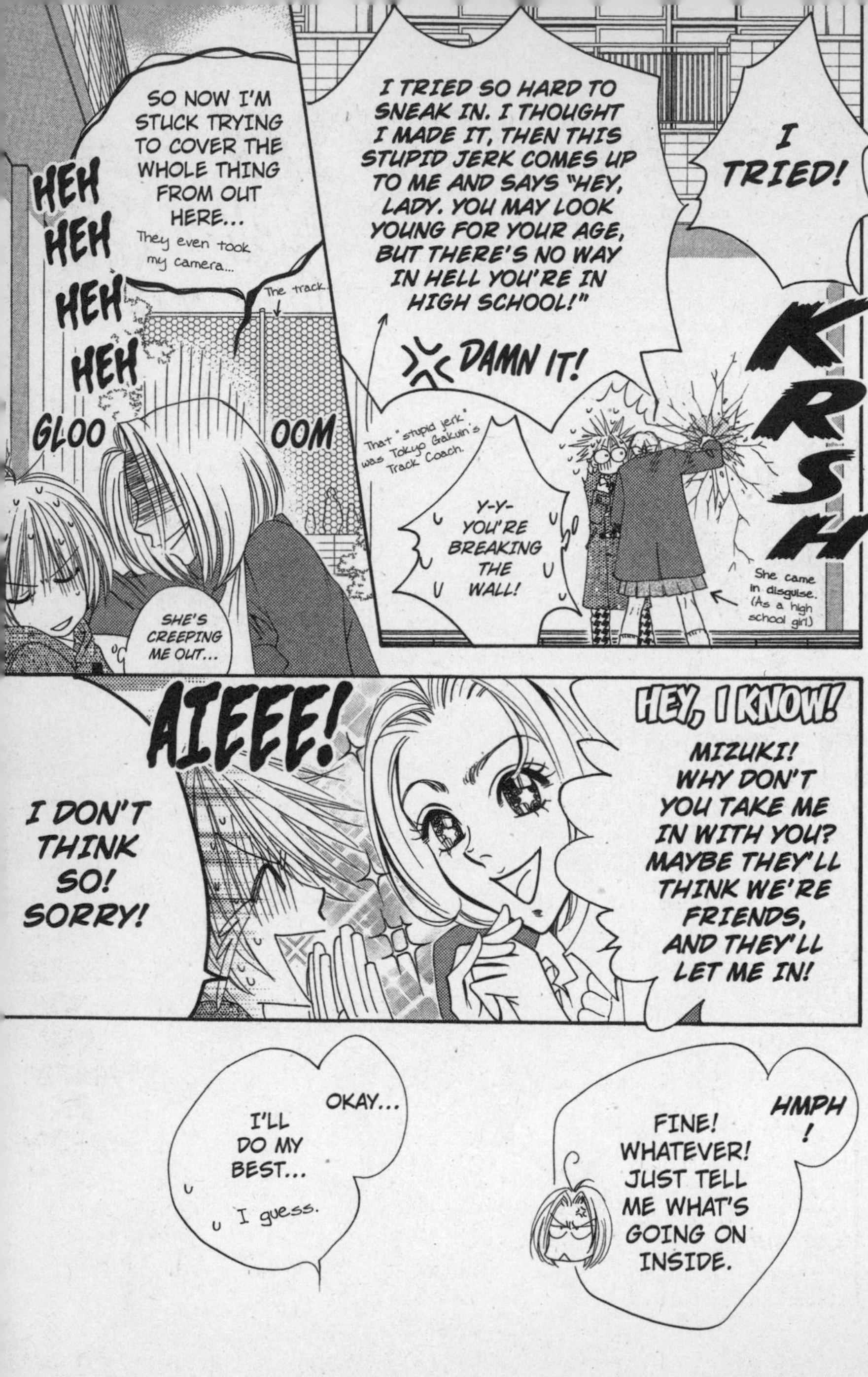
I TRIED SO HARD TO SNEAK IN. I THOUGHT I MADE IT, THEN THIS STUPID JERK COMES UP TO ME AND SAYS "HEY, LADY. YOU MAY LOOK YOUNG FOR YOUR AGE, BUT THERE'S NO WAY IN HELL YOU'RE IN HIGH SCHOOL!"
I TRIED!
KRSH
DAMN IT!
That "stupid jerk" was Tokyo Gakuin's Track Coach.
Y-Y-YOU'RE BREAKING THE WALL!
She came in disguise. (As a high school girl)
SO NOW I'M STUCK TRYING TO COVER THE WHOLE THING FROM OUT HERE...
They even took my camera...
The track.
HEH HEH HEH HEH
GLOO OOM
SHE'S CREEPING ME OUT...
HEY, I KNOW!
MIZUKI! WHY DON'T YOU TAKE ME IN WITH YOU? MAYBE THEY'LL THINK WE'RE FRIENDS, AND THEY'LL LET ME IN!
AIEEE!
I DON'T THINK SO! SORRY!
HMPH!
FINE! WHATEVER! JUST TELL ME WHAT'S GOING ON INSIDE.
OKAY...
I'LL DO MY BEST...
I guess.

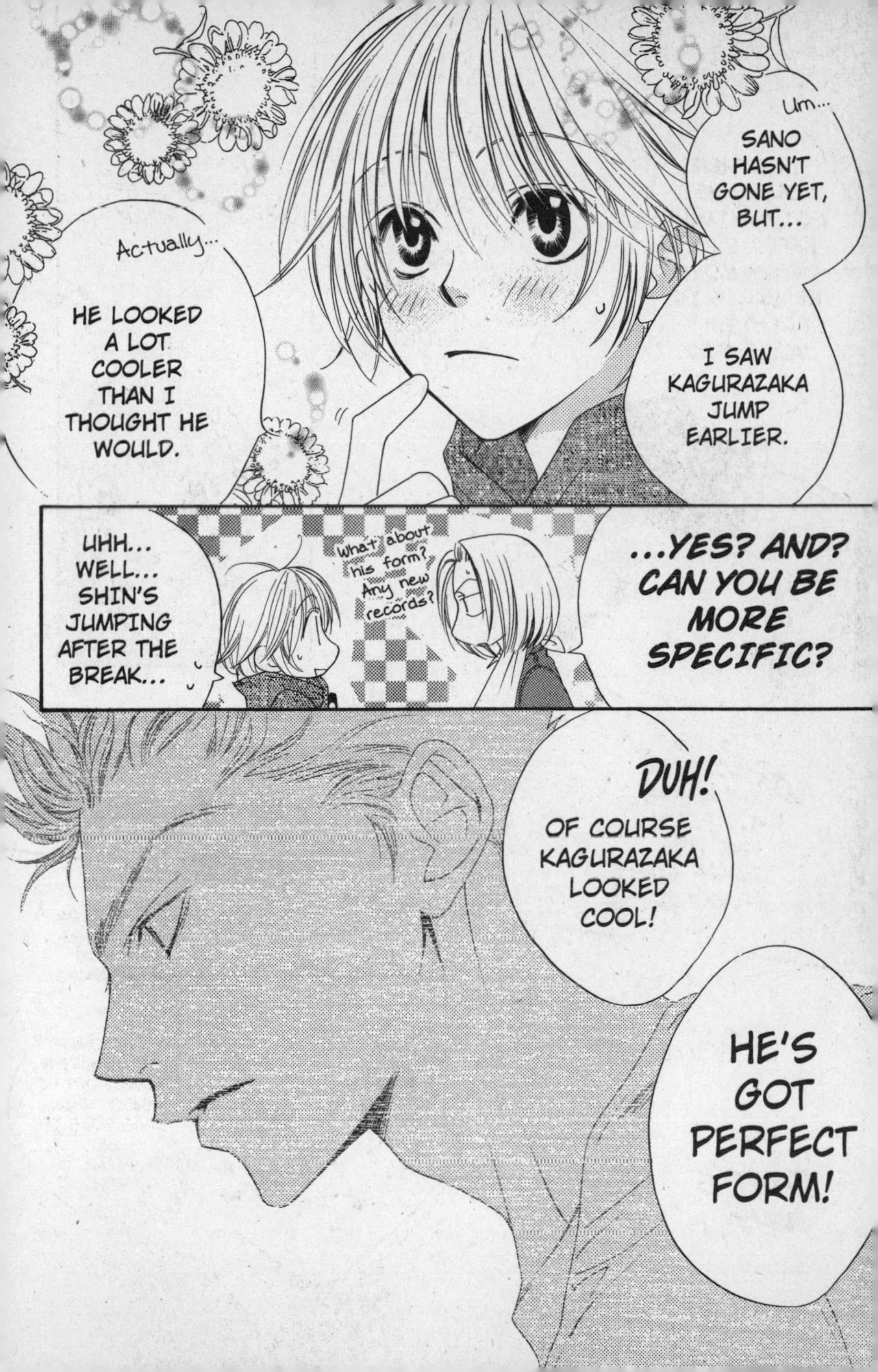
Um...
SANO HASN'T GONE YET, BUT...
I SAW KAGURAZAKA JUMP EARLIER.
Actually...
HE LOOKED A LOT COOLER THAN I THOUGHT HE WOULD.
...YES? AND? CAN YOU BE MORE SPECIFIC?
What about his form? Any new records?
UHH... WELL... SHIN'S JUMPING AFTER THE BREAK...
DUH!
OF COURSE KAGURAZAKA LOOKED COOL!
HE'S GOT PERFECT FORM!

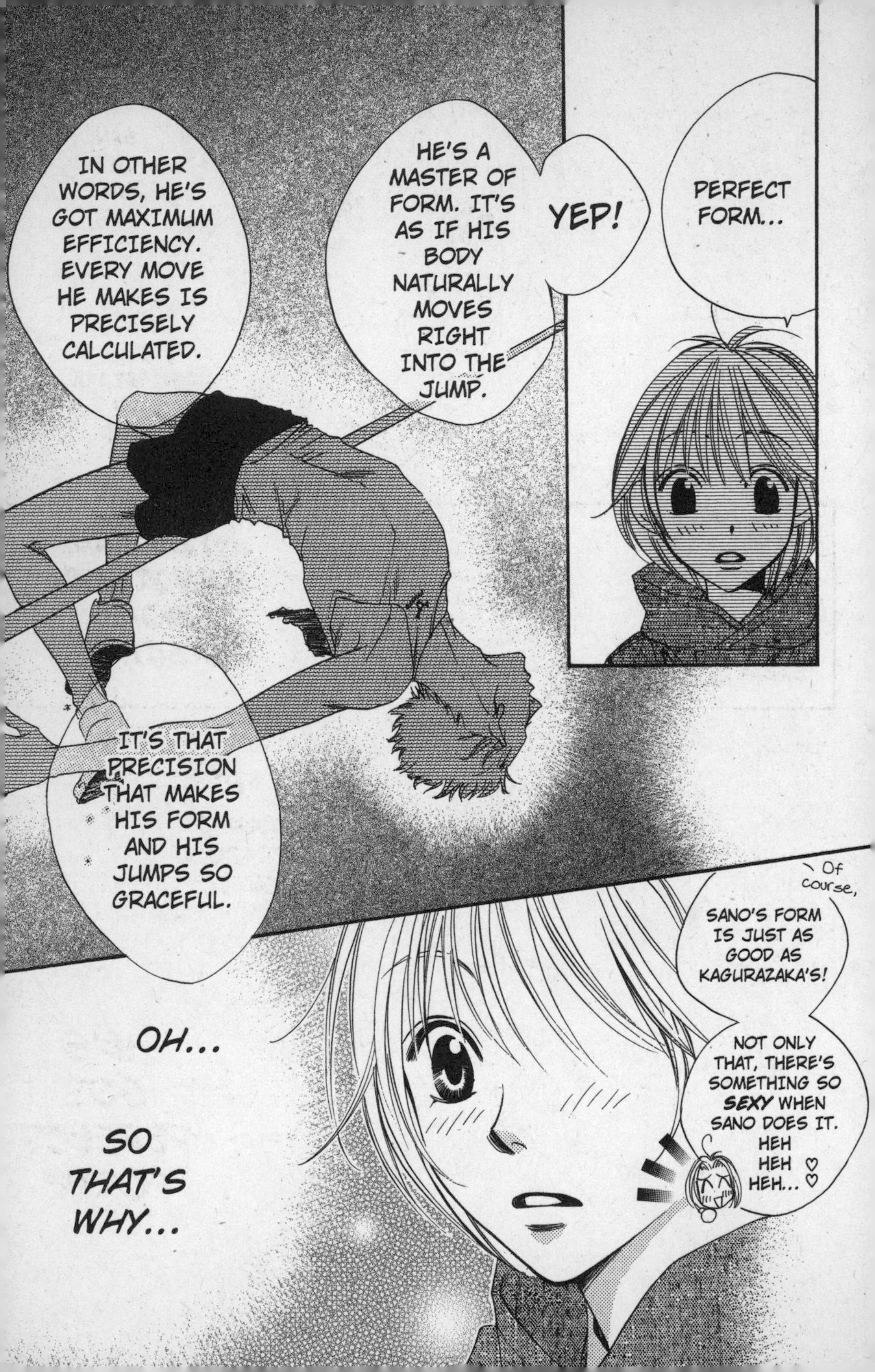
PERFECT FORM...
YEP!
HE'S A MASTER OF FORM. IT'S AS IF HIS BODY NATURALLY MOVES RIGHT INTO THE JUMP.
IN OTHER WORDS, HE'S GOT MAXIMUM EFFICIENCY. EVERY MOVE HE MAKES IS PRECISELY CALCULATED.
IT'S THAT PRECISION THAT MAKES HIS FORM AND HIS JUMPS SO GRACEFUL.
Of course,
SANO'S FORM IS JUST AS GOOD AS KAGURAZAKA'S!
NOT ONLY THAT, THERE'S SOMETHING SO SEXY WHEN SANO DOES IT. HEH HEH ♡ HEH... ♡
OH...
SO THAT'S WHY...

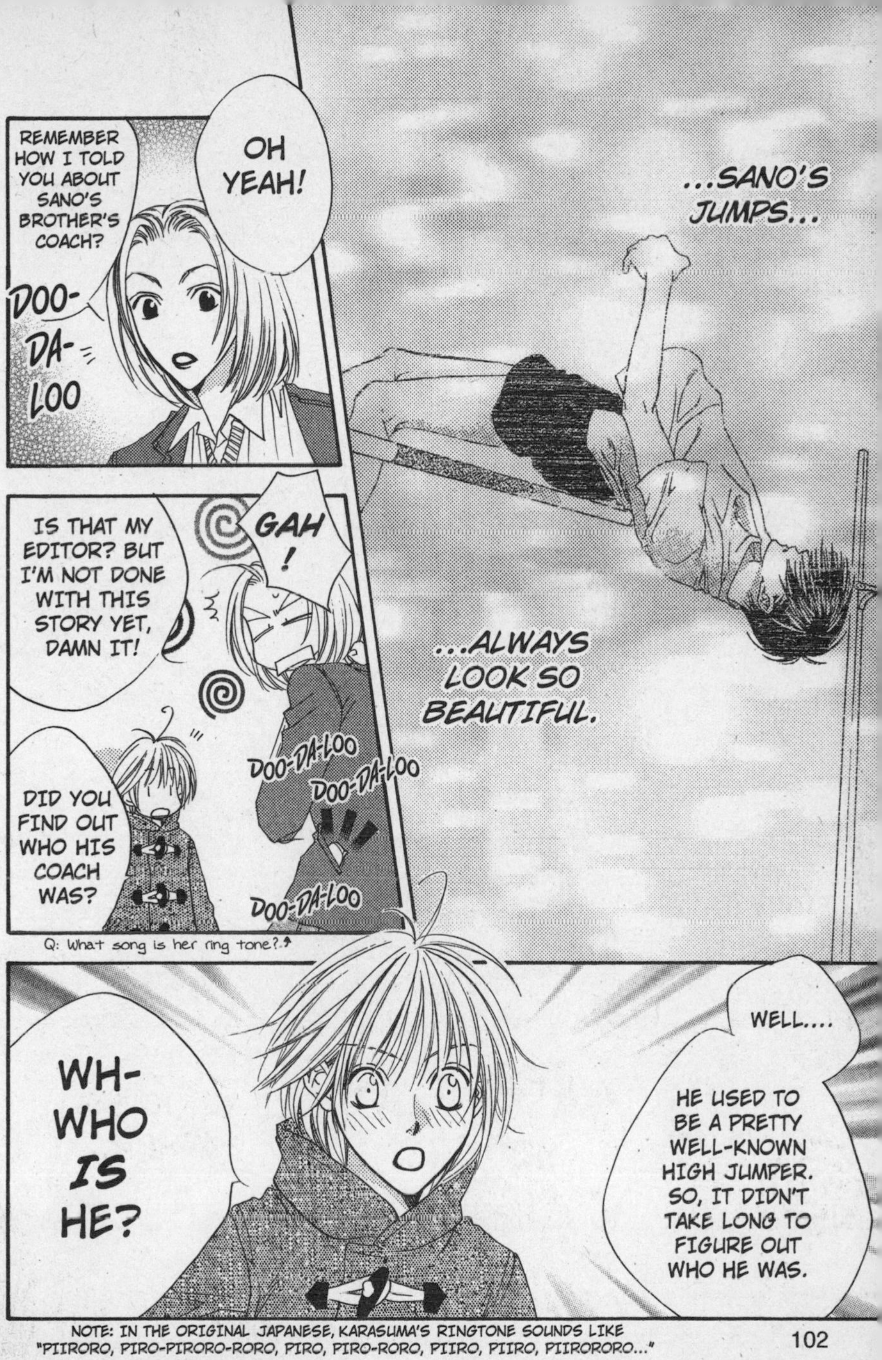
...SANO'S JUMPS...
...ALWAYS LOOK SO BEAUTIFUL.
OH YEAH!
REMEMBER HOW I TOLD YOU ABOUT SANO'S BROTHER'S COACH?
DOO-DA-LOO
GAH!
IS THAT MY EDITOR? BUT I'M NOT DONE WITH THIS STORY YET, DAMN IT!
DOO-DA-LOO
DOO-DA-LOO
DOO-DA-LOO
DID YOU FIND OUT WHO HIS COACH WAS?
Q: What song is her ring tone?
WELL....
HE USED TO BE A PRETTY WELL-KNOWN HIGH JUMPER. SO, IT DIDN'T TAKE LONG TO FIGURE OUT WHO HE WAS.
WH-WHO IS HE?

NOTE: IN THE ORIGINAL JAPANESE, KARASUMA'S RINGTONE SOUNDS LIKE "PIIRORO, PIRO-PIIRORO-RORO, PIRO, PIRO-RORO, PIIRO, PIIRO, PIIROROR0..."

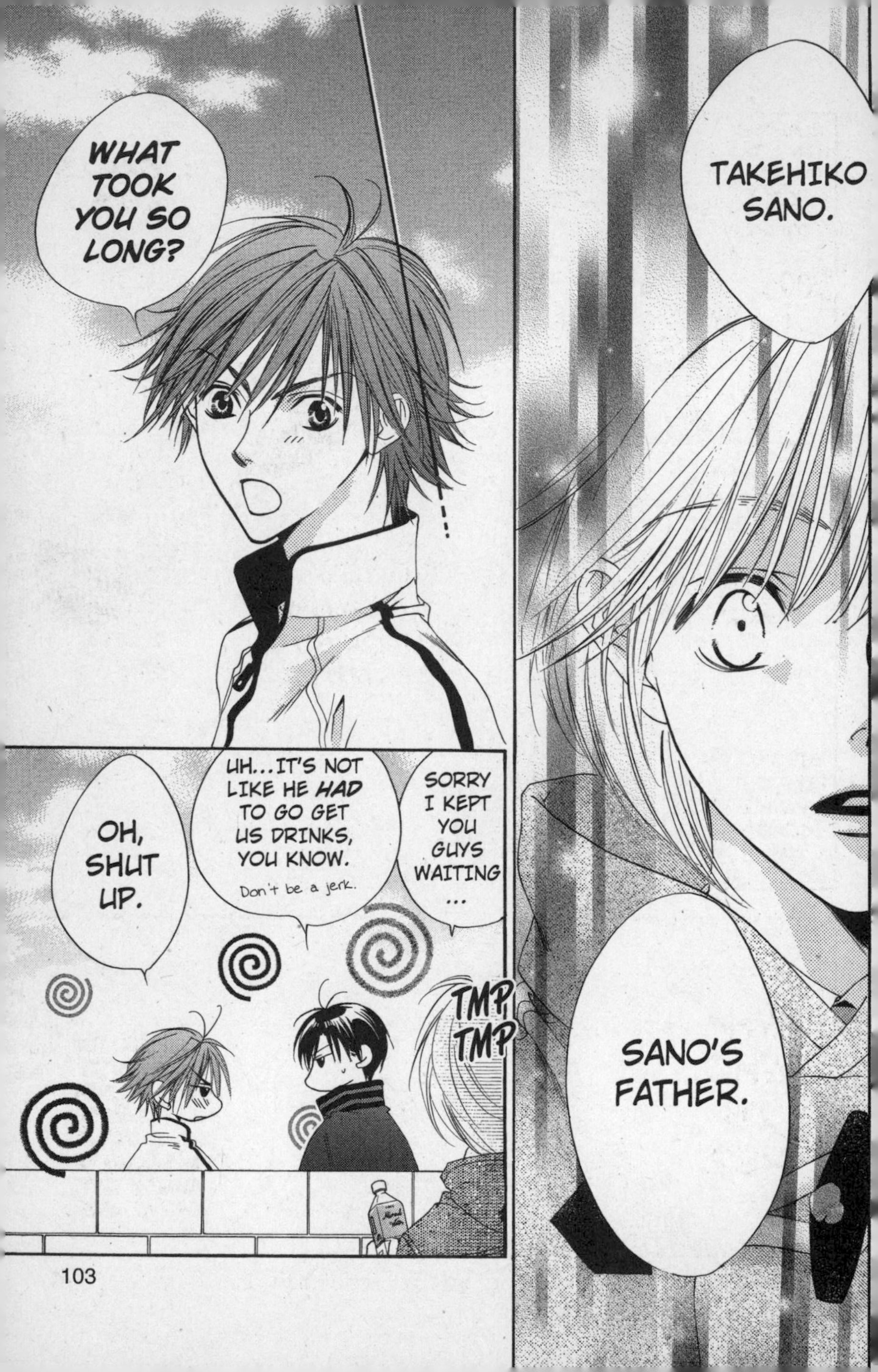
TAKEHIKO SANO.
SANO'S FATHER.
WHAT TOOK YOU SO LONG?
SORRY I KEPT YOU GUYS WAITING...
TMP TMP
UH...IT'S NOT LIKE HE *HAD* TO GO GET US DRINKS, YOU KNOW.
Don't be a jerk.
OH, SHUT UP.

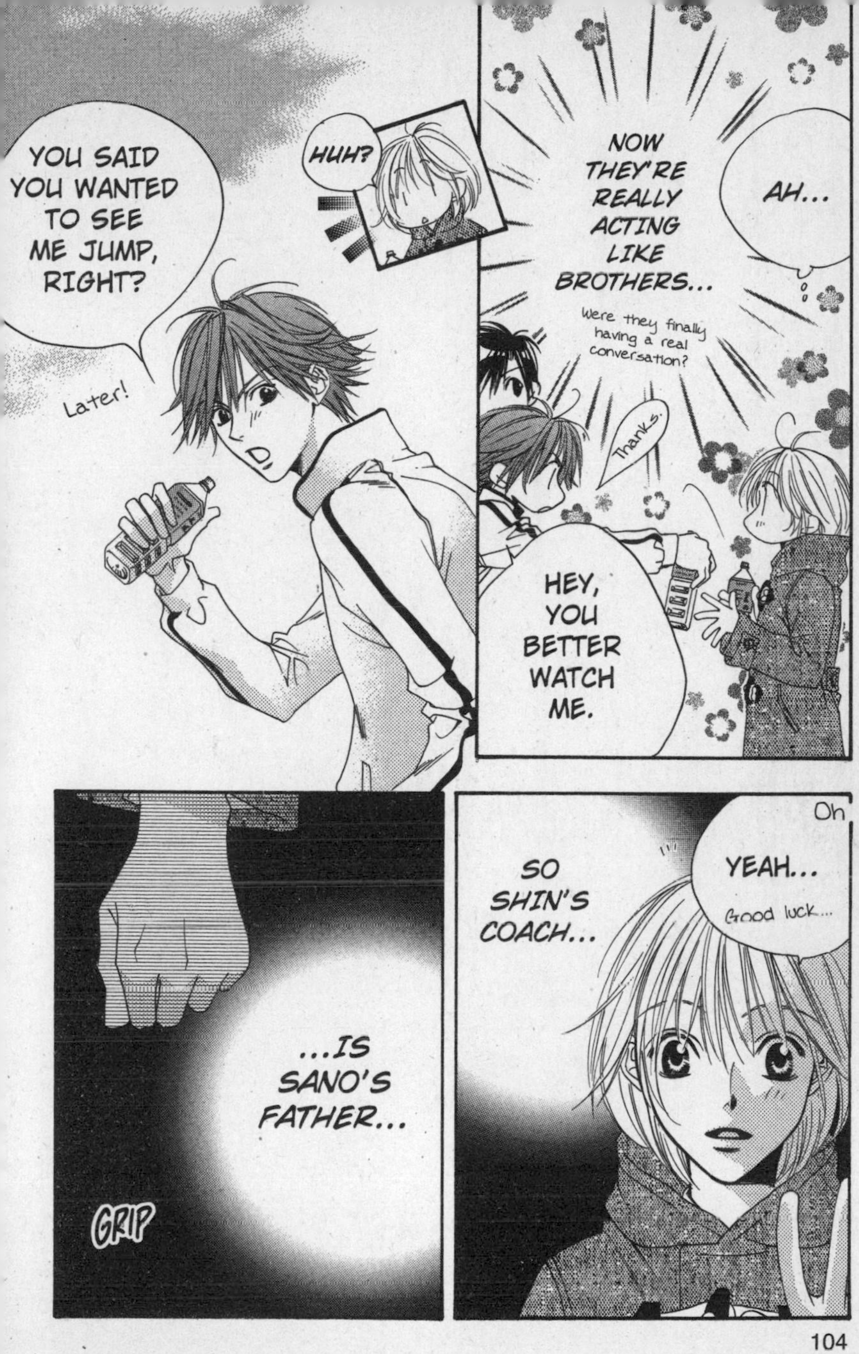
AH...
NOW THEY'RE REALLY ACTING LIKE BROTHERS...
Were they finally having a real conversation?
Thanks.
HEY, YOU BETTER WATCH ME.
HUH?
YOU SAID YOU WANTED TO SEE ME JUMP, RIGHT?
Later!
Oh
YEAH...
Good luck...
SO SHIN'S COACH...
...IS SANO'S FATHER...
GRIP

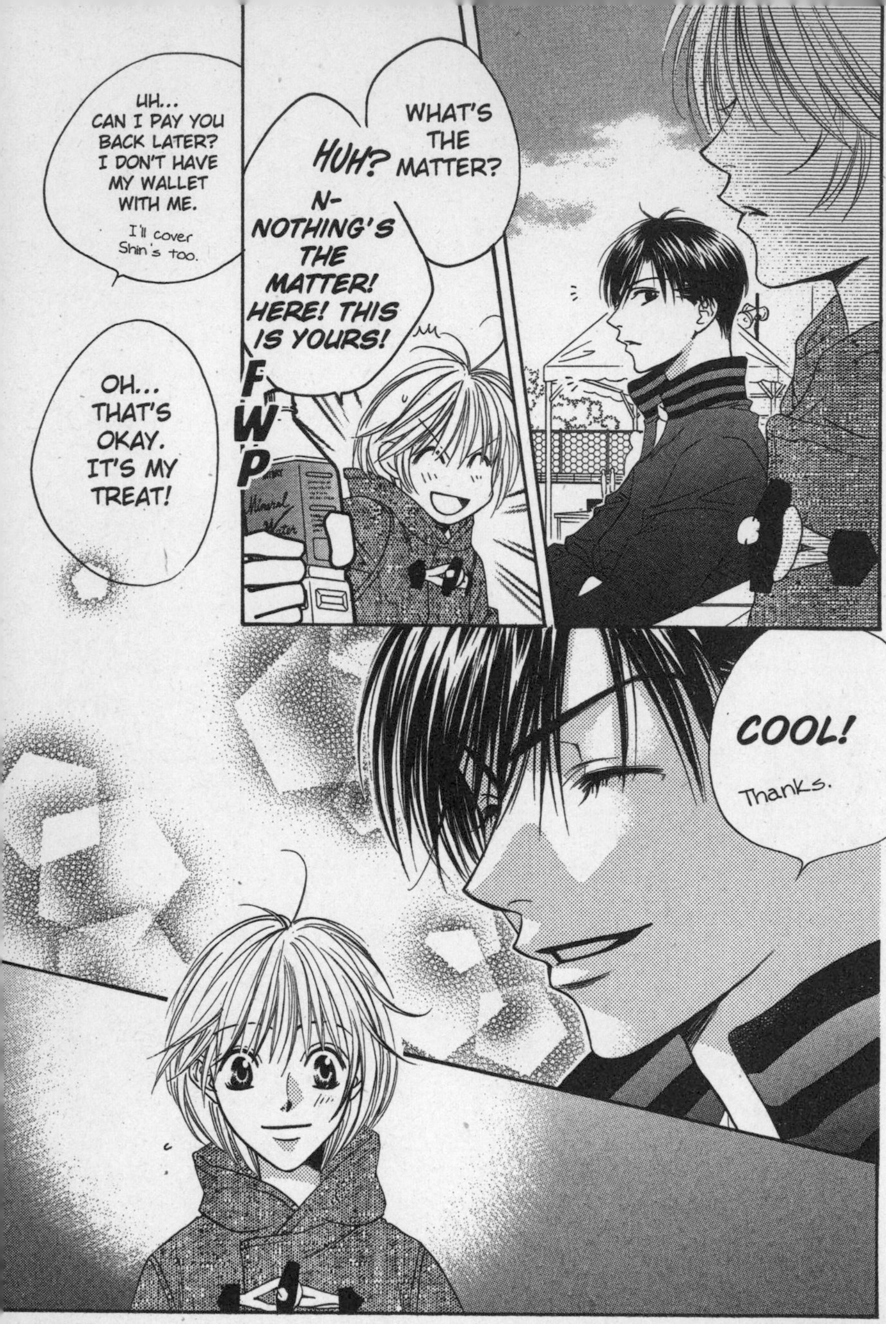
WHAT'S THE MATTER?
HUH?
N- NOTHING'S THE MATTER! HERE! THIS IS YOURS!
FWP
UH... CAN I PAY YOU BACK LATER? I DON'T HAVE MY WALLET WITH ME.
I'll cover Shin's too.
OH... THAT'S OKAY. IT'S MY TREAT!
COOL!
Thanks.

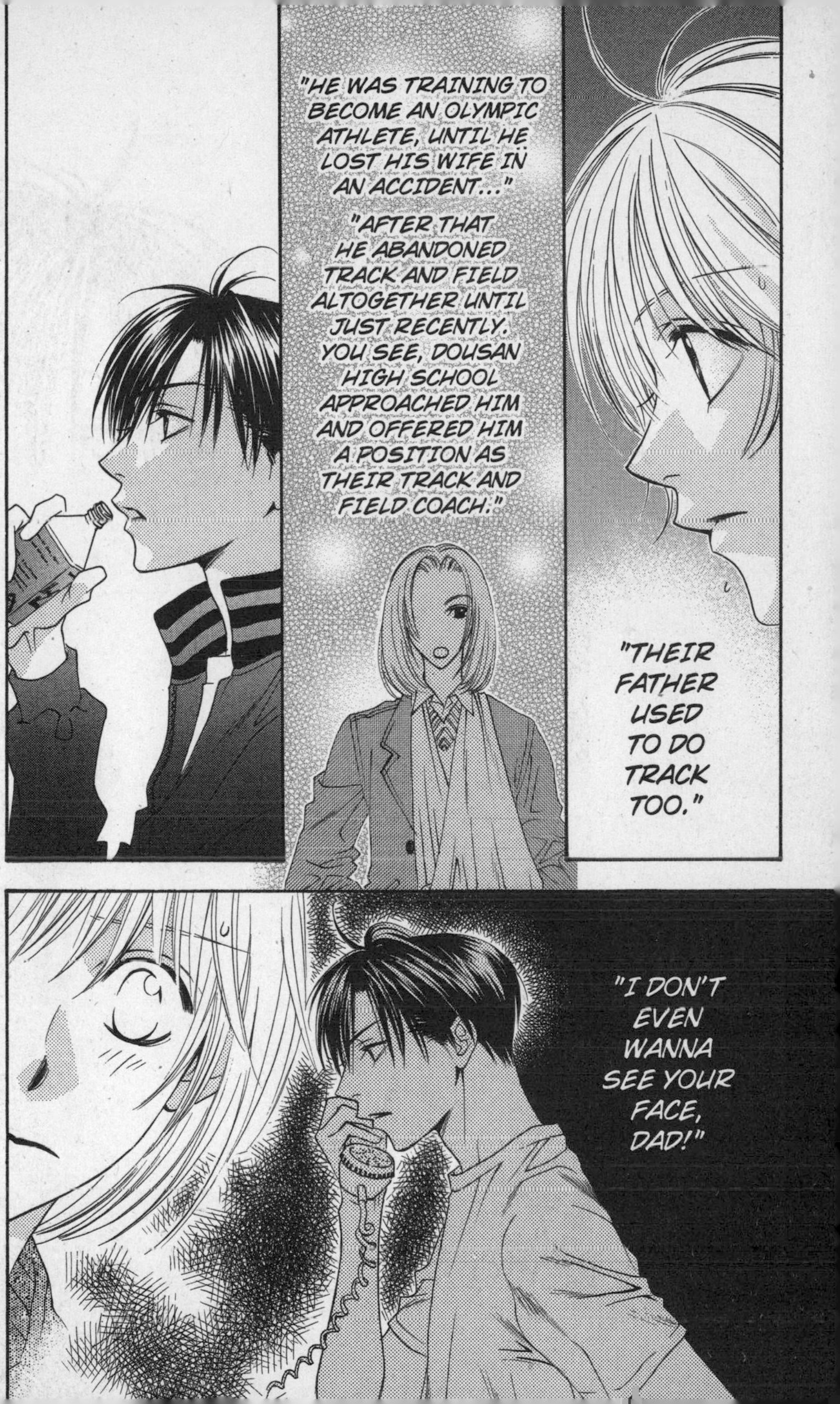
"THEIR FATHER USED TO DO TRACK TOO."
"HE WAS TRAINING TO BECOME AN OLYMPIC ATHLETE, UNTIL HE LOST HIS WIFE IN AN ACCIDENT..."
"AFTER THAT HE ABANDONED TRACK AND FIELD ALTOGETHER UNTIL JUST RECENTLY. YOU SEE, DOUSAN HIGH SCHOOL APPROACHED HIM AND OFFERED HIM A POSITION AS THEIR TRACK AND FIELD COACH."
"I DON'T EVEN WANNA SEE YOUR FACE, DAD!"

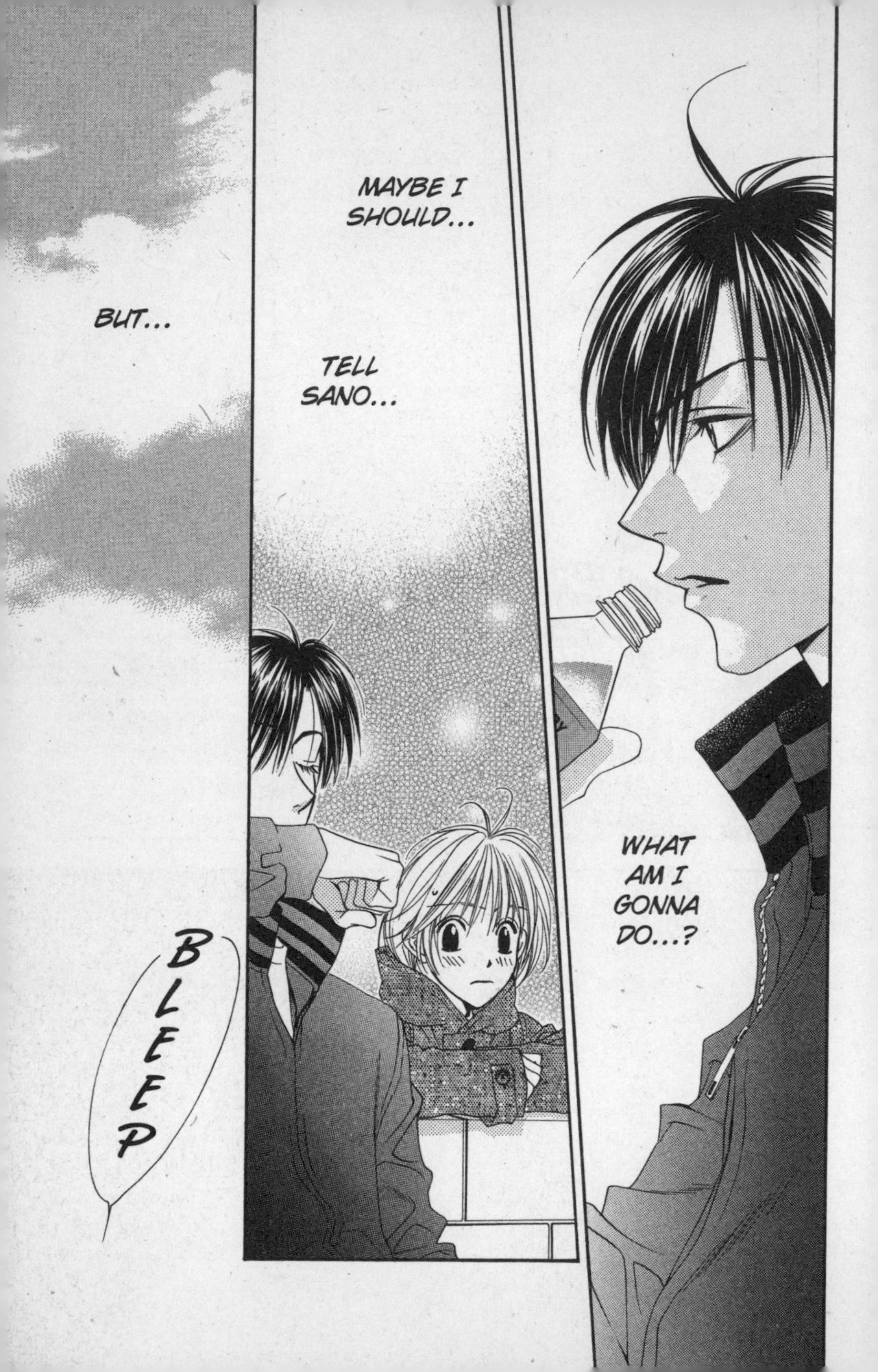
WHAT AM I GONNA DO...?
MAYBE I SHOULD...
TELL SANO...
BUT...
BLEEP

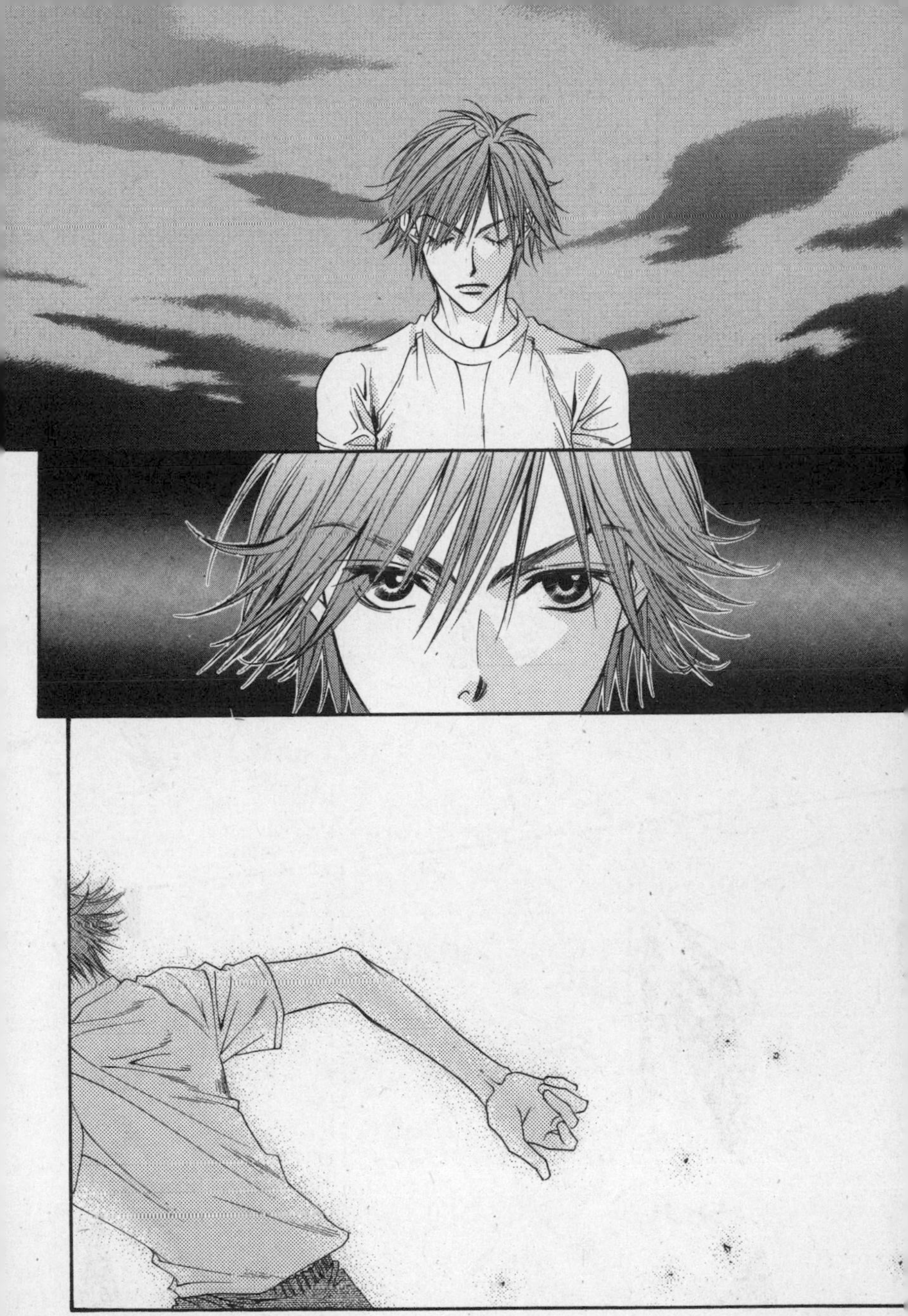

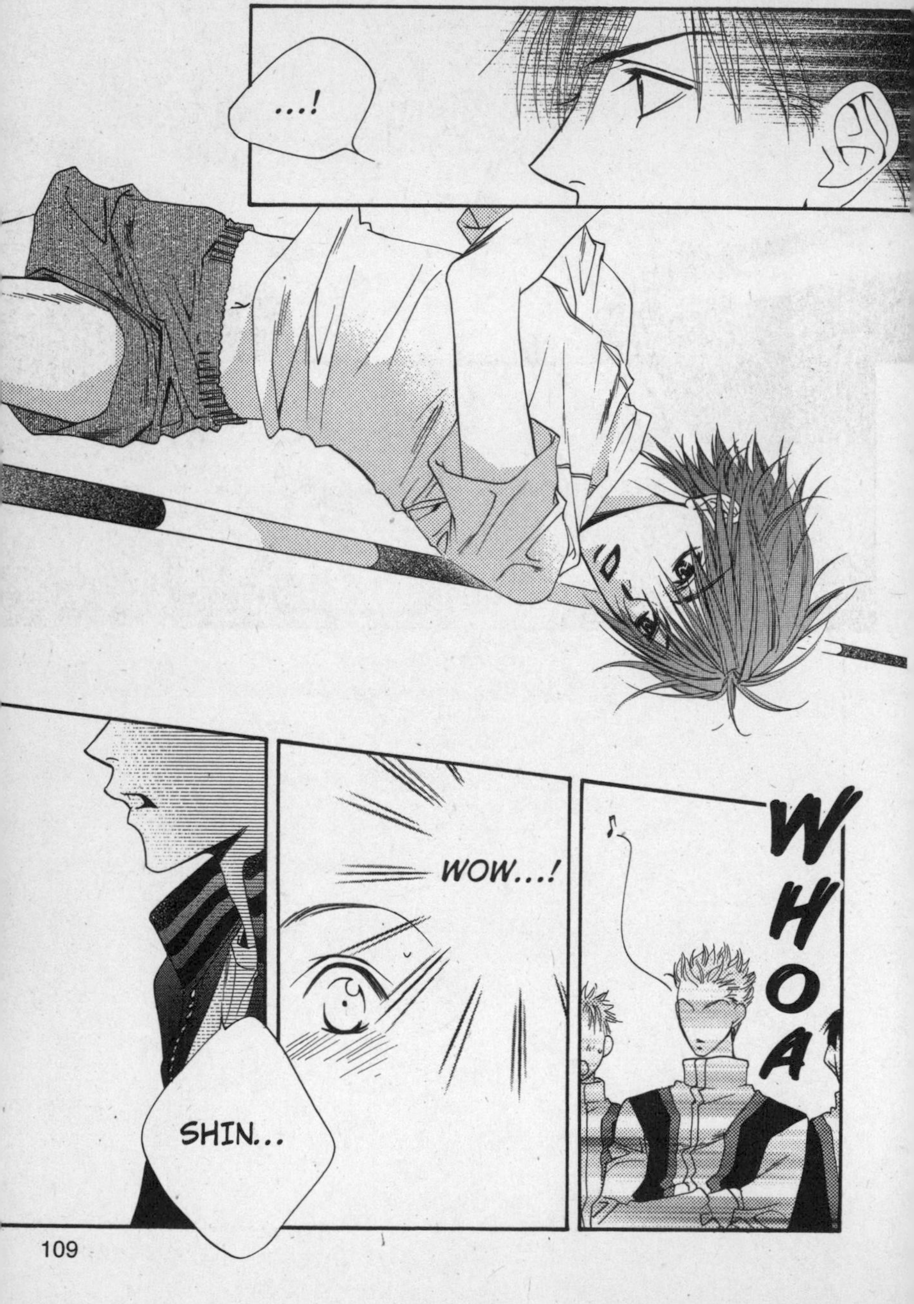
...!
WHOA
WOW...!
SHIN...

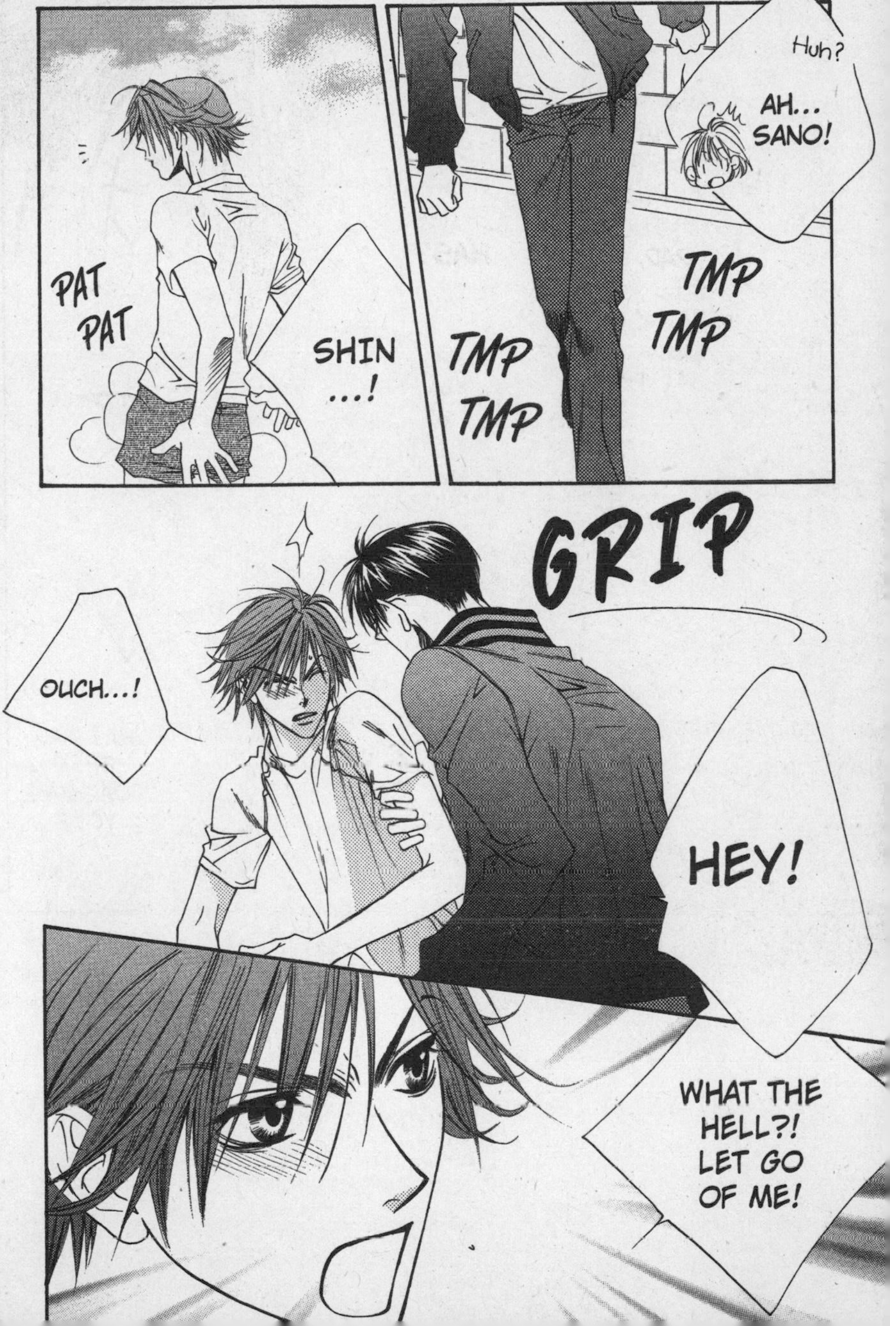
Huh?
AH... SANO!
TMP TMP
TMP TMP
PAT PAT
SHIN ...!
GRIP
OUCH...!
HEY!
WHAT THE HELL?! LET GO OF ME!

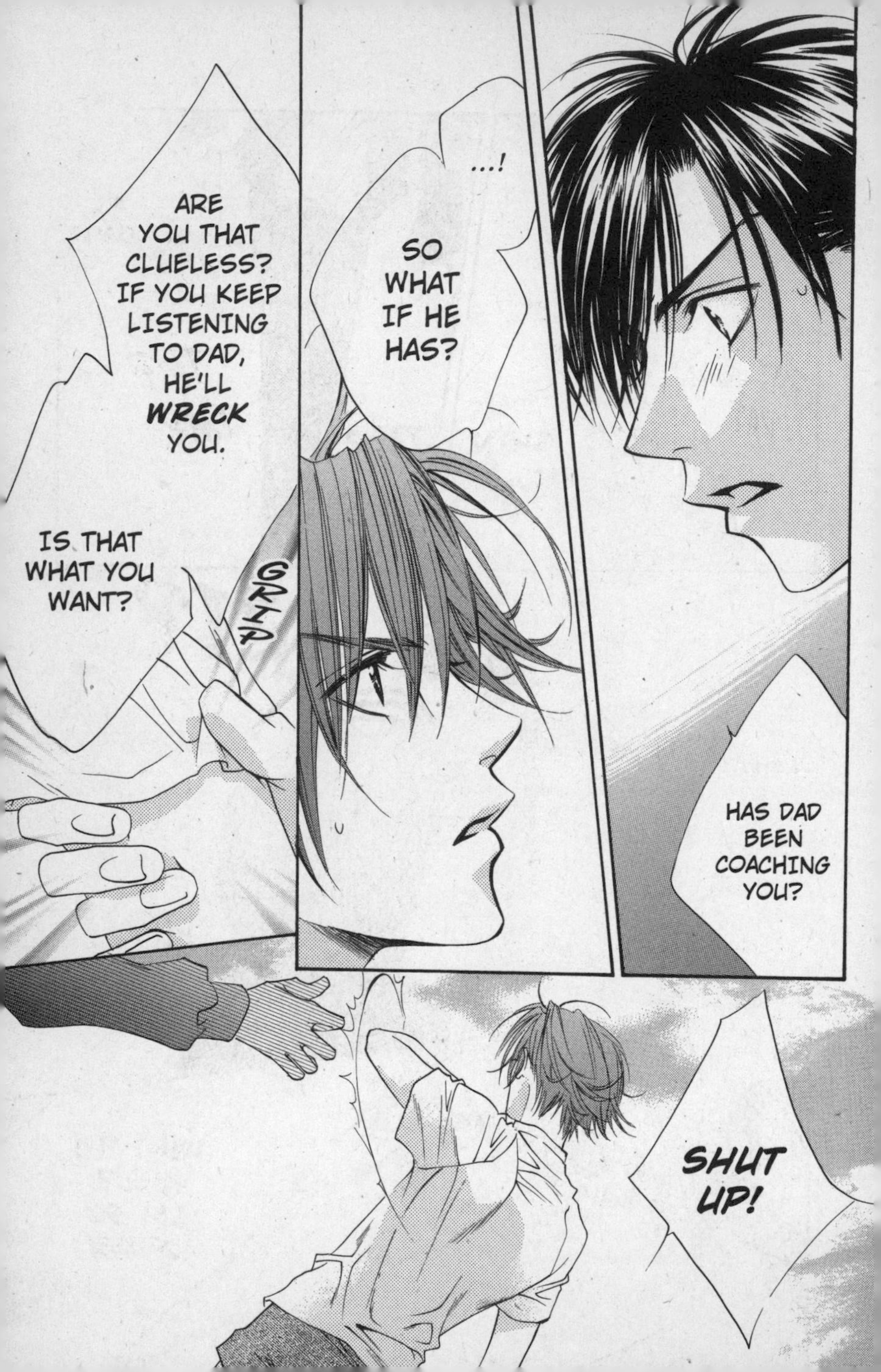
HAS DAD BEEN COACHING YOU?
...!
SO WHAT IF HE HAS?
ARE YOU THAT CLUELESS? IF YOU KEEP LISTENING TO DAD, HE'LL WRECK YOU.
GRIP
IS THAT WHAT YOU WANT?
SHUT UP!

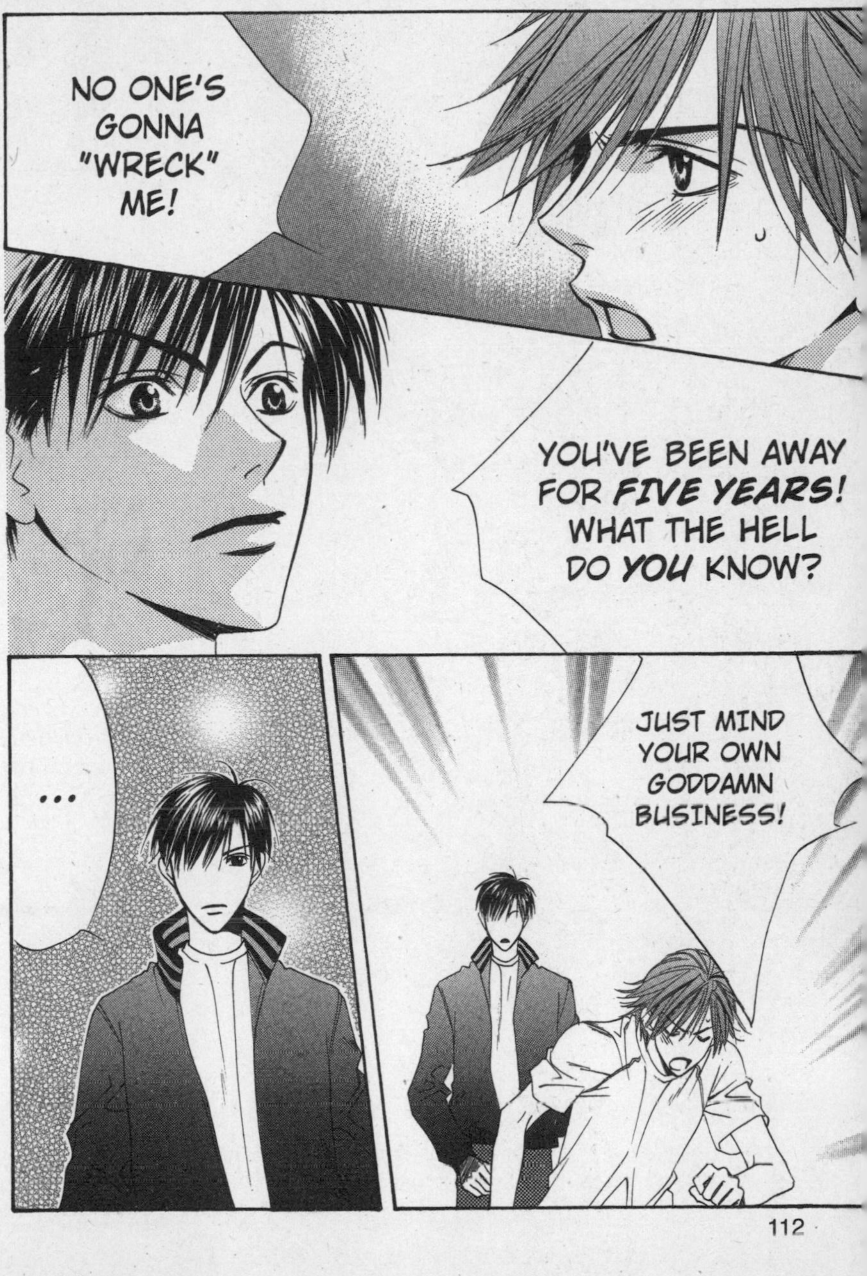
NO ONE'S GONNA "WRECK" ME!
YOU'VE BEEN AWAY FOR FIVE YEARS! WHAT THE HELL DO YOU KNOW?
JUST MIND YOUR OWN GODDAMN BUSINESS!
...

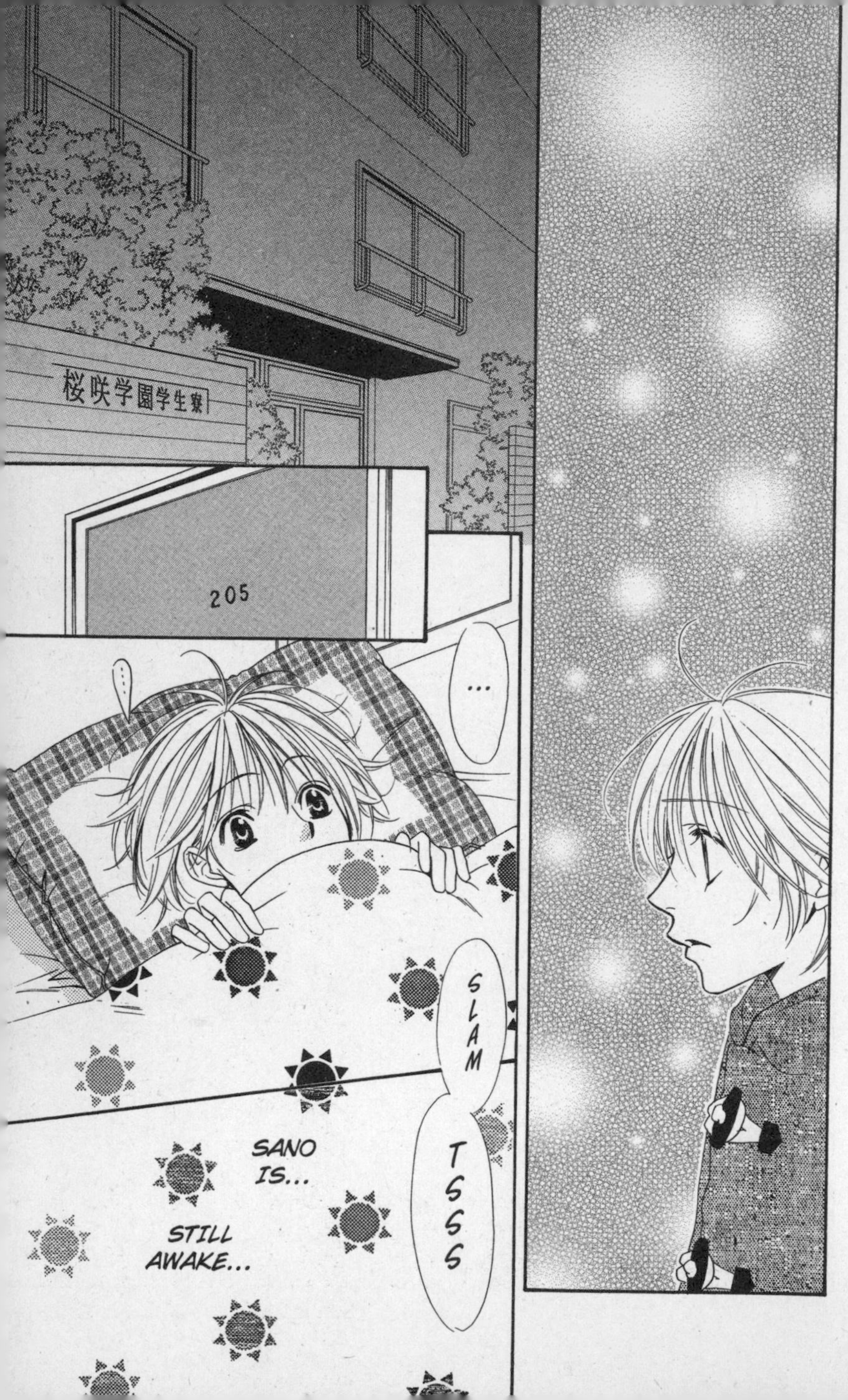
桜咲学園学生寮
205
...
SLAM
TSSS
SANO IS...
STILL AWAKE...

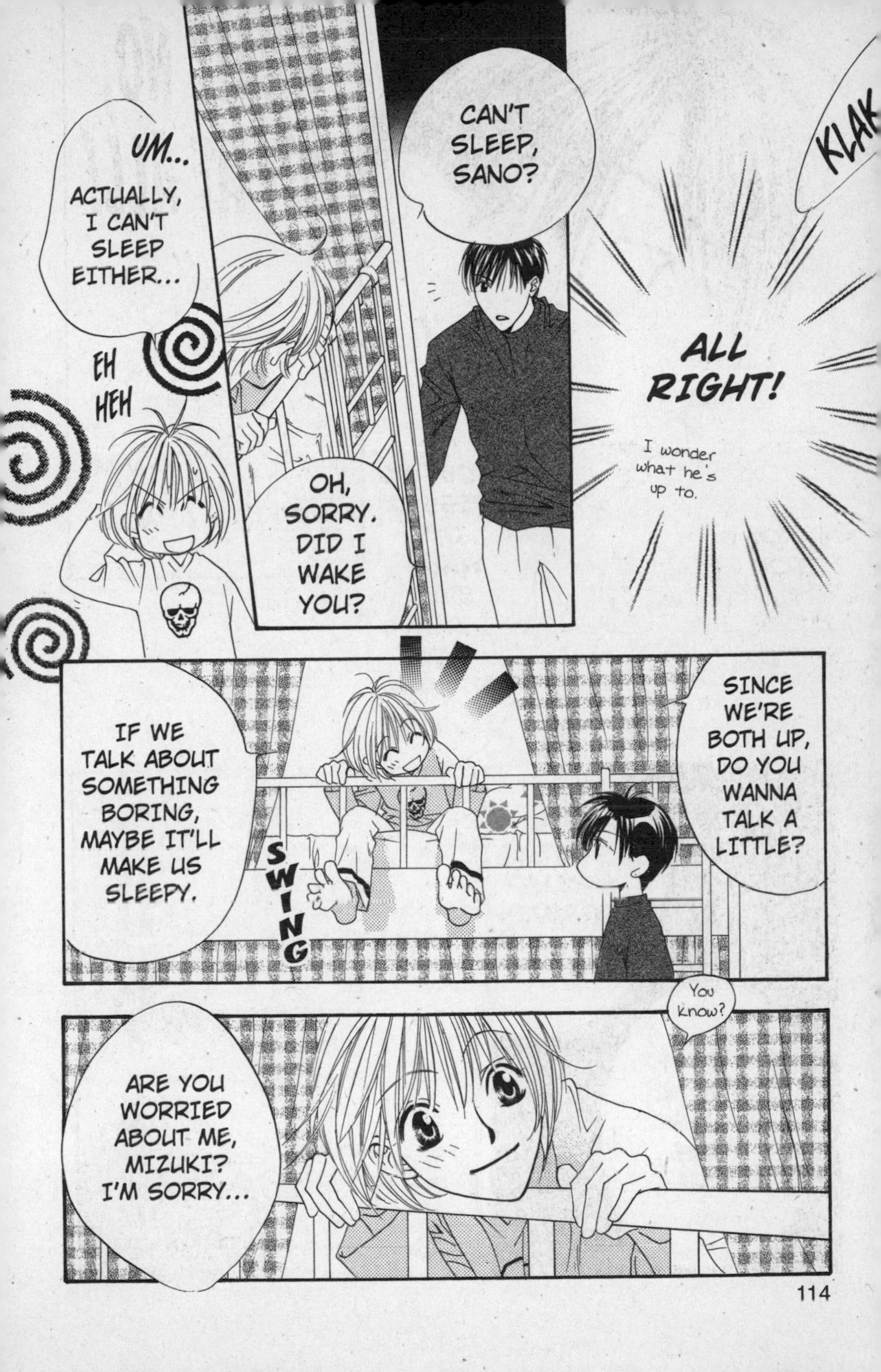
KLAK
CAN'T SLEEP, SANO?
OH, SORRY. DID I WAKE YOU?
UM... ACTUALLY, I CAN'T SLEEP EITHER...
EH HEH
ALL RIGHT!
I wonder what he's up to.
SINCE WE'RE BOTH UP, DO YOU WANNA TALK A LITTLE?
SWING
IF WE TALK ABOUT SOMETHING BORING, MAYBE IT'LL MAKE US SLEEPY.
You know?
ARE YOU WORRIED ABOUT ME, MIZUKI? I'M SORRY...

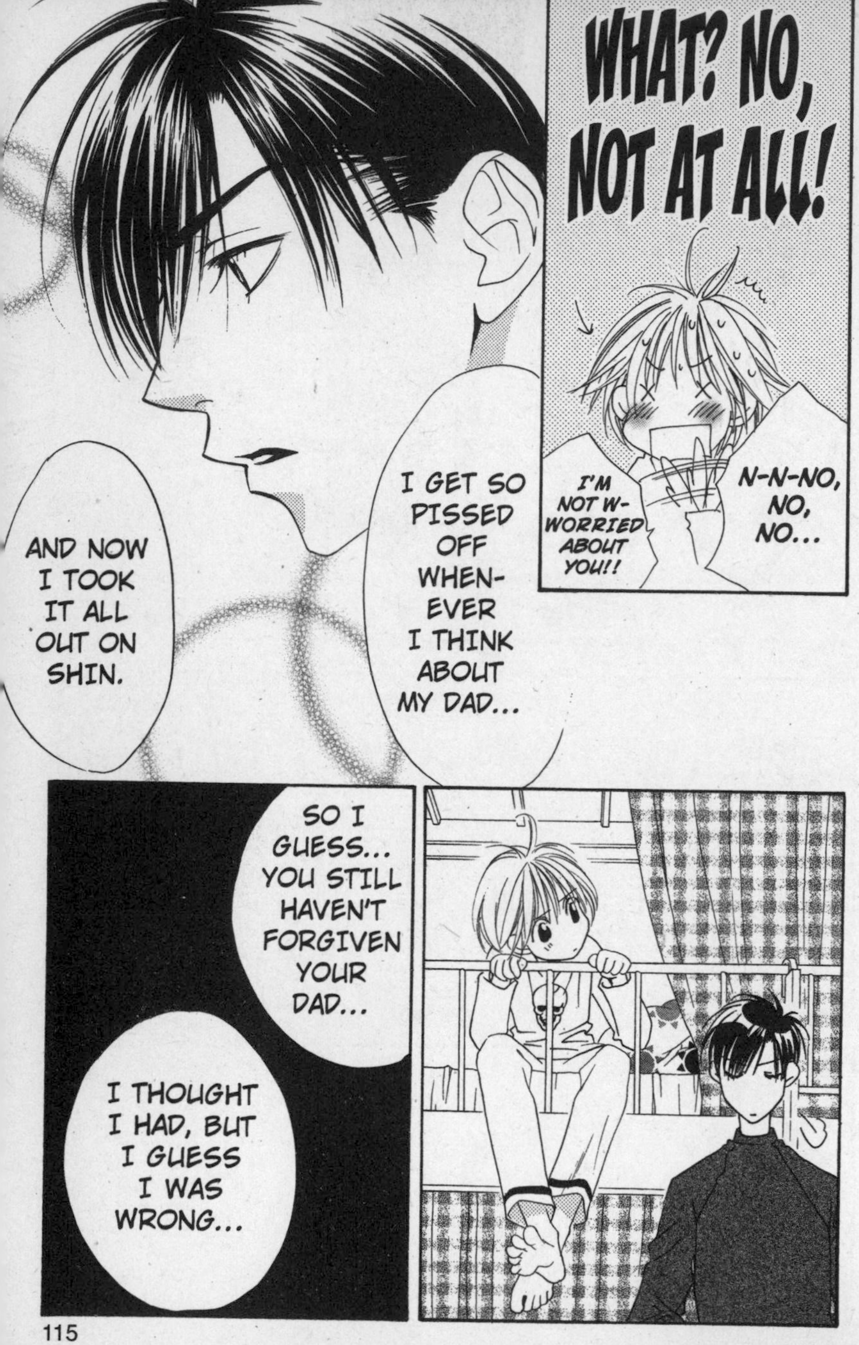
WHAT? NO, NOT AT ALL!
N-N-NO, NO, NO...
I'M NOT W-WORRIED ABOUT YOU!!
I GET SO PISSED OFF WHENEVER I THINK ABOUT MY DAD...
AND NOW I TOOK IT ALL OUT ON SHIN.
SO I GUESS... YOU STILL HAVEN'T FORGIVEN YOUR DAD...
I THOUGHT I HAD, BUT I GUESS I WAS WRONG...

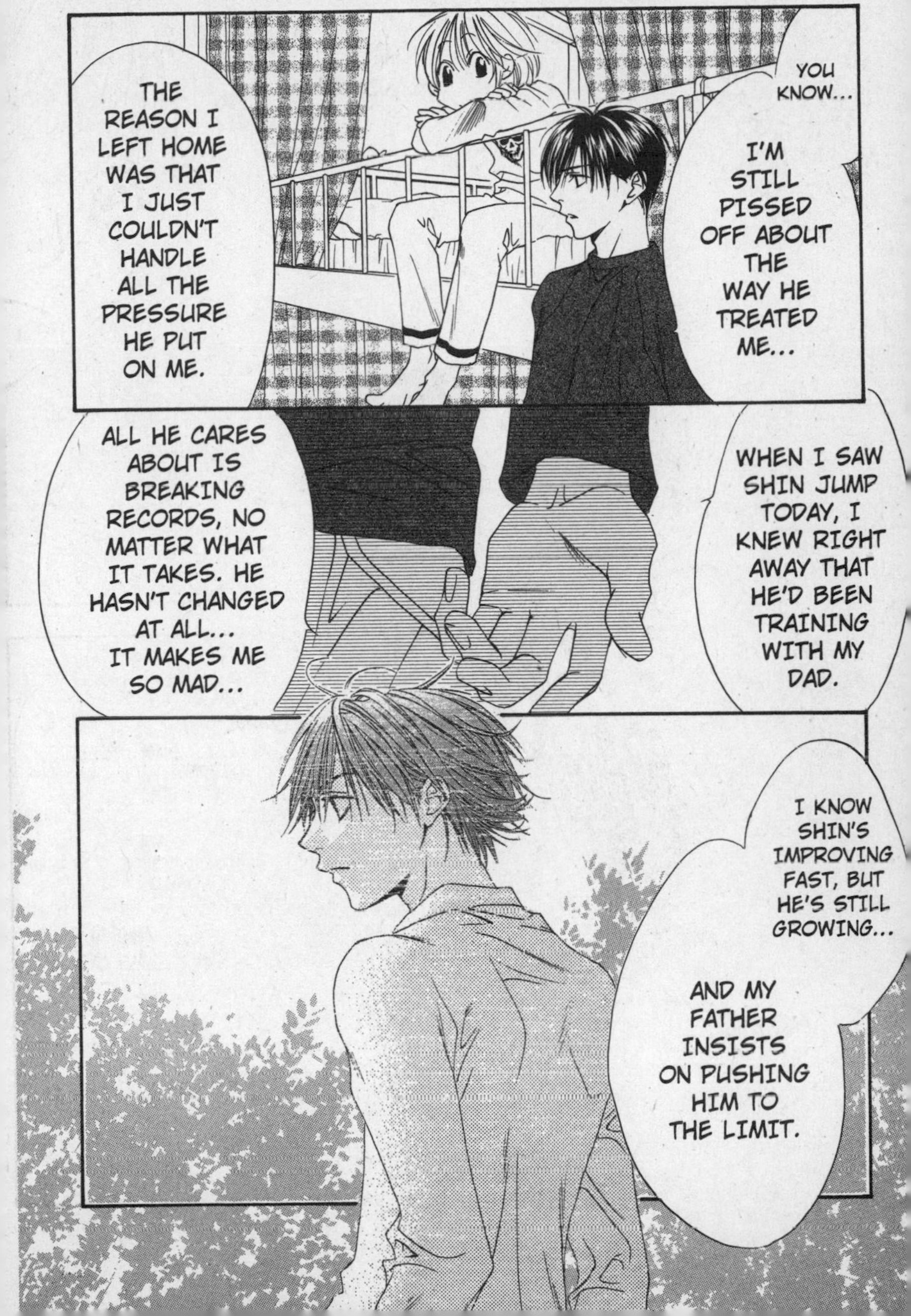
YOU KNOW...
I'M STILL PISSED OFF ABOUT THE WAY HE TREATED ME...
THE REASON I LEFT HOME WAS THAT I JUST COULDN'T HANDLE ALL THE PRESSURE HE PUT ON ME.
WHEN I SAW SHIN JUMP TODAY, I KNEW RIGHT AWAY THAT HE'D BEEN TRAINING WITH MY DAD.
ALL HE CARES ABOUT IS BREAKING RECORDS, NO MATTER WHAT IT TAKES. HE HASN'T CHANGED AT ALL... IT MAKES ME SO MAD...
I KNOW SHIN'S IMPROVING FAST, BUT HE'S STILL GROWING...
AND MY FATHER INSISTS ON PUSHING HIM TO THE LIMIT.

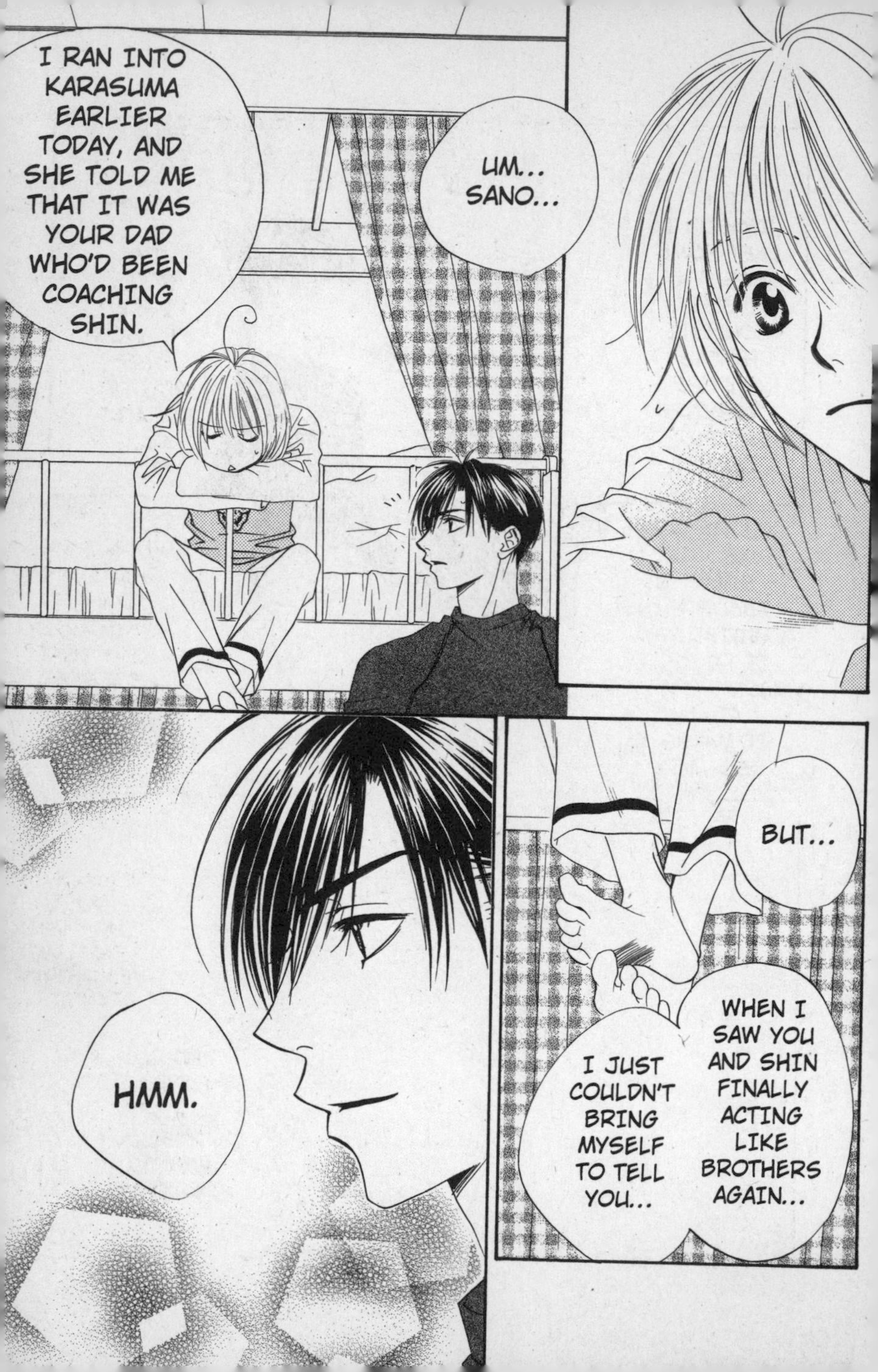
UM... SANO...
I RAN INTO KARASUMA EARLIER TODAY, AND SHE TOLD ME THAT IT WAS YOUR DAD WHO'D BEEN COACHING SHIN.
BUT...
WHEN I SAW YOU AND SHIN FINALLY ACTING LIKE BROTHERS AGAIN...
I JUST COULDN'T BRING MYSELF TO TELL YOU...
HMM.

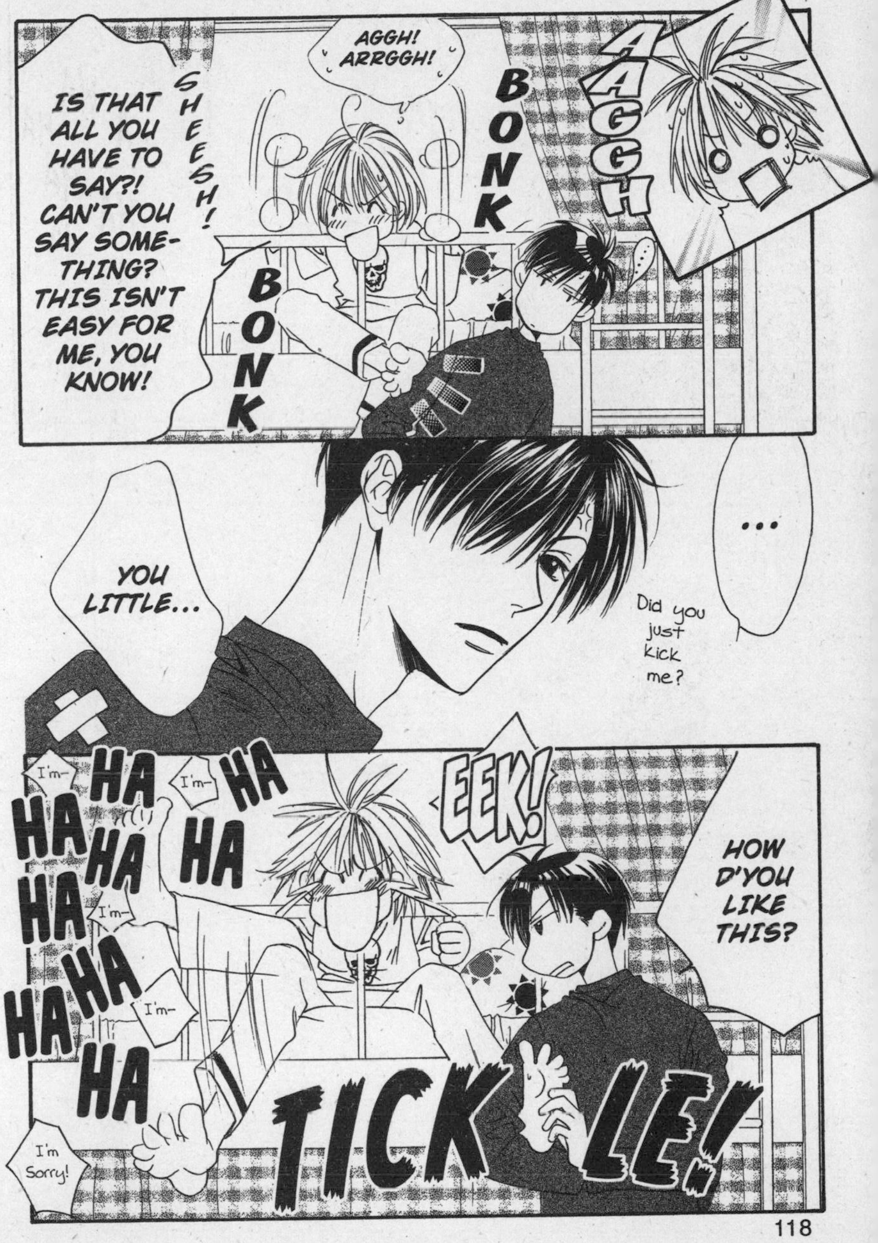
AAGGH
BONK
AGGH! ARRGGH!
SHEESH!
IS THAT ALL YOU HAVE TO SAY?! CAN'T YOU SAY SOME-THING? THIS ISN'T EASY FOR ME, YOU KNOW!
BONK
...
Did you just kick me?
YOU LITTLE...
HOW D'YOU LIKE THIS?
EEK!
TICKLE!
HA HA
HA
I'm-
HA HA HA HA HA HA HA HA
I'm-
I'm-
I'm-
I'm Sorry!

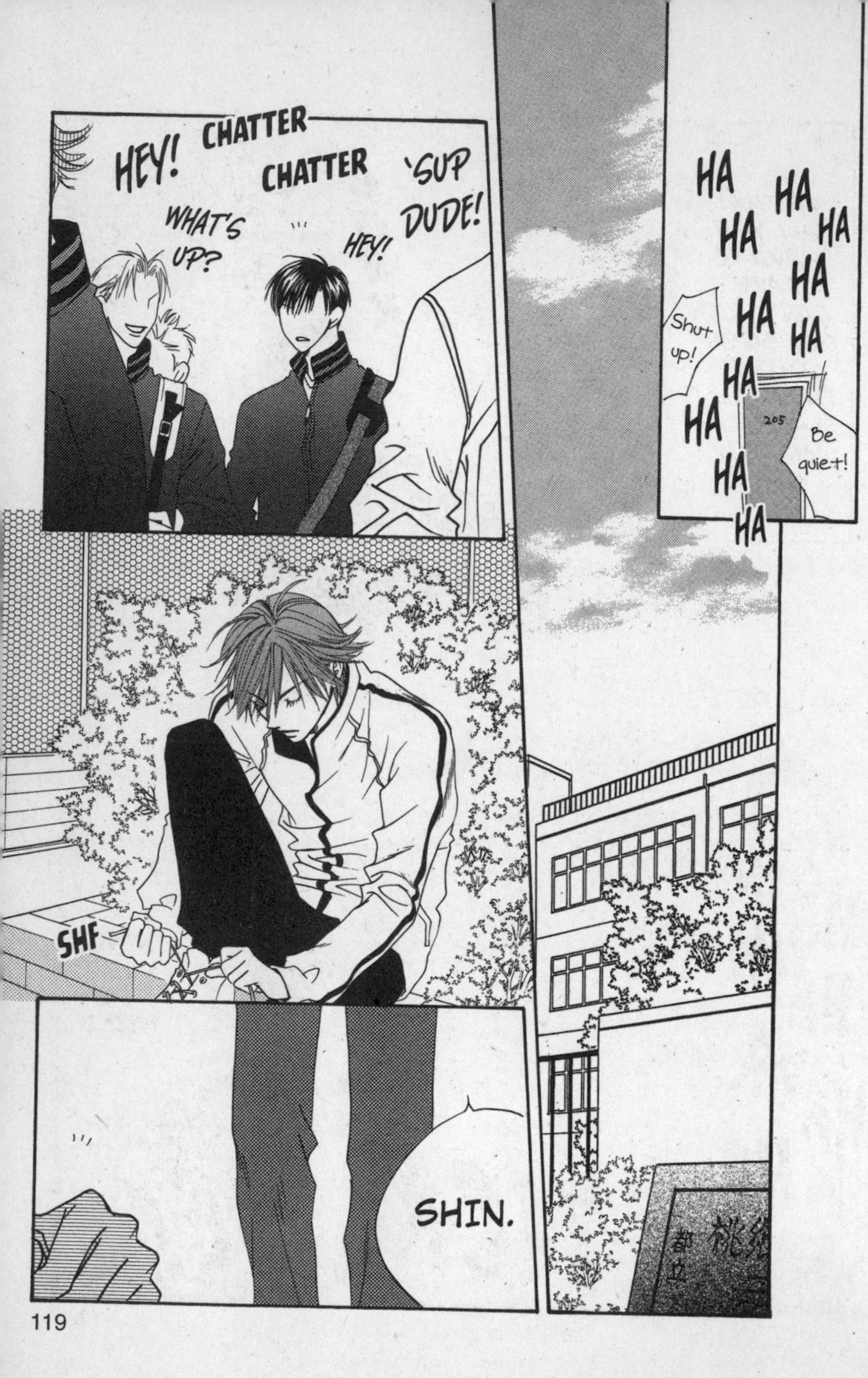
HA HA HA HA HA HA HA HA HA HA HA
Shut up!
Be quiet!
'SUP DUDE!
CHATTER
HEY!
CHATTER
HEY!
WHAT'S UP?
SHF
SHIN.

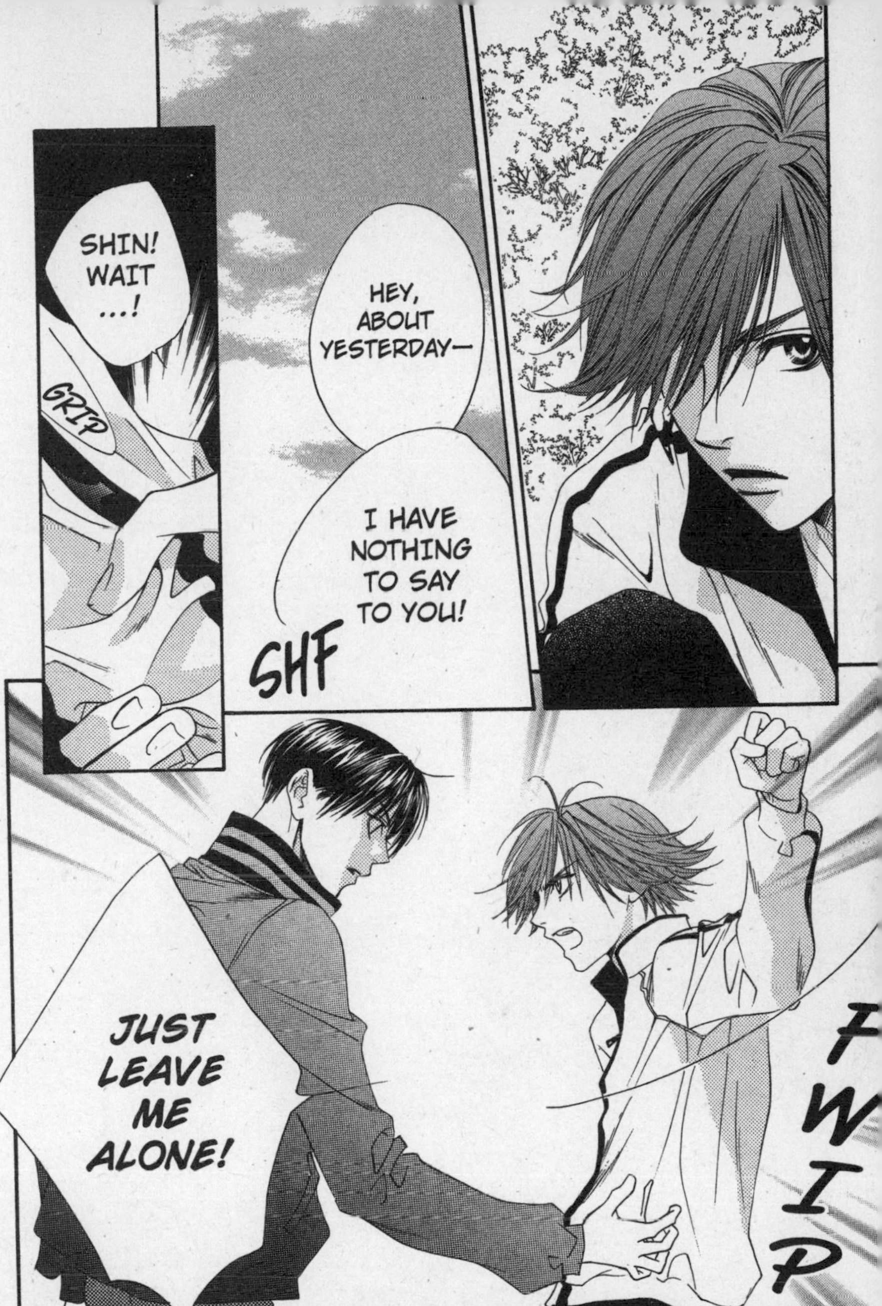
HEY, ABOUT YESTERDAY—
I HAVE NOTHING TO SAY TO YOU!
SHF
SHIN! WAIT ...!
GRIP
JUST LEAVE ME ALONE!
FWIP

HANA-KIMI CHAPTER 89/END

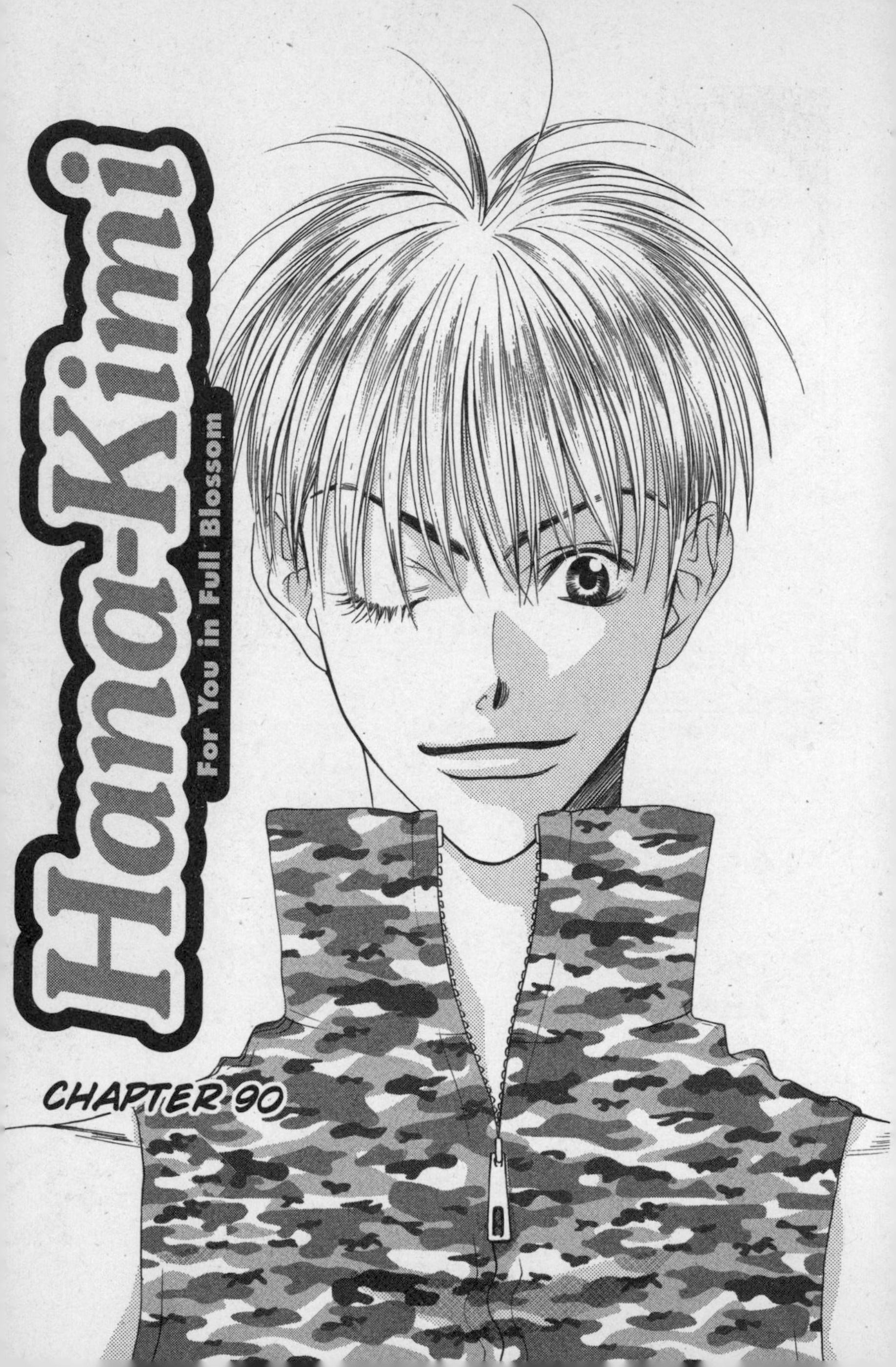
Hana-Kimi
For You in Full Blossom
CHAPTER 90

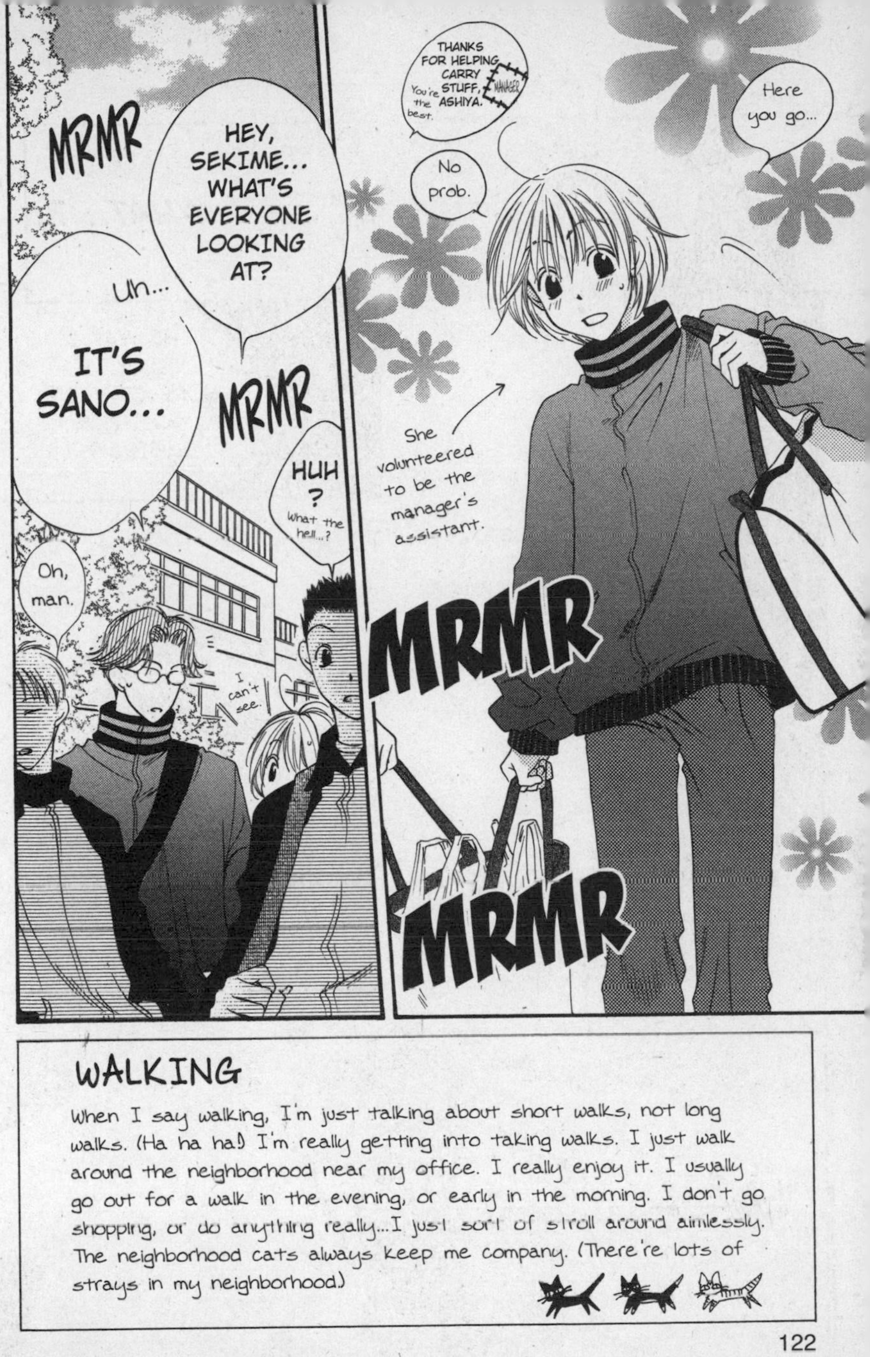
Here you go...
THANKS FOR HELPING CARRY STUFF, ASHIYA.
MANAGER
You're the best.
No prob.
She volunteered to be the manager's assistant.
MRMR
MRMR
HEY, SEKIME... WHAT'S EVERYONE LOOKING AT?
MRMR
Uh...
IT'S SANO...
MRMR
HUH? What the hell...?
Oh, man.
I can't see.

WALKING

When I say walking, I'm just talking about short walks, not long walks. (Ha ha ha!) I'm really getting into taking walks. I just walk around the neighborhood near my office. I really enjoy it. I usually go out for a walk in the evening, or early in the morning. I don't go shopping, or do anything really...I just sort of stroll around aimlessly. The neighborhood cats always keep me company. (There're lots of strays in my neighborhood.)

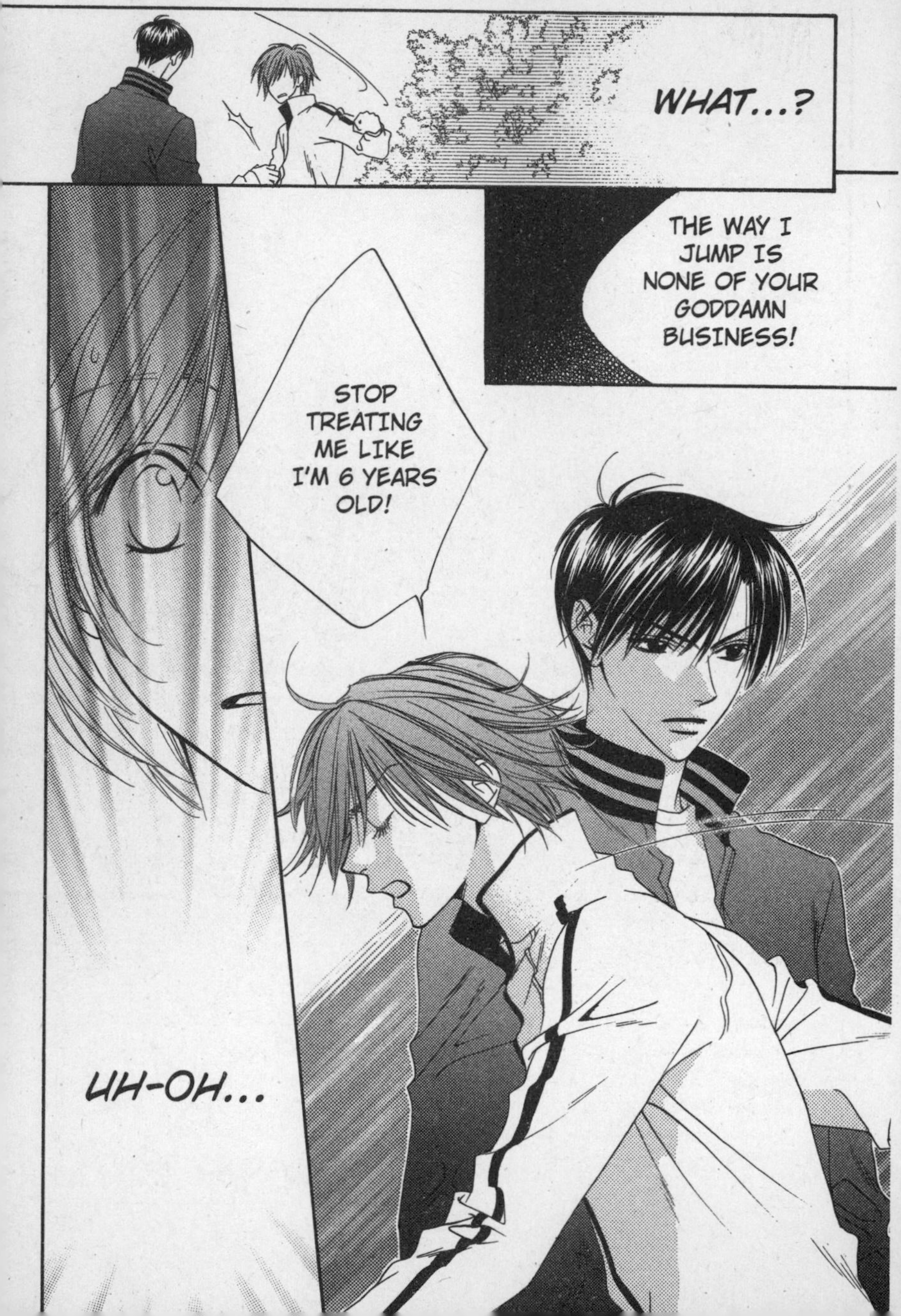
WHAT...?
THE WAY I JUMP IS NONE OF YOUR GODDAMN BUSINESS!
STOP TREATING ME LIKE I'M 6 YEARS OLD!
UH-OH...

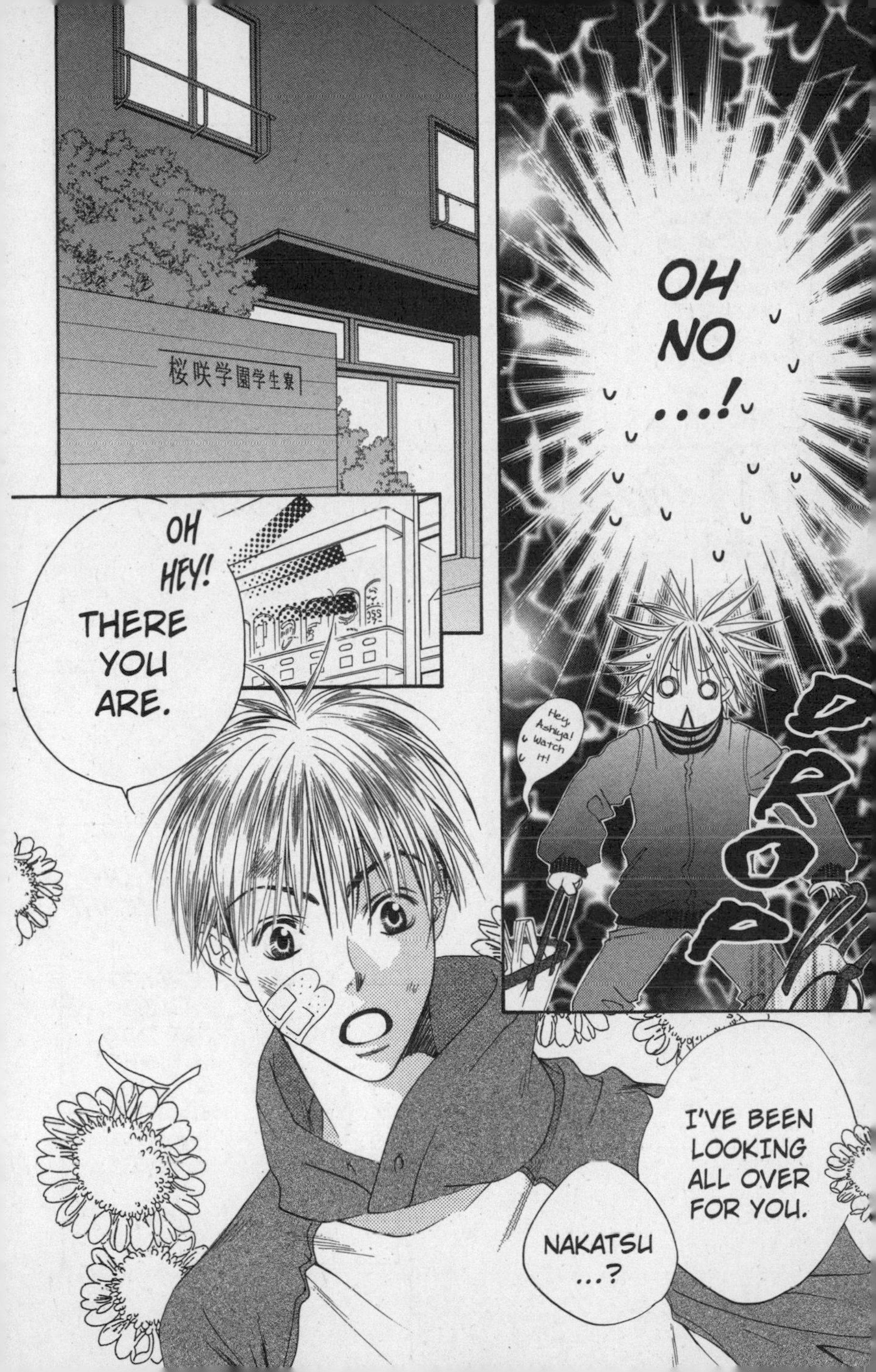
OH NO ...!
Hey, Ashiya! Watch it!
DROP
桜咲学園学生寮
OH HEY! THERE YOU ARE.
I'VE BEEN LOOKING ALL OVER FOR YOU.
NAKATSU ...?

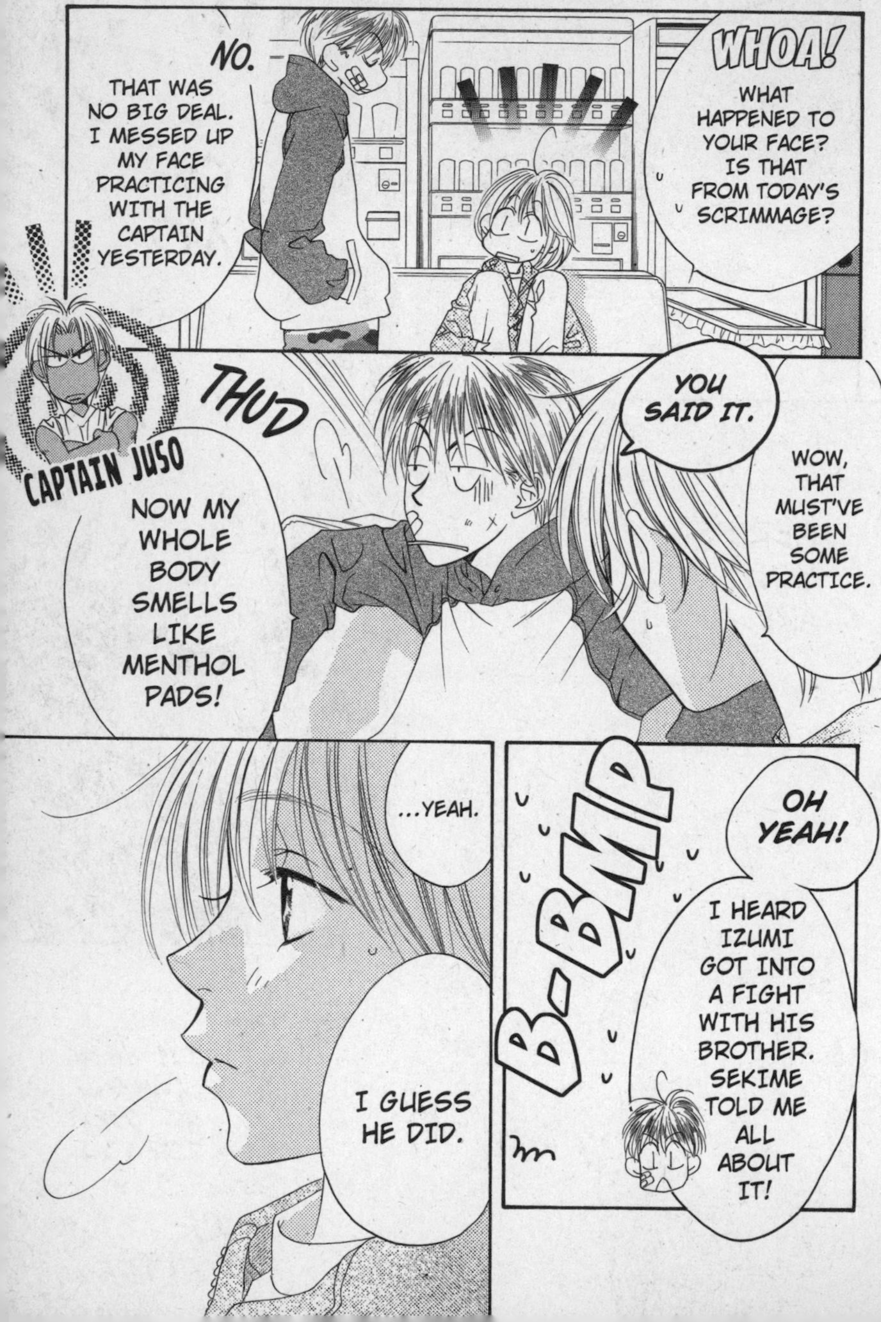
WHOA!
WHAT HAPPENED TO YOUR FACE? IS THAT FROM TODAY'S SCRIMMAGE?
NO.
THAT WAS NO BIG DEAL. I MESSED UP MY FACE PRACTICING WITH THE CAPTAIN YESTERDAY.
WOW, THAT MUST'VE BEEN SOME PRACTICE.
YOU SAID IT.
THUD
NOW MY WHOLE BODY SMELLS LIKE MENTHOL PADS!
CAPTAIN JUSO
OH YEAH!
I HEARD IZUMI GOT INTO A FIGHT WITH HIS BROTHER. SEKIME TOLD ME ALL ABOUT IT!
B-BMP
...YEAH.
I GUESS HE DID.

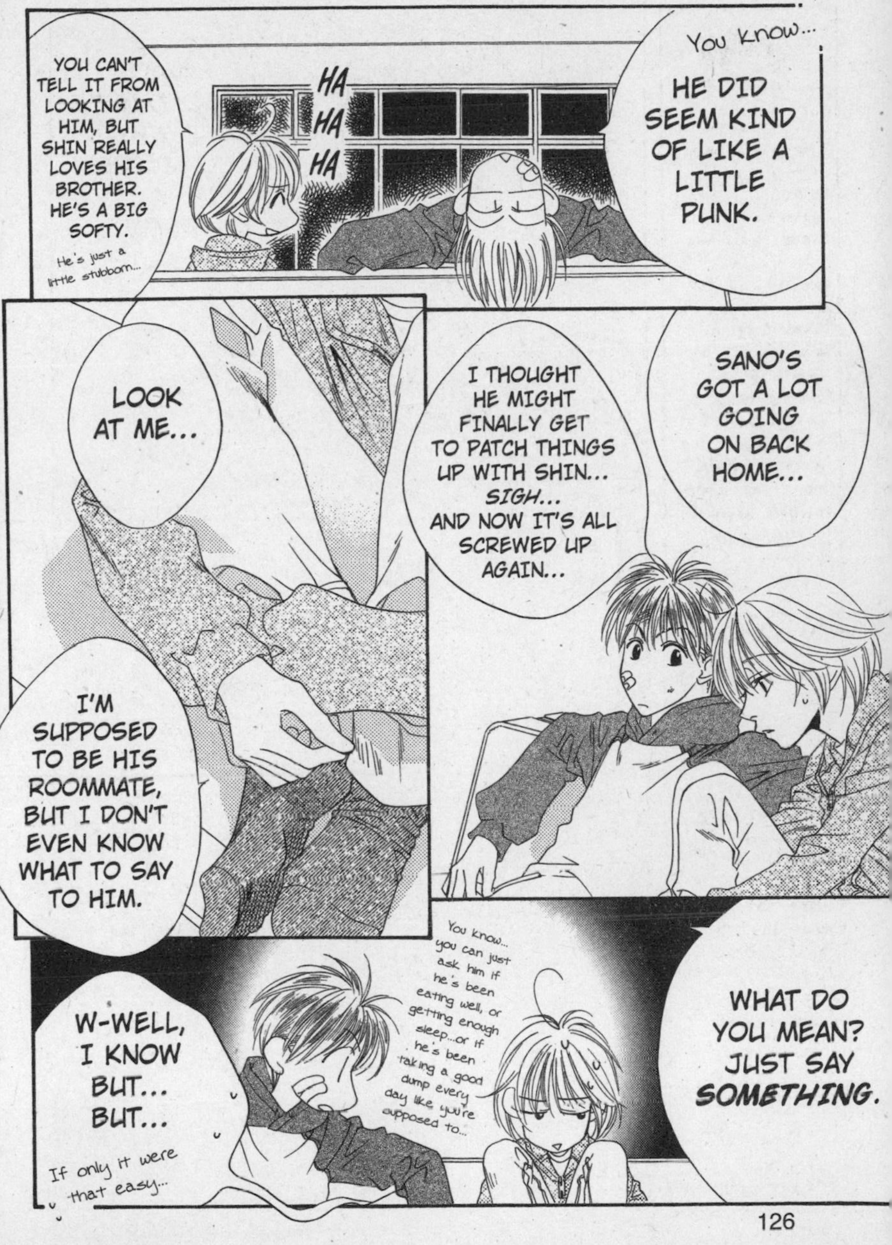
You know...
HE DID SEEM KIND OF LIKE A LITTLE PUNK.
HA HA HA
YOU CAN'T TELL IT FROM LOOKING AT HIM, BUT SHIN REALLY LOVES HIS BROTHER. HE'S A BIG SOFTY.
He's just a little stubborn...
SANO'S GOT A LOT GOING ON BACK HOME...
I THOUGHT HE MIGHT FINALLY GET TO PATCH THINGS UP WITH SHIN... SIGH... AND NOW IT'S ALL SCREWED UP AGAIN...
LOOK AT ME...
I'M SUPPOSED TO BE HIS ROOMMATE, BUT I DON'T EVEN KNOW WHAT TO SAY TO HIM.
WHAT DO YOU MEAN? JUST SAY SOMETHING.
You know... you can just ask him if he's been eating well, or getting enough sleep...or if he's been taking a good dump every day like you're supposed to...
W-WELL, I KNOW BUT... BUT...
If only it were that easy...

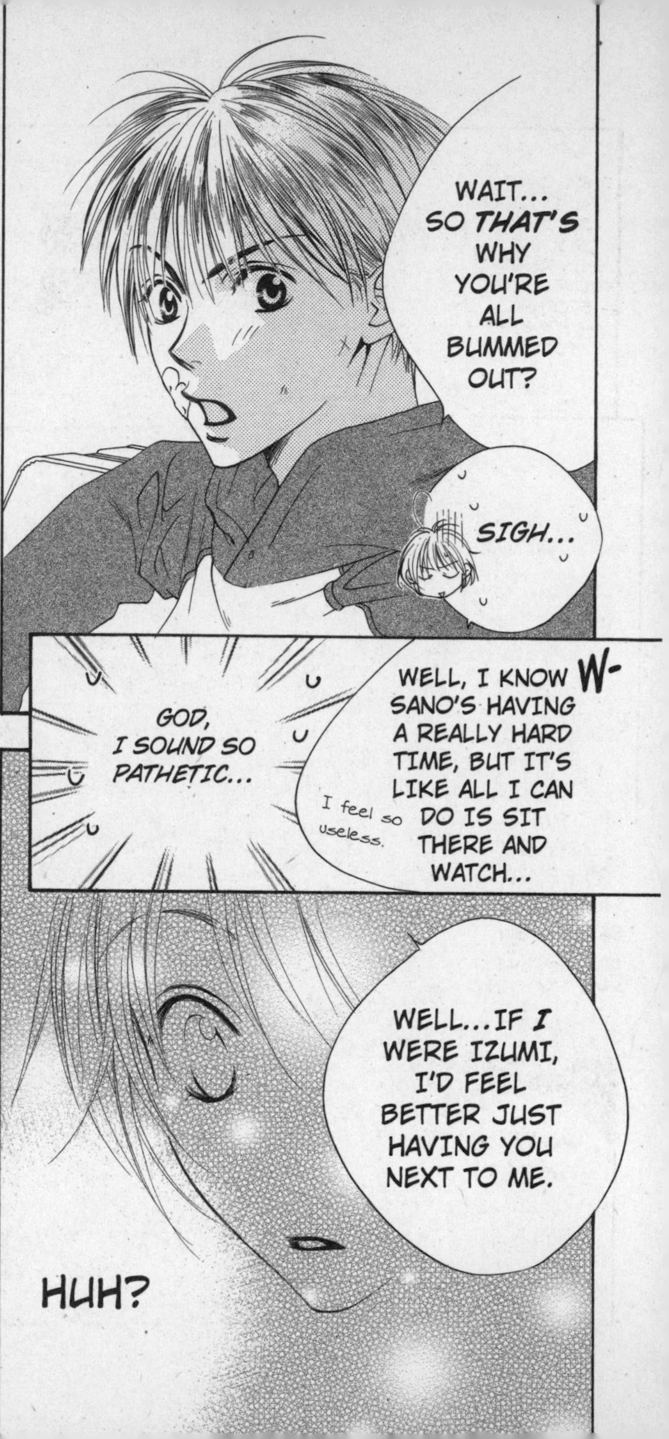
WAIT... SO *THAT'S* WHY YOU'RE ALL BUMMED OUT?
SIGH...
W-
WELL, I KNOW SANO'S HAVING A REALLY HARD TIME, BUT IT'S LIKE ALL I CAN DO IS SIT THERE AND WATCH...
I feel so useless.
GOD, I SOUND SO PATHETIC...
WELL...IF *I* WERE IZUMI, I'D FEEL BETTER JUST HAVING YOU NEXT TO ME.
HUH?

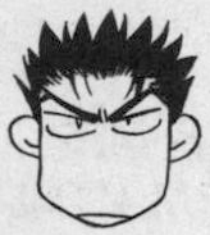

Megumi Tennoji

Birthday: August 26th
Grade: Third Year Japanese H.S. (equivalent of 12th grade in America)
Blood Type: A
Sign: Virgo
Height: 183cm
Favorite Food: Nikujaga (Stewed Potatoes and Beef)
Least Favorite Foods: Fast Food
Favorite Celebrity: Kanna Amasaki
Flower: Lotus

Birthday: July 2nd
Grade: Second Year Japanese H.S. (equivalent of 11th grade in America)
Blood Type: B
Sign: Cancer
Height: 179cm
Favorite Food: Grilled Cow Tongue
Least Favorite Food: Tomatoes
Favorite Celebrities: Any Older Women
Flower: Hibiscus

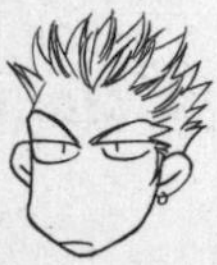

Shingo Kagurazaka

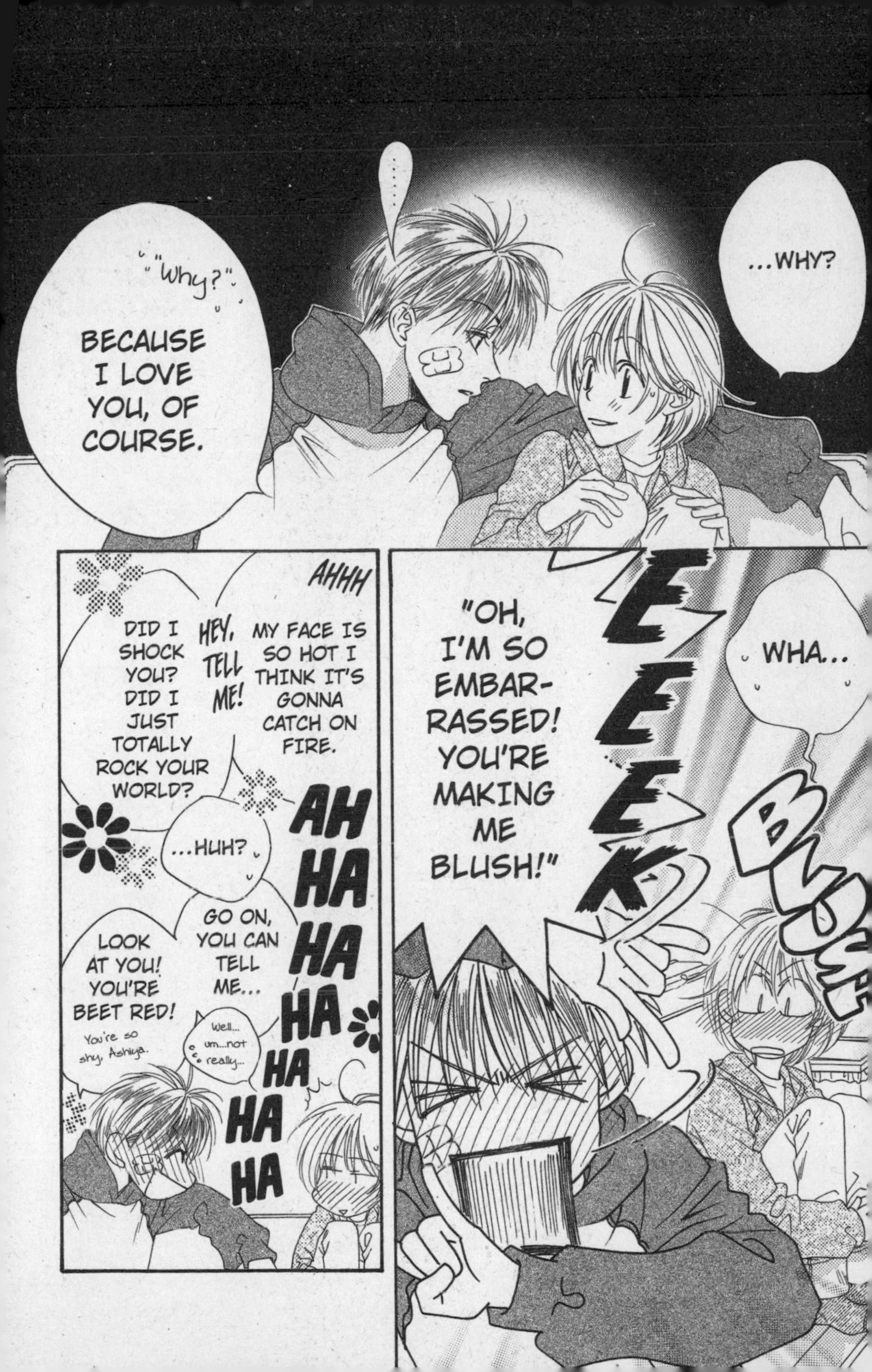
...WHY?
"Why?"
BECAUSE I LOVE YOU, OF COURSE.
WHA...
EEEEK
"OH, I'M SO EMBARRASSED! YOU'RE MAKING ME BLUSH!"
AHHH
MY FACE IS SO HOT I THINK IT'S GONNA CATCH ON FIRE.
HEY, TELL ME!
DID I SHOCK YOU? DID I JUST TOTALLY ROCK YOUR WORLD?
AH HA HA HA HA HA HA HA
...HUH?
GO ON, YOU CAN TELL ME...
LOOK AT YOU! YOU'RE BEET RED!
You're so shy, Ashiya.
Well... um...not really...

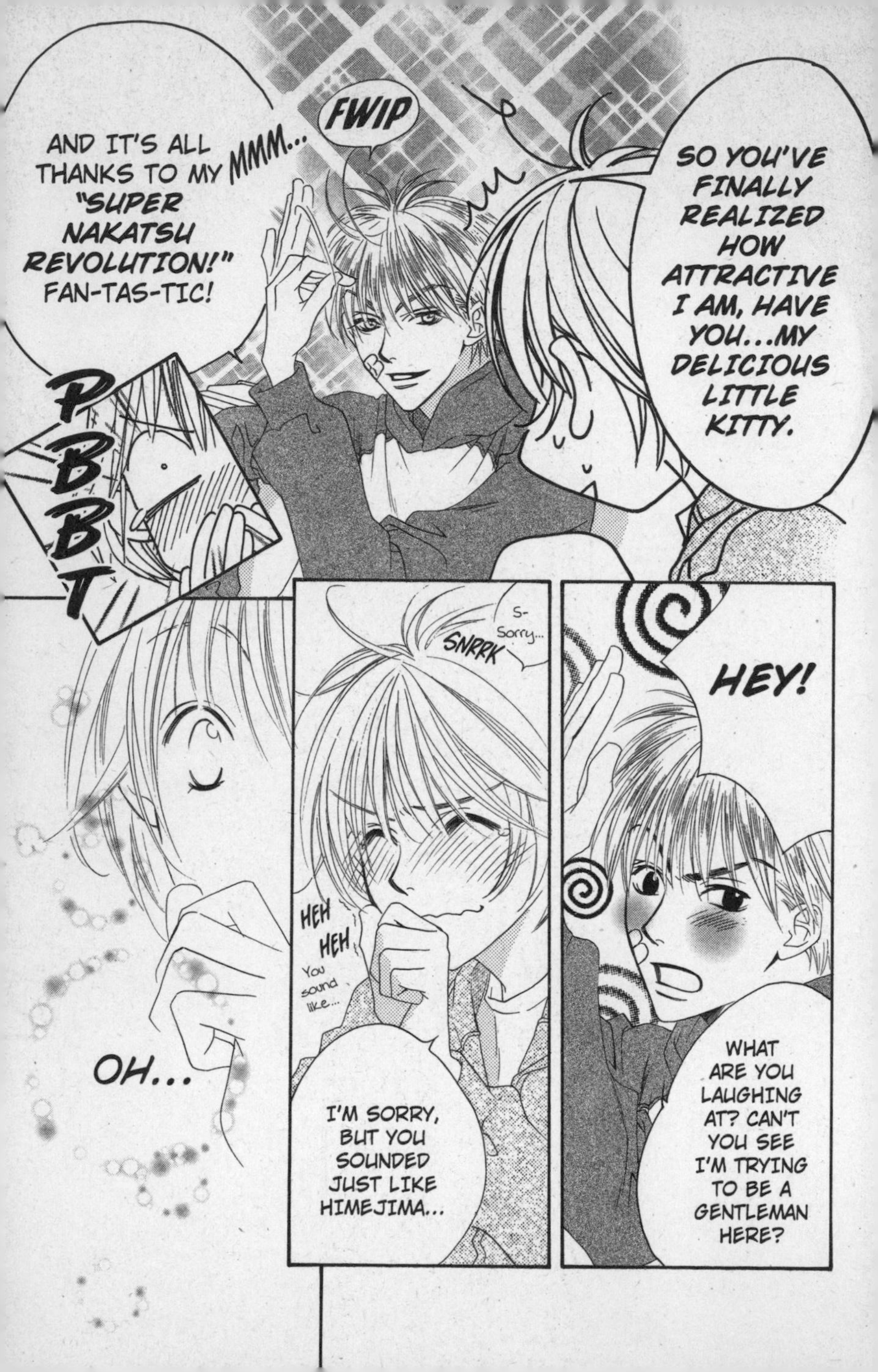
SO YOU'VE FINALLY REALIZED HOW ATTRACTIVE I AM, HAVE YOU...MY DELICIOUS LITTLE KITTY.
FWIP
MMM...
AND IT'S ALL THANKS TO MY "SUPER NAKATSU REVOLUTION!" FAN-TAS-TIC!
PBBBT
HEY!
WHAT ARE YOU LAUGHING AT? CAN'T YOU SEE I'M TRYING TO BE A GENTLEMAN HERE?
S-Sorry...
SNRRK
HEH HEH
You sound like...
I'M SORRY, BUT YOU SOUNDED JUST LIKE HIMEJIMA...
OH...

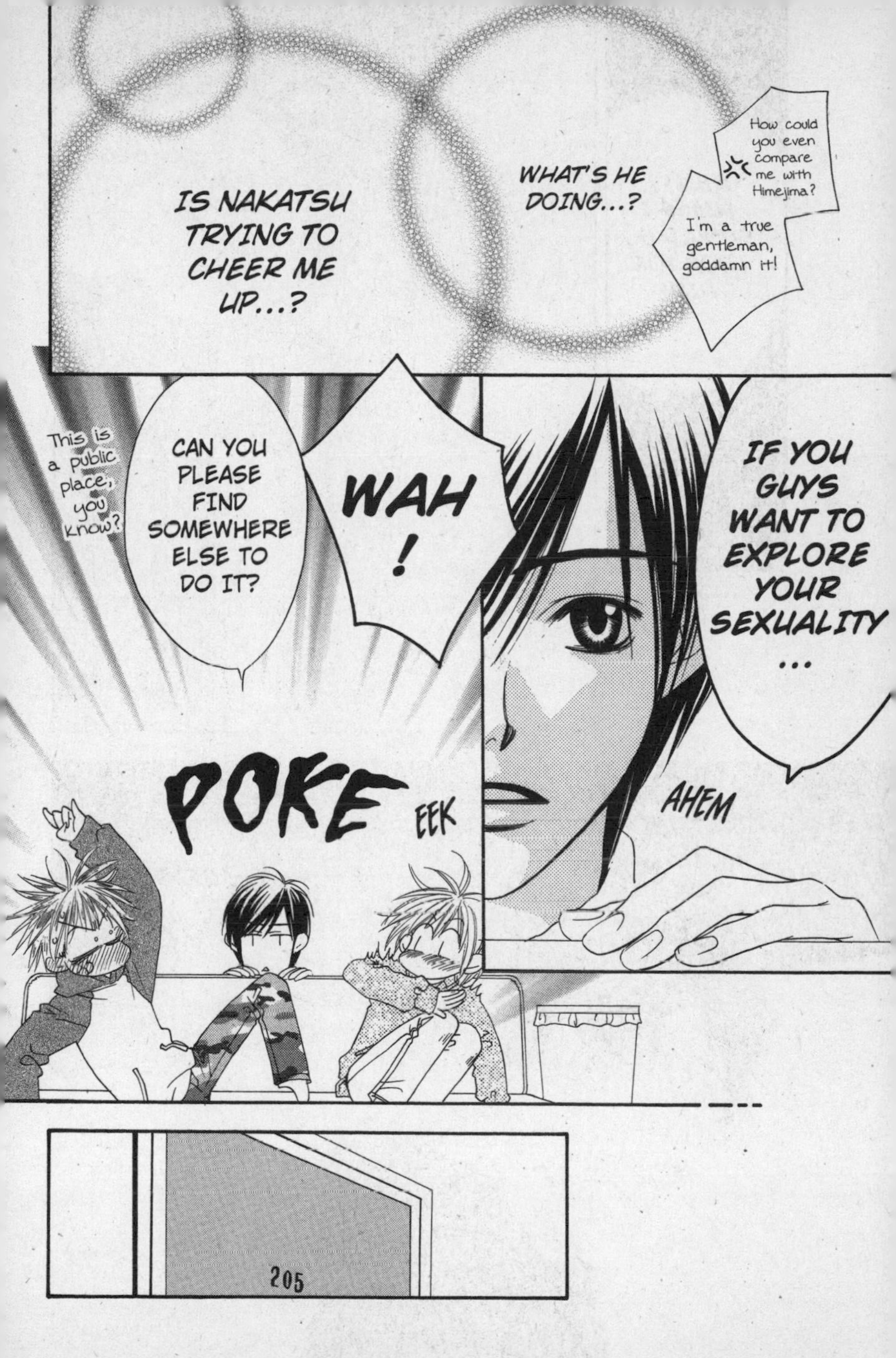
How could you even compare me with Himejima?
I'm a true gentleman, goddamn it!
WHAT'S HE DOING...?
IS NAKATSU TRYING TO CHEER ME UP...?
IF YOU GUYS WANT TO EXPLORE YOUR SEXUALITY ...
AHEM
WAH!
CAN YOU PLEASE FIND SOMEWHERE ELSE TO DO IT?
This is a public place, you know?
POKE
EEK

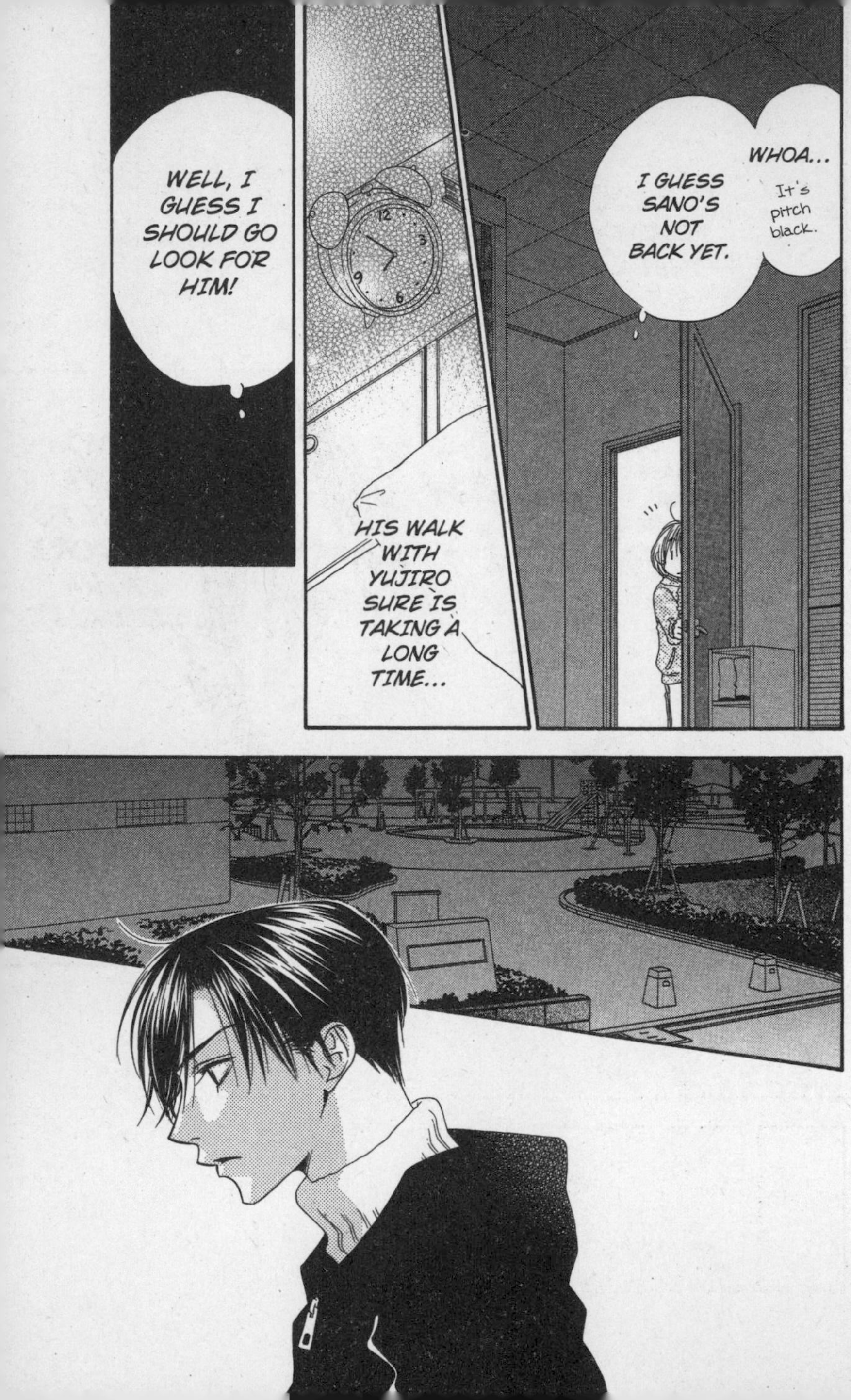
WHOA...
It's pitch black.
I GUESS SANO'S NOT BACK YET.
HIS WALK WITH YUJIRO SURE IS TAKING A LONG TIME...
WELL, I GUESS I SHOULD GO LOOK FOR HIM!

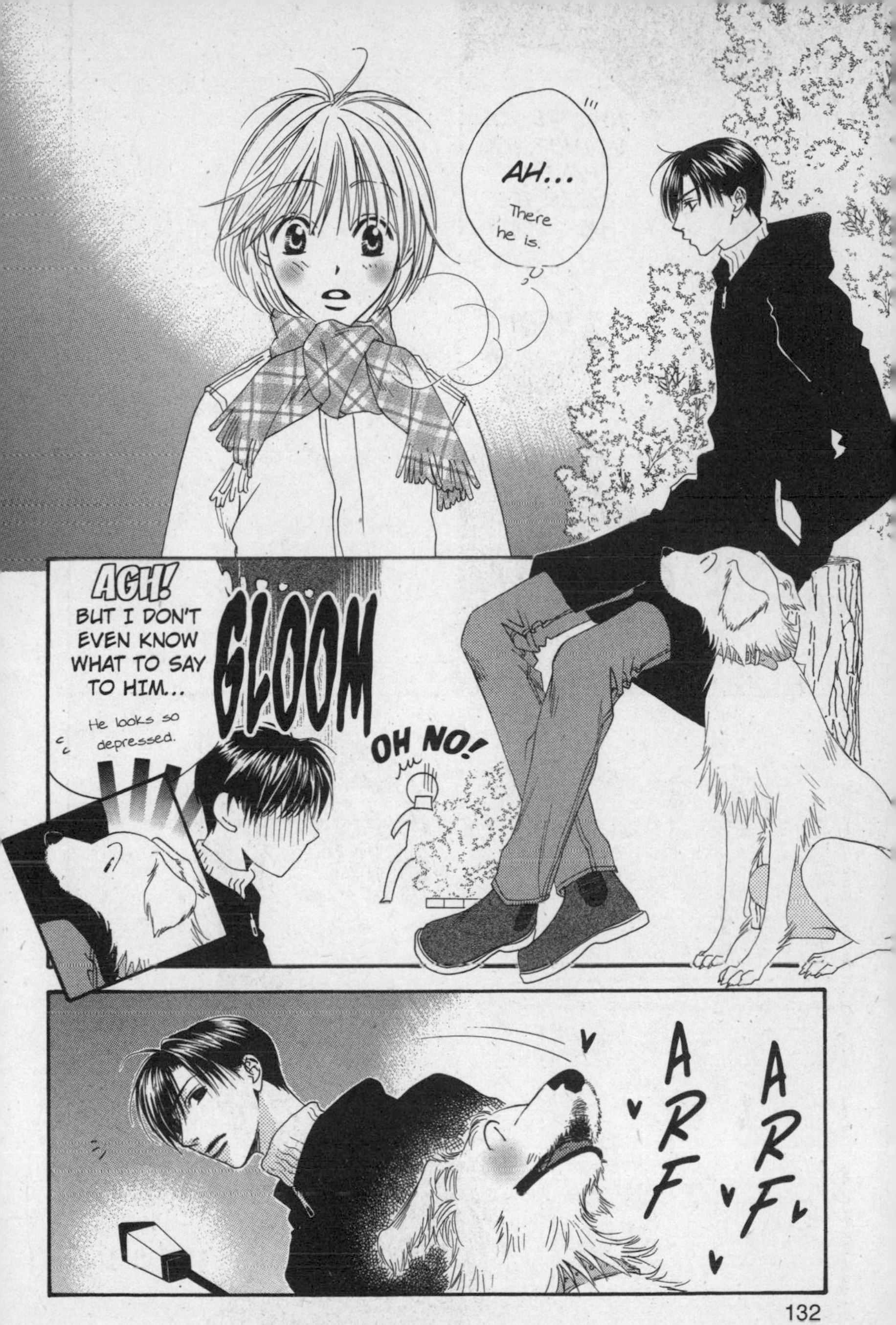
AH... There he is.
AGH! BUT I DON'T EVEN KNOW WHAT TO SAY TO HIM...
He looks so depressed.
GLOOM
OH NO!
ARF ARF

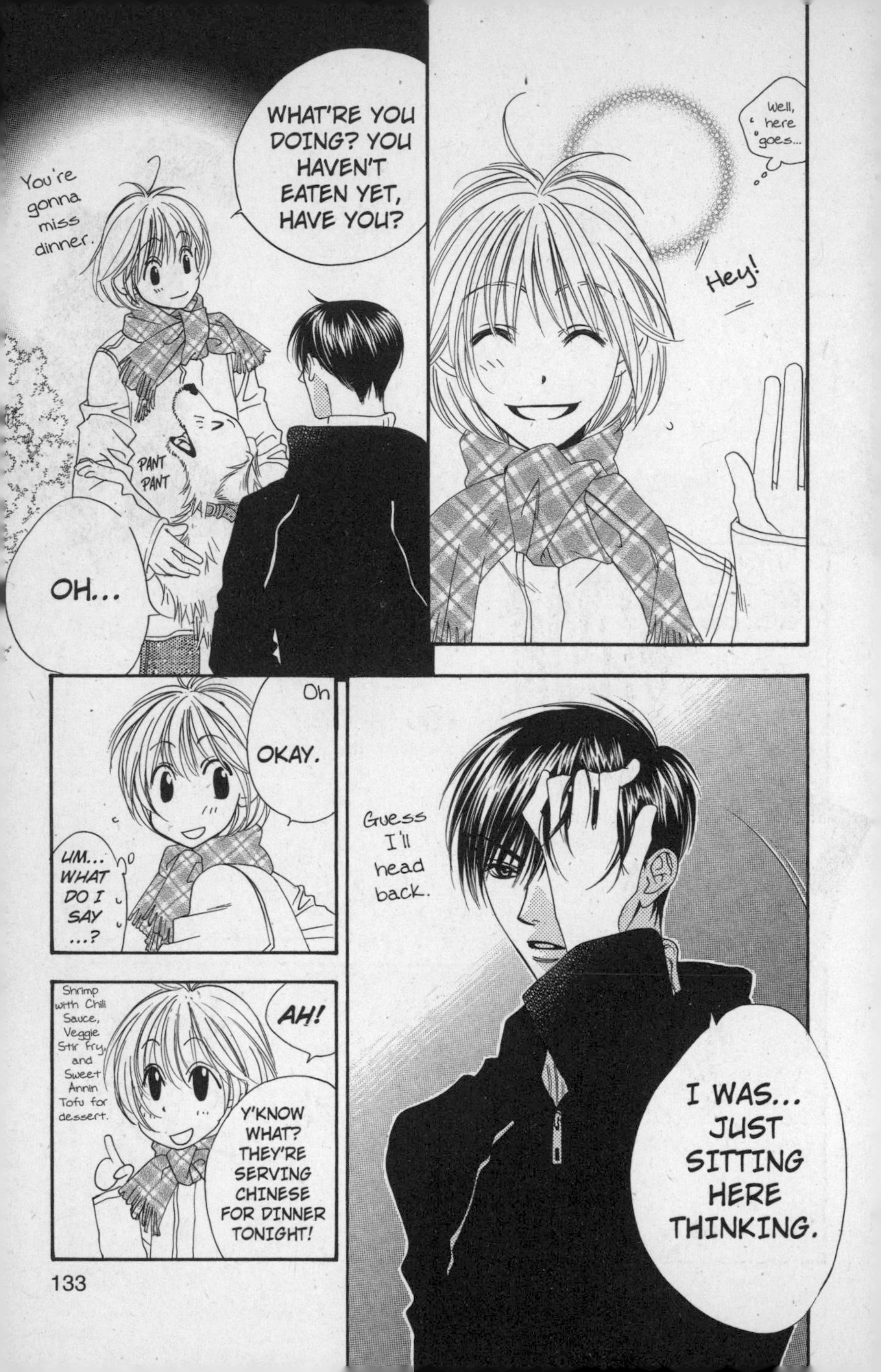
Well, here goes...
Hey!
WHAT'RE YOU DOING? YOU HAVEN'T EATEN YET, HAVE YOU?
You're gonna miss dinner.
PANT PANT
OH...
I WAS... JUST SITTING HERE THINKING.
Oh
OKAY.
Guess I'll head back.
UM... WHAT DO I SAY ...?
AH!
Shrimp with Chili Sauce, Veggie Stir Fry, and Sweet Annin Tofu for dessert.
Y'KNOW WHAT? THEY'RE SERVING CHINESE FOR DINNER TONIGHT!

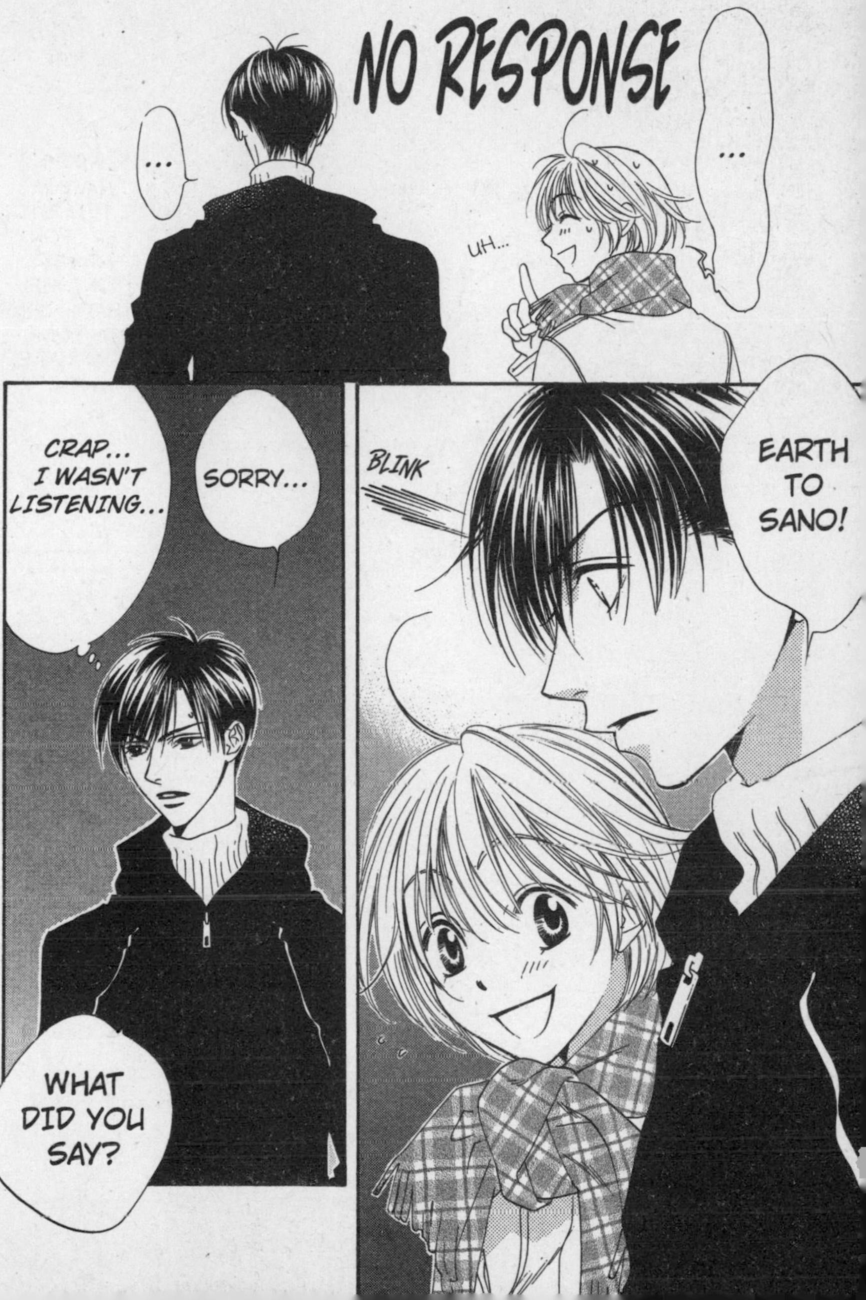
...
NO RESPONSE
UH...
...
EARTH TO SANO!
BLINK
SORRY...
CRAP... I WASN'T LISTENING...
WHAT DID YOU SAY?

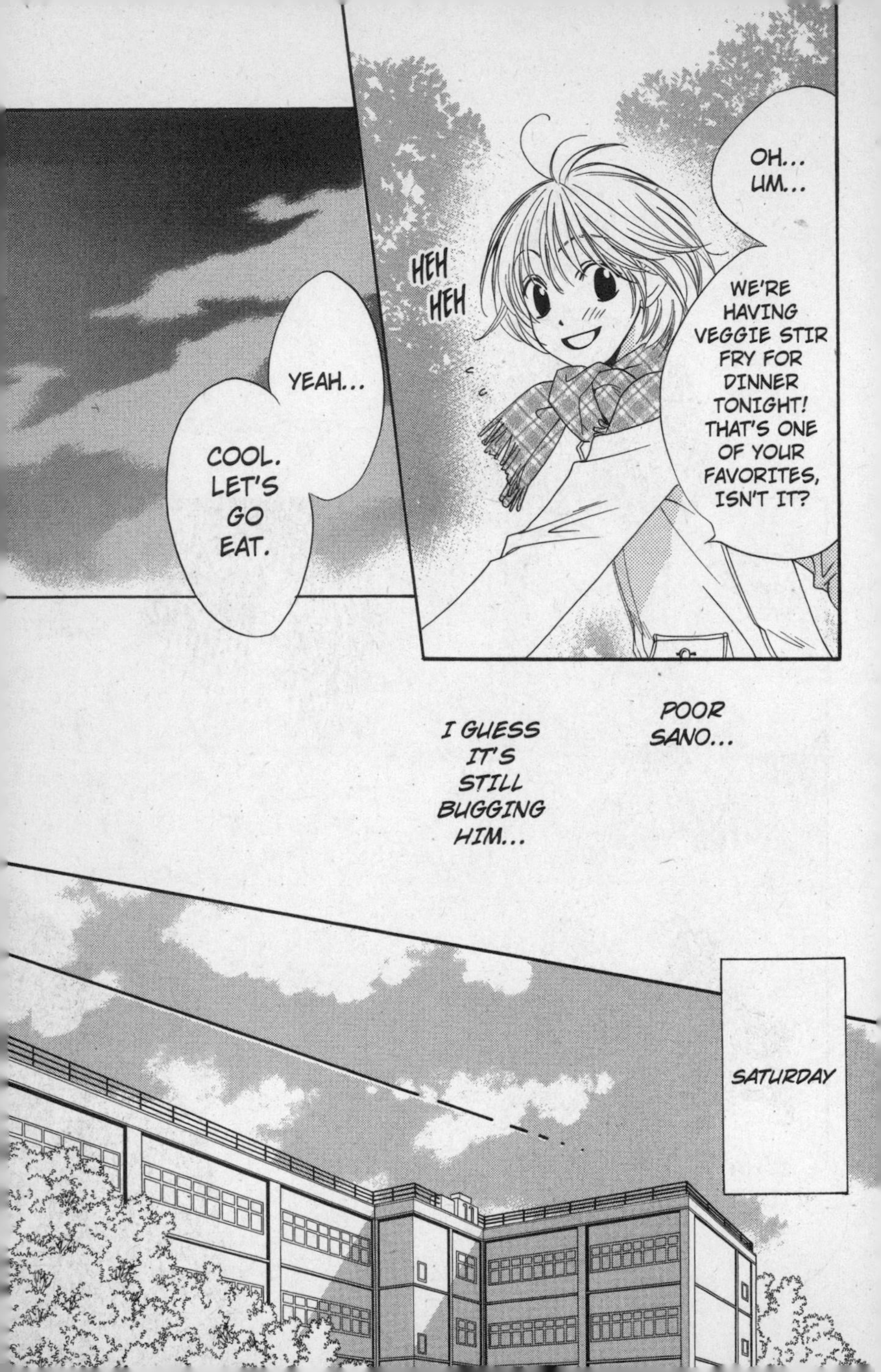
OH... UM...
WE'RE HAVING VEGGIE STIR FRY FOR DINNER TONIGHT! THAT'S ONE OF YOUR FAVORITES, ISN'T IT?
HEH HEH
YEAH...
COOL. LET'S GO EAT.
POOR SANO...
I GUESS IT'S STILL BUGGING HIM...
SATURDAY

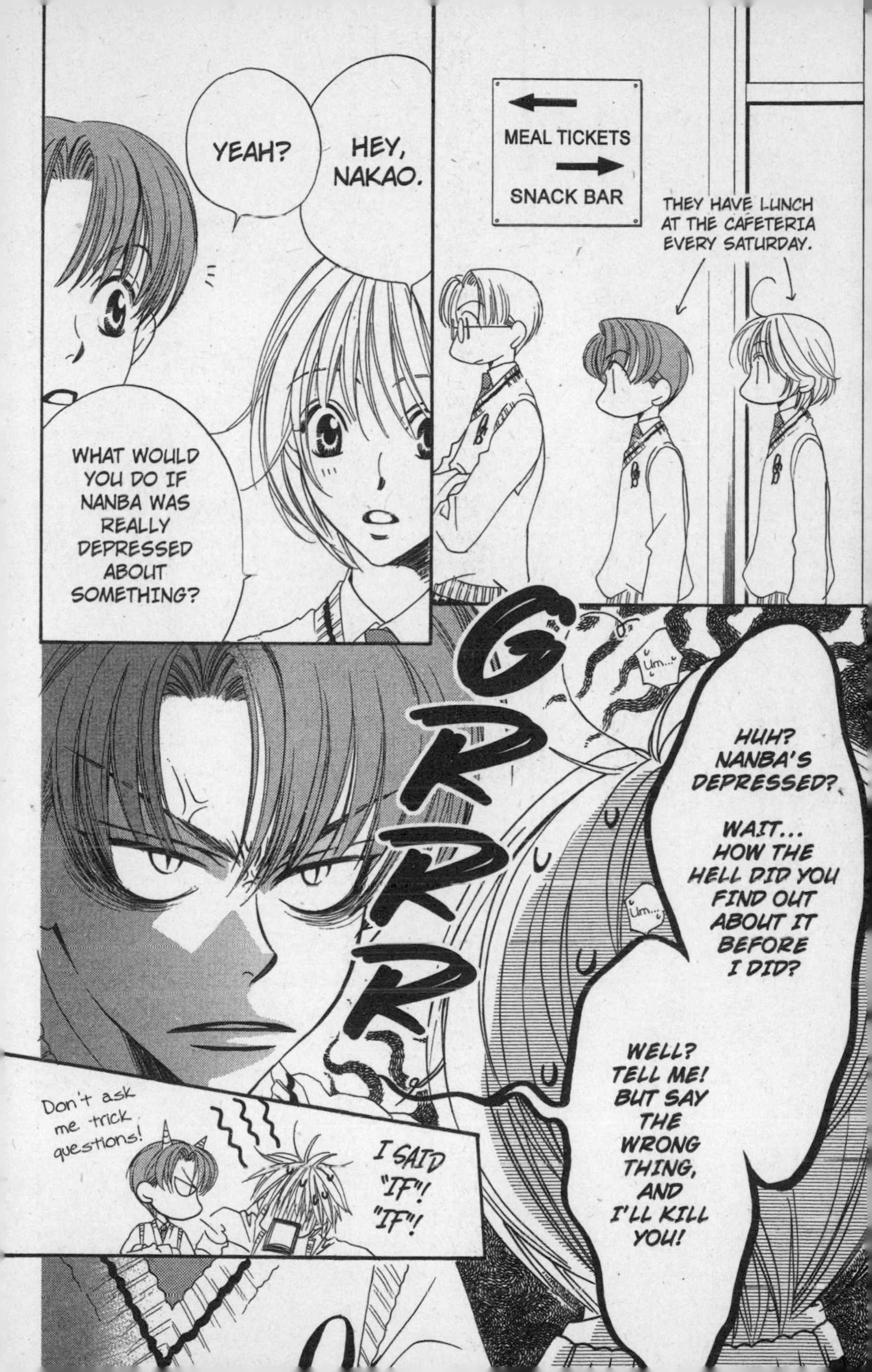
MEAL TICKETS
SNACK BAR
THEY HAVE LUNCH AT THE CAFETERIA EVERY SATURDAY.
HEY, NAKAO.
YEAH?
WHAT WOULD YOU DO IF NANBA WAS REALLY DEPRESSED ABOUT SOMETHING?
GRRRR
Um...
Um...
HUH? NANBA'S DEPRESSED?
WAIT... HOW THE HELL DID YOU FIND OUT ABOUT IT BEFORE I DID?
WELL? TELL ME! BUT SAY THE WRONG THING, AND I'LL KILL YOU!
I SAID "IF"! "IF"!
Don't ask me trick questions!

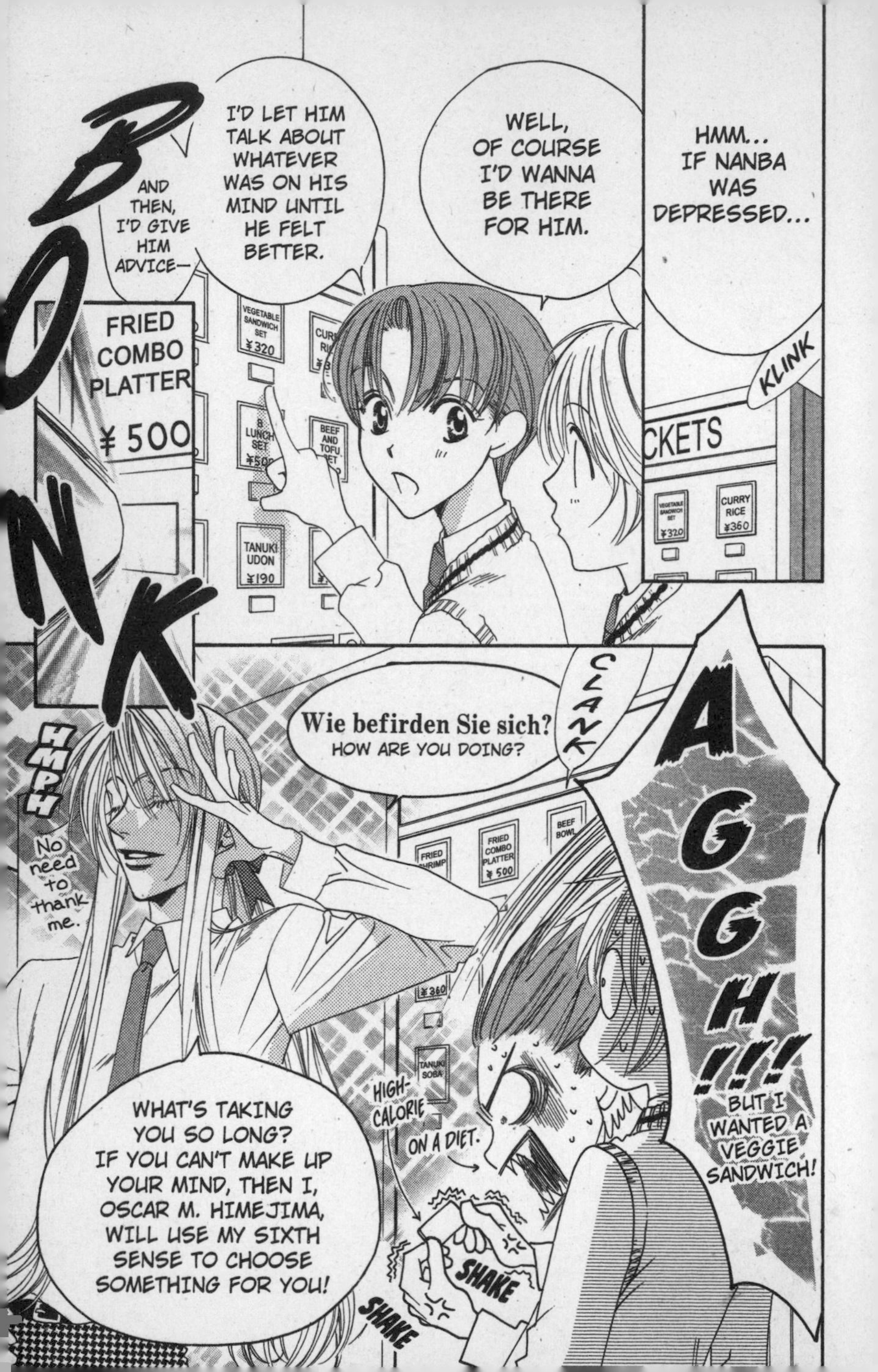
HMM... IF NANBA WAS DEPRESSED...
KLINK
CKETS
VEGETABLE SANDWICH SET ¥320
CURRY RICE ¥360
WELL, OF COURSE I'D WANNA BE THERE FOR HIM.
I'D LET HIM TALK ABOUT WHATEVER WAS ON HIS MIND UNTIL HE FELT BETTER.
AND THEN, I'D GIVE HIM ADVICE—
FRIED COMBO PLATTER ¥500
TANUKI UDON ¥190
BONK
AGGH!!!
BUT I WANTED A VEGGIE SANDWICH!
CLANK
Wie befirden Sie sich?
HOW ARE YOU DOING?
HMPH
No need to thank me.
FRIED COMBO PLATTER ¥500
BEEF BOWL
FRIED SHRIMP
TANUKI SOBA
HIGH-CALORIE
ON A DIET.
WHAT'S TAKING YOU SO LONG? IF YOU CAN'T MAKE UP YOUR MIND, THEN I, OSCAR M. HIMEJIMA, WILL USE MY SIXTH SENSE TO CHOOSE SOMETHING FOR YOU!
SHAKE
SHAKE

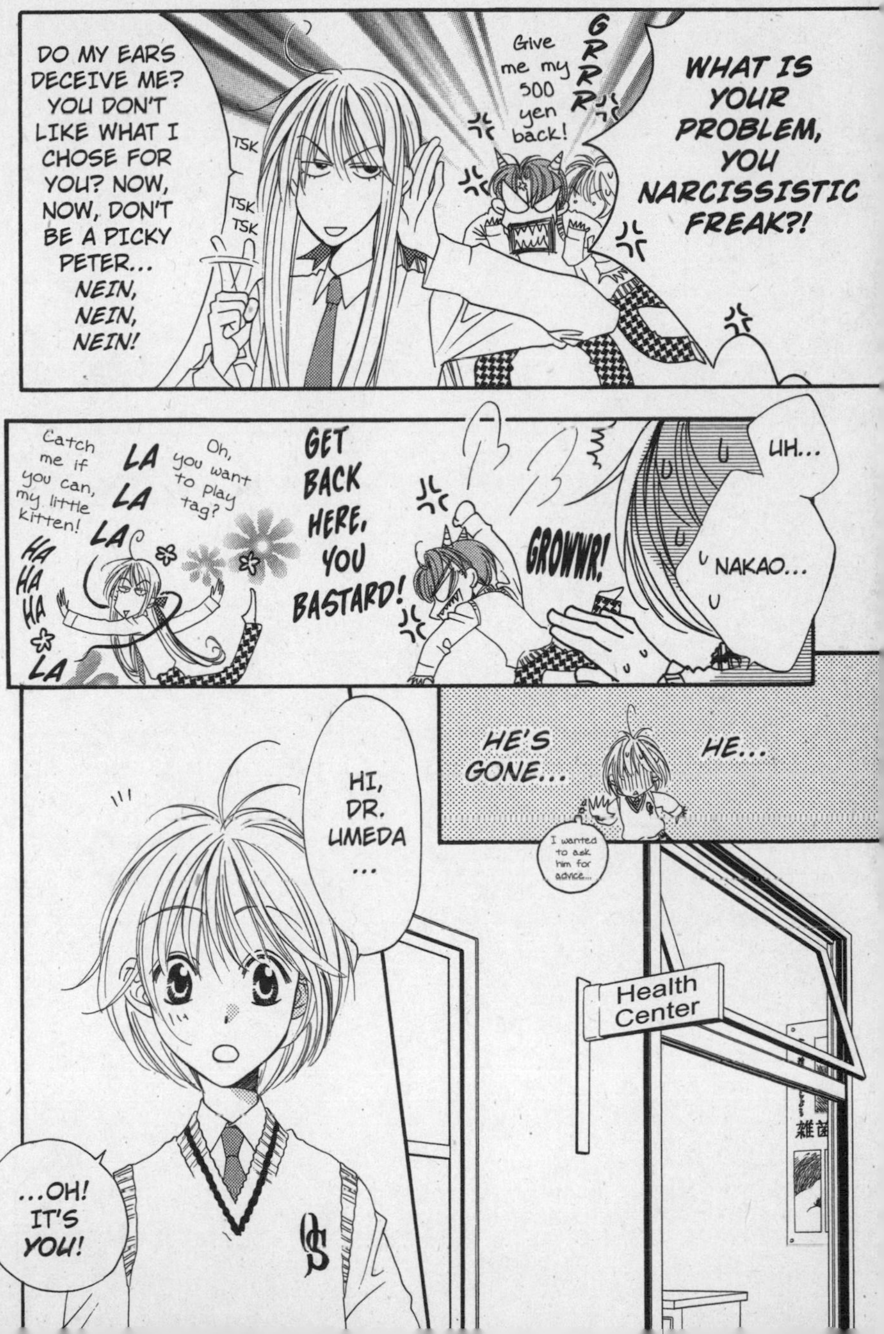
WHAT IS YOUR PROBLEM, YOU NARCISSISTIC FREAK?!
GRRR
Give me my 500 yen back!
DO MY EARS DECEIVE ME? YOU DON'T LIKE WHAT I CHOSE FOR YOU? NOW, NOW, DON'T BE A PICKY PETER... NEIN, NEIN, NEIN!
TSK TSK TSK
UH...
NAKAO...
GROWWR!
GET BACK HERE, YOU BASTARD!
Oh, you want to play tag?
Catch me if you can, my little kitten!
LA LA LA
HA HA HA LA
HE...
HE'S GONE...
I wanted to ask him for advice...
Health Center
HI, DR. UMEDA...
...OH! IT'S YOU!

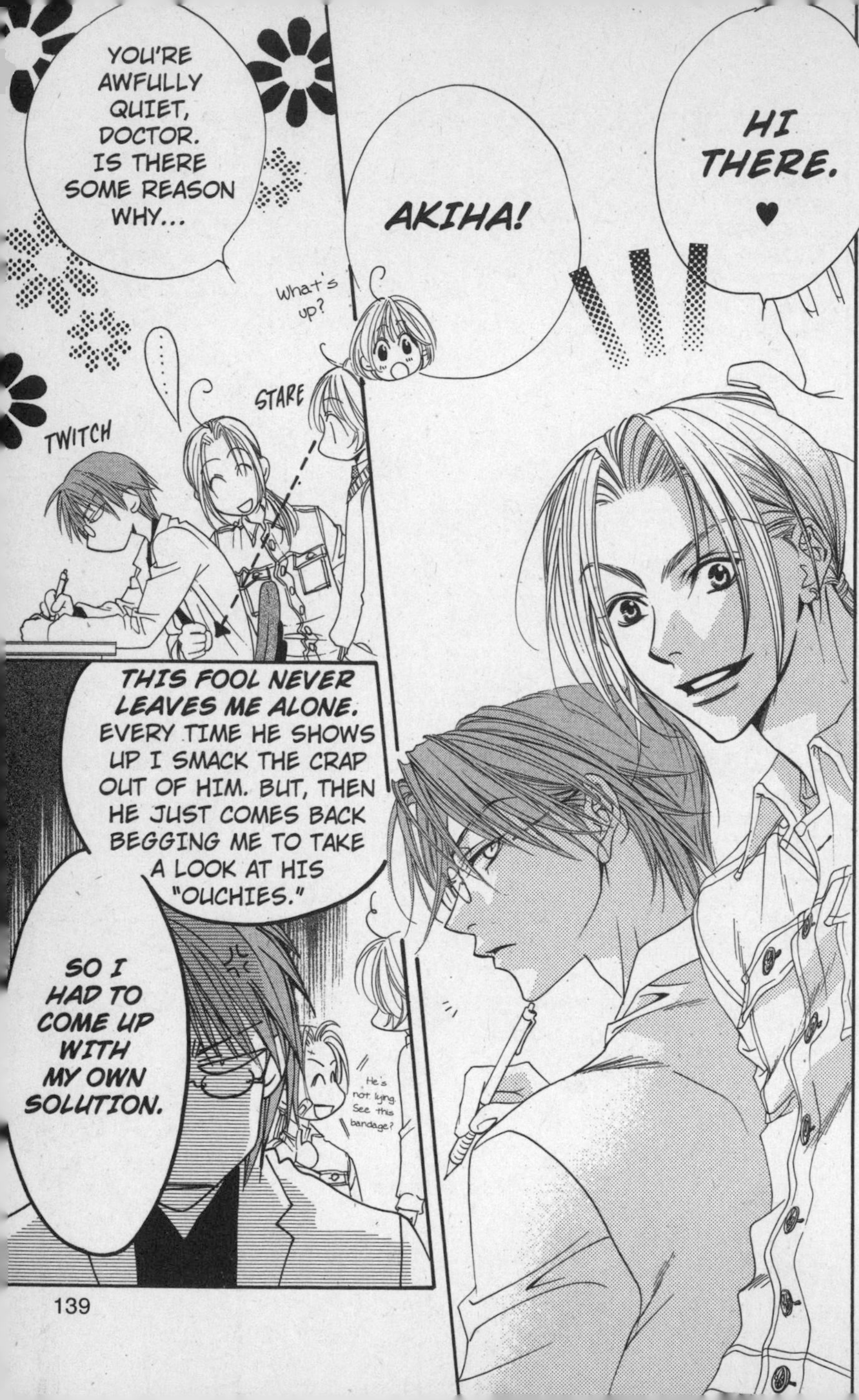
HI THERE. ♥
AKIHA!
YOU'RE AWFULLY QUIET, DOCTOR. IS THERE SOME REASON WHY...
What's up?
...
STARE
TWITCH
THIS FOOL NEVER LEAVES ME ALONE. EVERY TIME HE SHOWS UP I SMACK THE CRAP OUT OF HIM. BUT, THEN HE JUST COMES BACK BEGGING ME TO TAKE A LOOK AT HIS "OUCHIES."
SO I HAD TO COME UP WITH MY OWN SOLUTION.
He's not lying. See this bandage?

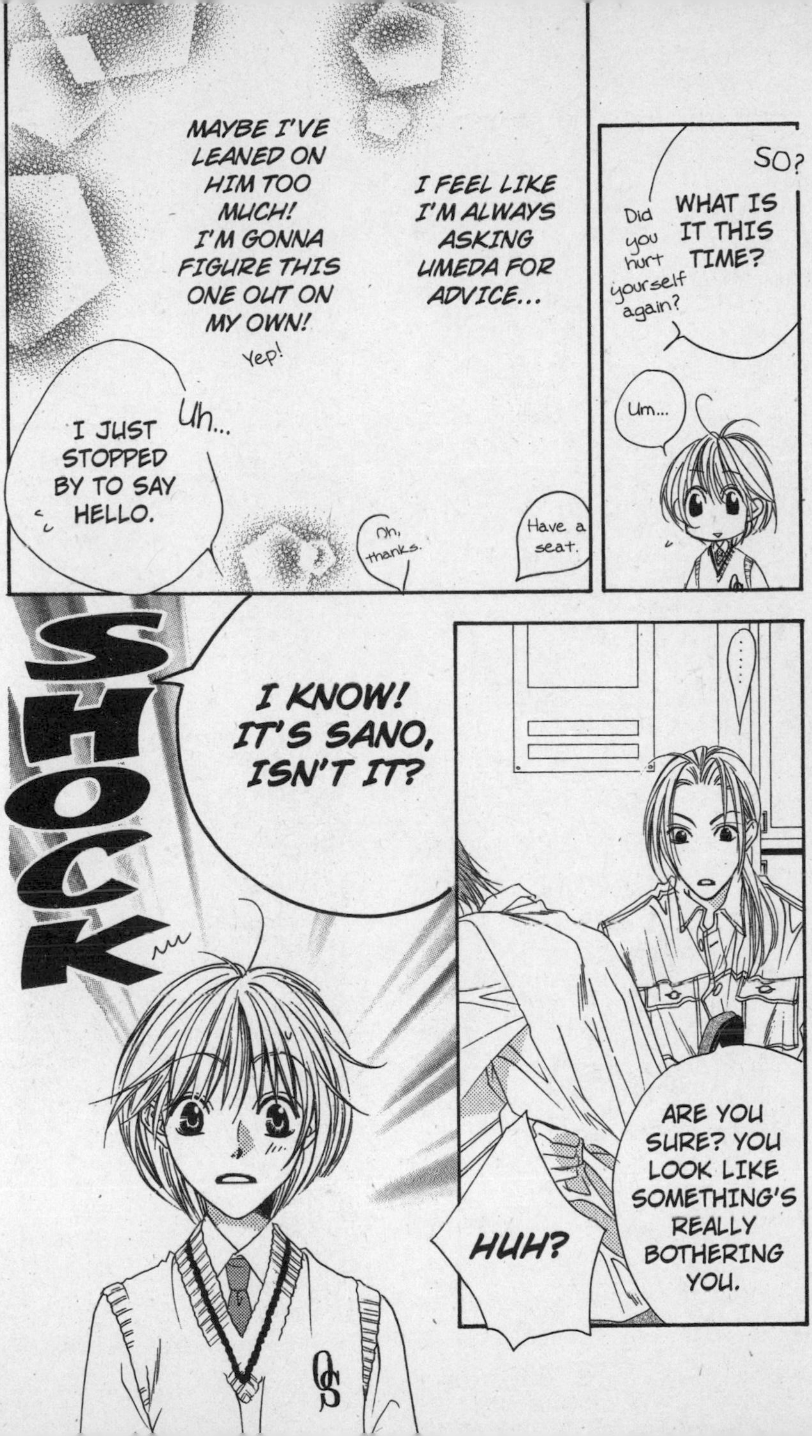
SO? WHAT IS IT THIS TIME?
Did you hurt yourself again?
Um...
I FEEL LIKE I'M ALWAYS ASKING UMEDA FOR ADVICE...
Have a seat.
Oh, thanks.
MAYBE I'VE LEANED ON HIM TOO MUCH! I'M GONNA FIGURE THIS ONE OUT ON MY OWN!
Yep!
Uh...
I JUST STOPPED BY TO SAY HELLO.
......
ARE YOU SURE? YOU LOOK LIKE SOMETHING'S REALLY BOTHERING YOU.
HUH?
I KNOW! IT'S SANO, ISN'T IT?
SHOCK

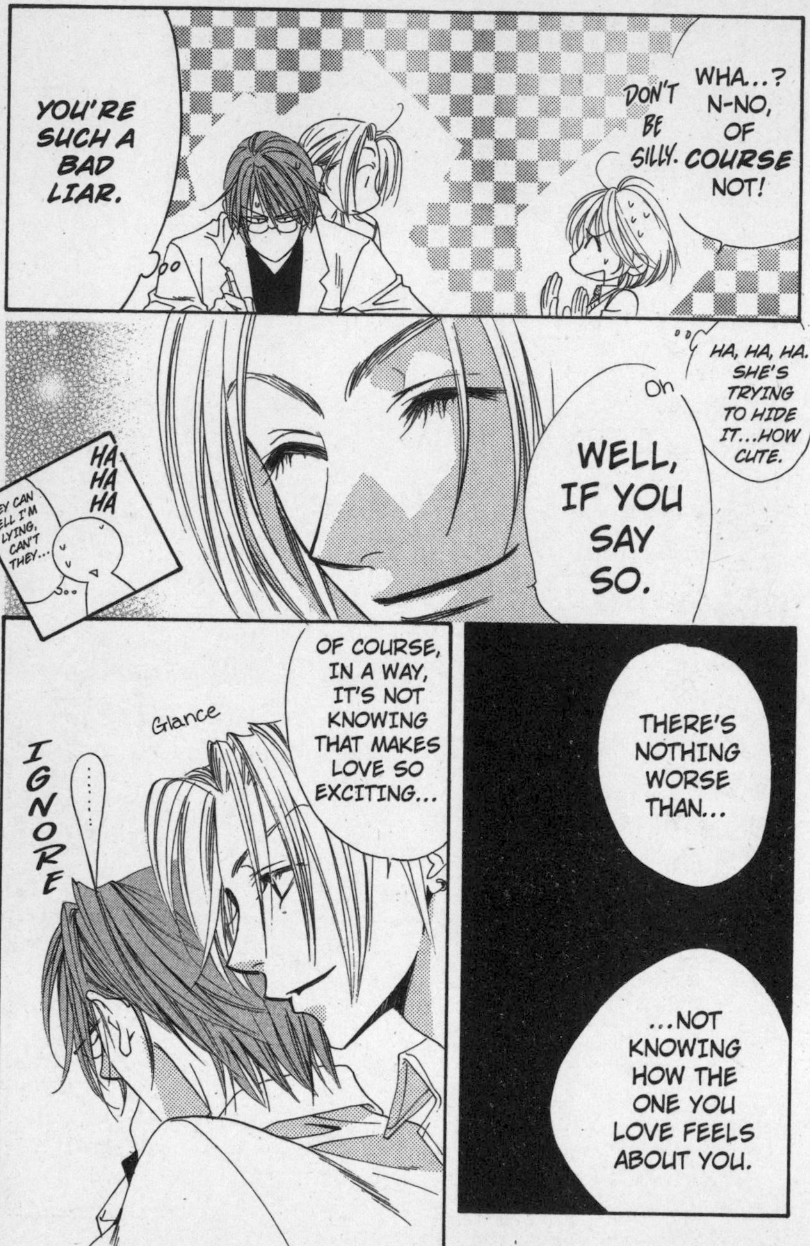
WHA...? N-NO, OF COURSE NOT!
DON'T BE SILLY.
YOU'RE SUCH A BAD LIAR.
HA, HA, HA. SHE'S TRYING TO HIDE IT...HOW CUTE.
Oh
WELL, IF YOU SAY SO.
HA HA HA
THEY CAN TELL I'M LYING, CAN'T THEY...
THERE'S NOTHING WORSE THAN...
...NOT KNOWING HOW THE ONE YOU LOVE FEELS ABOUT YOU.
OF COURSE, IN A WAY, IT'S NOT KNOWING THAT MAKES LOVE SO EXCITING...
Glance
IGNORE
......

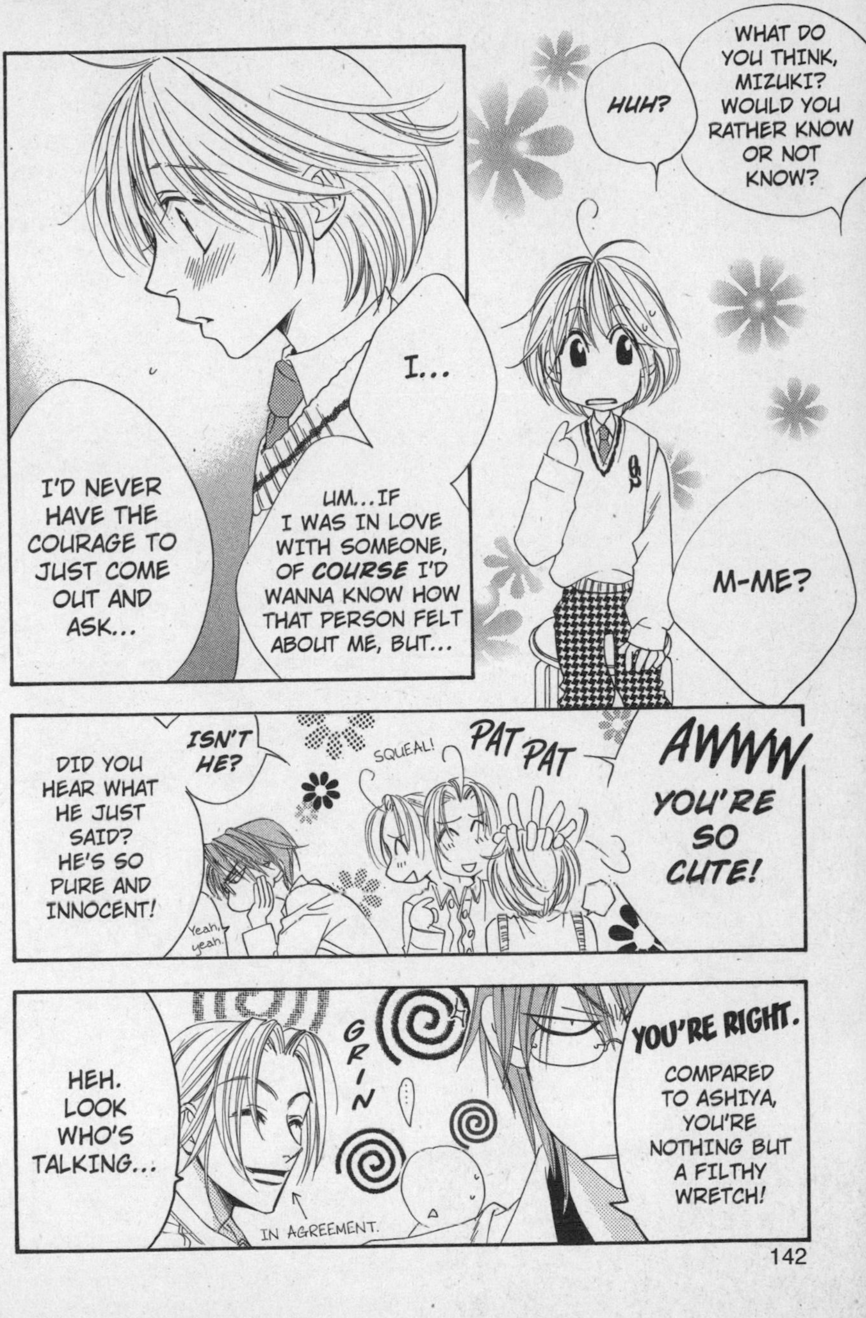
WHAT DO YOU THINK, MIZUKI? WOULD YOU RATHER KNOW OR NOT KNOW?
HUH?
M-ME?
I...
UM...IF I WAS IN LOVE WITH SOMEONE, OF COURSE I'D WANNA KNOW HOW THAT PERSON FELT ABOUT ME, BUT...
I'D NEVER HAVE THE COURAGE TO JUST COME OUT AND ASK...
AWWW
YOU'RE SO CUTE!
PAT PAT
SQUEAL!
DID YOU HEAR WHAT HE JUST SAID? HE'S SO PURE AND INNOCENT!
ISN'T HE?
Yeah, yeah.
YOU'RE RIGHT.
COMPARED TO ASHIYA, YOU'RE NOTHING BUT A FILTHY WRETCH!
GRIN
...
IN AGREEMENT.
HEH. LOOK WHO'S TALKING...

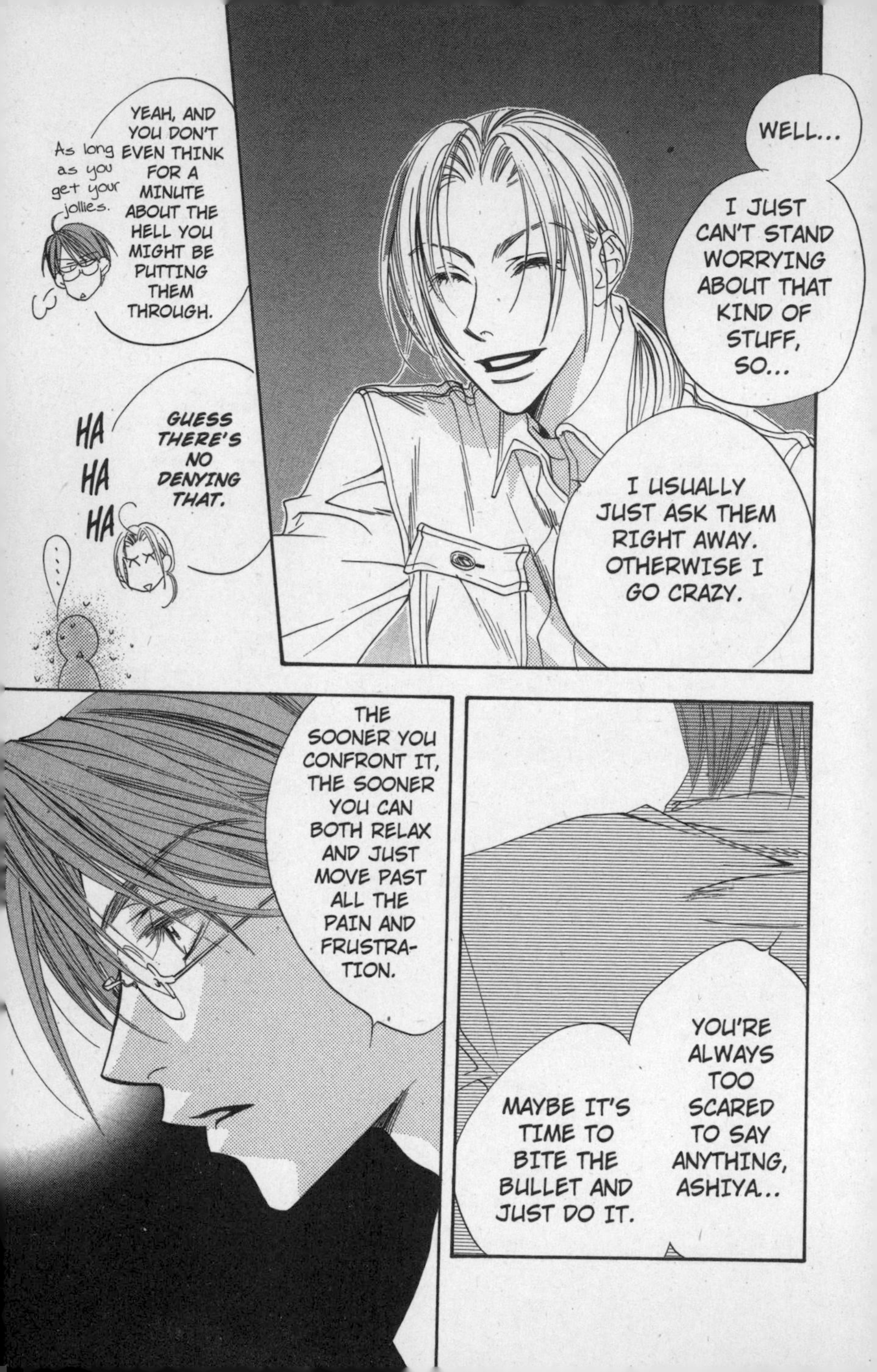
WELL...
I JUST CAN'T STAND WORRYING ABOUT THAT KIND OF STUFF, SO...
I USUALLY JUST ASK THEM RIGHT AWAY. OTHERWISE I GO CRAZY.
YEAH, AND YOU DON'T EVEN THINK FOR A MINUTE ABOUT THE HELL YOU MIGHT BE PUTTING THEM THROUGH.
As long as you get your jollies.
HA HA HA
GUESS THERE'S NO DENYING THAT.
YOU'RE ALWAYS TOO SCARED TO SAY ANYTHING, ASHIYA...
MAYBE IT'S TIME TO BITE THE BULLET AND JUST DO IT.
THE SOONER YOU CONFRONT IT, THE SOONER YOU CAN BOTH RELAX AND JUST MOVE PAST ALL THE PAIN AND FRUSTRA-TION.

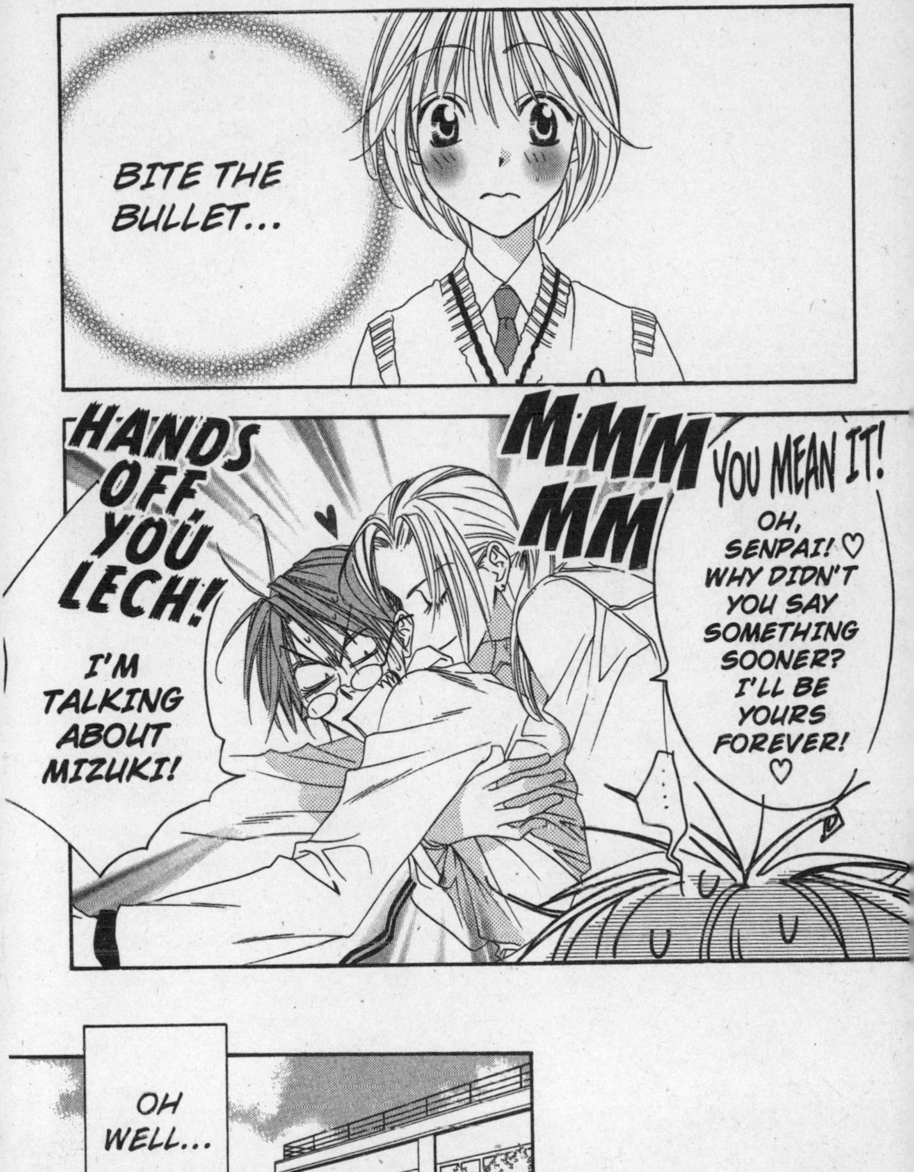
BITE THE BULLET...
YOU MEAN IT!
OH, SENPAI! ♡ WHY DIDN'T YOU SAY SOMETHING SOONER? I'LL BE YOURS FOREVER! ♡
MMM MM
HANDS OFF, YOU LECH!
I'M TALKING ABOUT MIZUKI!
OH WELL...

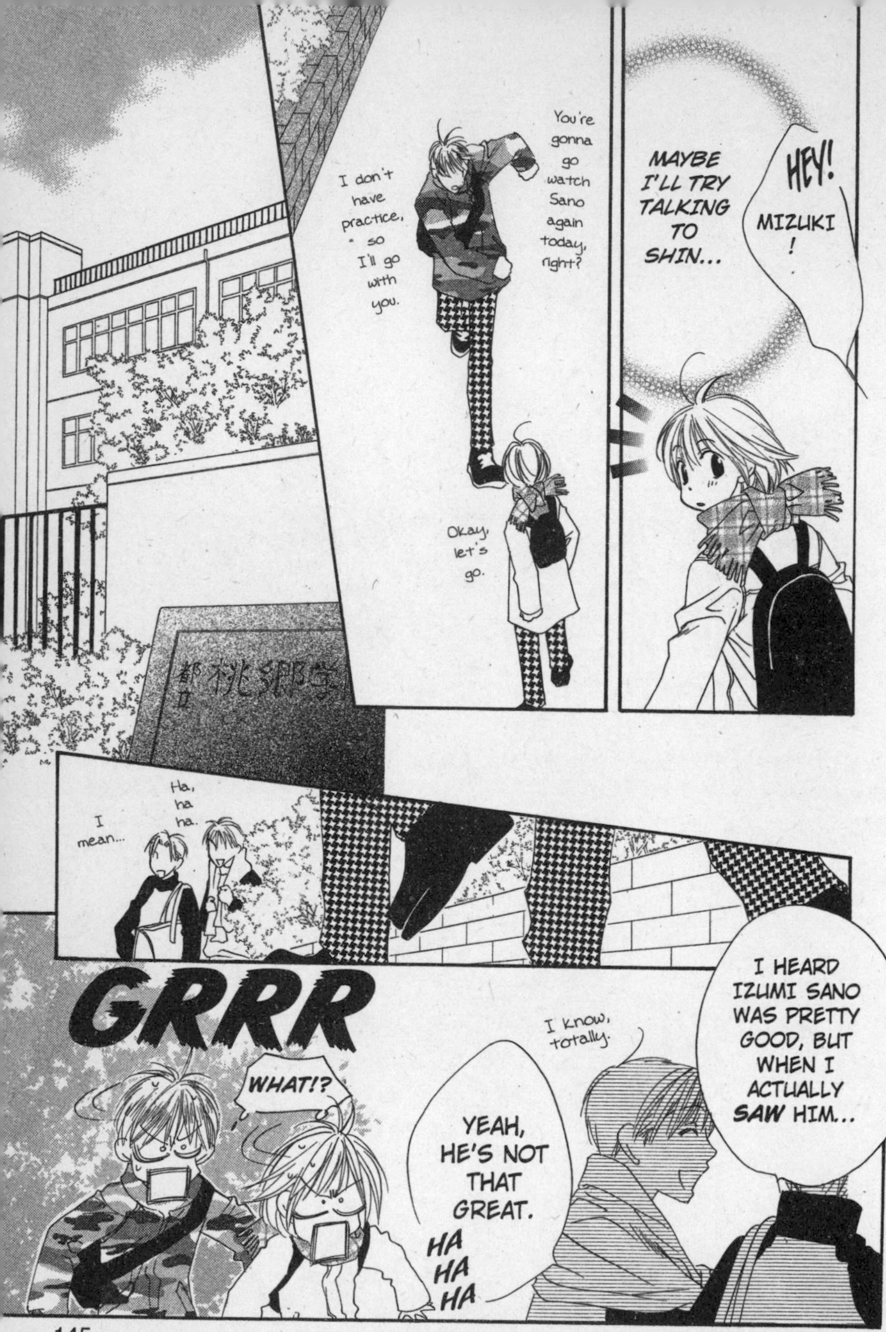
HEY!
MIZUKI!
MAYBE I'LL TRY TALKING TO SHIN...
You're gonna go watch Sano again today, right?
I don't have practice, so I'll go with you.
Okay, let's go.
Ha, ha ha.
I mean...
I HEARD IZUMI SANO WAS PRETTY GOOD, BUT WHEN I ACTUALLY SAW HIM...
I know, totally.
YEAH, HE'S NOT THAT GREAT.
HA HA HA
WHAT!?
GRRR

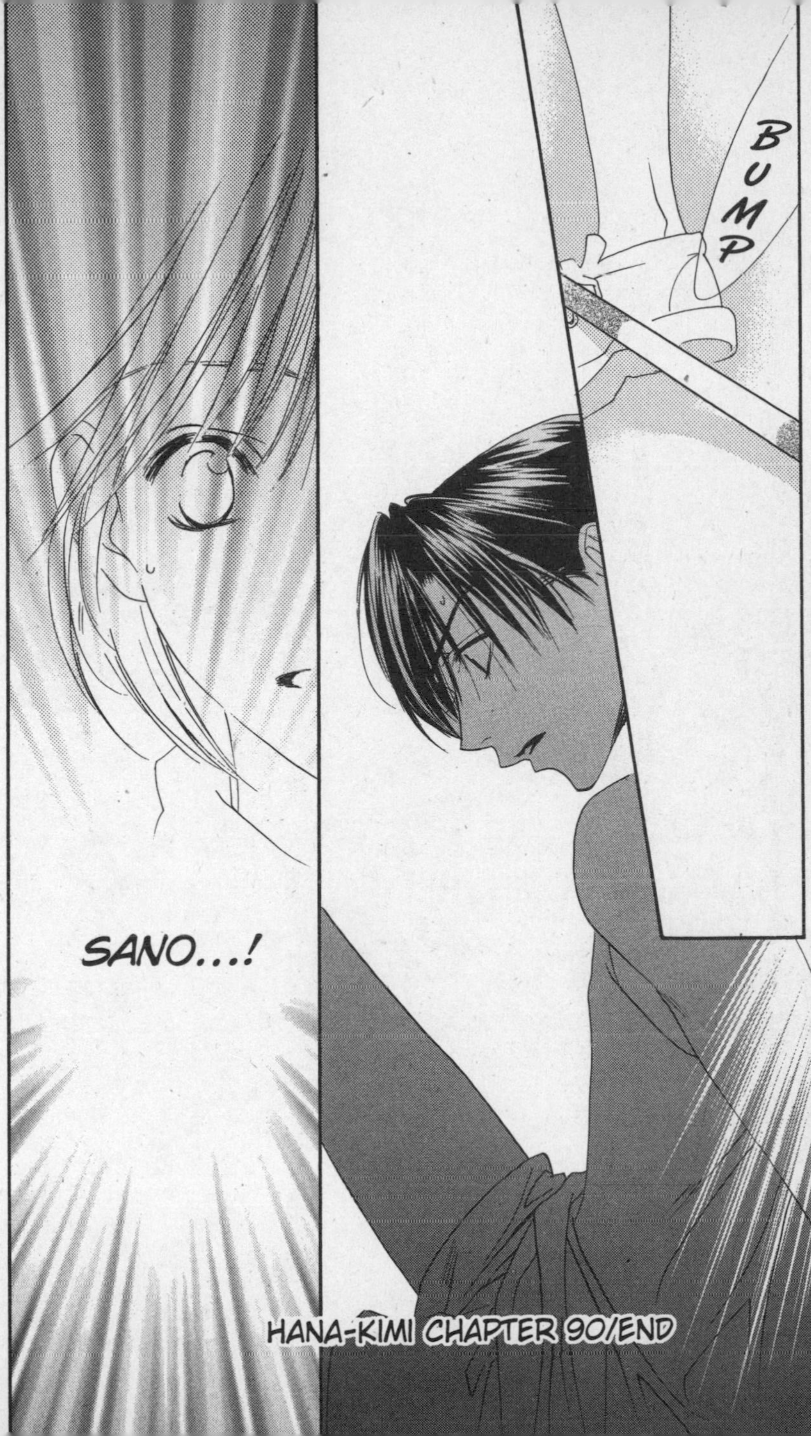
BUMP
SANO...!
HANA-KIMI CHAPTER 90/END

Hana-Kimi

For You in Full Blossom

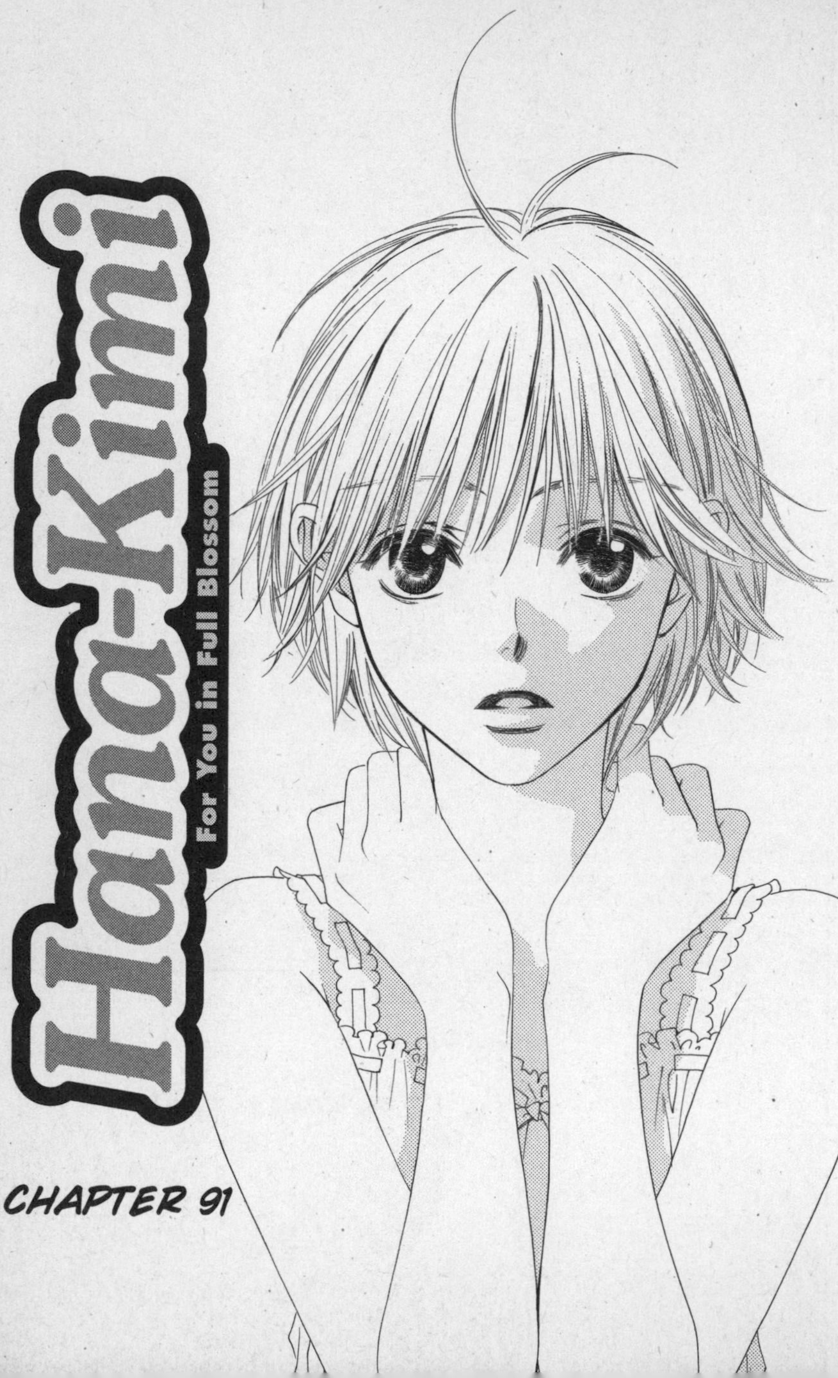

CHAPTER 91

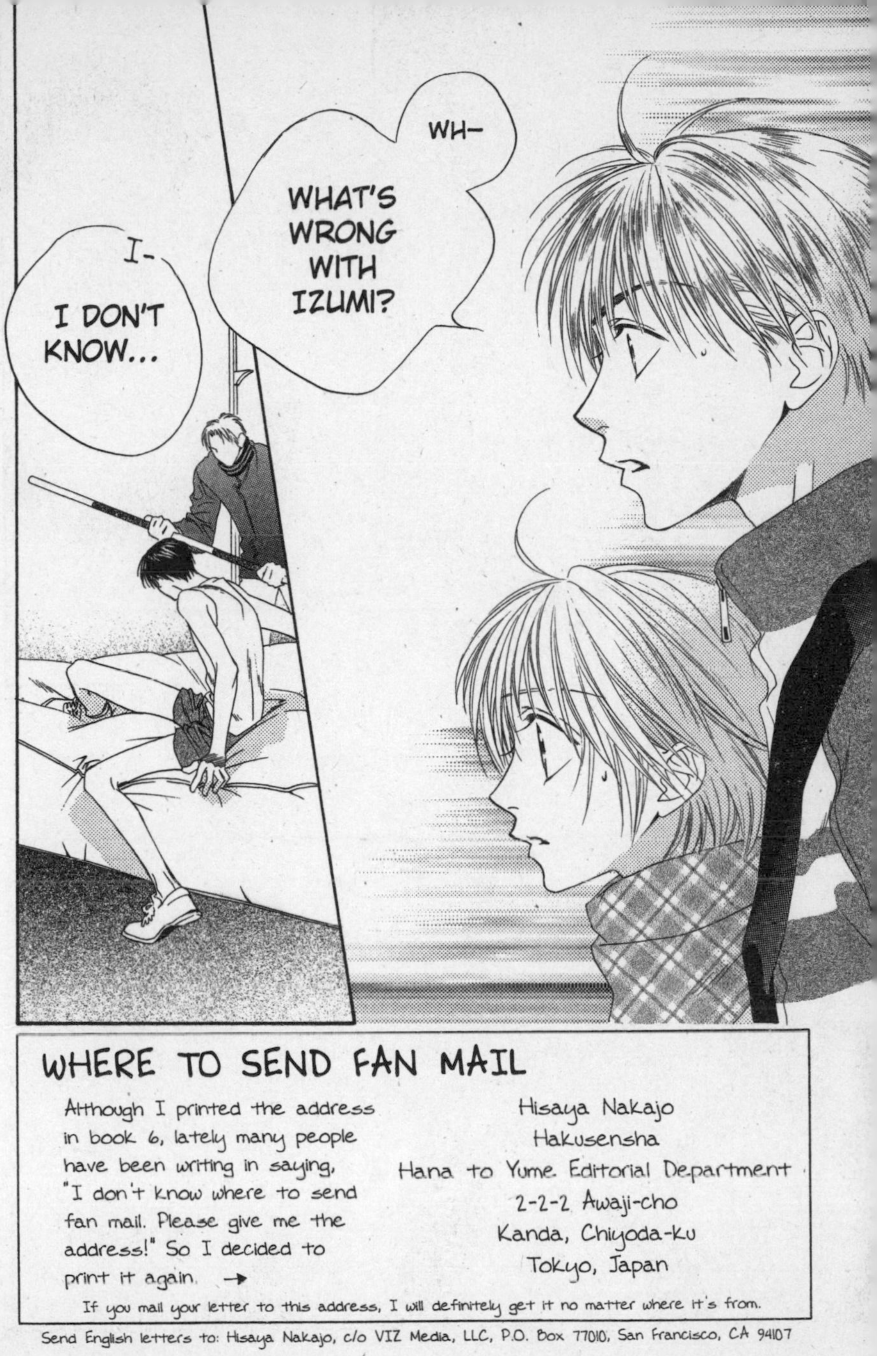
WH-
WHAT'S WRONG WITH IZUMI?
I-
I DON'T KNOW...

WHERE TO SEND FAN MAIL

Although I printed the address in book 6, lately many people have been writing in saying, "I don't know where to send fan mail. Please give me the address!" So I decided to print it again. →

Hisaya Nakajo
Hakusensha
Hana to Yume Editorial Department
2-2-2 Awaji-cho
Kanda, Chiyoda-ku
Tokyo, Japan

If you mail your letter to this address, I will definitely get it no matter where it's from.

Send English letters to: Hisaya Nakajo, c/o VIZ Media, LLC, P.O. Box 77010, San Francisco, CA 94107

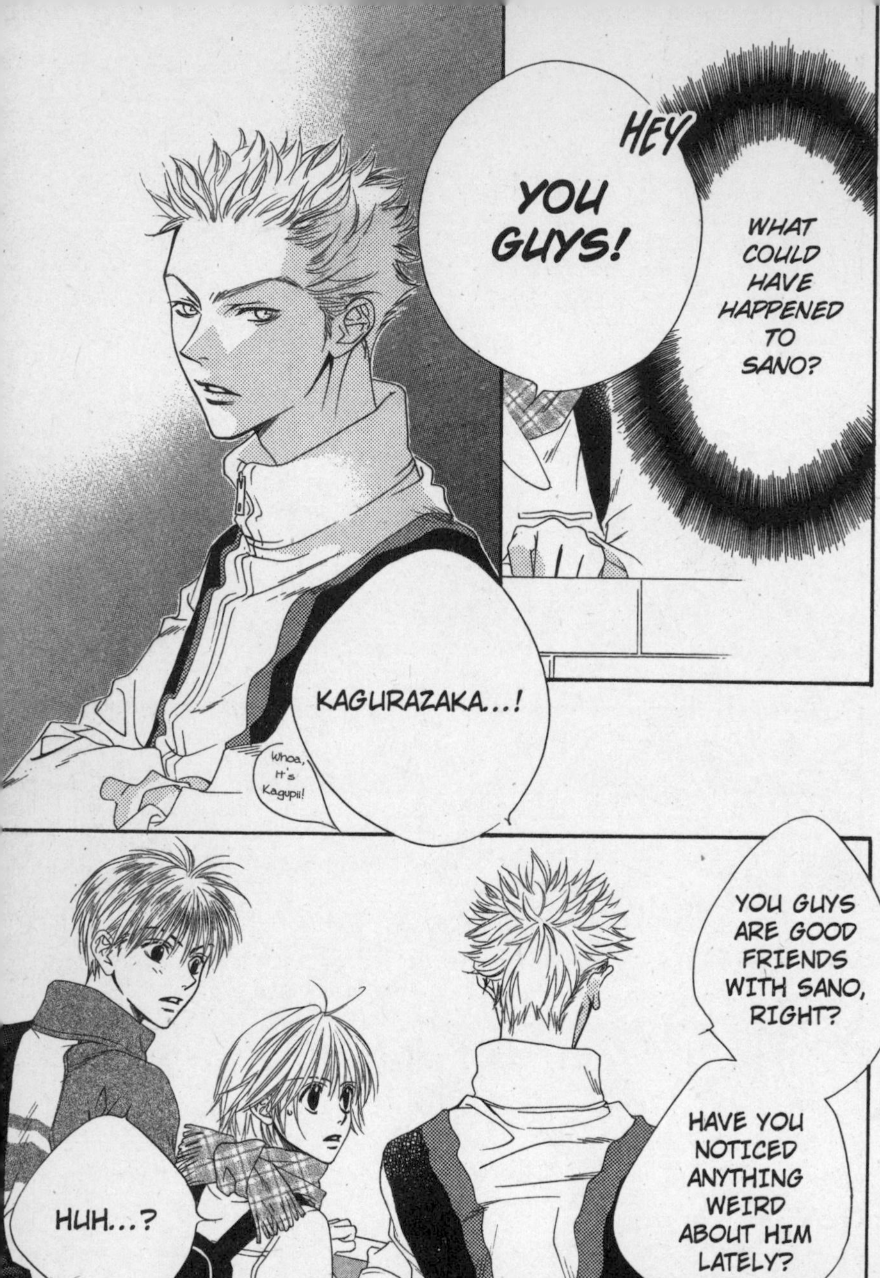
WHAT COULD HAVE HAPPENED TO SANO?
HEY YOU GUYS!
KAGURAZAKA...!
Whoa, it's Kagupii!
YOU GUYS ARE GOOD FRIENDS WITH SANO, RIGHT?
HAVE YOU NOTICED ANYTHING WEIRD ABOUT HIM LATELY?
HUH...?

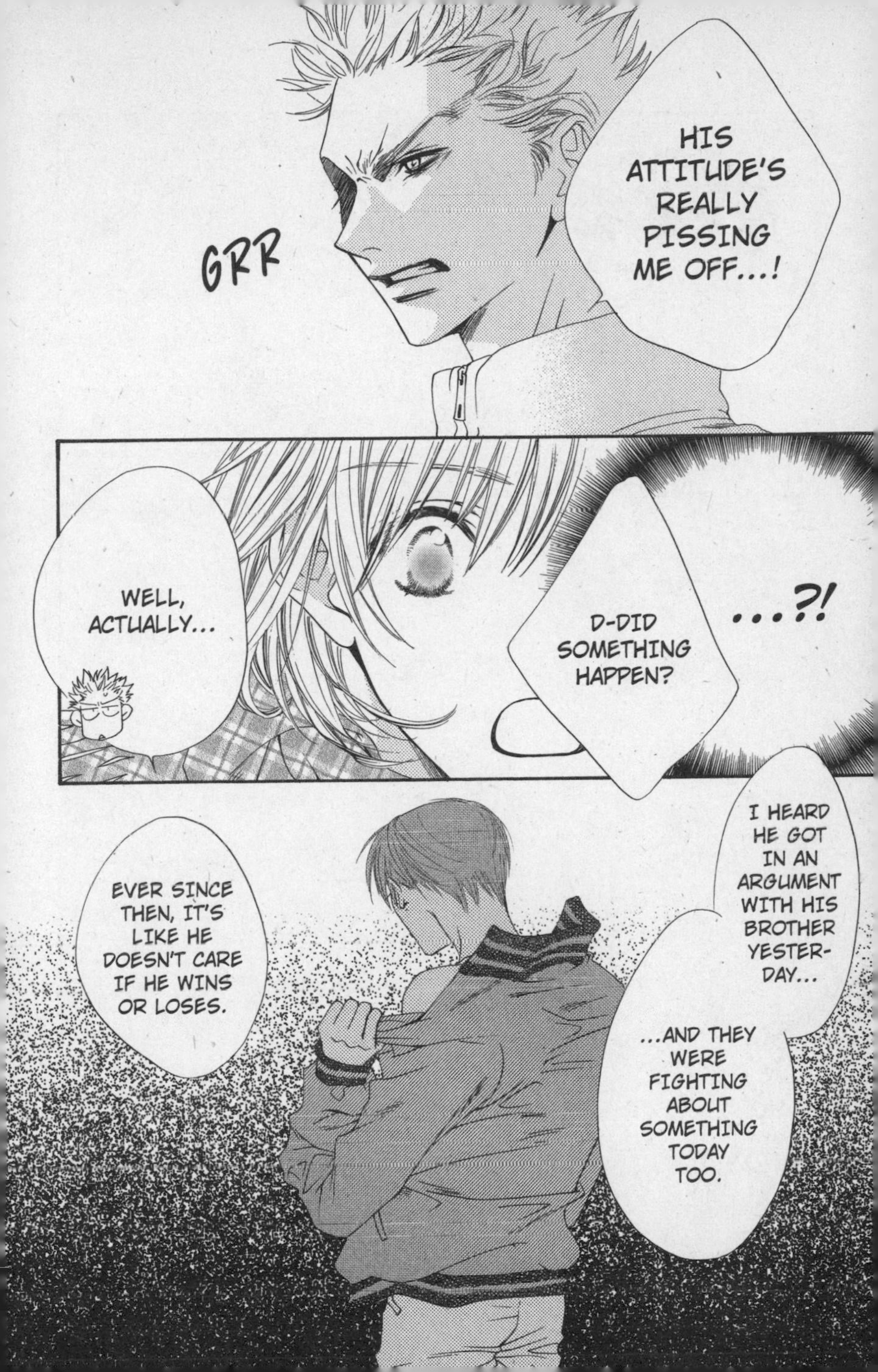
HIS ATTITUDE'S REALLY PISSING ME OFF...!
GRR
...?!
D-DID SOMETHING HAPPEN?
WELL, ACTUALLY...
I HEARD HE GOT IN AN ARGUMENT WITH HIS BROTHER YESTER-DAY...
...AND THEY WERE FIGHTING ABOUT SOMETHING TODAY TOO.
EVER SINCE THEN, IT'S LIKE HE DOESN'T CARE IF HE WINS OR LOSES.

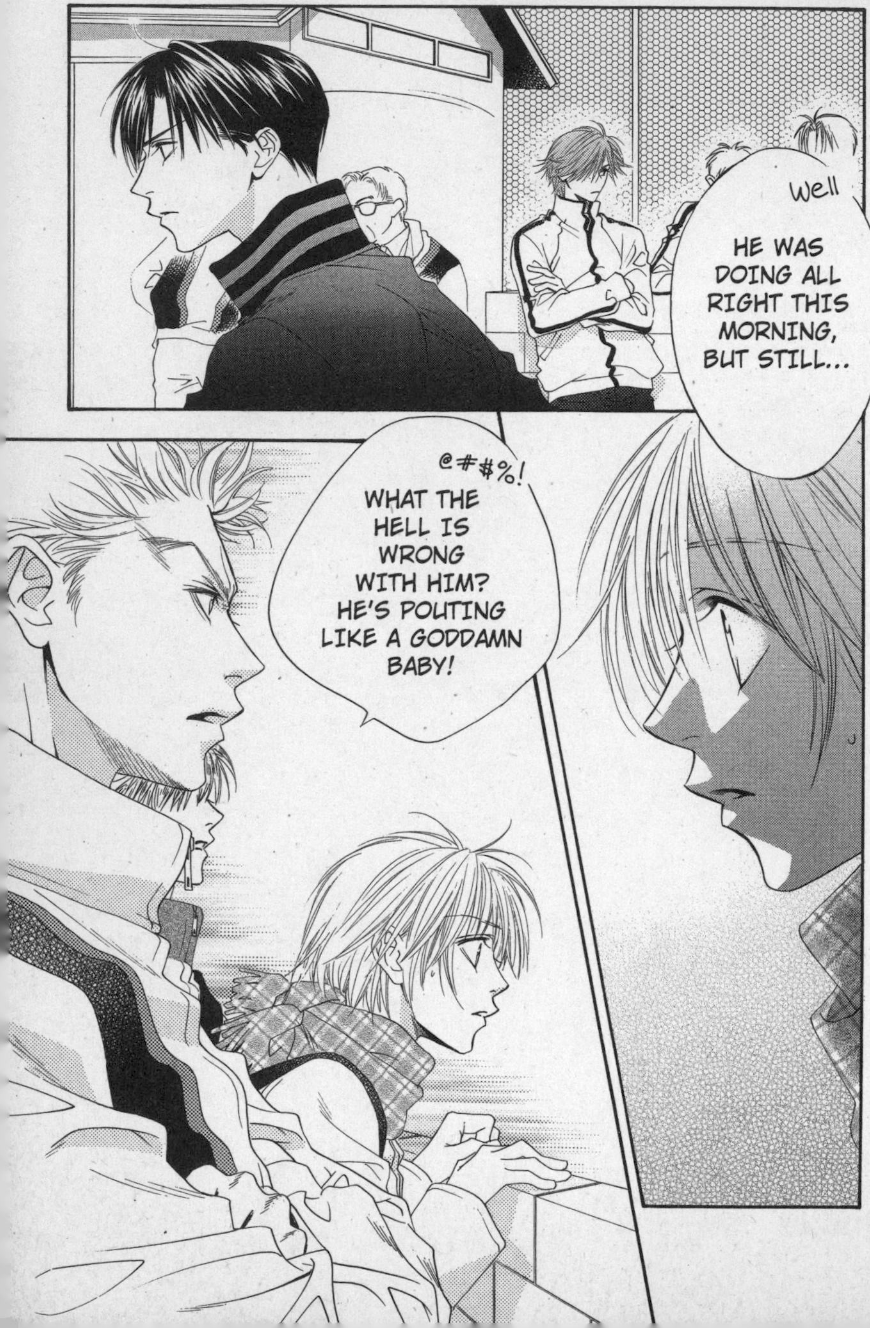
Well
HE WAS DOING ALL RIGHT THIS MORNING, BUT STILL...
@#$%!
WHAT THE HELL IS WRONG WITH HIM? HE'S POUTING LIKE A GODDAMN BABY!

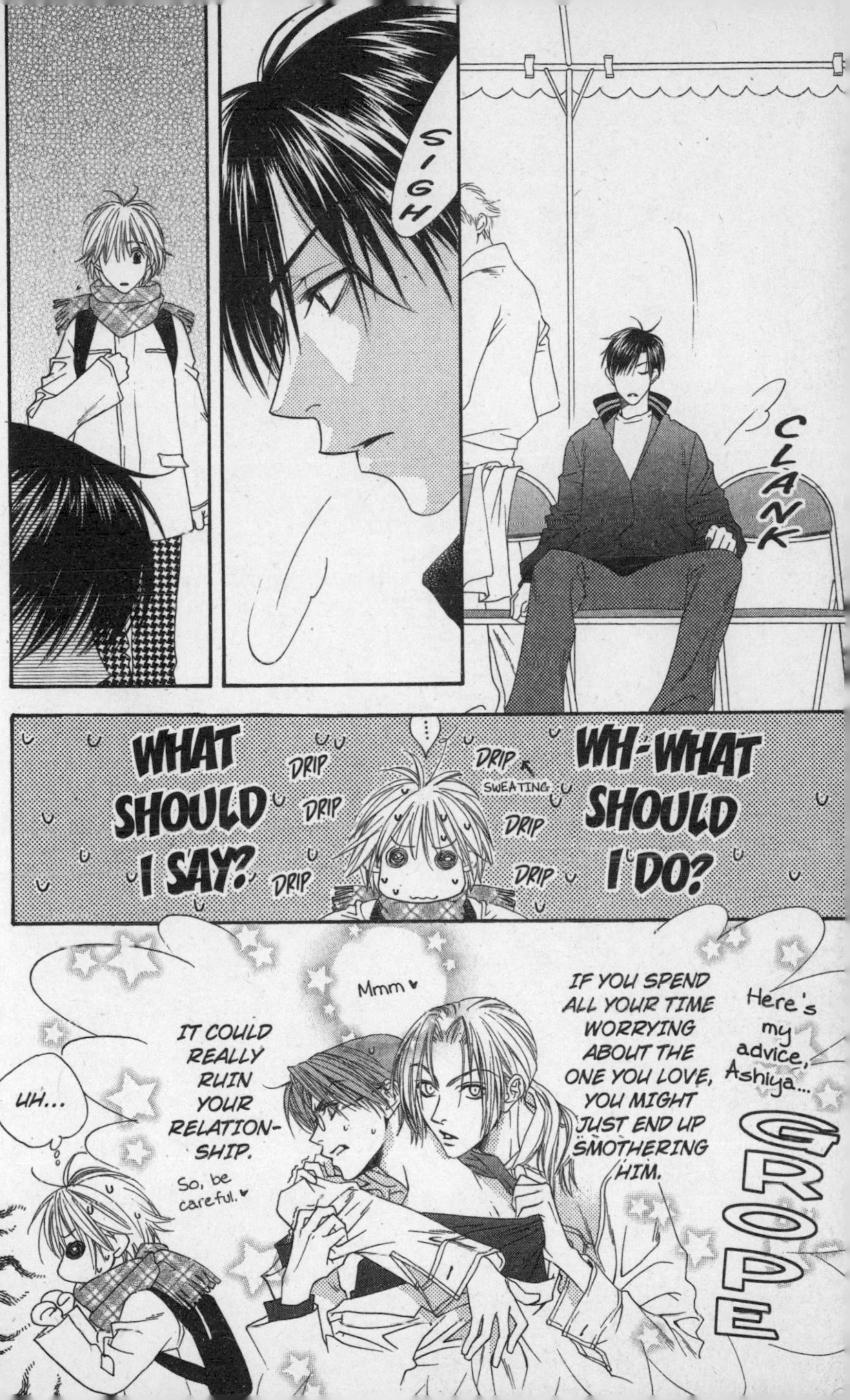
CLANK
SIGH
WH-WHAT SHOULD I DO?
DRIP
SWEATING
DRIP
DRIP
DRIP
DRIP
DRIP
WHAT SHOULD I SAY?
Here's my advice, Ashiya...
GROPE
IF YOU SPEND ALL YOUR TIME WORRYING ABOUT THE ONE YOU LOVE, YOU MIGHT JUST END UP SMOTHERING HIM.
Mmm
IT COULD REALLY RUIN YOUR RELATION-SHIP.
So, be careful.
UH...

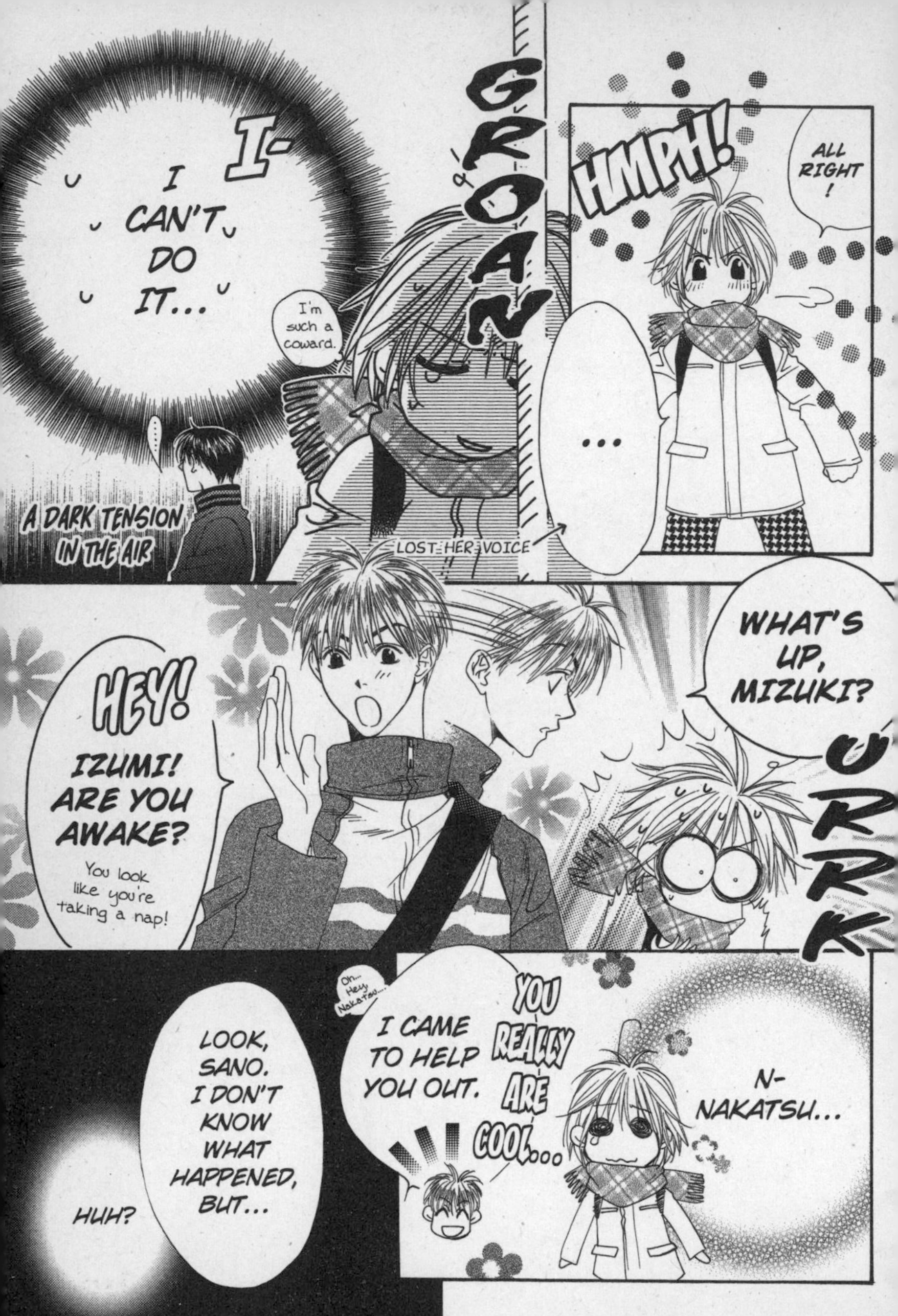
HMPH!
ALL RIGHT!
...
LOST HER VOICE
I-
I CAN'T DO IT...
GROAN
I'm such a coward.
A DARK TENSION IN THE AIR
WHAT'S UP, MIZUKI?
URRK
HEY!
IZUMI! ARE YOU AWAKE?
You look like you're taking a nap!
N-NAKATSU...
YOU REALLY ARE COOL...
I CAME TO HELP YOU OUT.
Oh... Hey Nakatsu...
LOOK, SANO. I DON'T KNOW WHAT HAPPENED, BUT...
HUH?

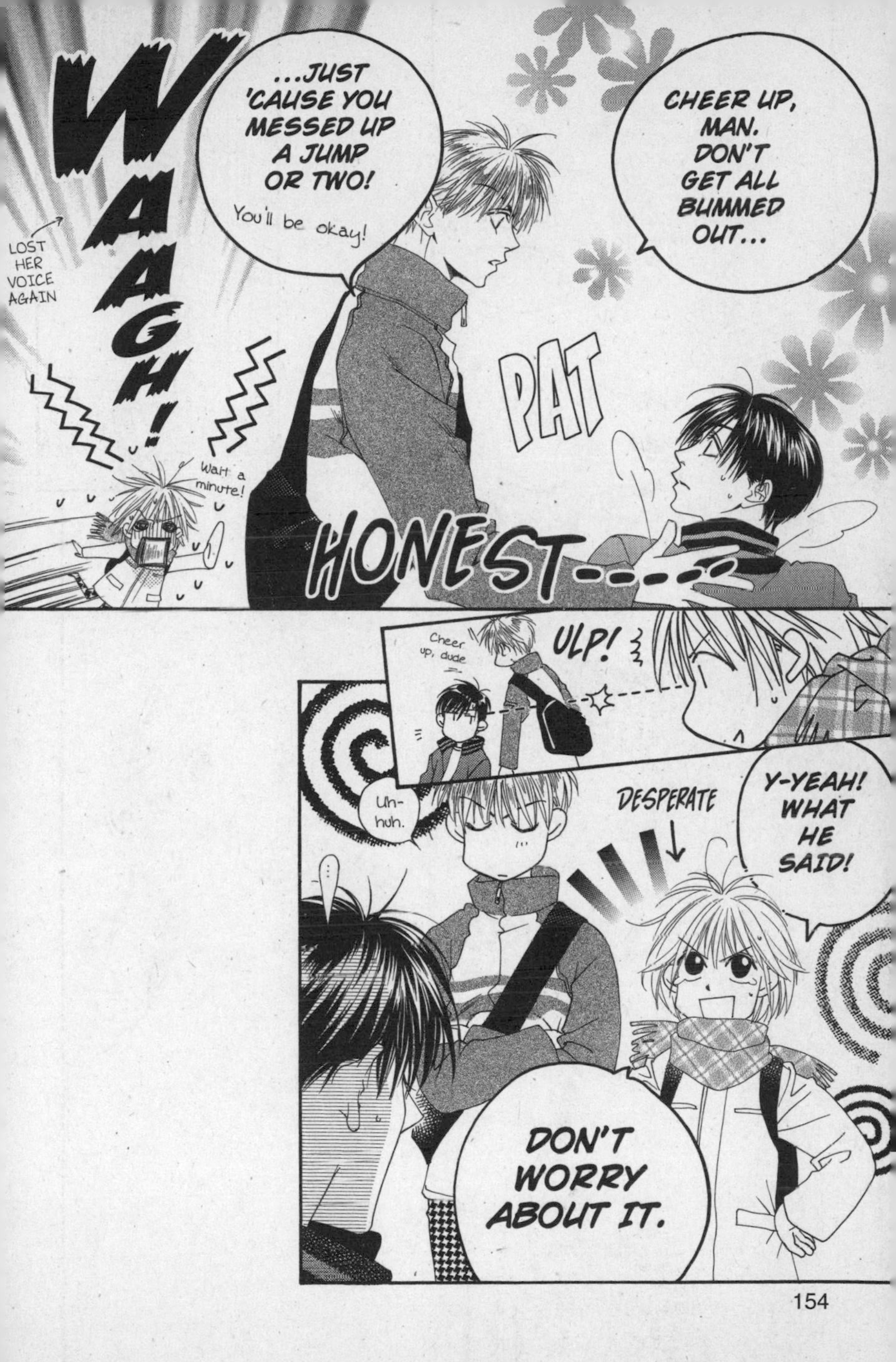
CHEER UP, MAN. DON'T GET ALL BUMMED OUT...
...JUST 'CAUSE YOU MESSED UP A JUMP OR TWO!
You'll be okay!
PAT
HONEST-----
WAAGH!
LOST HER VOICE AGAIN
Wait a minute!
ULP!
Cheer up, dude
Y-YEAH! WHAT HE SAID!
DESPERATE
Uh-huh.
...
DON'T WORRY ABOUT IT.

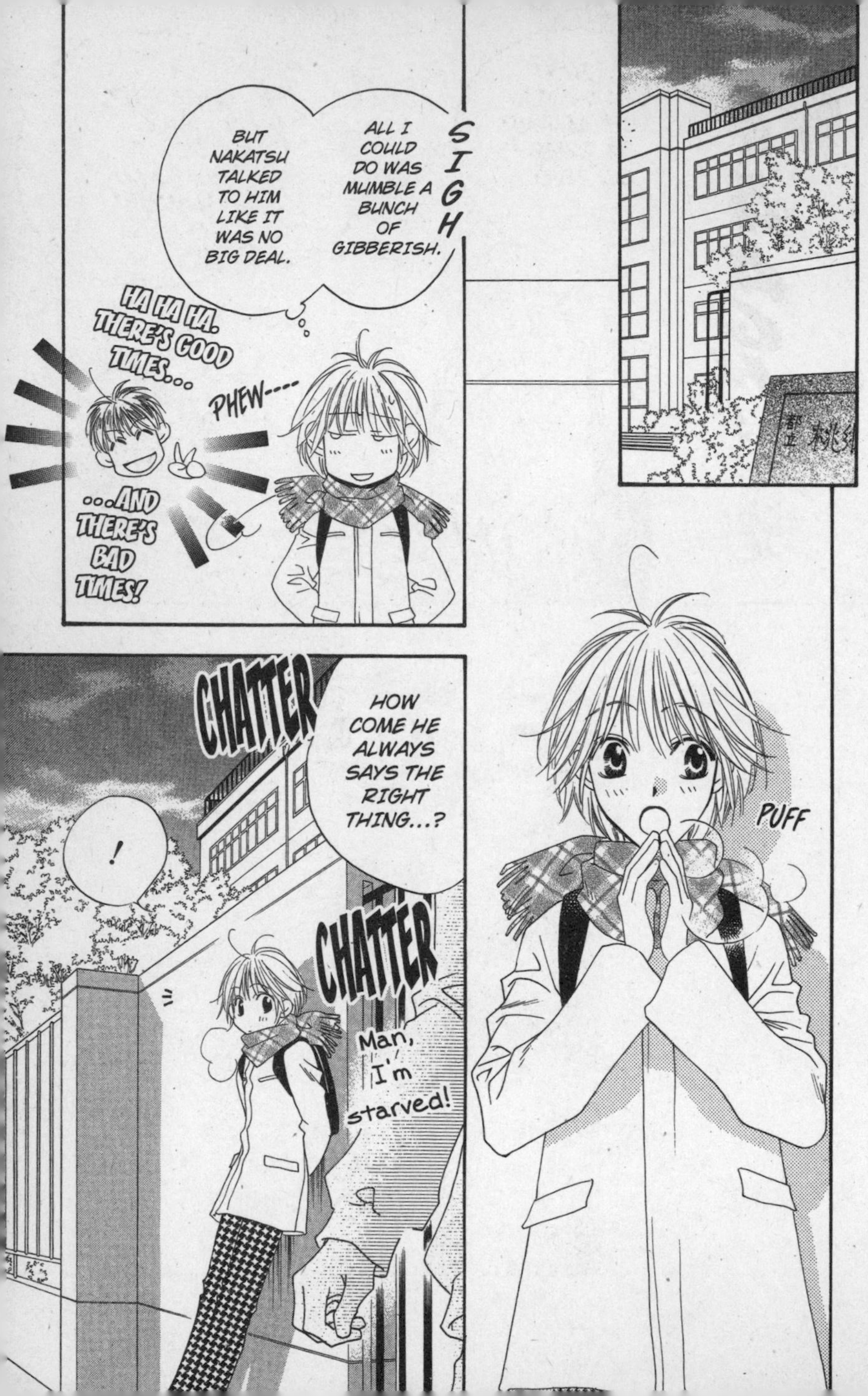

都立
SIGH
ALL I COULD DO WAS MUMBLE A BUNCH OF GIBBERISH.
BUT NAKATSU TALKED TO HIM LIKE IT WAS NO BIG DEAL.
HA HA HA. THERE'S GOOD TIMES...
PHEW----
...AND THERE'S BAD TIMES!
PUFF
HOW COME HE ALWAYS SAYS THE RIGHT THING...?
CHATTER
!
CHATTER
Man, I'm starved!

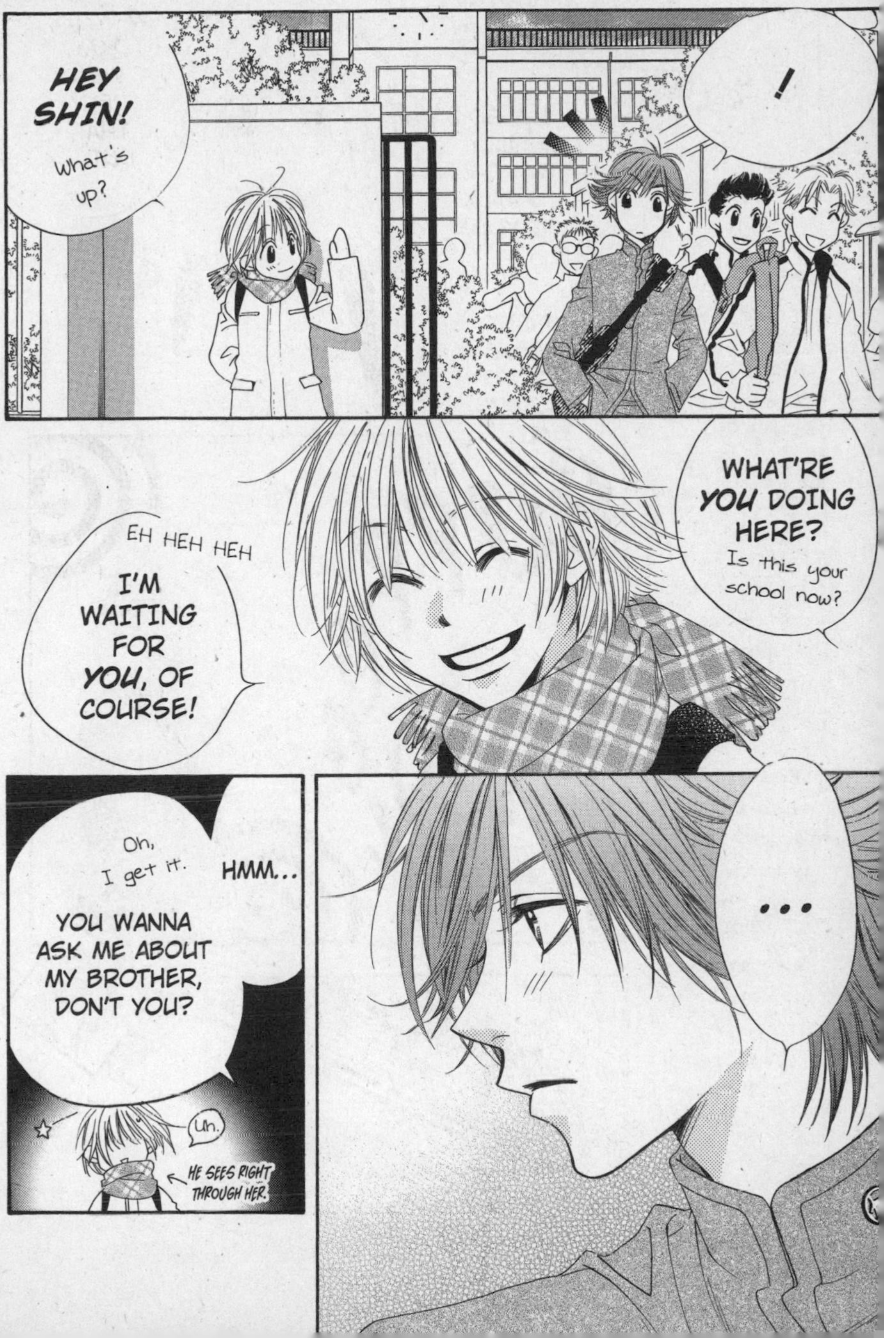
!
HEY SHIN! What's up?
WHAT'RE YOU DOING HERE? Is this your school now?
EH HEH HEH
I'M WAITING FOR YOU, OF COURSE!
...
HMM...
Oh, I get it.
YOU WANNA ASK ME ABOUT MY BROTHER, DON'T YOU?
Uh.
HE SEES RIGHT THROUGH HER.

PEEP PEEP

「See you」

So, did you guys enjoy the character profiles? (I didn't have enough time to draw the image flowers) If there are any other characters whose profiles you'd like to see, please let me know. Maybe I'll do them next time. (Next time?) See you in book 17!

Bye bye!

-- Hisayo Nakajo

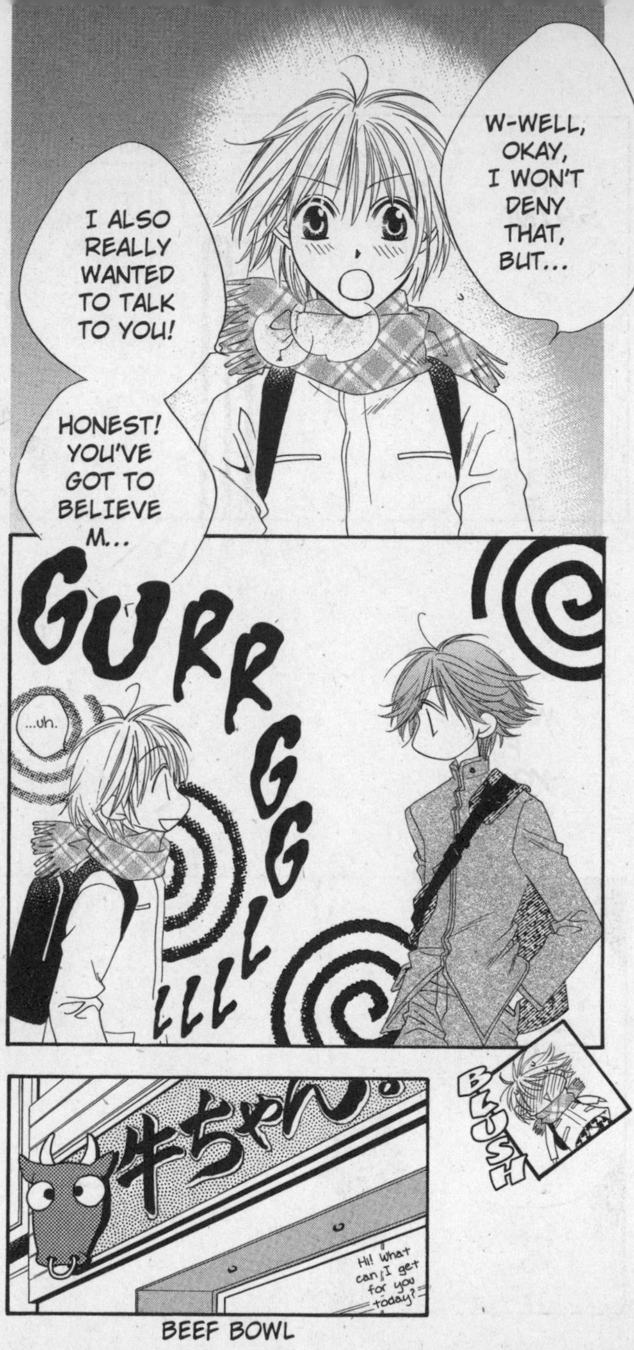

W-WELL, OKAY, I WON'T DENY THAT, BUT...
I ALSO REALLY WANTED TO TALK TO YOU!
HONEST! YOU'VE GOT TO BELIEVE M...
GURRGGLLLL
...uh.
BLUSH
牛ちゃん
Hi! What can I get for you today?

BEEF BOWL

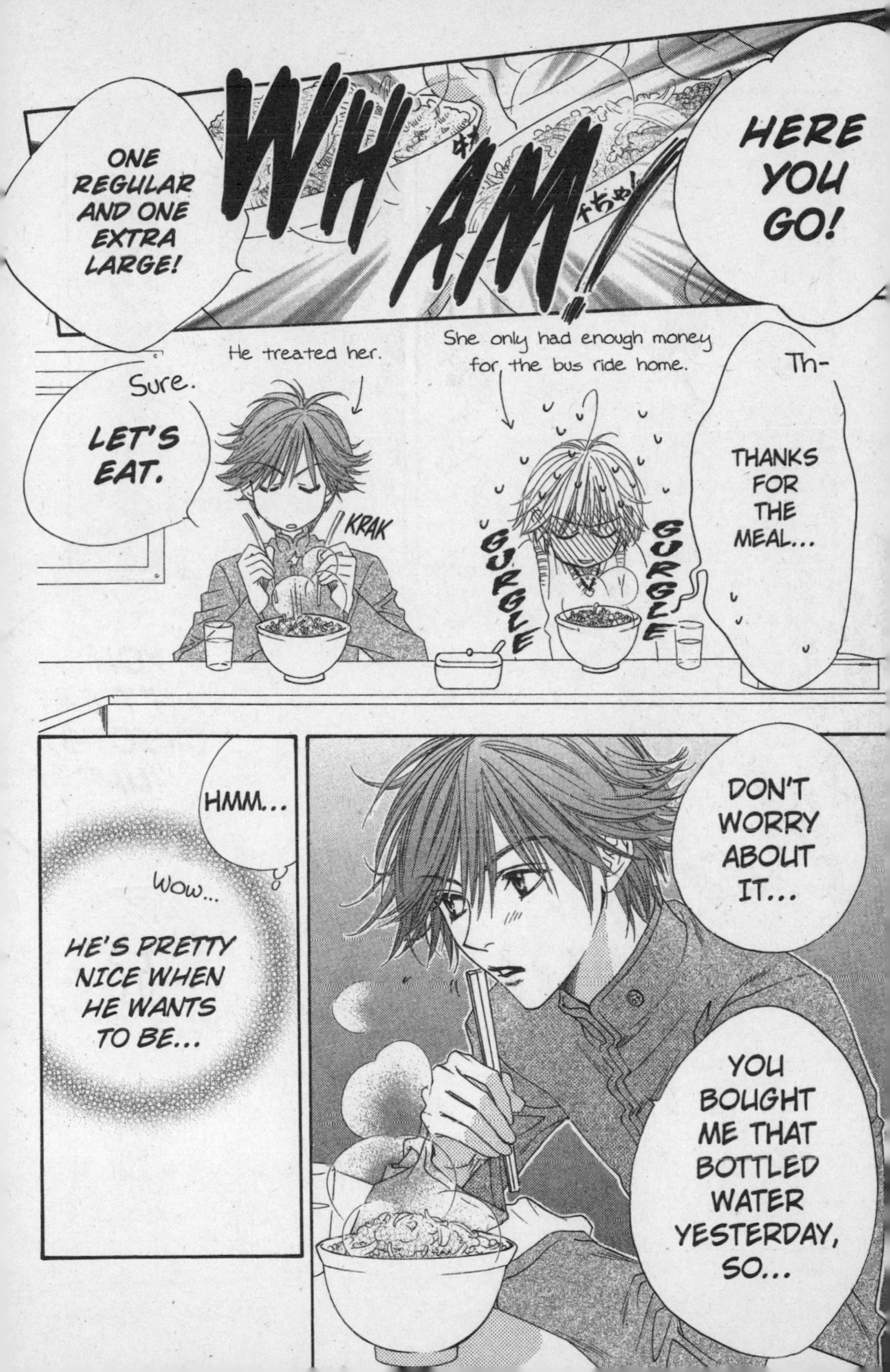
HERE YOU GO!
WHAM!
ONE REGULAR AND ONE EXTRA LARGE!
Th-
THANKS FOR THE MEAL...
She only had enough money for the bus ride home.
GURGLE
GURGLE
KRAK
He treated her.
Sure.
LET'S EAT.
DON'T WORRY ABOUT IT...
YOU BOUGHT ME THAT BOTTLED WATER YESTERDAY, SO...
HMM...
Wow...
HE'S PRETTY NICE WHEN HE WANTS TO BE...

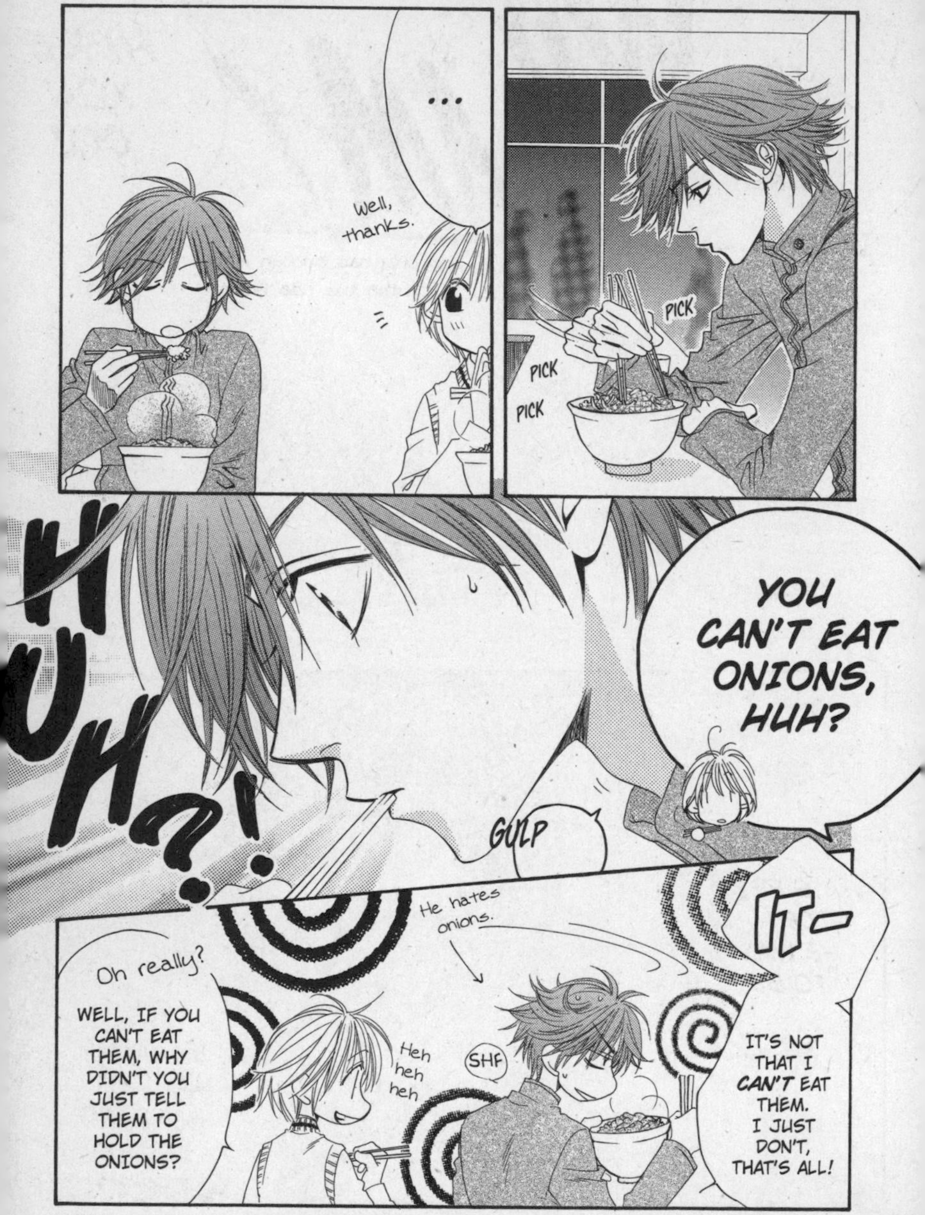
PICK
PICK
PICK
...
Well, thanks.
YOU CAN'T EAT ONIONS, HUH?
GULP
HUH?!
IT-
IT'S NOT THAT I CAN'T EAT THEM. I JUST DON'T, THAT'S ALL!
SHF
He hates onions.
Heh heh heh
Oh really?
WELL, IF YOU CAN'T EAT THEM, WHY DIDN'T YOU JUST TELL THEM TO HOLD THE ONIONS?

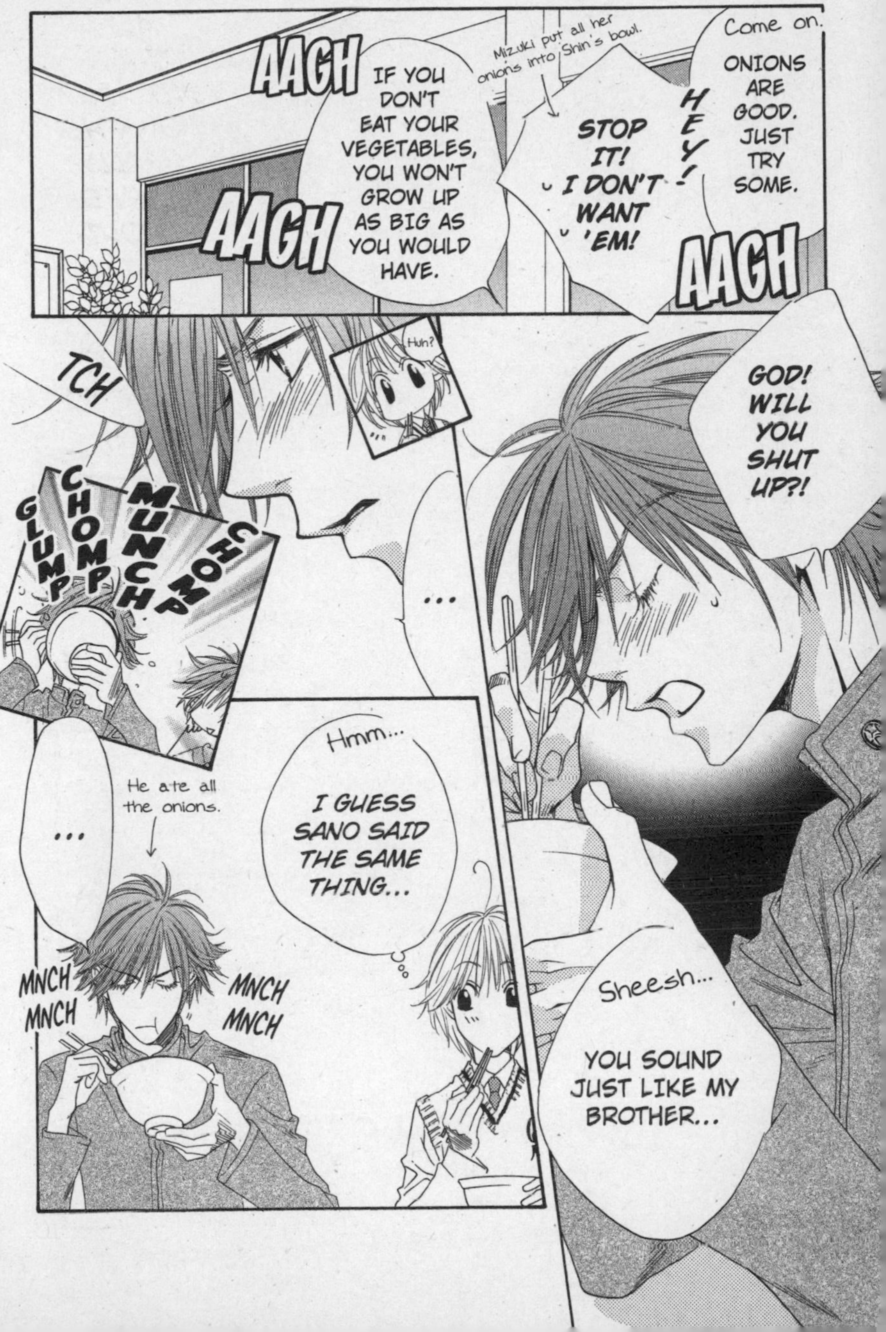

Come on.
ONIONS ARE GOOD. JUST TRY SOME.
HEY!
AAGH
STOP IT! I DON'T WANT 'EM!
Mizuki put all her onions into Shin's bowl.
IF YOU DON'T EAT YOUR VEGETABLES, YOU WON'T GROW UP AS BIG AS YOU WOULD HAVE.
AAGH
AAGH
GOD! WILL YOU SHUT UP?!
Sheesh...
YOU SOUND JUST LIKE MY BROTHER...
Huh?
TCH
...
CHOMP
MUNCH
CHOMP
GLUMP
Hmm...
I GUESS SANO SAID THE SAME THING...
MNCH MNCH
MNCH MNCH
He ate all the onions.
...

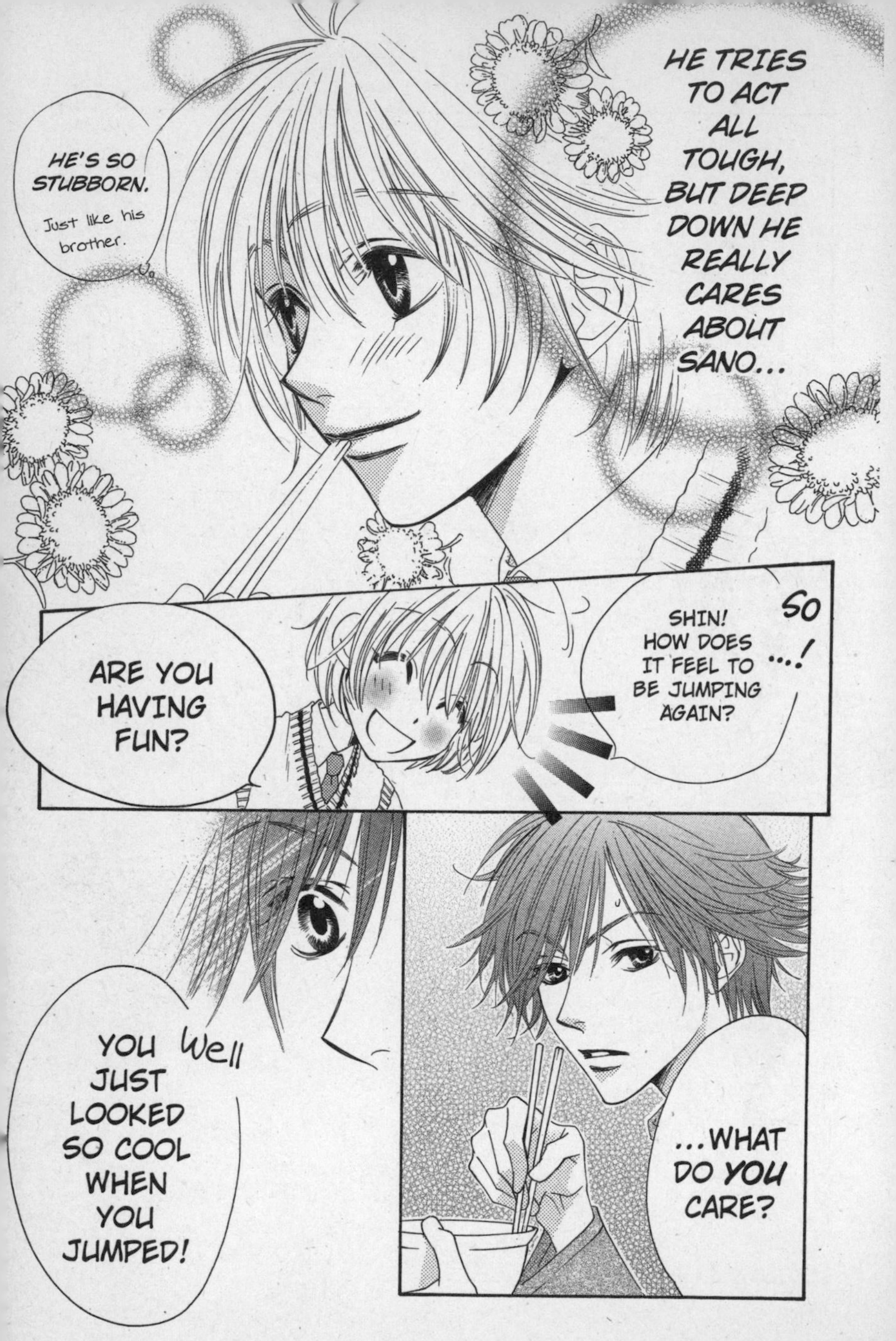
HE TRIES TO ACT ALL TOUGH, BUT DEEP DOWN HE REALLY CARES ABOUT SANO...
HE'S SO STUBBORN.
Just like his brother.
So...!
SHIN! HOW DOES IT FEEL TO BE JUMPING AGAIN?
ARE YOU HAVING FUN?
...WHAT DO *YOU* CARE?
Well
YOU JUST LOOKED SO COOL WHEN YOU JUMPED!

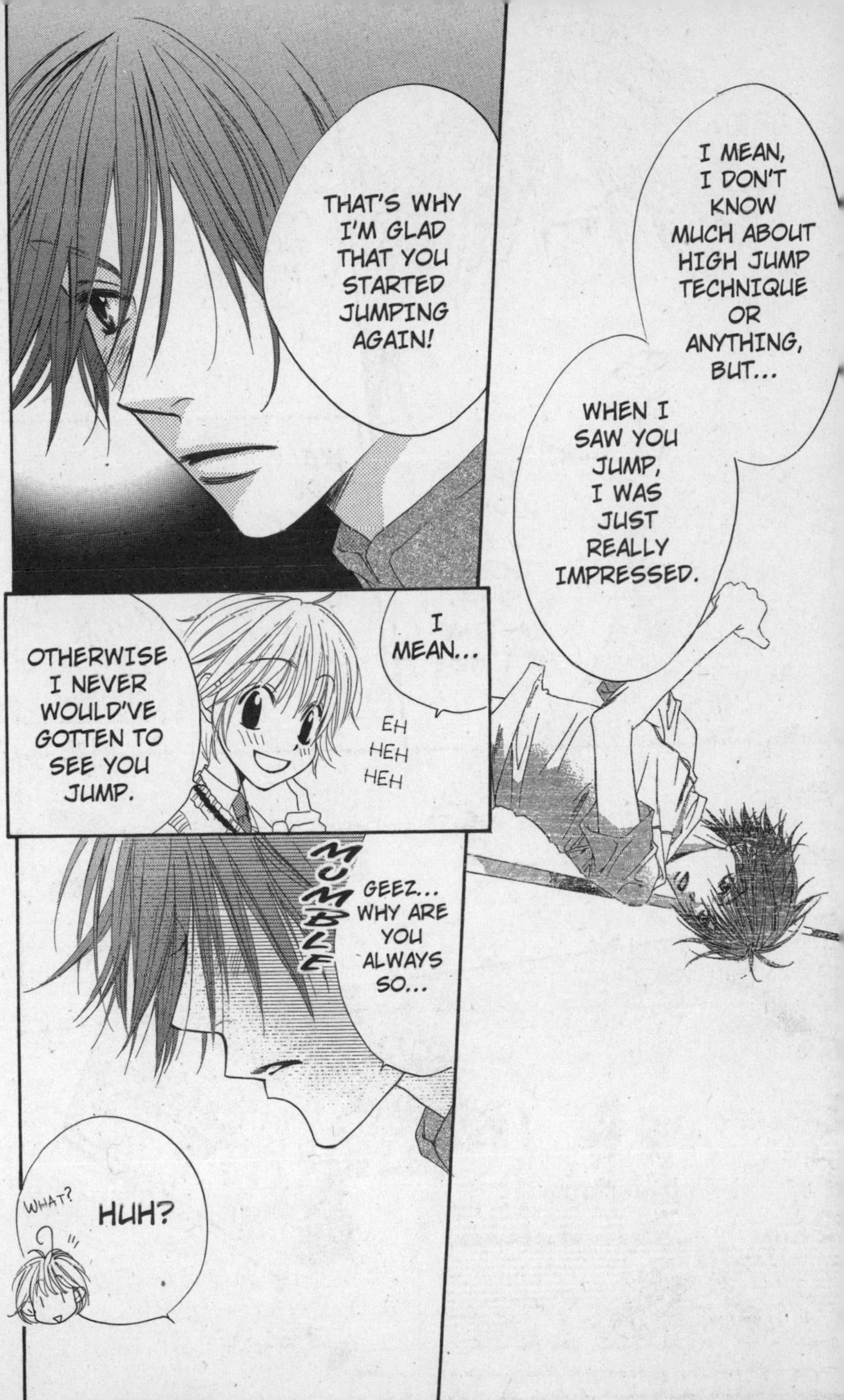

I MEAN, I DON'T KNOW MUCH ABOUT HIGH JUMP TECHNIQUE OR ANYTHING, BUT...
WHEN I SAW YOU JUMP, I WAS JUST REALLY IMPRESSED.
THAT'S WHY I'M GLAD THAT YOU STARTED JUMPING AGAIN!
I MEAN...
EH HEH HEH
OTHERWISE I NEVER WOULD'VE GOTTEN TO SEE YOU JUMP.
MUMBLE
GEEZ... WHY ARE YOU ALWAYS SO...
HUH?
WHAT?

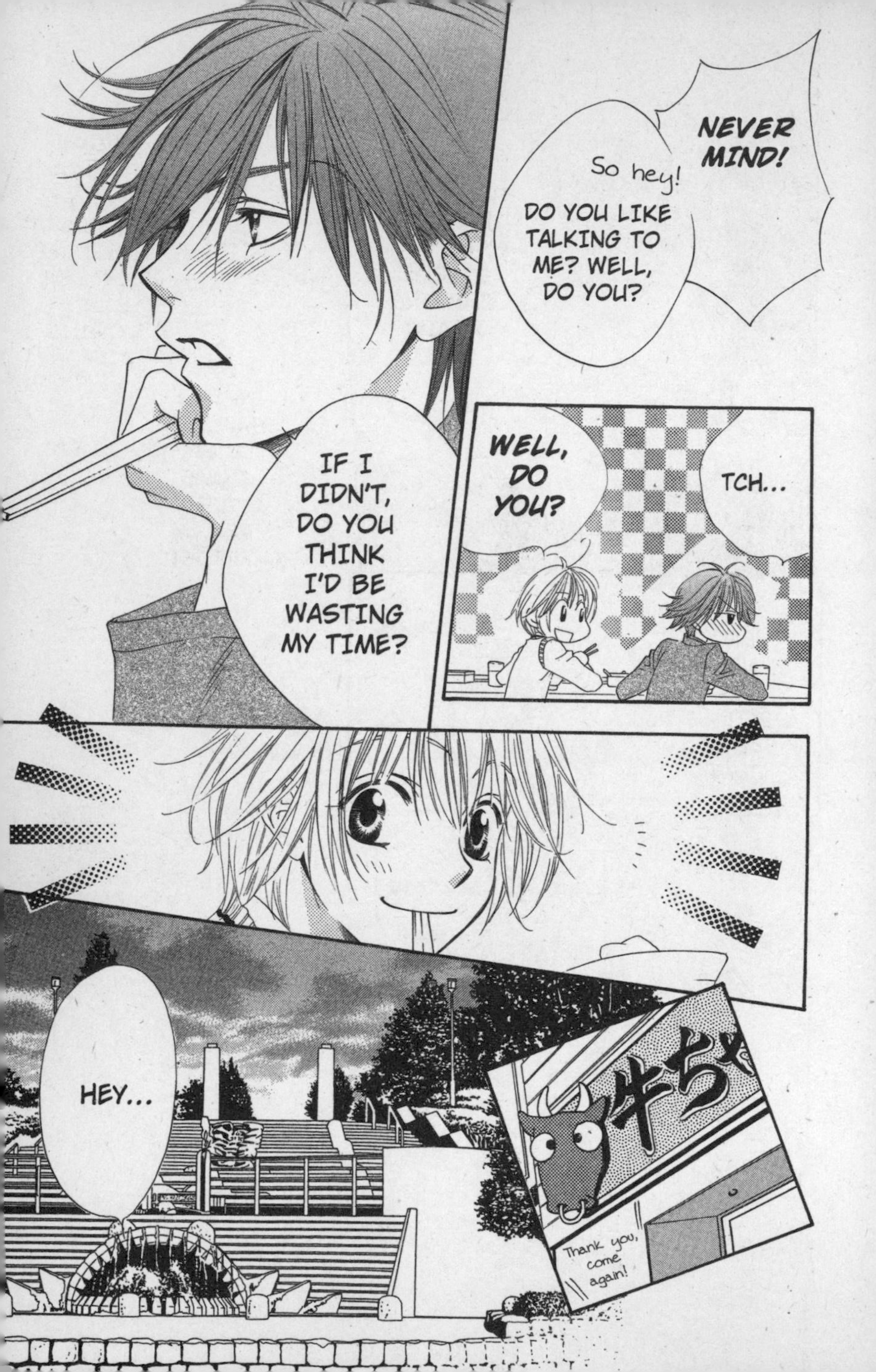
NEVER MIND!
So hey!
DO YOU LIKE TALKING TO ME? WELL, DO YOU?
TCH...
WELL, DO YOU?
IF I DIDN'T, DO YOU THINK I'D BE WASTING MY TIME?
Thank you, come again!
HEY...

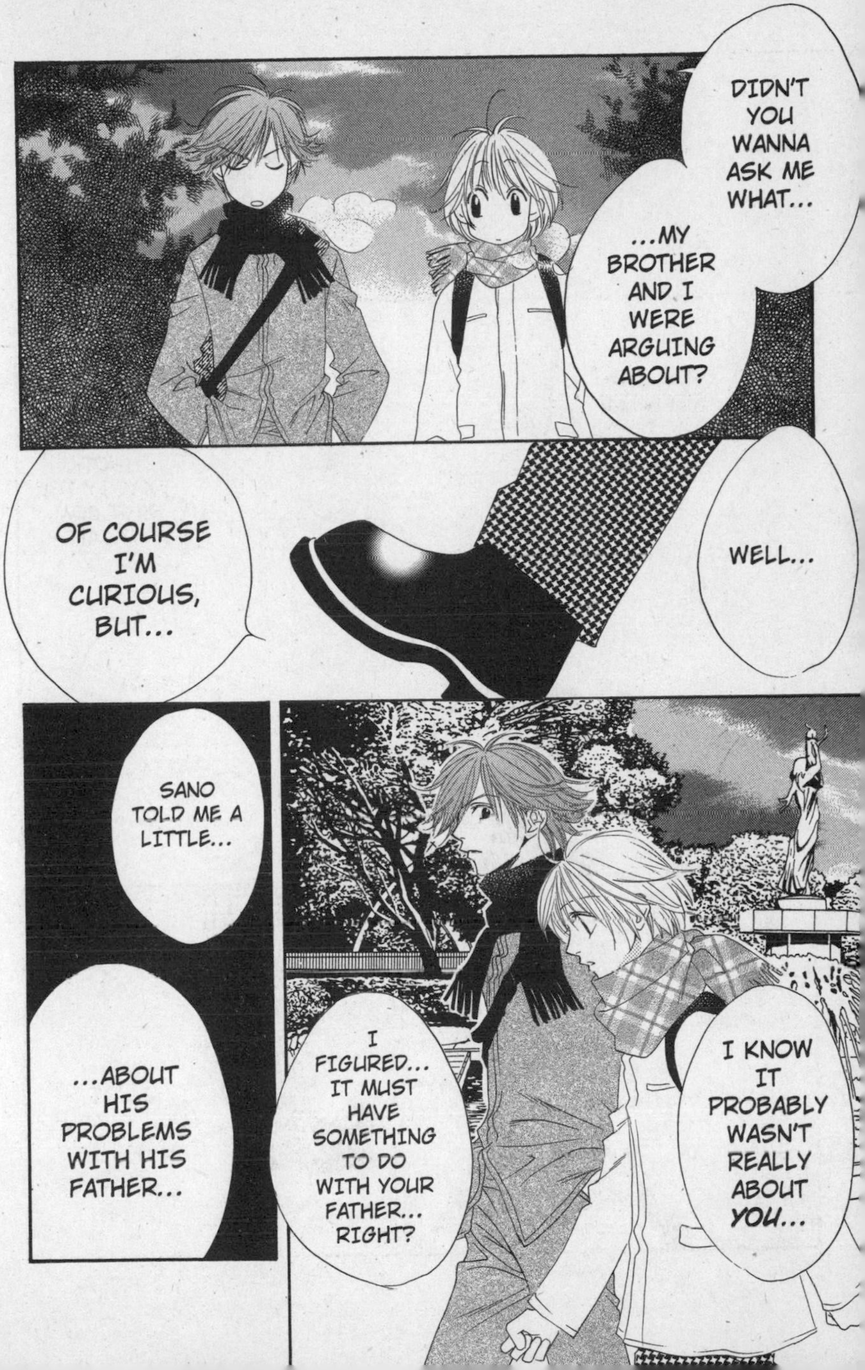
DIDN'T YOU WANNA ASK ME WHAT...
...MY BROTHER AND I WERE ARGUING ABOUT?
WELL...
OF COURSE I'M CURIOUS, BUT...
I KNOW IT PROBABLY WASN'T REALLY ABOUT *YOU*...
I FIGURED... IT MUST HAVE SOMETHING TO DO WITH YOUR FATHER... RIGHT?
SANO TOLD ME A LITTLE...
...ABOUT HIS PROBLEMS WITH HIS FATHER...

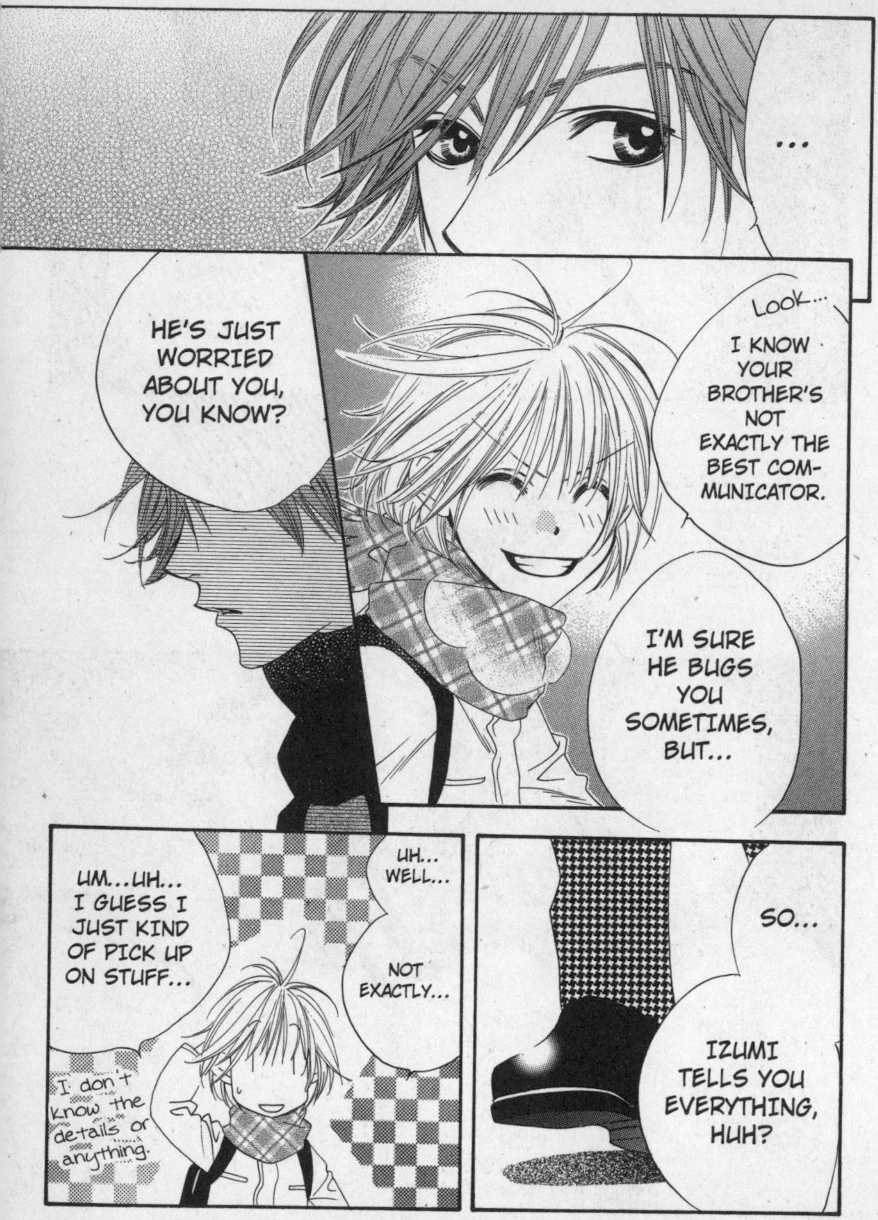
...
Look...
I KNOW YOUR BROTHER'S NOT EXACTLY THE BEST COM-MUNICATOR.
I'M SURE HE BUGS YOU SOMETIMES, BUT...
HE'S JUST WORRIED ABOUT YOU, YOU KNOW?
SO...
IZUMI TELLS YOU EVERYTHING, HUH?
UH... WELL...
NOT EXACTLY...
UM...UH... I GUESS I JUST KIND OF PICK UP ON STUFF...
I don't know the details or anything.

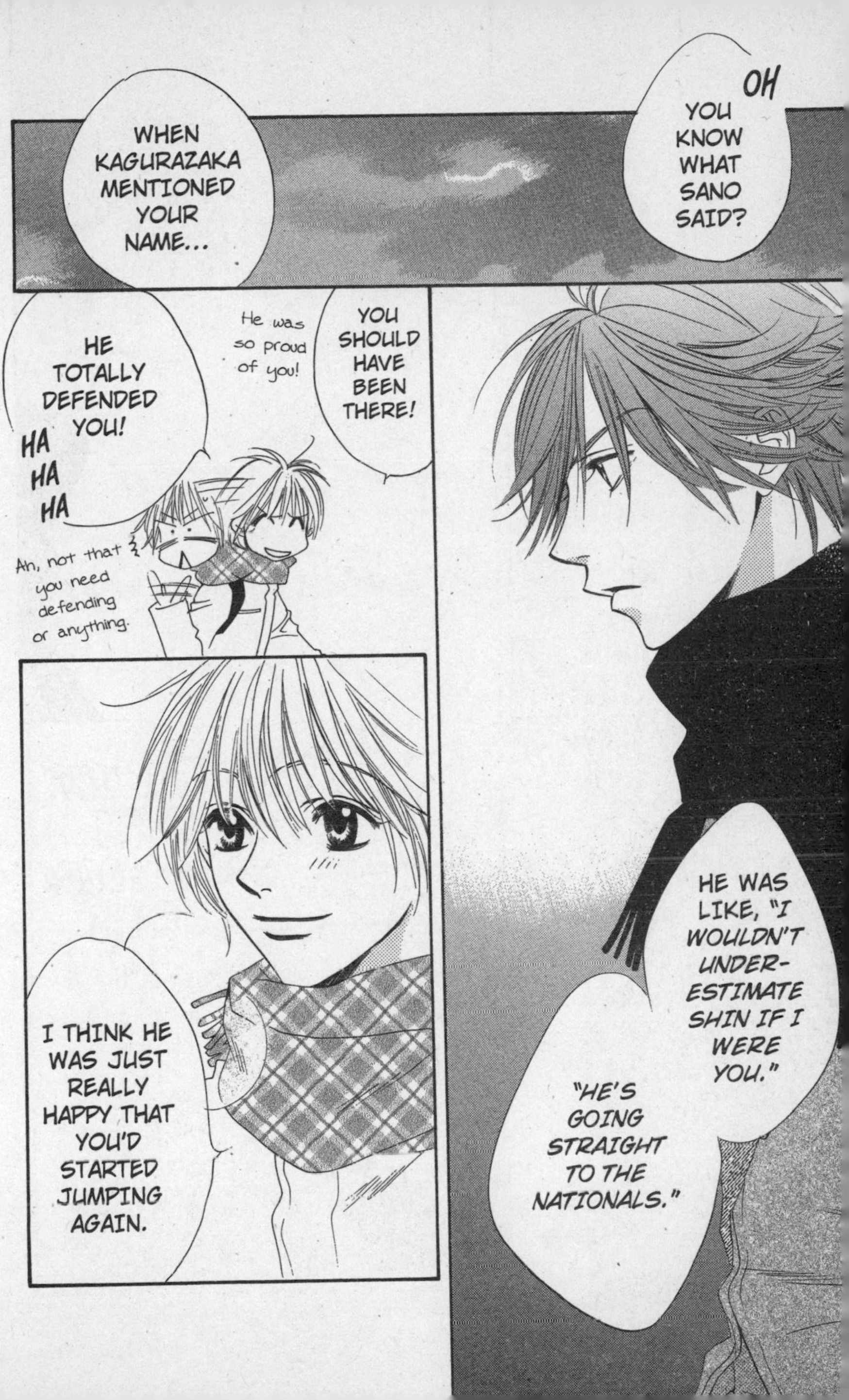
OH
YOU KNOW WHAT SANO SAID?
WHEN KAGURAZAKA MENTIONED YOUR NAME...
HE WAS LIKE, "I WOULDN'T UNDER-ESTIMATE SHIN IF I WERE YOU."
"HE'S GOING STRAIGHT TO THE NATIONALS."
YOU SHOULD HAVE BEEN THERE!
He was so proud of you!
HE TOTALLY DEFENDED YOU!
HA HA HA
Ah, not that you need defending or anything.
I THINK HE WAS JUST REALLY HAPPY THAT YOU'D STARTED JUMPING AGAIN.

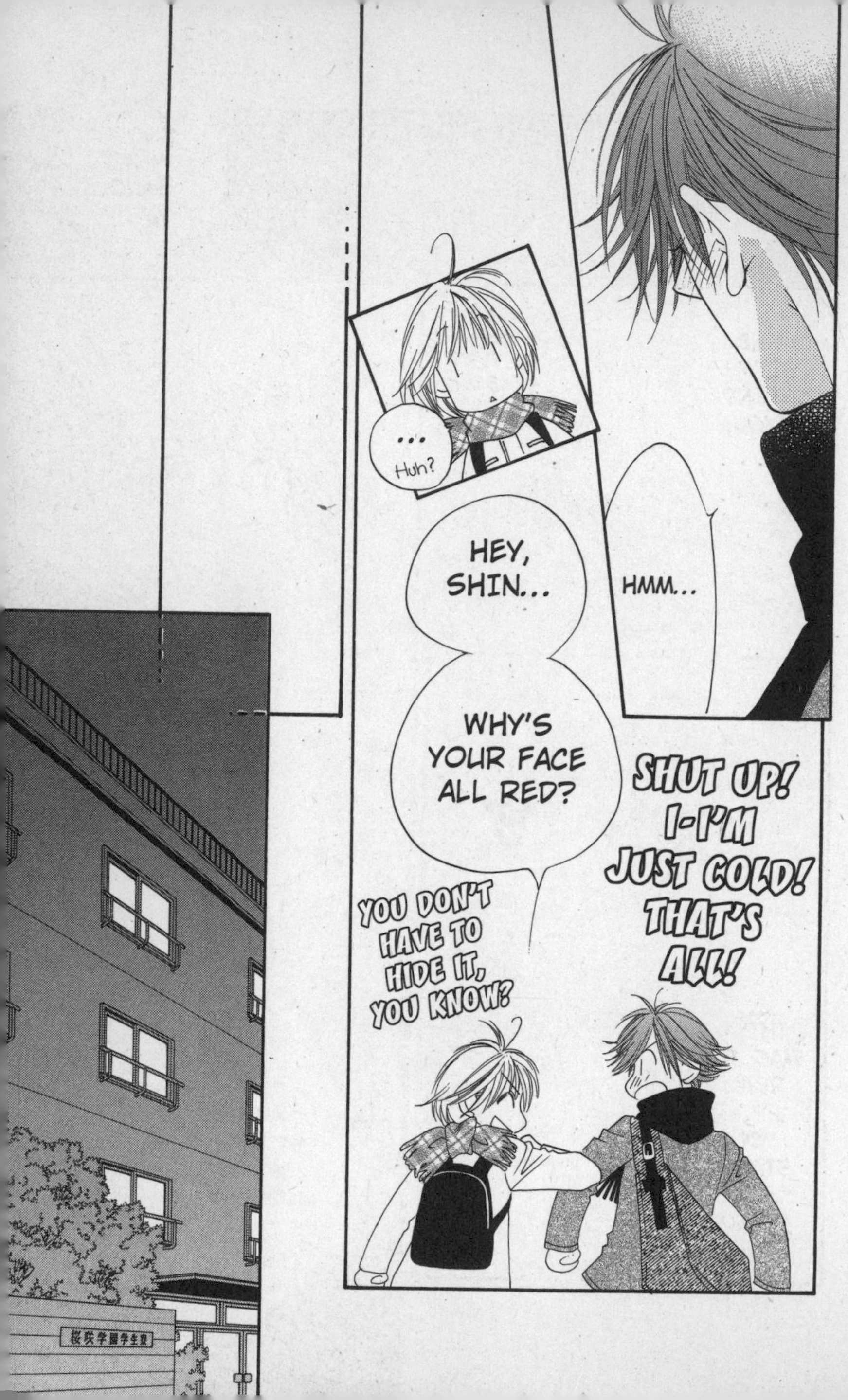
HMM...
...
Huh?
HEY, SHIN...
WHY'S YOUR FACE ALL RED?
SHUT UP! I-I'M JUST COLD! THAT'S ALL!
YOU DON'T HAVE TO HIDE IT, YOU KNOW?
桜咲学園学生寮

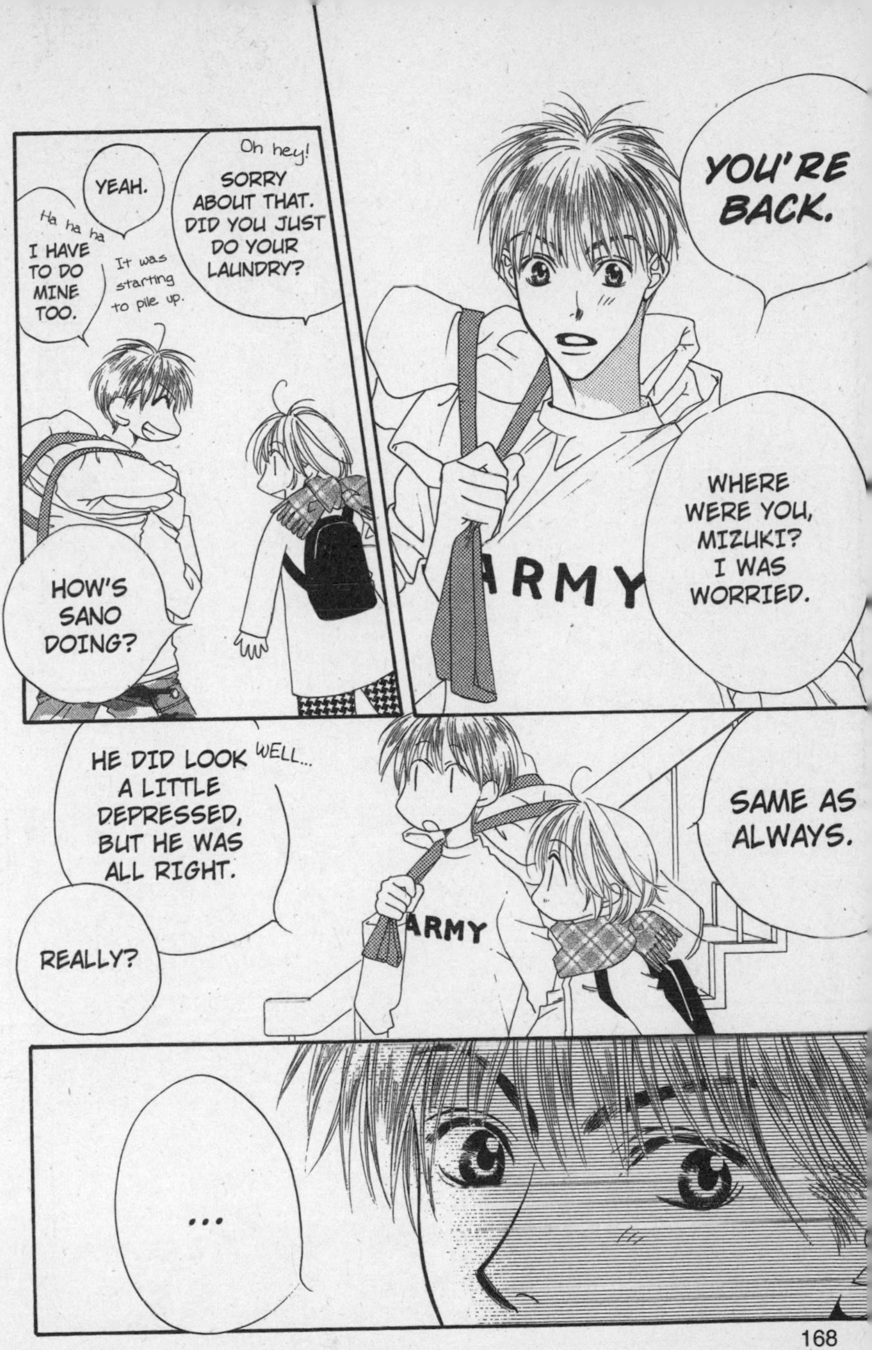
YOU'RE BACK.
WHERE WERE YOU, MIZUKI? I WAS WORRIED.
Oh hey!
SORRY ABOUT THAT. DID YOU JUST DO YOUR LAUNDRY?
YEAH.
It was starting to pile up.
Ha ha ha
I HAVE TO DO MINE TOO.
HOW'S SANO DOING?
SAME AS ALWAYS.
WELL...
HE DID LOOK A LITTLE DEPRESSED, BUT HE WAS ALL RIGHT.
REALLY?
...

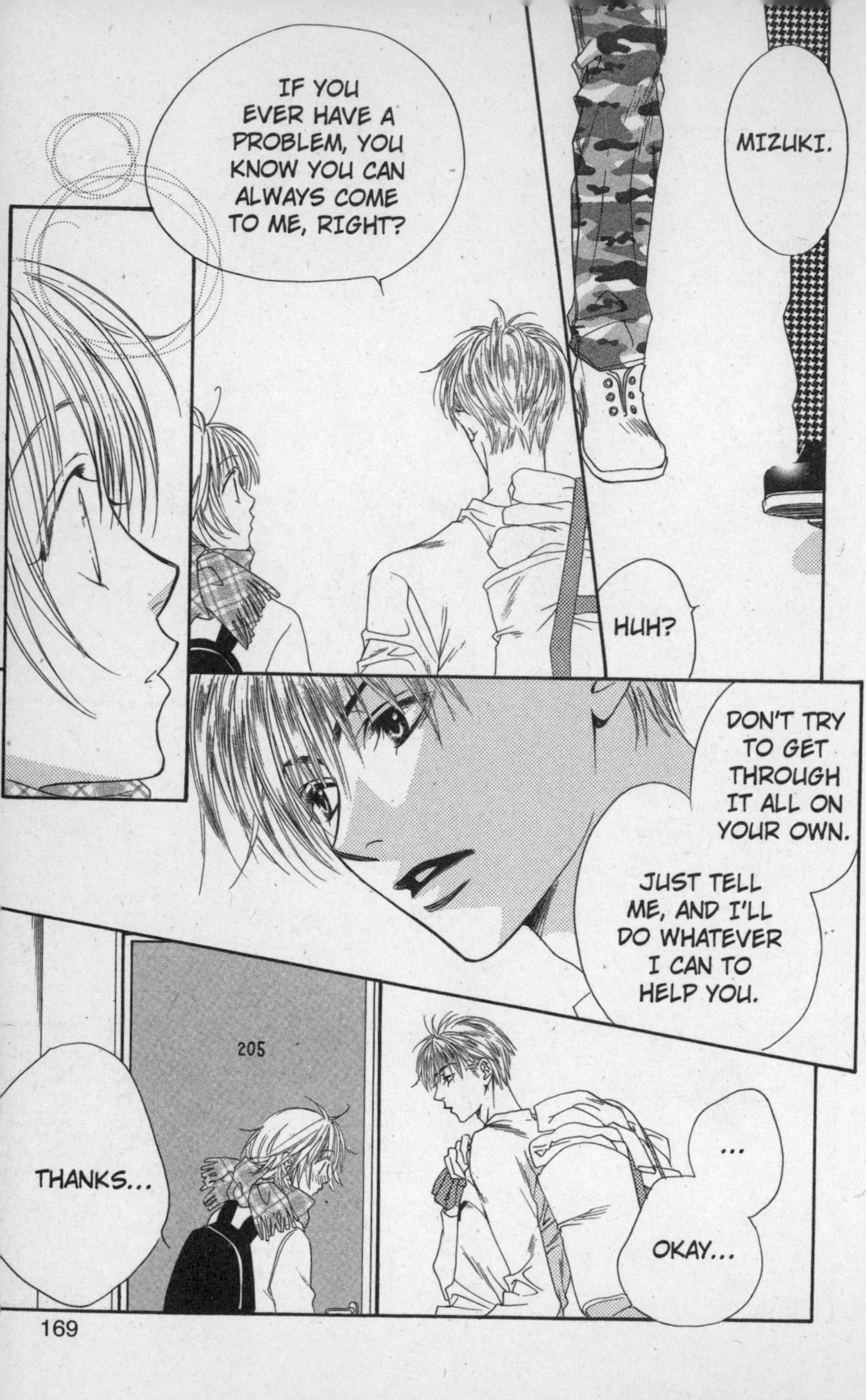
MIZUKI.
HUH?
IF YOU EVER HAVE A PROBLEM, YOU KNOW YOU CAN ALWAYS COME TO ME, RIGHT?
DON'T TRY TO GET THROUGH IT ALL ON YOUR OWN.
JUST TELL ME, AND I'LL DO WHATEVER I CAN TO HELP YOU.
205
...
OKAY...
THANKS...

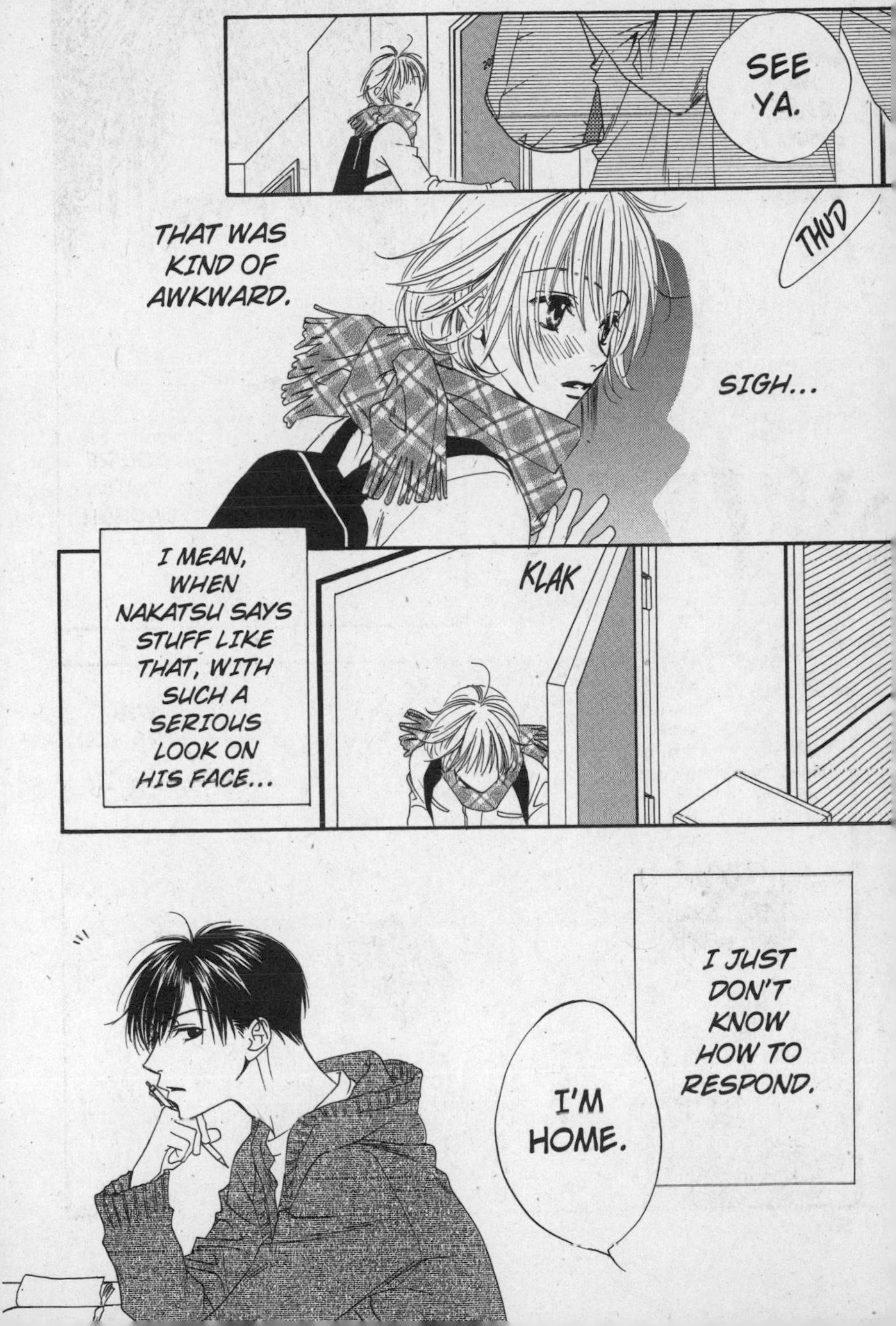
SEE YA.
THUD
THAT WAS KIND OF AWKWARD.
SIGH...
KLAK
I MEAN, WHEN NAKATSU SAYS STUFF LIKE THAT, WITH SUCH A SERIOUS LOOK ON HIS FACE...
I JUST DON'T KNOW HOW TO RESPOND.
I'M HOME.

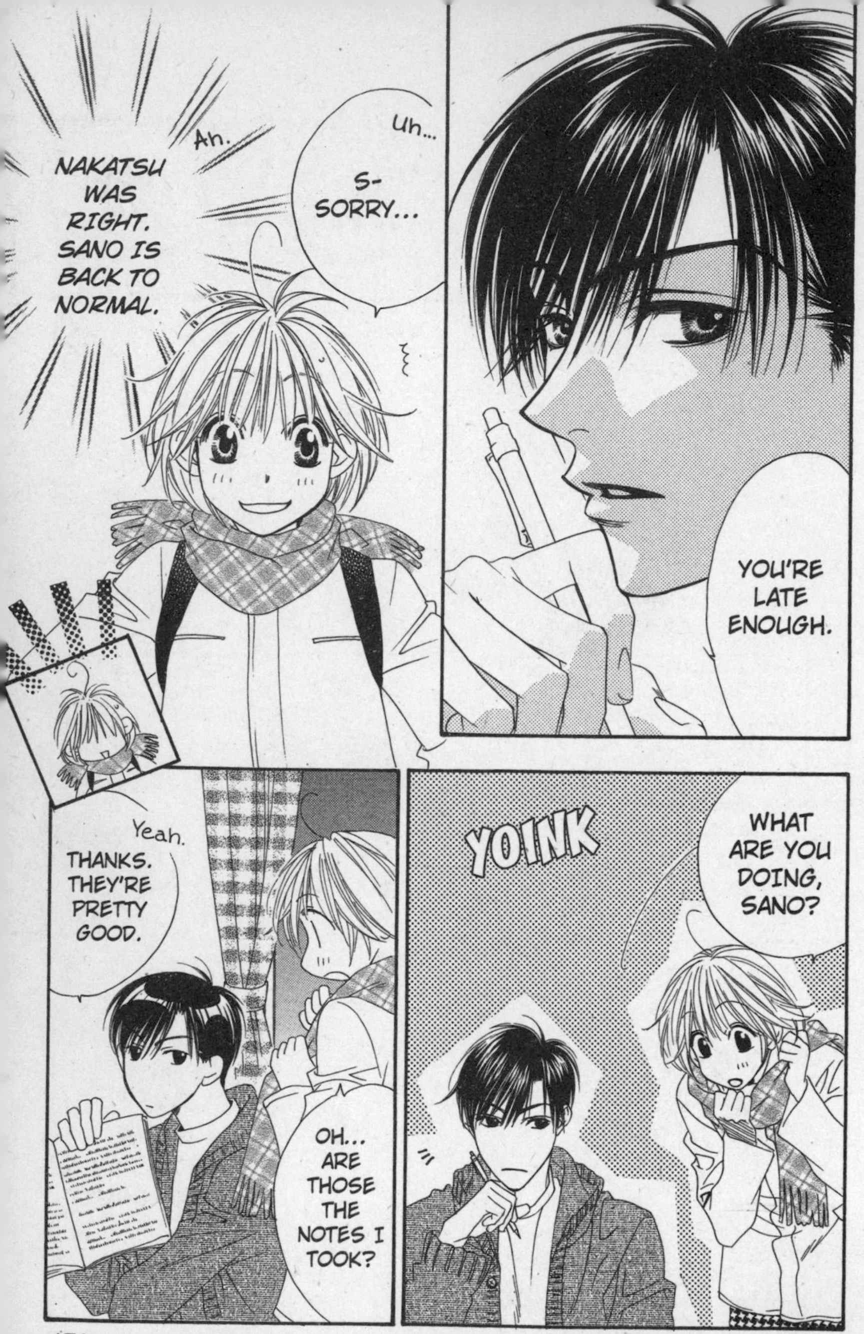
YOU'RE LATE ENOUGH.
Uh...
S-SORRY...
Ah.
NAKATSU WAS RIGHT. SANO IS BACK TO NORMAL.
YOINK
WHAT ARE YOU DOING, SANO?
OH... ARE THOSE THE NOTES I TOOK?
Yeah.
THANKS. THEY'RE PRETTY GOOD.

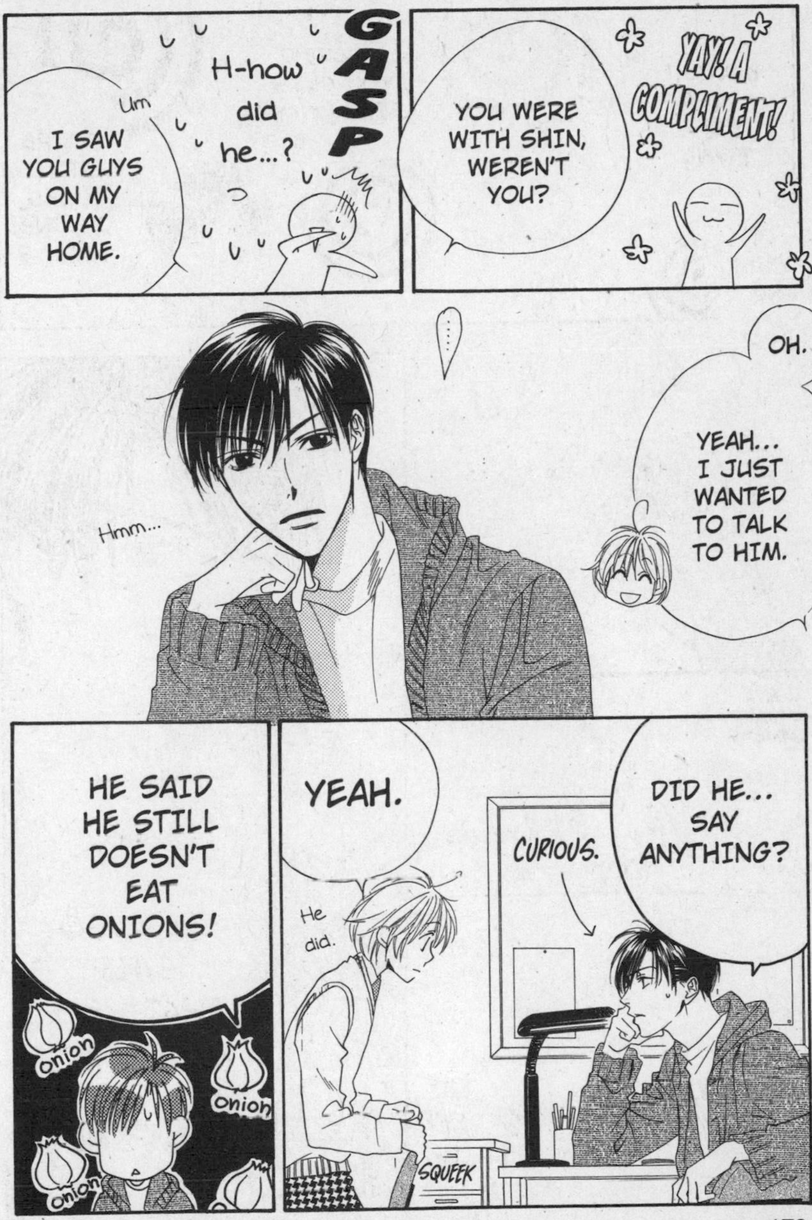
YAY! A COMPLIMENT!
YOU WERE WITH SHIN, WEREN'T YOU?
GASP
H-how did he...?
Um
I SAW YOU GUYS ON MY WAY HOME.
OH.
YEAH... I JUST WANTED TO TALK TO HIM.
......
Hmm...
DID HE... SAY ANYTHING?
CURIOUS.
YEAH.
He did.
SQUEEK
HE SAID HE STILL DOESN'T EAT ONIONS!
onion
onion
onion

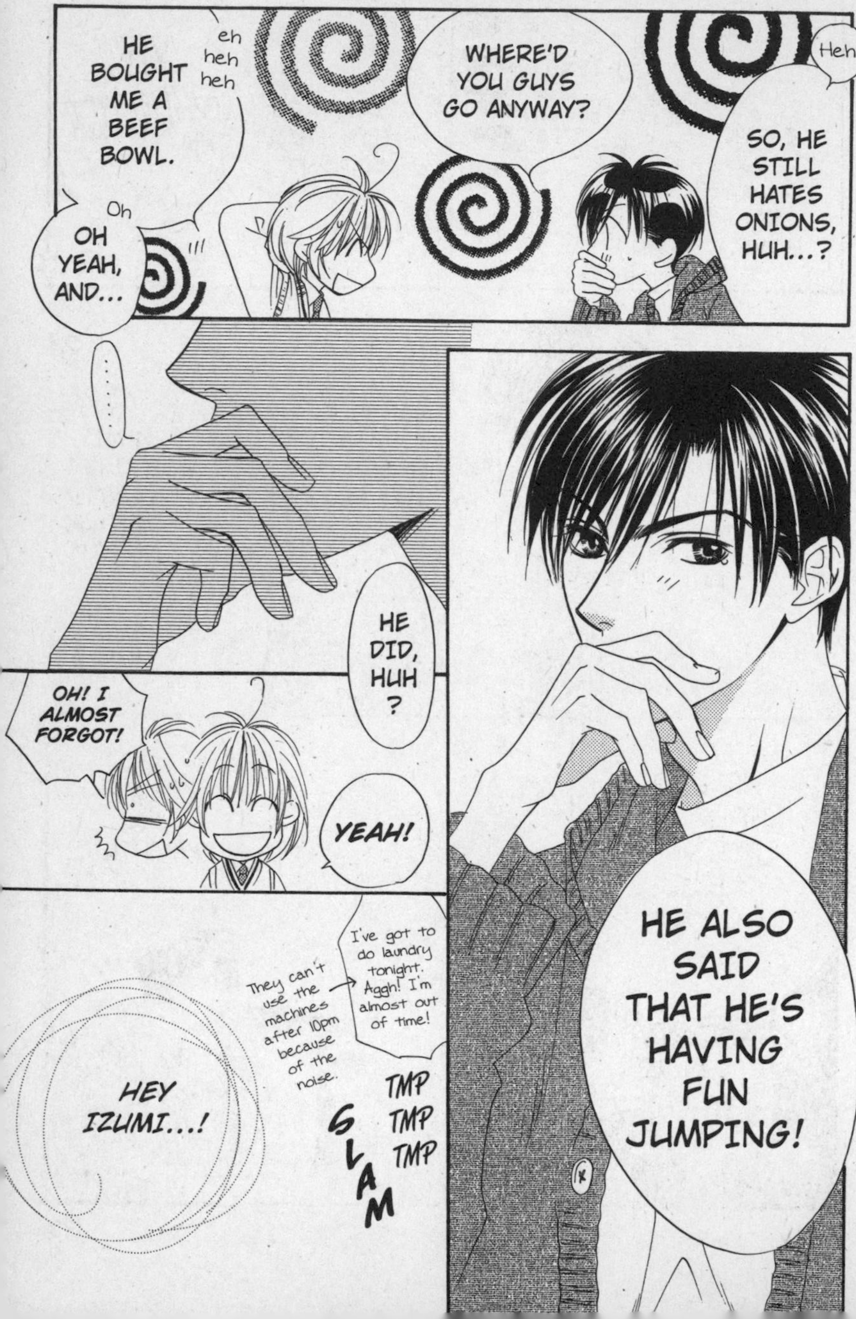
Heh
SO, HE STILL HATES ONIONS, HUH...?
WHERE'D YOU GUYS GO ANYWAY?
eh heh heh
HE BOUGHT ME A BEEF BOWL.
Oh
OH YEAH, AND...
HE ALSO SAID THAT HE'S HAVING FUN JUMPING!
......
HE DID, HUH?
YEAH!
OH! I ALMOST FORGOT!
I've got to do laundry tonight. Aggh! I'm almost out of time!
They can't use the machines after 10pm because of the noise.
TMP TMP TMP
SLAM
HEY IZUMI...!

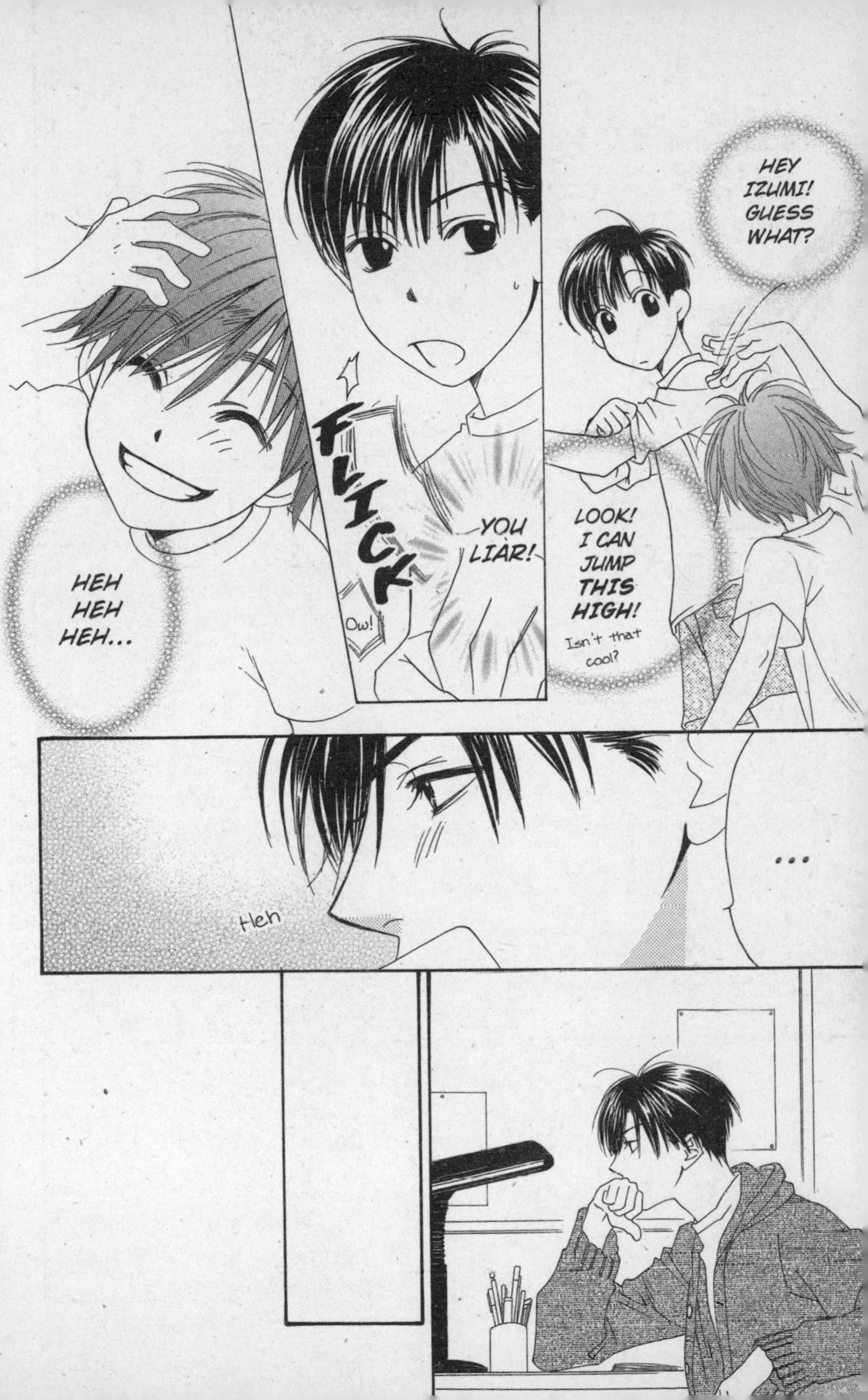
HEY IZUMI! GUESS WHAT?
LOOK! I CAN JUMP THIS HIGH!
Isn't that cool?
FLICK
YOU LIAR!
Ow!
HEH HEH HEH...
...
Heh

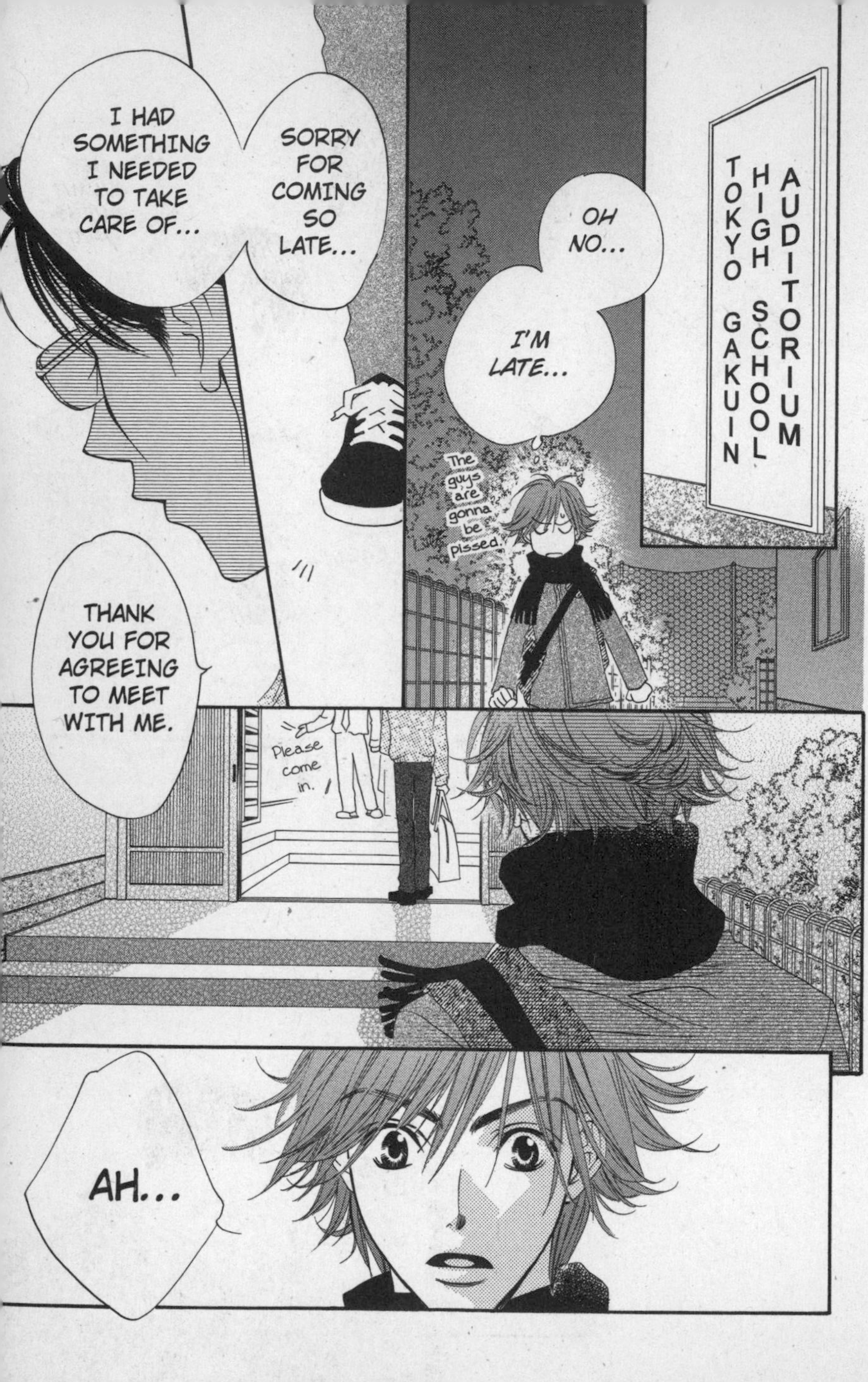
TOKYO GAKUIN HIGH SCHOOL AUDITORIUM
OH NO...
I'M LATE...
The guys are gonna be pissed.
SORRY FOR COMING SO LATE...
I HAD SOMETHING I NEEDED TO TAKE CARE OF...
THANK YOU FOR AGREEING TO MEET WITH ME.
Please come in.
AH...

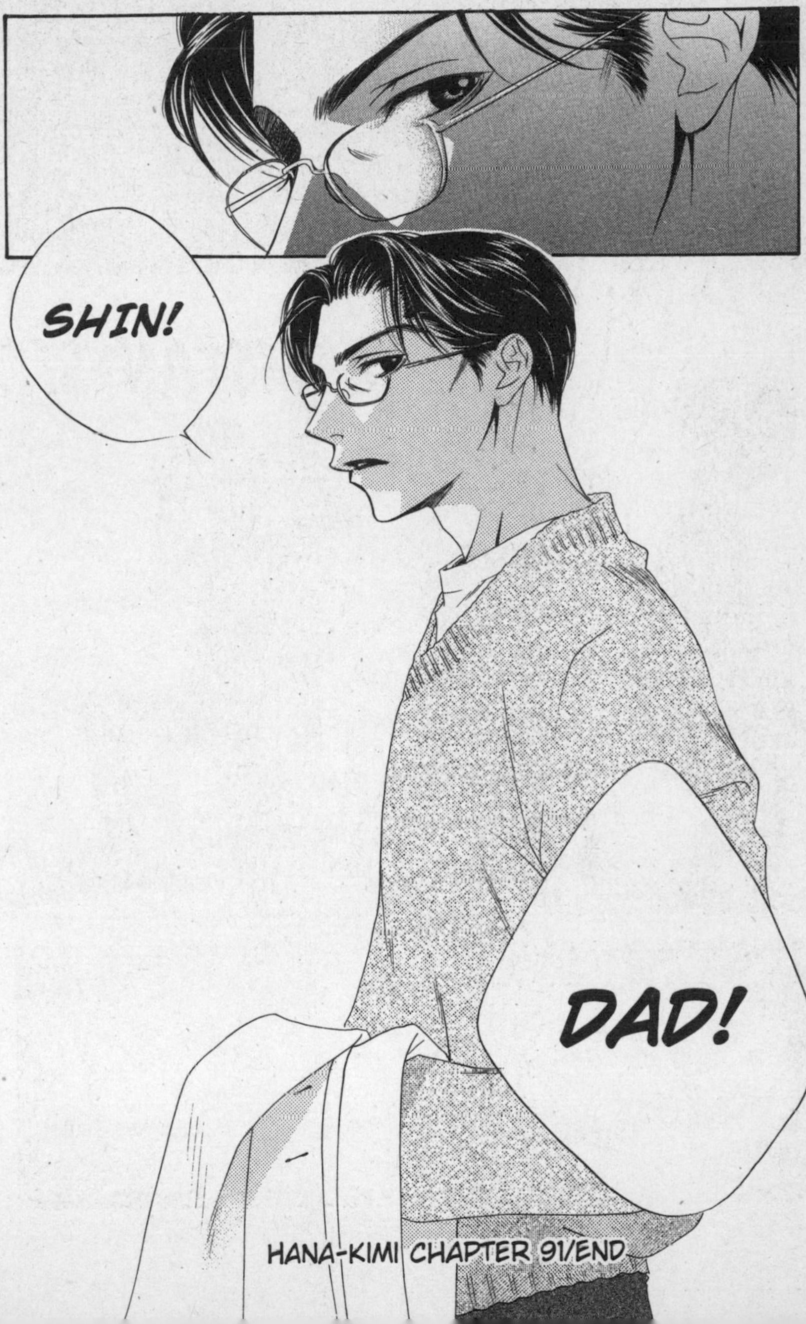
SHIN!
DAD!
HANA-KIMI CHAPTER 91/END

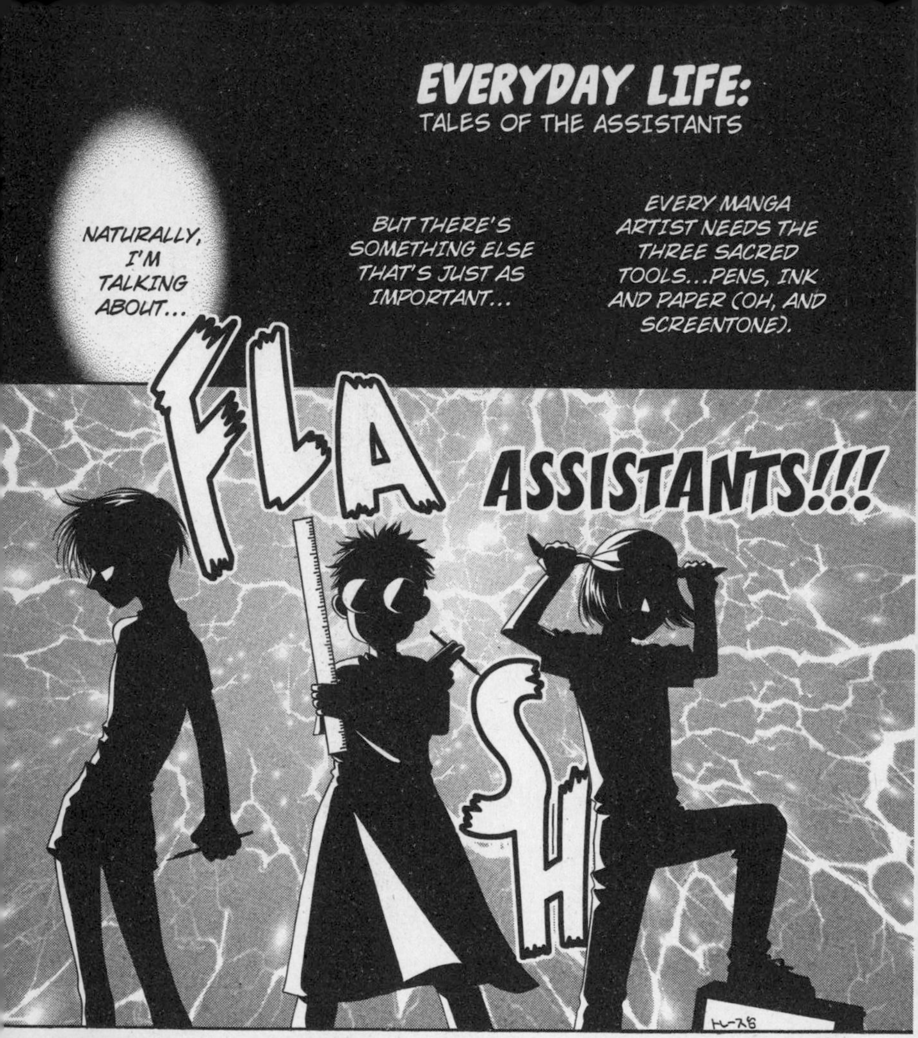
EVERYDAY LIFE:
TALES OF THE ASSISTANTS
EVERY MANGA ARTIST NEEDS THE THREE SACRED TOOLS...PENS, INK AND PAPER (OH, AND SCREENTONE).
BUT THERE'S SOMETHING ELSE THAT'S JUST AS IMPORTANT...
NATURALLY, I'M TALKING ABOUT...
FLASH
ASSISTANTS!!!
トレース台

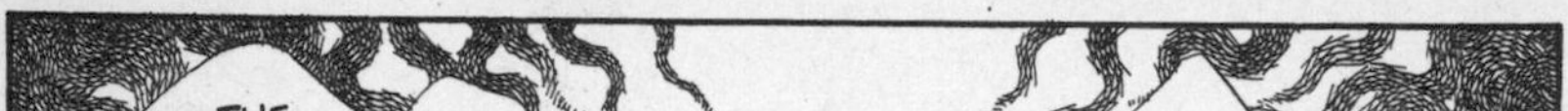
HEY!
Fill in the background!
WHAT'S WITH...
...THE CREEPY SCREEN-TONE AROUND US?

*HEADBAND="RED ORCA"

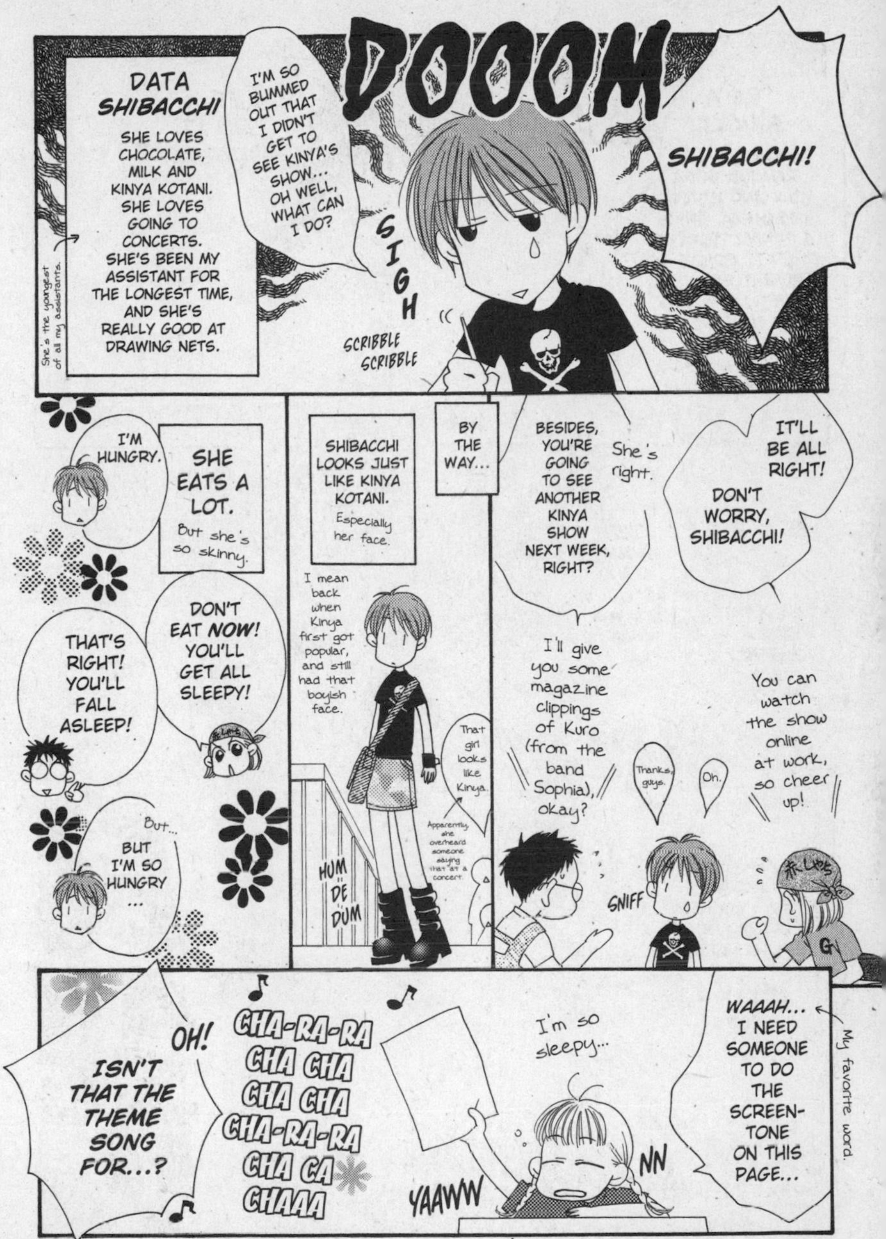
SHIBACCHI!
DOOOM
I'M SO BUMMED OUT THAT I DIDN'T GET TO SEE KINYA'S SHOW... OH WELL, WHAT CAN I DO?
SIGH
SCRIBBLE SCRIBBLE
DATA SHIBACCHI
SHE LOVES CHOCOLATE, MILK AND KINYA KOTANI. SHE LOVES GOING TO CONCERTS. SHE'S BEEN MY ASSISTANT FOR THE LONGEST TIME, AND SHE'S REALLY GOOD AT DRAWING NETS.
She's the youngest of all my assistants.
IT'LL BE ALL RIGHT!
DON'T WORRY, SHIBACCHI!
She's right.
BESIDES, YOU'RE GOING TO SEE ANOTHER KINYA SHOW NEXT WEEK, RIGHT?
You can watch the show online at work, so cheer up!
Oh.
Thanks, guys.
I'll give you some magazine clippings of Kuro (from the band Sophia), okay?
SNIFF
BY THE WAY...
SHIBACCHI LOOKS JUST LIKE KINYA KOTANI.
Especially her face.
I mean back when Kinya first got popular, and still had that boyish face.
That girl looks like Kinya.
Apparently, she overheard someone saying that at a concert.
HUM DE DUM
SHE EATS A LOT.
But she's so skinny.
I'M HUNGRY.
DON'T EAT NOW! YOU'LL GET ALL SLEEPY!
THAT'S RIGHT! YOU'LL FALL ASLEEP!
But...
BUT I'M SO HUNGRY...
WAAAH... I NEED SOMEONE TO DO THE SCREEN-TONE ON THIS PAGE...
My favorite word.
I'm so sleepy...
NN
YAAWN
CHA-RA-RA CHA CHA CHA CHA CHA-RA-RA CHA CA CHAAA
OH!
ISN'T THAT THE THEME SONG FOR...?

↖ Hisaya Nakajo getting sleepy (after a meal)

↖ "Advancing to the next level" music...

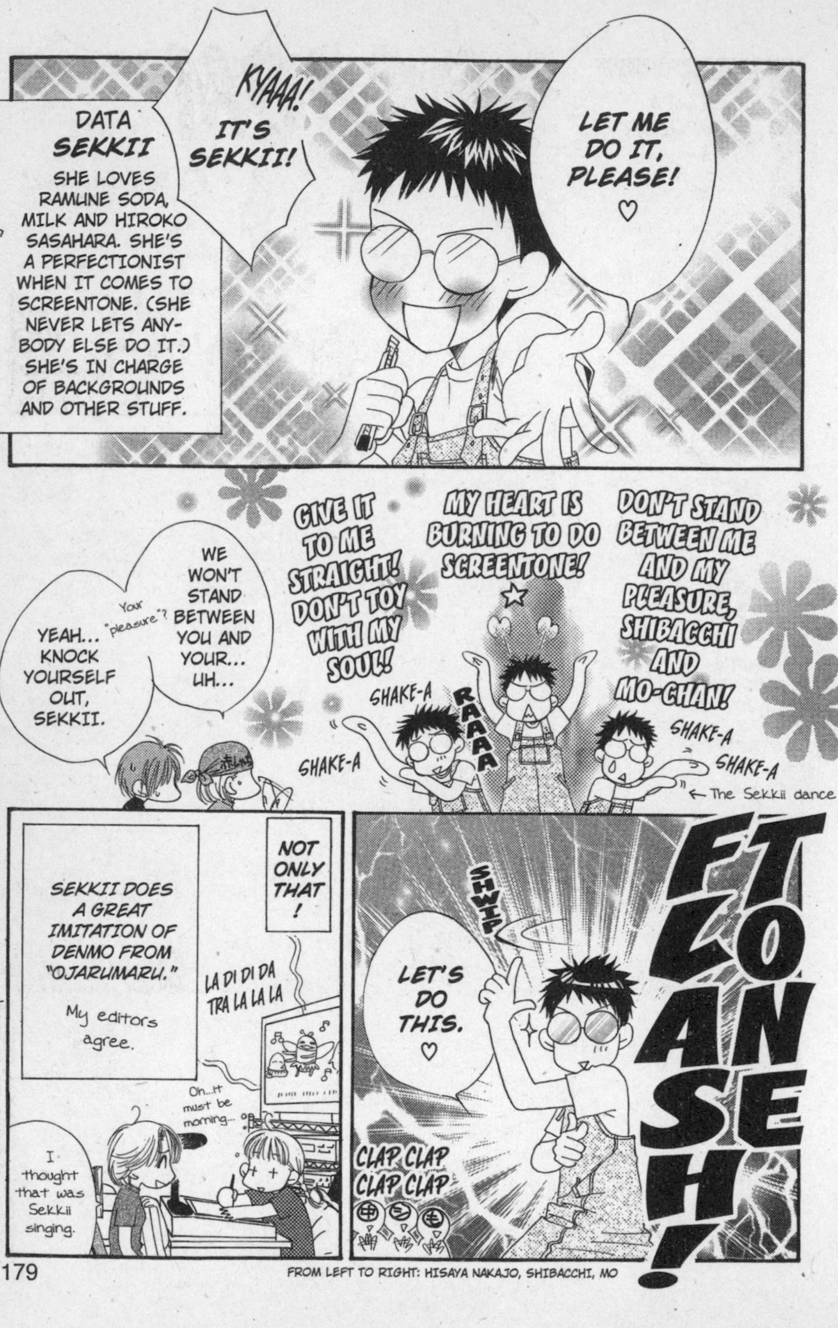
LET ME DO IT, PLEASE! ♡
KYAAA!
IT'S SEKKII!
DATA SEKKII
SHE LOVES RAMUNE SODA, MILK AND HIROKO SASAHARA. SHE'S A PERFECTIONIST WHEN IT COMES TO SCREENTONE. (SHE NEVER LETS ANYBODY ELSE DO IT.) SHE'S IN CHARGE OF BACKGROUNDS AND OTHER STUFF.
DON'T STAND BETWEEN ME AND MY PLEASURE, SHIBACCHI AND MO-CHAN!
MY HEART IS BURNING TO DO SCREENTONE! ☆
GIVE IT TO ME STRAIGHT! DON'T TOY WITH MY SOUL!
SHAKE-A
SHAKE-A
RAAAA
SHAKE-A
SHAKE-A
WE WON'T STAND BETWEEN YOU AND YOUR... UH...
Your "pleasure"?
YEAH... KNOCK YOURSELF OUT, SEKKII.
← The Sekkii dance
FT LO AN SE H!
SHWIP
LET'S DO THIS. ♡
CLAP CLAP CLAP CLAP
NOT ONLY THAT!
SEKKII DOES A GREAT IMITATION OF DENMO FROM "OJARUMARU."
My editors agree.
LA DI DI DA TRA LA LA
Oh...it must be morning...
I thought that was Sekkii singing.

FROM LEFT TO RIGHT: HISAYA NAKAJO, SHIBACCHI, MO

You can hear Sekkii scream when you listen to Hiroko Sasahara's live album. (During the encore)

* The assistants are all asleep.

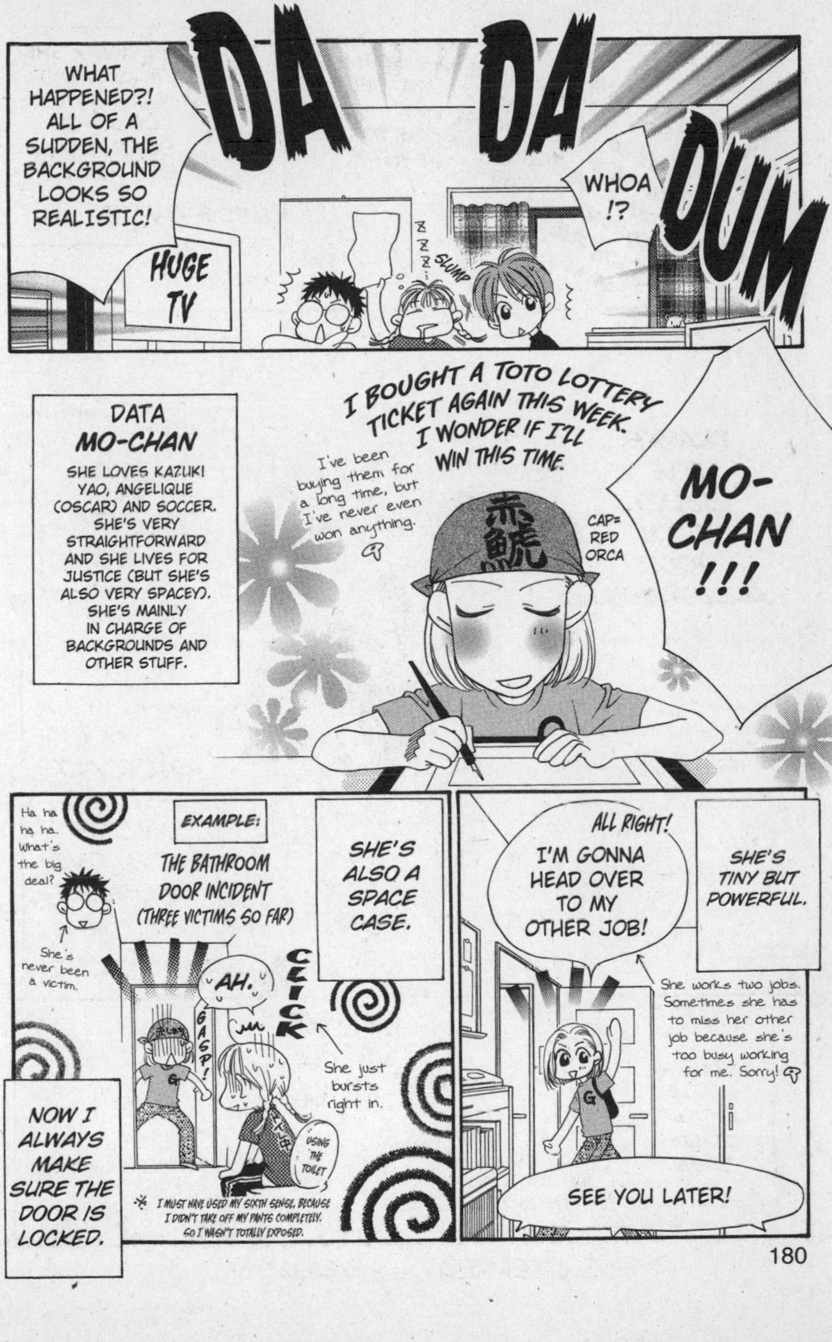
DA DA DUM
WHOA !?
SLUMP
HUGE TV
WHAT HAPPENED?! ALL OF A SUDDEN, THE BACKGROUND LOOKS SO REALISTIC!
MO-CHAN !!!
I BOUGHT A TOTO LOTTERY TICKET AGAIN THIS WEEK. I WONDER IF I'LL WIN THIS TIME.
I've been buying them for a long time, but I've never even won anything.
CAP= RED ORCA
DATA MO-CHAN
SHE LOVES KAZUKI YAO, ANGELIQUE (OSCAR) AND SOCCER. SHE'S VERY STRAIGHTFORWARD AND SHE LIVES FOR JUSTICE (BUT SHE'S ALSO VERY SPACEY). SHE'S MAINLY IN CHARGE OF BACKGROUNDS AND OTHER STUFF.
SHE'S TINY BUT POWERFUL.
ALL RIGHT!
I'M GONNA HEAD OVER TO MY OTHER JOB!
She works two jobs. Sometimes she has to miss her other job because she's too busy working for me. Sorry!
SEE YOU LATER!
SHE'S ALSO A SPACE CASE.
EXAMPLE:
THE BATHROOM DOOR INCIDENT (THREE VICTIMS SO FAR)
Ha ha ha, ha. What's the big deal?
She's never been a victim.
CLICK
AH.
GASP!
She just bursts right in.
USING THE TOILET
※ I MUST HAVE USED MY SIXTH SENSE, BECAUSE I DIDN'T TAKE OFF MY PANTS COMPLETELY. SO I WASN'T TOTALLY EXPOSED.
NOW I ALWAYS MAKE SURE THE DOOR IS LOCKED.

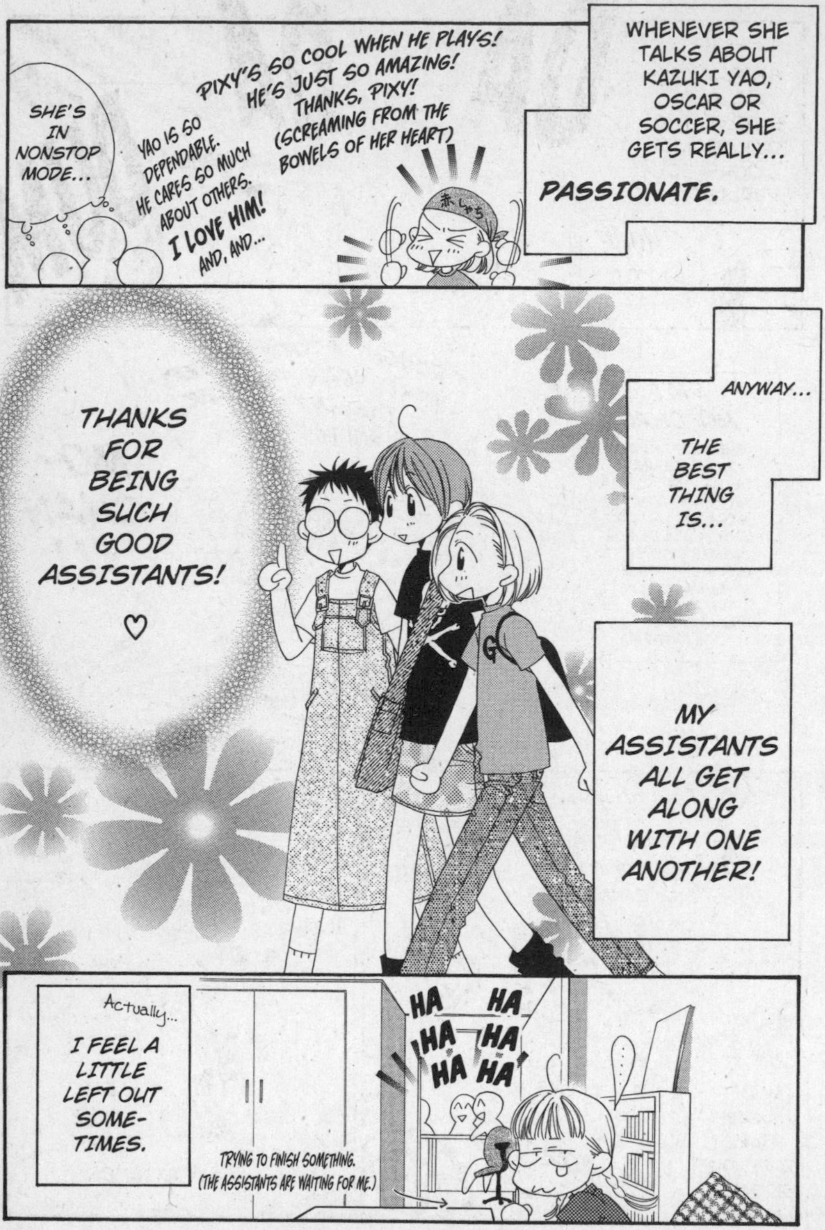

WHENEVER SHE TALKS ABOUT KAZUKI YAO, OSCAR OR SOCCER, SHE GETS REALLY...
PASSIONATE.
PIXY'S SO COOL WHEN HE PLAYS! HE'S JUST SO AMAZING! THANKS, PIXY! (SCREAMING FROM THE BOWELS OF HER HEART)
赤しゃち
YAO IS SO DEPENDABLE. HE CARES SO MUCH ABOUT OTHERS. I LOVE HIM! AND, AND...
SHE'S IN NONSTOP MODE...
ANYWAY...
THE BEST THING IS...
MY ASSISTANTS ALL GET ALONG WITH ONE ANOTHER!
THANKS FOR BEING SUCH GOOD ASSISTANTS! ♡
HA HA HA HA HA HA
Actually...
I FEEL A LITTLE LEFT OUT SOME-TIMES.
TRYING TO FINISH SOMETHING. (THE ASSISTANTS ARE WAITING FOR ME.)

EVERYDAY LIFE/END

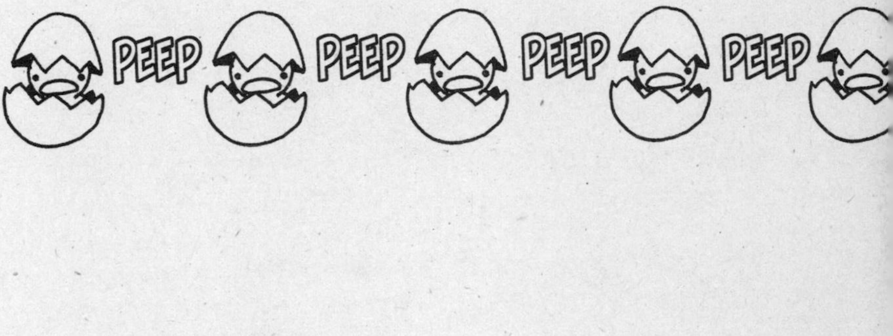
PEEP
PEEP
PEEP
PEEP

ABOUT THE AUTHOR

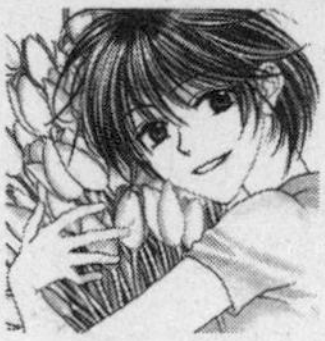

Hisaya Nakajo's manga series **Hanazakari no Kimitachi he** (For You in Full Blossom, casually known as **Hana-Kimi**) has been a hit since it first appeared in 1997 in the shôjo manga magazine **Hana to Yume** (Flowers and Dreams). In Japan, two **Hana-Kimi** art books and several "drama CDs" have been released. Her other manga series include **Missing Piece** (2 volumes) and **Yumemiru Happa** (The Dreaming Leaf, 1 volume).

Hisaya Nakajo's website:
www.wild-vanilla.com

IN THE NEXT VOLUME ...

Sano's father is back, and it isn't a happy reunion. Soon, the two brothers are set on a collision course, and Mizuki must try to mend their broken family while they compete for the upcoming track meet. Will Shin, Sano or Kagurazuka come out on top? But as Sano focuses on winning, Nakatsu takes the opportunity to move even closer to the girl—I mean boy—he loves...

森
いつものメニューはじめるぞ 油売ってないで さっさと来い
――待てよ
アンタ また……っ
森にも 強制して 無茶させてんじ ないのかよ……

COMING APRIL 2007!